THE BIG FOUR AND THE DEVELOPMENT OF THE ACCOUNTING PROFESSION IN CHINA

STUDIES IN THE DEVELOPMENT OF ACCOUNTING THOUGHT

Series Editor: Gary Previts

Recent Volumes:

Volume 6:	Doing Accounting History: Contributions to the Development of Accounting Thought
Volume 7:	Accounting: How to Meet the Challenges of Relevance and Regulation
Volume 8:	The Life and Writings of Stuart Chase (1888–1985): From an Accountant's Perspective
Volume 9:	Seekers of Truth: The Scottish Founders of Modern Public Accountancy
Volume 10:	The Contributions of John Lansing Carey to the Profession of Accountancy
Volume 11:	Abraham J. (Abe) Briloff: A Biography
Volume 12:	Early Warning and Quick Response: Accounting in the Twenty-First Century
Volume 13:	Gerhard G. Mueller: Father of International Accounting Education
Volume 14A:	A Global History of Accounting, Financial Reporting and Public Policy: Europe
Volume 14B:	A Global History of Accounting, Financial Reporting and Public Policy: Americas
Volume 14C:	A Global History of Accounting, Financial Reporting and Public Policy: Asia and Oceania
Volume 14D:	A Global History of Accounting, Financial Reporting and Public Policy: Middle East and Africa
Volume 15:	Understanding Accounting Academic Research: Before and After Sarbanes-Oxley

STUDIES IN THE DEVELOPMENT OF ACCOUNTING THOUGHT VOLUME 16

THE BIG FOUR AND THE DEVELOPMENT OF THE ACCOUNTING PROFESSION IN CHINA

BY

PAUL L. GILLIS

Guanghua School of Management, Peking University, Beijing, China

Published with the support of

THE UNIVERSITY OF SYDNEY
THE ACCOUNTING FOUNDATION

Emerald

United Kingdom – North America – Japan
India – Malaysia – China

Emerald Group Publishing Limited
Howard House, Wagon Lane, Bingley BD16 1WA, UK

First edition 2014

British Library Cataloguing in Publication Data
A catalogue record for this book is available from the British Library

ISBN: 978-1-78350-485-5
ISSN: 1479-3504 (Series)

CONTENTS

ACKNOWLEDGMENTS

> Live as if you were to die tomorrow. Learn as if you were to live forever.
> –Mahatma Gandhi

This project was born following my decision to take early retirement after a 28-year career at PricewaterhouseCoopers. While my golf handicap plunged in the lazy months that followed my retirement, I soon hungered for intellectual stimulation, if only to ward off the early onset of Alzheimer's disease. What began as an interesting hobby has blossomed into a rewarding second career in academia.

This book is based on the research I did for my doctoral thesis at Macquarie Graduate School of Management in Sydney, Australia. I was honored to receive the Emerald/EFMD Outstanding Doctoral Research Award for Interdisciplinary Accounting Research in 2011.

I am thankful to my colleagues at Peking University who created the perfect environment for me to pursue this study. Stacy Chen and Wennie Wei, promising doctoral students at Peking University, provided invaluable research assistance.

My doctoral supervisor, Richard Petty, also served as the President of CPA Australia, which gave him an understanding of the issues that are presented in this book that few academics possess. Gary Previtts, editor of this series, encouraged me to turn my work into this book and helped me to find the resources to update my research.

Most importantly, I am thankful for the wonderful support of my tiger wife, Grace Tang. Grace is a partner at PricewaterhouseCoopers and was incredibly helpful as a sounding board as the research progressed. She also helped me to gain access to her clients and her contacts in other firms.

I dedicate this book to the thousands of Big Four accountants who built an accounting profession in China. I am blessed with the opportunity to tell their story. They have done remarkable things, and the world is better off for it.

LIST OF ABBREVIATIONS

AA	Arthur Andersen
ARB	Accounting Research Bulletin
ASBE	Accounting Standards for Business Enterprises
ASE	American Stock Exchange
AY	Arthur Young
BEDC	Beijing Economic Development Corporation
C&L	Coopers & Lybrand
CAS	Chinese Accounting Standards
CASB	Chinese Auditing Standards Board
CCER	China Center for Economic Research at Peking University
CEPA	Closer Economic Partnership Arrangement
CICPA	Chinese Institute of Certified Public Accountants
CITIC	China International Trade and Investment Corporation
CPA	Certified Public Accountant
CPC	Communist Party of China
CR	Concentration ratio
CSRC	China Securities Regulatory Commission
DHS	Deloitte, Haskins and Sells
DTT	Deloitte Touche Tohmatsu
E&E	Ernst & Ernst
E&Y	Ernst & Young
EU	European Union
FESCO	Foreign Enterprise Human Resource Services Company
FIN 46	FASB Interpretation No. 46
GAAP	Generally accepted accounting principles
GDP	Gross domestic product
HHI	Herfindahl–Hirschman Index
HKEx	Hong Kong Exchange and Clearing Limited
HKFRS	Hong Kong Financial Reporting Standards
HKICPA	Hong Kong Institute of Certified Public Accountants
HKSE	Hong Kong Stock Exchange
IAASB	International Auditing and Assurance Standards Board
IAS	International Accounting Standards

IASB	International Accounting Standards Board
IASC	International Accounting Standards Committee
ICP	Internet content provider
IFRS	International Financial Reporting Standards
IPO	Initial public offering
KWTF	Kwan Wong Tan and Fong
LBM	Lowe, Bingham, and Matthews
LLP	Limited liability partnership
MOFTEC	Ministry of Foreign Trade and Economic Cooperation
NYSE	New York Stock Exchange
PCAOB	Public Company Accounting Oversight Board
PMM	Peat Marwick Mitchell
PPP	Purchasing power parity
PRC	People's Republic of China
PSF	Professional service firms
PW	Price Waterhouse
PwC	PricewaterhouseCoopers
SOE	State-owned enterprise
SUFE	Shanghai University of Finance and Economics
TR	Touche Ross
UK	The United Kingdom of Great Britain and Northern Ireland
US	The United States
WFOE	Wholly foreign-owned enterprise
WTO	World Trade Organization

LIST OF TABLES

CHAPTER 1

INTRODUCTION

> From the 1990s when they entered China quite cautiously to the beginning of this new century when they lord themselves arrogantly across China, only ten years have they used in China doing all the things which might have taken them several decades ... or more than 100 years if in other countries.
>
> – Ding Pingzhun, Director General of the Chinese Institute of Certified Public Accountants (Ding, 2006b, p. 83)

1.1. INTRODUCTION

This is a study of how an elite transnational group of large accounting firms (known today as the Big Four[1]) came to dominate the market for auditing services in China and how indigenous firms have struggled to break their domination. The study draws from Gramsci's (1935/1971) theory of hegemony, and argues that the Big Four, as part of a globalizing transnational capital class, has dominated indigenous firms by bringing to China an ideology that came to be accepted as "common sense." By winning this battle of ideology, the Big Four gained access to the coercive power of the state, and to the power of transnational institutions that have subsumed part of the power of the state. Indigenous firms have pursued a counter-hegemonic strategy of undermining the ideological superiority of the Big Four through the infiltration and modification of institutional arrangements following what Rudi Dutschke (1969) called "the long march through the institutions."

China's rapid development into a major economic power late in the 20th century is a remarkable event in world history. Few events in history have had such a dramatic effect on the lives of so many people in such a short period. Economic historian Angus Maddison estimated that China had about a quarter of the world's real gross domestic product (GDP) in terms of purchasing power parity (PPP) in the first century, a share that would grow to a third by 1820 (Maddison, 2003). Over the next 160 years, foreign incursions, civil war, the failure to participate effectively in the industrial revolution, followed by the adoption of communism resulted in China's share of global GDP falling to a low of 4.6%. In December 1978 Deng Xiaoping launched China on a program of economic reforms called the Four Modernizations, hoping to transform China into an economic power by the early 21st century. The cornerstone of the reforms was the transformation of the economy from a centrally planned system to "socialism with Chinese characteristics." Over the past 30 years of reform, socialism with Chinese characteristics took on all of the trappings of capitalism, with large capital markets and a largely market-driven economy that retains significant state influence. China began to climb back toward its historic position in the world economy, and by 2010 had the second largest national economy by GDP (PPP) and is forecast by the International Monetary Fund to pass the United States in 2016 (Barboza, 2010; Weisbrot, 2011). Foreign investment flooded into China in the late 20th century and formerly state-owned enterprises (SOEs) transformed into powerful multinational enterprises and sought capital on the world's stock exchanges.

China's emergence as an economic power involved massive social transformation. Reforms altered the cognitive orientations of society and modified fundamental existential and normative postulates, values, and ethics. The Chinese developed a new *weltanschauung* or worldview – a new way of interpreting and interacting with the world (Hiebert, 2008). New concepts of the role of government and business, and of China's role in the world needed to be developed and assimilated into Chinese society. Implicit in the construction of a new worldview was the contemporaneous development and modification of China's institutions. While none of China's institutions, including education, legal, commercial, government, and social, escaped transformational change during this period, some institutions did not exist and were created anew. Among the newly created institutions were certain professions that had not risen to significance in Communist China – professions that most prominently include accountants, lawyers, and other capitalistic professionals such as investment bankers, financial printers, and valuation experts. As China's new economy ventured into the uncharted territory of a market economy, it needed these new institutions to provide the normative and regulative forces needed to guide development.

China had developed a public accounting profession in the early decades of the 20th century, only to inter it together with other artifacts of capitalism following the Communist Revolution in 1949. As China began to open up to the world in the 1980s, it resurrected the public accounting profession to serve the needs of the developing market economy. Burgeoning interest by foreign companies eager to "sell one aspirin to one billion Chinese" led to eight of the largest international accounting firms setting up tiny offices in China that would provide advice to potential foreign investors. The Chinese, however, kept the auditing market to themselves and set up state-owned accounting firms to audit the new foreign investors.

On the night of June 4, 1989, tanks rolled into Tiananmen Square and squelched popular demands for political reforms. Foreign investors fled China and reforms paused during a period of introspection by Chinese leaders uncertain about whether to retreat to their familiar communist ideology or to advance toward further reform. Cognizant of the breakup of the Soviet Union, Deng Xiaoping ended the debate with a call for the acceleration of reforms during his famed Southern Tour in 1992, and an amazing period in global economic history began. Foreign investment flooded into China, making it the second largest destination (after the United States) for the two decades to follow. China reopened its stock exchanges to help state-owned enterprises raise capital. The economy rapidly privatized. Many Chinese companies began to list on international stock exchanges in order to raise capital and to import foreign corporate governance principles with the expectation that these reforms would improve the competitiveness of Chinese companies in world markets.

The acceleration of reform created the opportunity for the Big Four to capture the rapidly expanding accounting markets. Foreign investors starting businesses in China wanted to use their own accounting firms rather than a state-owned firm. Investment bankers advising Chinese companies seeking international stock listings told the companies to start by hiring the Big Four to get their accounts in order. In 1992, the Big Four won the right to audit in China, provided they entered into a joint venture with a state institution. The Big Four and their joint ventures rapidly secured the lion's share of audits related to foreign direct investment (FDI) and international listings, leading to a dominant position in the market.

Concerned about losing their market to foreigners, local firms and regulators embarked on a series of reforms that were intended to return the auditing markets to Chinese control. China adopted international accounting and auditing standards, and separated the state-owned audit firms from the state in order to make them independent of their clients, following international practices. The concept of creating a Chinese Big Four captivated some Chinese regulators; other regulators believed that the international Big Four was best suited to serve China's economic aspirations.

As the millennium approached, China's leaders sought to reach their long-held goal of becoming a full member of the global community by obtaining membership in the World Trade Organization (WTO). While accession to WTO was mostly a process of removing market barriers, Chinese accounting regulators saw an opportunity to localize the accounting profession by forcing the Big Four to practice in entities controlled by local CPAs, as was the practice in most WTO member countries. The Big Four outmaneuvered Chinese negotiators and persuaded the American and European government representatives to carve out a special exception permitting them to keep their China practices under foreign control.

Following China's accession to WTO the economy expanded anew. Chinese companies developed a voracious appetite for capital, and in 2009 seven of the ten largest global initial public offerings (IPOs) were from China (PricewaterhouseCoopers, 2010a). The Big Four, unleashed from their state-owned joint venture partners, grew into substantial firms of over 4,000 professional staff each and the firms began to talk of the not-too-far-off days when the Chinese firms would rival their American firms as the largest in the Big Four networks (Lee, 2007).

The Big Four faced great pressure to localize their practices, and in 2012 were forced to turn over ownership control of their audit practices to local CPAs. A boom in listings of private companies both in China and abroad collapsed in the wake of widespread accounting scandals and auditing failures. Chinese, American, and Hong Kong regulators sparred over how to regulate transnational activities of Chinese companies.

Chinese local firms, supported by the Chinese Institute of Certified Public Accountants (CICPA), began to lobby for greater support in their competition against the Big Four. The CICPA put forth policy recommendations, ultimately accepted by the State Council, China's highest executive organ, which called for 10 large Chinese CPA firms capable of serving China's multinational corporations globally. One of the strategies sanctioned by the State Council was for China's local firms to align with second-tier global firms, and by 2012 a proposed merger of the Chinese member firms of RSM and Crowe Horwath will vault the firm ahead of Ernst & Young and KPMG to become China's third largest accounting firm. The rapid ascension and strong government support of local firms raises the future possibility that the Big Four will not dominate the Chinese accounting profession in the same way it has dominated most markets in the world.

1.2. THE PURPOSE AND SIGNIFICANCE OF THIS BOOK

The purpose of this book is to document and understand the historical development of the accounting profession in China with a focus on the role of the Big Four accounting firms. This research is necessary to understand how accounting markets develop in emerging economies and to understand how the forces of globalization shape the competitive structure and regulation of these markets. The book will also provide insight into the future development of the accounting profession in China. Should indigenous firms successfully challenge the hegemony of the Big Four in China there may be implications for accounting markets globally.

1.2.1. How This Study Contributes to the Literature

I have positioned this book within a body of research that has addressed the development of the accounting profession in China. Western scholars began to turn their attention to the development of the modern accounting profession in China in the early 1990s, approximately a decade after China first opened up. Substantive papers on modern Chinese accounting begin to appear in the mid- to late 1990s, nearly 20 years after the profession was reestablished. Most early papers chronicled the current state of the profession. These papers were primarily descriptive, with the apparent purpose being to introduce Chinese accounting to the academy.

1.2.1.1. Extant Research Related to the Development of the CPA Profession in China

Xiang (1998) explained how the transition of China's economy was influencing China's accounting reforms and standards. He found that accounting reforms lagged managerial reforms in China. Lin (1998), one of the more prolific scholars on Chinese accounting, published one of the first important papers. This paper focused on the process of internationalization of the CPA profession in China. He found evidence of this in improved qualification standards for CPAs, the establishment and consolidation of professional organizations, the implementation of professional standards and training, and the opening up of the market to foreigners. The major problems the profession faced at that time were independence, quality, lack of competition, a weak legal environment, and poor enforcement of standards.

A number of similar papers reported on early developments in the profession in China (Bai, 1988; Chan & Rotenberg, 1999; Lau & Yang, 1990; Scapens & Hao, 1995; Tang, Chow, & Cooper, 1994; Tang & Lau, 2000). Hilmy (1999) concludes that accounting reforms were a response to political pressure to improve the economy.

Hao (1999) documented the development of the CPA profession from 1918 to the mid-1990s. He found the state to be the dominant player in the development of the profession. Foreign influences were more significant than community and market forces. He contrasted the development of the Chinese profession to that in the Czech Republic and observed that the Big Nine firms had failed to dominate in China as they had in the Czech Republic.

International influences on the development of accounting in China are a common theme in the extant literature. Early articles by Fang and Tang (1991) and Ge (1993) explained how increasing internationalization described the early development of the profession. A different type of article was written by Yunwei Tang (2000) and published in *Accounting Horizons*. Tang was a noted Chinese accounting professor, International Accounting Fellow with the International Accounting Standards Committee (IASC), senior partner of Da Hua, Shanghai's largest CPA firm, and Chairman of Price Waterhouse Da Hua, PW's joint venture firm in Shanghai. Tang observed the difficulty experienced in setting accounting standards in China, the need to accept international practice, and the importance of developing the skills of people. This article and three others he authored (Tang, 1997a, 1997b, 1999) provide a perspective on this period by an actor inside the emerging institution.

The first attempt to write a book length modern history of accounting in China fell short. Allen Huang and Ronald Ma's (2001) covers the period from 1949 to 2000, but its 122 page length results in it merely pointing out the major events. It is strongest in its coverage of Mao era accounting, a topic rarely considered by others. Coverage of the role of the international firms is absent. Lu and Saunders (2005) wrote about the history of Chinese public accounting from the 1900s to the present. The article simply reported key events and did not provide any meaningful analysis or interpretation.

Several significant historical publications have been written in Chinese. The two volumes of D. Y. Gao's (1982b, 1988) *General History of Chinese Accounting* predate the significant institutional developments of the profession that occurred in the 1990s, as does the work of Li and Wang (1989). The memoirs of Ding Pingzhun (2006a, 2006b, 2008) are a five-volume set that include many source documents related to his service as Director

General of the CICPA during the key periods of development of the profession. These documents, while often exhibiting an extreme bias, provide remarkable insight into the workings of the Chinese government bureaucracy and political system. This book makes extensive use of these memoirs.[2]

Rask, Chu, and Gottschang (1998), writing in the economic literature, described the role of accounting in the transition of China's economy. They observed that enterprises operating under market forces were outperforming SOEs, and that western accounting practices were necessary for a market economy.

This book extends extant research that has examined the development of the profession in China in three ways. First, this book examines the development of the CPA profession over a longer period of time and in considerable detail. Because much of the extant research was conducted before 2000, it does not consider the significant development of the profession and China's economy in the first decade of the 21st century. This book fills that gap. Second, it further explains how international institutions shaped China's accounting institutions, and in particular, how the Big Four served as agents of change. Finally, the focus of this book is on the role of the Big Four, a frequently ignored actor in extant research.

1.2.1.2. Role of the Big Four

Most extant research on Chinese accounting has focused on institutional developments such as the gradual adoption of international standards and has not focused on the role of firms in the development of the profession. Research that does consider accounting firms as important actors in the development of the profession has principally looked at indigenous firms, ignoring the "elephant in the room" presented by the much larger Big Four firms (Dai, Lau, & Yang, 2000; Lu, Ji, & Aiken, 2009). A conception that the Big Four are insignificant players in the Chinese audit market has developed and persisted.

This (arguably nationalistic) bias against considering the impact of the presence of the Big Four can be traced to Hao (1999, p. 300) who wrote: "At the date of this writing, it appears that the Big Five cannot be expected to play a dominant role in the formation of a Chinese accountancy community in the near future." Yapa and Hao (2007, p. 33) updated Hao (1999) based on a series of interviews in Beijing in 2005, reaching a dubious conclusion, albeit one consistent with Hao (1999):

> However, according to available information, despite the PRC's openness to the outside world, it appears that "Big Four" and other international accounting firms cannot be

expected to play a prominent role in the development of the Chinese accountancy profession in the near future.

The authors appear to have based their conclusion largely on Tang's (1999) report that the international firms had a market share of about 15% at the undisclosed time when Tang collected his data. Data that was readily available when Yapa and Hao prepared their study would have indicated that the Big Four firms had a significant market share when measured by revenues or by market capitalization audited. The authors further indicate that regulations forbid the international Big Four from doing statutory audit or accounting work in China, yet they acknowledge the firms can open representative offices, establish joint ventures, and accept member firms. The authors appear to fail to understand that the Big Four typically practice in one of these forms in most countries in the world.

Helen Yee (2009, 2012) has addressed the development of the CPA profession in China in the 1980s and early 1990s. She states that the international accounting firms did not have much influence in China in the 1990s. She suggests that it would be worthwhile to explore the uneasy relationship between the state and the international accounting firms on the development of the accounting profession after 2001, following China's admission to the WTO. This book shows that the influence of the international firms began long before 2001, but it does answer Yee's call for study of the role of international firms in China.

Lu et al. (2009) critically evaluated the significance of governmental dominance in Chinese accounting development. They examined the role of government over three periods of Chinese development – until 1949, 1949–1979, and 1979 to the present, with an emphasis on the most recent history. They concluded that government played a dominant, near exclusive, role in shaping the accounting profession. The article reaches some questionable conclusions by completely ignoring the presence and influence of international firms and institutions in China. For example, they state that there is no independent accounting profession in China because of the influence of the state and that most clients are SOEs. This ignores the reality of the existence of sizable international accounting firms that are clearly independent of the state and the reality that by 2002 the non-state sector would produce over two-thirds of China's GDP (Asian Development Bank, 2002). While the paper does acknowledge that outside forces have influenced the development of accounting (in particular the worldwide trend toward IFRS), the authors maintain that the government still maintains controlling powers and is likely to do so in the foreseeable future.

The paper fails to even mention the presence of international CPA firms in China, the role of the WTO, and how international capital markets have shaped China's accounting markets.

This refrain was most recently repeated by Simunic and Wu (2009, p. 21) who call for auditing research in the Chinese environment because "the market share of the Big Four firms is quite low." The present book will correct those misconceptions and explain the prominent role played by the Big Four in the development of the Chinese accounting profession. In this study, the author observed what appears to be a nationalistically driven resentment of the Big Four's presence in China by Chinese academics. This resentment has led to bias in presenting research results. By exposing the facts, this book will contribute to the eradication of this source of bias.

1.2.1.3. Globalization

I have also positioned this book within the body of research addressing globalization and accounting, a field that is itself a subset of globalization research within the discipline of the political economy. It answers Poullaos's (2004) call for greater engagement between critical accounting researchers and the globalization literature. Samsonova (2009, p. 529) conceives of globalization as "not merely something that is imposed or exerted but rather as something that is a product of the cross-border collaborative agency of state as well as non-state actors, both individual and collective." This book follows Samsonova's perspective of globalization, and focuses on the roles of state and non-state actors in the process of developing and globalizing China's accounting profession. In this respect it extends Suddaby, Cooper, and Greenwood (2007) by providing a field-level account of how the Big Four and transnational institutions like the WTO have subsumed some of the power of state regulators. It also explains the role of transnational accounting firms in the processes of globalization, extending to a new geography similar studies conducted in Greece (Caramanis, 1999, 2002, 2005); New Zealand (Baskerville & Hay, 2010); and Eastern Europe (Cooper, Greenwood, Hinings, & Brown, 1998; Samsonova, 2009).

Cooper and Robson (2006) observe that accounting historians have not always clearly stated the implications that the historical development of the profession in Britain and the United States might have in determining "... the likely strategies available to accountants in other parts of the world who are attempting to create a professional body, or others trying to resist such attempts" (p. 418). This book will attempt to avoid that shortcoming, and will address the likely strategies available to protagonists and counter-protagonists in future developing markets.

1.2.1.4. Marxism

This book brings accounting research informed by Gramsci's theory of hegemony back to its Marxist roots in class struggle. This book casts the struggle between the transnational capital class represented by the Big Four and the indigenous Chinese CPA firms in stock Marxist terms as the quintessential confrontation between the proletariat and the bourgeoisie. Fleischman and Radcliffe (2003, p. 16) remind Marxist accounting historians of their responsibility to update Marx as new stages of capitalism wax and wane. This book makes a modest contribution in this respect by providing a field-level account that applies Marxist theory to the conversion of China's Marxist/Leninist, communist/socialist-based economy to a form resembling capitalism.

This book also answers the call by McNally and Schwarzmantal (2009) for scholars of international relations to explain more broadly and more thoroughly the processes by which hegemonic consent by the subordinate class is obtained. This book also extends hegemonic research in accounting by providing a field-level account of how counter-hegemonic strategies are developed and executed.

1.2.2. Why This Book is Important

China's emergence as a world economic power increasingly intertwines the lives of nearly all people with China. Consequently, China's institutions have broad reaching influence. Accounting firms perform a normative and regulative function within society, and the Chinese CPA profession has increasing impact far beyond its local activities. Chinese companies have dominated the IPO market globally in recent years (PricewaterhouseCoopers, 2010a). China has become the second largest source of FDI, while remaining the second largest destination for the same. Chinese companies trade globally, and get into trade disputes globally. The CPA profession in China plays a key role in all of those activities, providing critical services that allow capital to flow and trade to continue. Understanding how the CPA profession in China fills these roles is the most important contribution of this book.

This book will be useful to a broad range of users. It will be of particular use to both domestic and international regulators of the accounting profession. Domination by the Big Four of global accounting markets is a matter of great concern for regulators worldwide (European Commission, 2009, 2010; General Accounting Office, 2003; Government Accountability Office, 2008; House of Lords, 2011). Because China is a relatively new market, we can see how globalization leads to market domination in a relatively short period. The examination of counter-hegemonic strategies by indigenous firms will inform the development of strategies to counter Big Four domination in markets globally. This book will help regulators in China to better understand how they are influenced, and to a certain extent controlled, by the transnational capital class and its supporting institutions. International regulators will be able to understand how emerging patterns of transnational regulation enable and constrict their powers and help them to identify how "regulatory holes" – gaps where transnational accounting firms escape regulation – come to exist. Although the scale of and institutional environment of China makes it a unique market among developing nations, this book will inform those involved with the development of the CPA profession in other emerging economies.

The findings of this book will be useful to accounting firms in their strategic planning. The Big Four will benefit from this book through gaining an understanding of the threats and opportunities that they face with respect to their market positions. Second-tier international firms will better understand how they can find the success in China that has eluded them elsewhere. Indigenous firms will better understand why they are dominated by the Big Four and how they can develop strategies to optimize their market position. This information will be useful to indigenous firms in other markets who face competition from globalizing market entrants.

1.3. THE RESEARCH QUESTION

The major research question of this thesis is: *How did the accounting profession in China develop during China's period of opening up and reform?*[3] I will answer that question by answering three subsidiary questions.

1.3.1. How did the Big Four Come to Dominate Chinese Accounting Markets?

Based on the findings in this book, I will argue that Chinese society chose to accept the Big Four as a means of reforming its economy and gaining acceptance in the global community. Chinese society decided to accept the neoliberal ideology of global markets that, from an accounting perspective, include international accounting and auditing standards, conventions as to the role and structure of accounting firms, and acceptance of the dominating role of the Big Four. I argue that the Big Four is a member of what the literature calls the globalizing transnational capital class, which gains access to and ultimate domination of local markets through the spread of its ideology, which in the present case is the neoliberal ideology of globalization (Carroll & Carson, 2003; Sklair, 1995, 1997, 2002; van der Pijl, 1984, 1998).

1.3.2. Why did the Big Four Come to Dominate Chinese Accounting Markets?

I will argue that the process of globalization has resulted in the shifting of spatial, ideational, and identification boundaries of the profession in a manner consistent with the theory developed by Suddaby et al. (2007). This theory posits that changing boundaries of the profession have resulted in a shift of power away from traditional state regulators to transnational forces such as the WTO and the Big Four firms. I argue that this shift in power led the Big Four to dominate the market in China.

1.3.3. How have Indigenous Firms Tried to Break the Dominance of the Big Four?

This book will examine the counter-hegemonic strategies and tactics used by local firms and their principal advocate, the CICPA. The book will find that the indigenous firms have primarily used a strategy of mimetic and normative isomorphism as a means of deepening contradictions related to the Big Four dominance of local markets.

1.4. OVERVIEW OF METHODOLOGY

This book is a critical historiography, conducted, in part, in the style of ethnography. The researcher has been engaged with the subject for over 30 years, first in a 28-year career with PricewaterhouseCoopers (PwC) that culminated in a leadership role in China, followed by a second career as an accounting professor at Peking University where he continued his interaction with the profession. The book uses a "bricolage," as the term is defined by Denzin and Lincoln (2000). With a bricolage, the researcher draws from different qualitative approaches to knowledge construction and uses them to build a bespoke methodology.

There are two primary methodological streams for this book. The first evaluates the structure of the profession in China using established methodologies for measuring market concentration. These methodologies allow comparison of the China accounting market to markets in other countries. The second stream constructs a history of the involvement of the Big Four in China. This portion of the book uses various archival data sources including news clippings, firm histories, and private records. Significant to the book are the memoirs of Ding Pingzhun, the former Secretary General of the CICPA. Ding has preserved documents that provide a rare insight into the thinking of Chinese bureaucrats during this historic time and allow this research to speak to "both sides of the story." Extensive interviews of people involved during the development of the CPA profession in China supplement the archival sources.

1.5. LIMITATIONS AND DELIMITATIONS

The modern CPA profession in China has developed over a 30-year period beginning in 1980. I decided to study this long period in order to identify and analyze phenomena that result in persistent changes, rather than those with temporary impact. A longer period of study also fills a gap in the literature for a comprehensive analysis of the development of the profession in China. This decision, however, results in a more superficial analysis than an examination of a shorter period would allow. In my opinion, the level of analysis is appropriate to the purpose of this book, yet I acknowledge that a more comprehensive analysis of shorter periods of development would yield further insights. I leave this to future research.

This book focuses on the role of the Big Four in China. This has biased the research design toward collecting and evaluating data related to the Big Four rather than indigenous firms. In large part, I have allowed the memoirs of former CICPA Director General Ding Pingzhun to speak for indigenous firms. While my research shows Ding Pingzhun to be a tireless advocate of indigenous firms, other voices might add to the analysis of indigenous firm responses to Big Four hegemony. Christine Chan (2008) has taken this up with her case study of the strategies of two indigenous firms competing with Big Four firms, but there is further work to be done.

This is a cross-cultural study. The important actors come from diverse backgrounds, including many of Western, Hong Kong, and Mainland Chinese origin. The researcher and author of this book is an American who has lived and worked in China since 1997. Bias is a major threat to cross-cultural studies. Constructs that are chosen may not be similarly defined in all cultural groups (van de Vijver & Leung, 1997). Data for this book included materials in both Chinese and English. Because I am not completely proficient in the Chinese language, I have relied on translations of Chinese materials. Translation introduces a new level of bias to research. The translation literature suggests that there is no one correct translation and that the translator is like Aladdin in the enchanted vaults: spoiled for choice (Bassnet, 1994).

1.6. ORGANIZATION OF THE BOOK

The organization of the remainder of this thesis is as follows: Chapter 2 explains the overall grounding of the study in Marxist theory, and explains and justifies the selection of Gramsci's theory of hegemony as the guiding theoretical foundation for the book. Chapter 3 evaluates extant literature related to the Big Four accounting firms with a focus on the globalizing impacts of these firms.

Chapters 4 through 7 present the findings of this study. Chapter 4 explains the early development of the profession. Chapter 5 explains the process by which the Big Four dominated the accounting profession in China. Chapter 6 explains how the Big Four have sustained their domination. This chapter also presents findings related to the market structure of the accounting profession in China. Chapter 7 outlines the counter-hegemonic strategies of the indigenous CPA profession.

Chapter 8 analyzes the findings and answers the three primary research questions: (1) How did the Big Four come to dominate Chinese accounting markets; (2) Why did the Big Four come to dominate Chinese accounting markets; (3) How have indigenous firms tried to break the hegemony of the Big Four?

Chapter 9 addresses the implications of the study. I present strategies to enhance or protect the respective positions of the three key groups of actors in this book: the Big Four, indigenous firms, and accounting regulators. I also present a series of recommendations of areas for further research in this field.

NOTES

1. Arthur Andersen (AA), Arthur Young (AY), Coopers & Lybrand (C&L), Deloitte Haskins and Sells (DHS), Ernst & Ernst (E&E), Peat Marwick Mitchell (PMM), Price Waterhouse (PW), and Touche Ross (TR) were collectively known as the Big Eight. The Big Nine added the European firm of Klyneld Main Goerdeler, which later merged with PMM to form KPMG. E&E merged with AY to form Ernst & Young (E&Y); C&L merged with PW to form PricewaterhouseCoopers (PwC); DHS merged with TR to form Deloitte Touche Tohmatsu (DTT); and AA failed to successively create the Big Six, the Big Five, and the present Big Four.
2. Quotations from Ding in this book have been translated from the original Chinese.
3. In 1978, China launched a policy of *openness and reform* that has guided China's development in the 30 + years since. The term *opening up* has come to refer to the acceptance of foreign investment in China and the increasing engagement of China with the world (Démurger, 2000).

CHAPTER 2

THEORETICAL FOUNDATIONS

> Classes struggle, some classes triumph, others are eliminated. Such is history; such is the history of civilization for thousands of years. To interpret history from this viewpoint is historical materialism; standing in opposition to this viewpoint is historical idealism.
>
> – Mao Zedong, "Cast Away Illusions, Prepare for Struggle": August 14, 1949 (Mao, 1961)

This chapter sets forth the theoretical foundations for the study. The chapter begins by positioning the study within historical critical accounting research. I evaluate alternative research paradigms and defend the selection of a Marxist approach. The chapter then explains Antonio Gramsci's theory of hegemony and counter-hegemony. The chapter concludes with a defense of the appropriateness of the theories of hegemony and counter-hegemony for the purposes of this study.

2.1. HISTORICAL CRITICAL ACCOUNTING RESEARCH

This research is positioned within the body of critical accounting research that answers Hopwood's (1978) call for studies "of accounting" rather than the traditional studies "in accounting." Critical accounting research aims to uncover the relationships between accounting and society by examining the circumstances surrounding the emergence and development of accounting practices (Burchell, Clubb, Hopwood, Hughes, & Nahapiet, 1980; Hopwood, 1988). Traditional accounting research focuses principally on positivistic analysis of economic factors, whereas critical accounting research expands this focus to include political, cultural, and societal parameters (Hopwood, 1987). Bryer (2005, p. 26) argues that "to unleash accounting history we must drop the neoclassical framework and engage with major social theorists, particularly Weber and Marx."

In the context of historical accounting research, the traditional approach has been to examine accounting in the historical context in which it operates in order to provide a basis for determining how ideas and practices influence society (Napier, 1998). The critical approach to accounting history seeks the same result through a greater emphasis on the political, cultural, and social context in which accounting develops (Gomes, 2008). Fleischman and Radcliffe (2003) observe that contemporary accounting historians have moved away from an older economic reductionism into a broader investigation of the cultural, social, and political foundations of industrial activity.

An important thread of historical accounting research has included research on the profession of accountancy and the firms and individuals who make up that profession. The accounting profession is a powerful and important institution in most societies and it has attracted considerable attention from scholars. Cooper and Robson (2006) argued that too many of the early studies of the role of the accounting profession in society were willing to accept the profession's own narrative that emphasized their public interest purpose. Burrage (1990, pp. 5–6) criticized much of the historical work on the professions:

> … historians focused on the creation, the domestic affairs, and of the corporate affairs of particular professions and therefore tended to concentrate on the elite of the profession and the issues that came to the attention of their governing bodies. They rarely sought to study the working practice of the rank and file members of the profession, rarely referred to other professions, rarely sought to relate changes in the profession to changes in the wider society and rarely therefore found any reason to criticize the profession. Their main task was to recount the success story of responsible leaders coping with the problems that faced the profession.

Burrage might criticize this study for many of the same reasons. Studies of the development of a profession necessarily focus on the activities of the elite of the profession, and that is because of the significant impact that the elite have on the process. The daily working practices of the rank and file shed little light on how institutions are formed. Based in part on his criticism, I have included many interviews of the rank and file in my data, but found little explanatory power in their observations of the process. I accept and respond to Burrage's other criticisms by relating the development of the profession in China to the broader changes taking place in

Chinese society as it opened up to the world, and by considering the impact of other professionals, particularly lawyers and investment bankers on the development of the accounting profession.

2.2. ALTERNATIVE THEORETICAL FOUNDATIONS FOR HISTORICAL ACCOUNTING RESEARCH

Fleischman and Radcliffe (2003) identify three prominent paradigms for accounting history studies: neoclassical or economic-rationalist; Foucauldian; and Marxist. Similarly, Goddard (2002) categorizes the literature on the relationship between the accounting profession and the state into three schools: Foucauldian, Weberian, and Marxist (and a fourth category that is a composite of these).

2.2.1. Non-Marxist Approaches

The neoclassical or economic-rationalist perspective has been the dominant traditional approach to accounting history studies. The neoclassical perspective holds that accounting change is a rational movement toward lower transaction costs and accordingly aligns well with traditional, positivistic accounting research.

Foucauldian approaches, based on the work of French postmodernist philosopher Michel Foucault, stress the importance of knowledge in the acquisition of power. According to Edward Said (1983, p. 216), Foucault's greatest contribution is explaining how "the will to exercise dominant control in society and history has also discovered a way to clothe, disguise, rarify and wrap itself systematically in the language of truth, discipline, rationality, utilitarian value and knowledge." Foucauldian approaches are useful in explaining professionalism and closure of accounting markets. In the present study, Foucault may help to explain how the expertise of the Big Four helped them to achieve a dominant position in the China accounting markets.

Foucauldian approaches stress the centrality of language in synthesizing power and knowledge. The Foucauldian school was characterized by Chua and Sinclair (1994) as analyzing how discursive and nondiscursive practices of accountants interconnect with diverse discourses and programs of governments. Armstrong (1991), however, points out that Foucauldian approaches reject any a priori correlation of interest with class. Since the central thesis of this study associates power with the class of the Big Four, the Foucauldian approach provides less explanatory power than Marxist approaches where class is central.

Closely related to Foucauldian approaches are Weberian approaches, based on the work of German sociologist and political economist Max Weber. Goddard (2002) argues that the Weberian school, illustrated by Chua and Poullaos (1993, 1998) and Walker and Shackleton (1998), downplays the materialistic base of Marxist approaches and instead relies more on closure theories of professions. Closure theories are powerful tools to explain the early development of accounting markets. In China, however, the accounting profession rapidly achieved closure following the opening up of the economy, most likely because of the rapid acceptance of Western practices. Accordingly, closure theory is not ideal for explaining how the Big Four came to dominate accounting practice in China.

2.2.2. Marxist Approaches

This study is informed by the Marxist tradition, a body of theory that is largely based on the writings of Marx, Engels, Lenin, Trotsky, Stalin, and Mao. From a historical perspective, Marx argued that industrial society emerged from a long process of class conflict that ultimately resulted in the capitalistic mode of production overthrowing the feudal system (Bryer, 2005). Fundamental to the Marxist tradition is the exploitation of the working class by capitalist firms and the "whole network of ideological and repressive state apparatuses that ultimately support the ruling class and the extant mode of production" (James, 2010, p. 697).

Much of Marxist-informed accounting research has focused on the partisan nature of accounting records and how accounting practices can suppress classes of people (Bryer, 2005, 2006; Hopper & Armstrong, 1991). Bryer (1999) has gone so far as to argue that Marx could provide us with a general theory of accounting based on these concepts.

This study, however, focuses not on how accounting technologies suppress working classes, but rather on how two classes of professional accountants emerged and how one class, the Big Four firms, came to dominate the other class, indigenous accounting firms. Marx and Engels (1846/1974, p. 77) argued that "all history is the history of class struggle," and this thesis argues that history of the accounting profession in China is no exception.

China is one of the few remaining countries in the world that claims to follow a Marxist/Leninist philosophy. The current constitution of the Communist Party of China states: "Marxism–Leninism brings to light the laws governing the development of the history of human society. Its basic tenets are correct and have tremendous vitality" (Communist Party of China, 2007). Marxism–Leninism's focus on the inherent class struggles of capitalism formed the ideological justification for China's experiments with communism. Marxism informs this study not because of China's ideological support for it and its significant impact on the ordering of Chinese society, but rather because it best explains the reemergence of capitalism in China under what the Communist Party calls Deng Xiaoping Theory and Jiang Zemin's Important Thought of Three Represents. Marx believed that feudalism would successively give way to capitalism, socialism, and communism. While it can be argued that Chinese communism did not reflect what Marx had in mind, the ironic use of Marxism in this study to explain the evolution of communism to state-sponsored capitalism in China could perhaps be described as a case of Marx being hoisted by his own petard.

2.2.2.1. Theory of Hegemony

Hegemony is a Marxist concept derived largely from the work of Antonio Gramsci, the first leader of the Italian Communist Party in the turbulent days of Mussolini's march to power. Gramsci worked for the Communist International[1] during 1923–1924 in Moscow and Vienna. He was later imprisoned in one of Mussolini's jails where he wrote his famous "Prison Notebooks" which are considered his most important contribution to Marxist theory (Sasson, 1991). Among Marxists, Gramsci is noted for his theory of cultural hegemony as the means to gaining class dominance. In his view, a new "Communist man" had to be created before any political revolution was possible. This led to a focus on the efforts of intellectuals in the fields of education and culture. Gramsci envisioned an extended campaign through society's institutions, including the government, the judiciary, the military, the schools, and the media. He also concluded that so long as the workers had a Christian soul, they would not respond to revolutionary appeals, so the critical agenda was to replace the Christian soul.

Gramsci's conception of hegemony is that a culturally diverse society can be dominated by one of its social classes. The ideas of the dominating class come to be accepted as the norm, perceived to benefit all of society while possibly only benefiting the dominating class. Williams (1960, p. 587) provides a comprehensive definition of hegemony:

> By "hegemony" Gramsci seems to mean a sociopolitical situation, in his terminology a "moment," in which the philosophy and practice of a society fuse or are in equilibrium; an order in which a certain way of life and thought is dominant, in which one concept of reality is diffused throughout society in all its institutional and private manifestations, informing with its spirit all taste, morality, customs, religious and political principles, and all social relations, particularly in their intellectual and moral connotations. An element of direction and control, not necessarily conscious, is implied. This hegemony corresponds to a state power conceived in stock Marxist terms as the dictatorship of a class.

Sikka and Willmott (2009) observe that the mechanisms of hegemony:

> … do not rely, in the first instance upon naked coercion but instead depend upon the processes of moral and cultural leadership provided by the institutions of civil society, notably education and the media and extending to the legitimating expertise provided by the inter alia accounting firms.

2.2.3. Hegemony of Consent

Most scholars who have interpreted Gramsci have concluded that the hegemony of consent is the distinguishing feature of hegemony over other forms of domination. Simon (1982, p. 21) explains hegemony as "a relation, not of domination by means of force, but of consent by means of political and ideological leadership." Bates (1975, p. 352) explains hegemony as "political leadership based on the consent of the led, a consent which is secured by the diffusion and popularization of the world view of the ruling class."

Consent to hegemony by the subordinate class is rarely active or even conscious. Weber (1922/1978, p. 21) suggests that such explicit consent would be unusual:

> In the great majority of cases, actual action goes on in a state of inarticulate half-consciousness or actual unconsciousness of its subjective meaning. The actor is more likely to "be aware" of it in a vague sense than he is to "know" what he is doing or be explicitly self-conscious about it. In most cases, his action is governed by impulse or habit. Only occasionally and in the uniform action of large numbers, often only in the case of a few individuals, is the subjective meaning of the action whether rational or irrational, brought clearly into consciousness. The ideal type of meaningful action where the meaning is fully conscious and explicit is a marginal case.

Hegemonic studies tend to infer the consent of the subordinate class from the absence of organized opposition to the hegemony. McNally and Schwarzmantal (2009) have called for scholars applying Gramscian theory to international relations to explain more thoroughly and more broadly the processes by which hegemonic consent is reached. This is likely a difficult task; particularly if one accepts Weber's view that people do not tend to be actively involved in such decisions. Instead, it is necessary to examine changes in ideology with a view toward understanding why the changes were not actively resisted, or if they were resisted, why the change was ultimately accepted.

Joseph (2002) observes that for a class to become hegemonic, it must have behind it the economic, political, and cultural conditions which allow it to put itself forward as leading. In the present study, the ideological changes that enabled Big Four hegemony were nested in broader ideological changes in society as it moved from the former economic system to one more based on capitalistic principles. Chinese society changed its ideology from a centrally planned and controlled Communist approach to a market-driven approach, and the Big Four participated in, benefited from, and influenced this change.

2.2.4. Hegemony of Coercion

The hegemony of consent is backed up from time to time by the hegemony of coercion. Gramsci viewed the state as playing a central role in organizing social and political life, which it achieves by providing cultural, ideological, and political leadership (Lehman & Tinker, 1987). Political society is derived from the coercive power of the state – conventionally understood to include laws, courts, military, police, and regulators. A group that has established hegemony of consent through ideological superiority may occasionally need the coercive power of the state to maintain that hegemony. The coercive power of the state is present in accounting principally through the regulation of the profession. Such regulations include standards for admission to the profession, accounting and auditing standards, and requirements as to the form of practice. Other coercive instruments of society such as police, courts, and prisons back up these regulations.

While the state in Gramsci's work was easily understood, the role of the state as it relates to the accounting profession has been subsumed by the emergence of new regulators that alter the traditional boundaries of professional regulation (Suddaby et al., 2007). Sklair (1995, 1998) considers the bureaucrats that make up these regulators (together with sympathetic local bureaucrats) as members of the transnational capital class (further discussed below). These new regulators include nongovernmental associations such as the International Accounting Standards Board (IASB) and the

WTO. While certain of these regulators set rules and standards, the ultimate enforcement of their rules and standards rests with the state, since only the state has the power to imprison or confiscate the property of those who choose to ignore rules and standards. For example, the IASB establishes International Financial Reporting Standards (IFRS). An actor can be compelled to follow such standards only if the state chooses to adopt the standard and to sanction noncompliance.

The accounting profession in China, particularly the Big Four, also faced multiple state actors. The increasing globalization of China's economy brings its companies and institutions into regulatory nexus with other jurisdictions. For example, a Chinese company that lists its shares in New York and London is subject to state securities regulation in all three countries. In this situation, China has the power to regulate the company because it is organized under Chinese laws and operates within China. United States and United Kingdom regulators gain regulatory nexus because they regulate all companies listed on their stock exchanges. By gaining the regulatory nexus to regulate companies listed on stock exchanges, countries also typically gain regulatory oversight on accountants who audit the companies listed on those exchanges.

2.2.5. Class

Marx used an essentially functionalist definition of class derived from the place of a function within the system. Marx identified the three great classes of modern capitalist societies to include wage-laborers, capitalists, and landowners, yet acknowledged that this class articulation does not emerge in a pure form. In determining what makes up a class, Marx suggested looking to the source of revenue of the social groups – wages, profit, and ground-rent in the case of the three great classes (Marx, 1867/1981).

Ollman (1993) argues that this definition of class is too simplistic for today's society because class represents a complex social relation. Individuals who share a social space and functions and assume over time common characteristics as regards income, lifestyle, political consciousness, and organization become members of a class. Ollman argues that class is a quality that attaches to individuals in the class and shapes the thinking and action of class members. While class is a quality attached to an individual, other qualities such as gender and nationality (arguably classes in themselves) also attach to the individual and moderate the influence of the class on the thinking and action of the class member.

2.2.5.1. Transnational Capital Class

Globalization in the later half of the 20th century has spawned a thread of research arguing for recognition of the emergence of a transnational capital class (Carroll & Carson, 2003; Kauppi & Madsen, 2013; Sklair, 1995, 1997, 2002; van der Pijl, 1984, 1998). The transnational capital class is theorized as a segment of the world bourgeoisie purported to represent transnational capital and the ideology of neoliberalism. It is transnational in the sense that it denotes economic and related social, political, and cultural processes that supersede nation-states (Robinson & Harris, 2000). Carroll and Carson (2003) found evidence of interlocking directorships in transnational organizations such as the World Economic Forum and argued that this illustrated how the transnational capital class influenced global policy.

Robinson and Harris (2000) argue that the transnational capital class is a global ruling class because it controls the levers of an emergent transnational state apparatus and of global decision-making. This is consistent with Suddaby et al.'s (2007) finding of emerging transnational regulation of the accounting industry. Robinson and Harris (2000, p. 12) maintain that the transnational capital class was in the process of constructing an historic hegemonic bloc:

> This historic bloc is composed of transnational corporations and financial institutions, the elites that manage the supranational economic planning agencies, major forces in the dominant political parties, media conglomerates, and technocratic elites and state managers in both North and South.

Robinson and Harris (2000) observe that most accounts (with the notable exception of Sklair who unlinks the class from geography) of the transnational capital class posit a national bourgeoisie that converges externally with national classes in other countries. Kaup (2013) argued that scholars need to discern between transnational elites who operate in local circuits of accumulation and those who participate in global circuits of accumulation. These accounts are consistent with the account presented in this study of the Big Four, where Big Four practices are organized on a national basis yet are integrated globally. Beaverstock (2004) found that expatriate professionals in law firms working side by side with local professionals created transnational communities. McNally and Schwarzmantal (2009, p. 24) explain how hegemony is established between the transnational capital class and local subordinate groups:

> Thus, those who subscribe to the logic of the transnational capital class, international hegemony is processed through the consensual relationships forged between transnational elites and their respective "national subordinate" classes.

This study will focus on the consensual relationships that develop between the Big Four and local accountants.

2.2.5.2. Transnational Epistemic Communities

Sklair (2002) includes globalizing professionals as one of four interlocking groups that make up the transnational capital class (also including corporations, globalizing bureaucrats and politicians, and merchants and media). Professionals in the transnational capital class would include accountants, lawyers, investment bankers, financial printers, and valuation experts. These professionals form epistemic communities, as defined by Haas (1992, p. 4):

> An epistemic community is a network of professionals with recognized expertise and competence in a particular domain and an authoritative claim to policy-relevant knowledge within that domain or issue area. Although an epistemic community may consist of professionals from a variety of disciplines and backgrounds, they have (1) a shared set of normative and principled beliefs which provide a value-based rationale for the social action of community members; (2) shared causal beliefs which are derived from their analysis of practices leading or contributing to a central set of problems in their domain and which then serve as the basis for elucidating the multiple linkages between possible policy actions and desired outcomes; (3) shared notions of validity – that is, intersubjective, internally defined criteria for weighing and validating knowledge in the domain of their expertise, and (4) a common policy enterprise – that is, a set of common practices associated with a set of problems to which their professional competence is directed, presumably out of the conviction that human welfare will be enhanced as a consequence.

Christensen, Newberry, and Potter (2010) argue that small epistemic communities of expert accountants have an outsized influence in guiding global accounting policy. The transnational epistemic communities of professionals are important to the establishment of hegemony, since they mutually reinforce the ideology of the transnational hegemonic class. For example, in the case of international listings of Chinese companies, international investment bankers, international lawyers and accountants expect, and often demand, the participation of each other, in part to manage risk, and in part because that is "the way it is done" – a mutually reinforcing ideology. Ramirez (2012) shows how the transnational elite infiltrate and transform the elite of previously insular professional communities to extend their regulatory influence across border.

2.2.6. Strata and Class

Robinson and Harris (2000) criticize Sklair (1995) for conflating strata with class, a criticism that would apply to this thesis as well. The argument is that the transnational capital class is simply an elite stratum of the capitalist class. Following Robinson and Harris's logic, the Big Four would not represent a separate class, rather an elite stratum of the class of professional accountants, or more broadly professionals, or the bourgeoisie. Robinson and Harris's own work undermine their argument, where they refer to the World Economic Forum as an acknowledged class organization because of the strict conditions of admission. A Gramscian (and Marxist) analysis is powerful for unaligned segment interests since it focuses on the conflict between the objectives of the segments. Regardless of whether we call a segment a stratum or a class, the Gramscian and Marxist concept of class applies to situations, such as the accounting profession in China, where the interests of the segments are potentially in conflict.

2.2.6.1. Class and the Accounting Profession

The premise of this thesis is that the accounting profession in China divided into two classes shortly after its inception. The first class consists of those accountants who organized into indigenous CPA firms in the 1980s. Over time, these accountants would become conscious of their new class as certified public accountants. The return of public accounting to China after its long hiatus created a class of domestic accountants where none was present before. The other class consisted of the Big Eight CPA firms that entered China at the same time. Well established in other countries, this class consisted of personnel who came to China with a clear consciousness of their class status, although newly hired employees might take some time to acquire class-consciousness.

Members of either the indigenous CPA class or the Big Eight CPA class were members of other classes as well. Indigenous CPAs might identify with classes based on geography, educational background, gender, or the state institution from which they came. The national origin, firm affiliation, and functional specialization such as audit or tax heavily influenced the perspectives of Big Eight accountants. As the Big Eight firms grew and employed increasing numbers of local employees, these employees would often have common traits with indigenous CPAs such as Chinese Communist Party memberships, educational backgrounds, and other social experiences. Within the Big Eight firms there would be additional classes including such divisions as expatriates versus locals, partners versus staff, and audit versus tax. Such divisions would be less pronounced in the indigenous firms in the early stages; however, there would soon arise class distinctions between smaller indigenous firms and those permitted to audit-listed companies.

Over time, the indigenous and Big Eight classes of accountants would become conscious of their different classes. The consciousness of a class is critical to Marxist theory, since it enables the class struggle that is at the heart of capitalism. Ollman (1993) describes class-consciousness as a type of group think, a collective, interactive approach to recognizing, labeling and coming to understand, and acting upon, the particular world that class members have in common. Class-consciousness sets forth the broad outline of class struggle and where one fits in it, establishes feelings of solidarity with other members of the class and a rational hostility toward opposition classes.

The identity of two primary classes of independent accountants is consistent with both Marx's and Ollman's approach to class. From a Marxist perspective the Big Four looked to different sources of revenue – mainly large internationally listed SOEs and foreign-invested enterprises while the indigenous firms focused on smaller SOEs and private companies. From Ollman's perspective of class, interviews with accountants in China clearly establish that Big Four accountants and local firm accountants perceive themselves as belonging to different groups.

Deng and Macve (2012) criticize the treatment of the Big Four as a class as defined in an earlier version of this work (Gillis, 2011a). While they acknowledge the insight that the Big Four represent part of a globalizing capitalistic class, they do not accept that the Big Four represent a class in the sense of a classic working-class struggle, noting that it was the Chinese government itself that encouraged the entry of the Big Four and that many local accountants came from the government. The Big Four may not represent a class in the classic working-class conception, but it can be argued that the Marxist conception of class, particularly in a Gramscian context, is not so narrowly limited. Deng and Macve have conflated the state with the class of local accountants.

Yee (2009) also conflates the state with a hegemonic class. In a Gramscian analysis, the state is the reservoir of coercive power accessible from time to time to support the hegemony of the dominating class. Yee uses the state as a proxy for a hegemonic class associated with the Communist Party of China and more particularly the bureaucrats who support the reform ideology of Deng Xiaoping.

2.2.7. Creation of Historic Blocs

Hegemony, once established, is rarely ephemeral but rather manifests itself in historic blocs. Simon (1982, p. 26) argued that once a hegemonic class has combined leadership in civil society with leadership in sphere of production, an "historic bloc" is established and may endure for an entire historic period. According to Worth (2002, p. 298):

> An historic bloc refers to the solid structure that is created when a hegemonic order is in place, its formation being dependent on the hegemony, which in turn "binds" or "glues" together all the other parts of society into a relationship which recognizes homogenous norms of political economic practices and culture.

The conditions for the creation of a hegemonic class are often established by an organic crisis. An organic crisis is one in which there is a breakdown of the social relations and institutions which hold society together and enable it to maintain and reproduce itself (Hall, 1984, p. 12). Gramsci (1935/1971, p. 178) maintained that such crises can only be resolved by the creation of a new hegemony and "sometimes last(s) for decades." Goddard (2002) argued that:

> During this period of instability and transition, the system of alliances forming the basis of the hegemony may have to undergo far-reaching changes and a process of restructuring if it is to survive. Such crises are often precipitated by failure of the ruling class in some large undertaking such as war, for which it demanded the consent and sacrifice of the people or as a result of the crisis in the sphere of production (Bates, 1975). The crisis will consist of a struggle to create a new balance of political forces, requiring a reshaping of state institutions as well as the formation of new ideologies. Unless effectively challenged, the ruling class will re-establish its hegemony, although a new historic bloc will be created. Historical development can therefore be seen as a series of organic crises followed by new historic blocs that establish hegemony over a period of relative stability.

Identification of organic crises has important methodological implications, since they serve to both establish and threaten hegemony. Organic crises are the catalysts for change.

The Big Four's hegemony over the accounting profession in America and much of the developed world has constituted an historic bloc since the early 20th century (Stevens, 1981). The series of corporate scandals in the early 2000s following the collapse of Enron were a major organic crisis that threatened the public accounting profession (Asthana, Balsam, & Kim, 2009). These corporate crises reshaped state institutions, creating in the United States the Public Company Accounting Oversight Board (PCAOB). They also led to new ideologies, such as new conceptions of independence that prohibited the firms from performing certain consulting services with audit clients. These new conceptions were institutionalized through laws. Three of the Big Four shed their consulting practices in the early 2000s and the Big Four survived the crisis, effectively forming a new historic bloc and maintaining their hegemony.

In China, the accounting profession emerged because of institutional reforms caused by the organic crisis brought about by the failure of the Cultural Revolution, which ultimately led to China's strategy to open up to the outside world. The next major organic crisis was marked by the events at Tiananmen Square in 1989, which led to the major economic reforms that created the economic and political conditions that enabled the Big Four to establish hegemony over the nascent profession. This study identifies two further organic crises – the opening and expansion of capital markets and China's entry into the WTO. Yee (2012) combines all of these events into a single organic crisis related to the transformation of China's economy to one that is market-driven.

2.2.8. Ideology

At the core of Gramsci's conception of hegemony is ideology. "Man is not ruled by force alone, but also by ideas" (Bates, 1975, p. 351). The hegemony of consent builds on the perceived ideological superiority of the ruling class. Bates (1975) equates hegemony with political leadership that is based on the consent of the led, a consent which is secured by the diffusion and popularization of the world view of the ruling class. Whichever class achieves this political leadership, or hegemony, will determine which range of outcomes prevails. Marx believed that "the economic base sets the range of possible outcomes, but free political and ideological activity is ultimately decisive in determining which alternative prevails" (Femia, 1986, p. 38).

Hegemony is not to be found in a purely instrumental alliance between classes which retain their individuality and own ideologies, but rather it involves the "creation of a higher synthesis so that all its elements fuse in a 'collective will' which becomes the protagonist for political action throughout that hegemony's entire duration" (Mouffe, 1979, p. 184). It is through ideology that this collective will is formed, since its very existence depends on the creation of ideological unity which will serve as "cement" (Gramsci, 1935/1971, p. 1380). The creation of ideological unity is not the product of a "titanic struggle between rival *Weltanschauungen*" but rather is a result of "practical engagements about shifts and modifications in common sense, or popular consciousness" (Hunt, 1990, p. 310).

Sallach (1974, p. 41) argues that the dominant class uses its privileged access to the primary ideological institutions to propagate values which reinforce its structural position:

> Such propagation involves not only the inculcation of its values and the censorship of heterodox views but also and especially the ability to define the parameters of legitimate discussion and debate over alternative beliefs, values and worldviews. Actually, censorship and direct inculcation are extreme instances in the hegemonic process (and frequently may be counterproductive). The most effective aspect of hegemony is found in the suppression of alternative views through the establishment of parameters that define what is legitimate, reasonable, sane, practical, good, true, and beautiful.

The reward for winning the battle for ideology is access to the coercive power of the state and the creation of a hegemonic class. Through ideology, the hegemonic class creates a dominant conception of reality enabling a particular form of power and domination to be stabilized and consent to be secured (Hall, 1983).

In the case of accounting, ideologies are often expressed as technologies. International accounting and auditing standards and the methods of organization and practice by accounting firms reflect the ideological consensus of society as to how accounting and auditing should be practiced. This ideology developed over the century and half history of the profession in the West and has become well entrenched in Western society. In China, however, this ideology was new and untested, and was contrary in many aspects to accepted Chinese ideologies. For example, the concept of an independent CPA firm owned by its partners is well accepted in the West yet was ideologically inconsistent with Chinese views on the role of the state and the appropriateness of private ownership.

In order for the Big Four to establish hegemony over the accounting profession, it needed to establish its ideology of how accounting and auditing should be organized and conducted as superior to alternatives based on Chinese ideologies. The Big Four needed to suppress alternative views that Chinese auditors could organize and practice under different ideologies than the West. The Big Four did this by successfully suppressing alternative views that indigenous firms could serve large Chinese multinational companies. Following Sallach's theory, they did this through their privileged access to the primary ideological institutions – investment banking, the international legal profession and foreign capital markets, as well as transnational agencies involved in setting accounting and auditing standards. Through this they succeeded in defining themselves to investors, companies, and the Chinese government that they were the only "legitimate, reasonable, sane, practical, good, true, and beautiful" choice. The Big Four also had the proper economic, political, and cultural conditions to enable itself to be put forward as leading (Joseph, 2002). Changing domestic attitudes toward capitalism and the role of foreigners in the economy enabled the Big Four to put forth its ideology.

2.2.9. Maintaining Hegemony

Hegemony is not only about securing dominance over other classes, but it is also about reproducing the social structures that have created the material conditions for an historic bloc. Joseph (2002) argues that the ruling bloc maintains its hegemony by advancing a dynamic of social reorganization and modernization. In the case of the Big Four, simply obtaining a dominant market position is not sufficient. If the firms fail to retain their existing clients and fail to win a dominant portion of new clients, they would rapidly lose their hegemony. Retaining and winning new clients requires firms to upgrade methodologies and create new services – which is the process of modernization in the accounting world.

Hunt (1990, p. 311) argues that a hegemonic class can never simply articulate the immediate interests of its own constituents. He maintained that to be dominant, the hegemonic class must "address and incorporate, if only partially, some aspects of the aspirations, interests, and ideology of subordinate groups." Hunt advances the idea that three mechanisms are involved in this process. First, the dominant ideology must contribute to securing a minimum standard of social life. In the case of accounting in China, this means that the Big Four could not take over the entire market, but rather must leave sufficient opportunity for the indigenous firms. Second, the dominant class must engage in a more or less self-conscious compromise to incorporate some aspect of the interests of the subordinate group. In a market situation, this may manifest itself in decisions to reject certain competitive tactics that, while potentially effective, might be excessively predatory. The third mechanism identified by Hunt is the need for the dominant hegemony to articulate values and norms such that they take on significant trans-class appeal. For example, proposals for the adoption of international accounting and auditing standards in China need to be articulated in a way that appeals to indigenous firms.

2.2.10. Counter-Hegemony

Subordinate groups often will resist the hegemony of the dominant class and attempt to end the historic bloc. Hunt (1990, p. 312) calls the process of breaking the hegemony of the dominant class counter-hegemony, and defines it as: "The process by which subordinate classes challenge the dominant hegemony and seek to supplant it by articulating an alternative hegemony." Hunt saw that process as a "reworking" or "refashioning" of the elements that are constitutive of the prevailing hegemony (p. 313).

The objective behind Gramsci's work was to guide the struggle against Italian fascists. Fundamental to Gramsci's struggle with Italian fascists was his view that militant oppositional politics entails much more than straightforward, frontal confrontation with the institutions of established power (Buttigieg, 1991). For Gramsci, hegemonic order could only be challenged by a passive revolution, where counter-hegemonic forces persistently challenge the overall ideology of the hegemony, and then serve to transform it over time (Worth, 2002). Evoking images of Mao Zedong's Long March of the Red Army, Rudi Dutschke (1969, p. 249) labeled this nonviolent approach to revolution "the long march through the institutions," a process of infiltrating institutions with the goal of a "subversive-critical deepening of the contradictions related to class interests." Gramsci (as quoted in Larrain (1983, p. 84)) pointed out that the process does not involve the creation of contradictions, but rather the deepening of the awareness and significance of existing contradictions: "It is not a question of introducing from scratch a scientific form of thought into everyone's individual life, but of renovating and making 'critical' an already existing activity."

This deepening of contradictions undermines the ideological foundations supporting the hegemonic class, ultimately facilitating revolution. Because hegemony requires acceptance of the ideological superiority of a particular class, Gramsci and Dutschke recognized that the best (and perhaps only) way of breaking the hegemony was to undermine and replace the ideology of the hegemonic class.

Following the reasoning of Gramsci and Dutschke, it is unlikely that indigenous Chinese CPA firms could alter the hegemony of the Big Four through a direct assault. Certainly, violent means of overthrow would be absurd. Because the Big Four's claim to ideological superiority had been widely accepted, it is also likely that any attempt to secure the coercive power of the state to force change would fail. Accordingly, the indigenous firms need to first take the "long march through the institutions." The objective of the "long march" would be to infiltrate the institutions that support the hegemony of the Big Four with the intent to undermine the ability of the Big Four to claim the legitimacy conferred by these institutions. For example, one of the claims to ideological superiority of the Big Four is their purported expertise in the application of international accounting and auditing standards. This claim has contributed to the

Big Four gaining exclusive access to internationally listed Chinese companies. Indigenous firms, supported by the CICPA and Chinese government, have begun to address this issue by adopting international accounting and auditing standards and becoming involved in the institutions that set these standards. These are major steps in the "long march through the institutions" that Gramsci and Dutschke considered fundamental to a successful counterrevolution. The counter-hegemonic efforts of indigenous firms seek to deepen nationalistic contradictions – "if we do the same work to the same standards, why do foreign rather than Chinese firms dominate the Chinese auditing profession?"

2.2.11. Hegemonic Projects

According to Joseph (2002), hegemony manifests itself at two levels – a deeper hegemony that operates at a structural level and surface hegemony which is embodied in conscious hegemonic projects. Hegemonic projects emerge from the deeper hegemonic conditions and the ideological superstructure. The consequence of a class establishing ideological superiority is that an ideational superstructure emerges in response to the existing social structure defined in terms of coercive economic and political social relations (Sallach, 1974). This ideological superstructure is the deeper layer of hegemony. At the surface, hegemony (and counter-hegemony) manifests itself in a series of hegemonic projects, which involve intention and agency on the part of specific social actors (Hunt, 1990).

Hegemonic projects are more easily observed than the deeper ideological superstructure because they involve actions. Because hegemonic projects are based upon that superstructure, they serve to illuminate the ideological basis for hegemony. The identification and analysis of hegemonic projects is a critical direction for the methodological design of this study.

2.2.12. Why Hegemony Is the Appropriate Theory for This Study

Gramsci and the theory of hegemony have been established as a "legitimate and useful approach to the study of accounting" (Goddard, 2002, p. 662). Goddard indicates that hegemonic approaches can make further contributions to the historical study of accounting in general by providing a rigorous theoretical methodology for the study of accounting in its social, political, and economic context.

Accounting scholars have used the theory of hegemony in a wide range of studies. The relationship between accounting and the state is a central topic. Cooper (1995) used the theory of hegemony to construct historical and material explanations for accounting's relationships with the state. Richardson (1989) used the theory of hegemony to explain corporatism in the regulation of Canadian accountants. Alawattage and Wickramasinghe (2008) consider the role of accounting in a political hegemony. Spence (2007, 2009) framed social and environmental reporting as a hegemonic process and then considered the counter-hegemonic role of social accounting. Other topics that have been evaluated using a theory of hegemony include: financial accountability in nongovernment organizations (Ahmed, Hopper, & Wickramsinghe, 2010); hegemony of public accountants over tax education in Canada (Warsame, 2006); and the role of Western hegemony in establishing accounting regulation in Gulf Cooperation Countries (Al-Qahtani, 2005). Xu, Cortese, and Zhang (2013) explained how accounting systems supported the establishment of a new hegemony by Mao Zedong in China.

Helen Yee's (2009) work applying the theory of hegemony to the development of the accounting profession in China is particularly relevant to this study. Yee examined the reemergence of public accounting in China in the early 1980s and, in particular, the political and ideological influences on the nascent profession. She found evidence that the political and ideological influence of the state permeated the accounting community, empowering the government to mobilize Chinese accountants in the implementation of its economic agenda. Yee's study does not consider the role of international accounting firms and transnational institutions because she examines the early 1980s, a period that preceded the establishment of Big Four hegemony.

There are some problems with Yee's analysis. As previously discussed, Yee conflates the state with a hegemonic class. Her treatment of public accountants as a subordinate class is premature, since her work focuses on a period when these accountants were just being deployed from state institutions and likely had not yet developed class-consciousness. Yee finds greater explanatory power by reference to Confucian principles of filial piety. She argues that the state provided a nurturing environment for the nascent profession that could be likened to the father and son relationship encompassed in the Confucian notion of *wu lun*. This book extends Yee by evaluating a much longer period (Yee through the early 1980s and this study through 2012). This book also focuses on the role of international firms and institutions in the development of the profession in China. While these firms and institutions were present during Yee's study, their influence would grow significantly in subsequent years. While this book results in significantly different findings than Yee, the difference is explainable given the different historical periods examined.

NOTE

1. The Communist International, commonly abbreviated as ComIntern and also known as the Third International, was an international communist organization, formed in Moscow in 1919, and which operated until 1943 (Borkenau & Aron, 1962).

CHAPTER 3

THE BIG FOUR

> Working through an intricate network of high-level contacts and special relationships, they operate at the seat of power and yet are often removed from the public eye. This influence is pervasive, touching the lives of every human being and impacting the decisions of governments, corporations, churches, rock stars, armies, hospitals, universities, museums, penitentiaries, poets and police.
>
> – Mark Stephens (1981, p. 2)

This chapter is a review and synthesis of the literature which examines the multinational business service firms currently known as the Big Four and which has studied the globalization of their activities. The Big Four are the principal actors in this study. Once known as the Big Eight, with their numbers reduced over the years due to mergers and the failure of Arthur Andersen (AA), they now number four.

This chapter begins with a brief history of the development of the Big Four and a snapshot of their present status. I then explain the structure of the Big Four, starting with the partnership structure that is the foundation of the firms, and leading to an explanation of how the Big Four structure their global networks. This analysis is critical to this study, because the international structures that existed enabled and constrained the entry of these firms into China. Following this analysis, I evaluate the literature that addresses how the Big Four have entered emerging markets. Finally, I briefly review the limited literature dealing with foreign law firms in China. The foreign legal profession has faced similar challenges to accounting in entering China, and it has been less successful in obtaining a significant market position.

The professions have long been a focus of sociological research because the autonomy and social status of individual professionals contrasts with the anonymity of impersonal markets and the rational character of bureaucracy (Abbott, 1988). The professionalization of accounting has been an important theme in academic research (see West (1996) for a review of this literature). Professional service firms have been an increasingly important sector in modern society and as a result have attracted a significant volume of academic research. Accounting firms and law firms have been studied in the bulk of that work, although other professions are increasingly being identified and examined (von Nordenflycht, 2010). The Big Four have been the focus of a large portion of professional service firm research mainly because they are large, influential organizations with a global reach. Larson (1977) wrote that the professions are a project in which an occupation attempts to translate its special knowledge and skills into social and economic rewards, and in that respect the Big Four have been very successful. The Big Four audit most public companies on stock exchanges globally, and are the advisor of choice to governments worldwide on economic and social issues (Cooper & Robson, 2009).

3.1. THE BIG FOUR

3.1.1. Historical Roots

Each of the Big Four firms traces its origins to the United Kingdom and the United States in the 19th century. PricewaterhouseCoopers typifies the development of the Big Four. Price Waterhouse, a predecessor firm, traces its origins to a sole practitioner, Samuel Lowell Price, who opened an office in London in 1849 in the early days of the profession. As capital flowed from Britain to America and to Britain's colonies, members of the British profession of chartered accountants periodically traveled to these locations on behalf of their clients. The British firms, including Price Waterhouse, began to establish a permanent presence in the United States (DeMond, 1951; Edwards, 1960; Stevens, 1981). As capital markets developed in the United States early in the 20th century, the British firms found a ready market for their skills. When US Steel first floated its investment securities in 1903, management hired the British firm of Price Waterhouse to certify their statements in order to make the investment more attractive for British investors (DeMond, 1951, pp. 58–64). Following World War II, Price Waterhouse expanded rapidly throughout the world by opening new offices or by aligning with local firms (Baskerville & Hay, 2010; Caramanis, 1999; Cooper, Greenwood, Hinings, & Brown, 1998; Way & Nield, 2002).

In 1982, Price Waterhouse World Firm was formed to coordinate the activities of Price Waterhouse firms worldwide. In 1998, Price Waterhouse merged with Coopers and Lybrand (which had followed a similar path) to form PricewaterhouseCoopers, the world's largest professional services firm (PricewaterhouseCoopers, 2010b). This merger was the final in a series of megamergers that reduced the Big Eight to the Big Five. In 2002, AA failed in the wake of a criminal conviction for its complicity in the Enron scandal and the Big Five became the Big Four (Toffler, 2003). The role of accountants in the collapse of Enron and other corporations in the early 2000s has presented a significant challenge to the legitimacy of the Big Four as stewards of corporate accountability (Carnegie & Napier, 2010).

3.1.2. Big Four Markets

The Big Four are large transnational organizations that tend to dominate accounting markets globally (General Accounting Office, 2003; Government Accountability Office, 2008; Minyard & Tabor, 1991; Narasimhan & Chung, 1998; Walker & Johnson, 1996). Stevens (1981, p. 2), in his popular book on the Big Eight, asks and answers this question:

> Who are the Big Eight? For starters they are huge multinational business organizations, the largest professional firms in the world, and some of the most influential financial powers on earth. They are Arthur Andersen; Arthur Young; Coopers & Lybrand; Deloitte Haskins and Sells; Ernst and Whinney; Peat, Marwick, Mitchell; Price Waterhouse and Touche Ross. Working through an intricate network of high-level contacts and special relationships, they operate at the seat of power and yet are often removed from the public eye. This influence is pervasive, touching the lives of every human being and impacting the decisions of governments, corporations, churches, rock stars, armies, hospitals, universities, museums, penitentiaries, poets and police. Even those who know of – or even work for – the Big Eight do not fully recognize the enormity of their presence. To put it simply, the Big Eight are into everything.

The Big Four have increased in scale considerably since Stevens called attention to the wide-ranging impact of these firms on society. By 2012, these firms collectively employed 693,503 people around the world and had combined revenue of $110.2 billion (Table 3.1). Each of the Big Four operates in at least 140 countries and have offices in nearly every commercial center in the world.

3.1.2.1. Assurance Services

The principal business line of the Big Four is assurance services, often referred to as auditing. Assurance mainly involves the auditing of financial

Table 3.1. Big Four 2012 Global Statistics.

	Revenue	Partners	Total Staff	Countries
PricewaterhouseCoopers	$31.5	9,359	180,529	158
Deloitte Touche Tohmatsu	31.3	9,948	193,359	162
Ernst & Young	24.4	a	167,225	140
KPMG	23.0	8,624	152,390	156
Total	$110.2		693,503	

[a]Not disclosed.
Source: Big Four websites.
Revenue in US$ billions.

Table 3.2. Big Four 2012 Global Revenue by Service Line (US$ Billions).

	PwC	DTT	EY	KPMG	Big Four
Assurance	$14.9	$13.0	$10.9	$10.3	$49.1
Tax	7.9	5.9	6.4	4.9	25.1
Advisory	8.7	12.4	7.1	7.9	36.1
Total	$31.5	$31.3	$24.4	$23.1	$110.3
Assurance	47%	41%	45%	45%	45%
Tax	25%	19%	26%	21%	23%
Advisory	28%	40%	29%	34%	32%
Total	100%	100%	100%	100%	100%

Source: Big Four websites.

information and the provision of a report expressing an opinion of the auditor as to whether the financial statements fairly present the position of the company in accordance with generally accepted accounting principles. Regulators of stock exchanges, tax collection bureaus, and corporate administration bureaus often require audit reports. Audit reports are usually made available to shareholders and to certain creditors, including banks, suppliers, and labor unions. Assurance services made up 45% of the revenue of the Big Four in 2012 (Table 3.2).

3.1.2.2. Tax Services

Tax services have long been an important secondary business line for the Big Four. Tax services include the preparation of tax returns, other tax compliance tasks, and tax planning and consulting. These services made up 23% of Big Four revenue in 2012 (Table 3.2).

3.1.2.3. Advisory Services

Advisory services are also commonly called consulting services. Consulting services grew from a range of 5% to 19% of revenue in 1977 to a range of 11–28% in 1984 (Previts, 1985). By 1999, Former SEC Chairman Levitt pointed out that the share of big accounting firm's revenues derived from consulting rose from one-third in 1993 to 51% in 1999 (Levitt, 2002, p. 8). Zeff (2003, p. 278) observed: "during the 1990s, the big firms expanded into global, multidisciplinary professional services firms that also happened to conduct audits." Concerns about whether auditors could be independent of their clients while providing significant consulting services led to regulatory reform in the United States in the form of the Sarbanes–Oxley Act of 2002. The new rules restricted the ability of accounting firms to provide consulting services to audit clients. In anticipation of these rules, three of the Big Four (with the exception of DTT) divested of their consulting practices by sale or public offering (Brock & Powell, 2005). The Big Four soon returned to consulting and, by 2012, advisory revenue had again climbed to 32% of Big Four revenue (Table 3.2). Accenture, spun out from AA, currently has 266,000 employees, more than any of the Big Four.

This study focuses on the assurance segment of the Big Four. It is in assurance services that the influence of the Big Four on global and national institutions is most pronounced. Assurance services, also commonly called auditing, are critical to the functioning of global capital markets. In the tax and advisory markets the Big Four play significant, often leading roles, but these markets are more competitive and less dominated by the Big Four. While tax and advisory services may result in a significant impact on the success of a company, they do not have the widespread influence on society of assurance services.

3.1.3. Characteristics of Big Four Partnerships

While international accounting firms rival some of the largest corporations in terms of the scale of their operations, they are significantly different from most multinational companies (Lowendahl, 2000). Understanding the structure of international accounting firms is a necessary step toward understanding how they expand into new markets. Most multinational businesses of the scale of the Big Four organize as corporations. These firms typically raise capital from shareholders, usually by issuing shares that trade on major stock exchanges. The shareholders select a Board of Directors that hires managers to administer the business. When multinational enterprises expand internationally, they typically form a wholly owned subsidiary in that location and managers are either locally hired or seconded into the new subsidiary. Profits that are not reinvested locally are paid as a dividend to the parent company, and become available for distribution to shareholders or for use in other parts of the business.

The Big Four firms initially established themselves as partnerships owned by partners who were the senior practitioners in the firms. The firms raised capital from the partners themselves. Accounting laws in most jurisdictions institutionalized this practice by prohibiting the ownership of accounting firms by non-accountants. As partners retire, the firm returns their capital, typically from funds raised from newly admitted and existing partners. In this manner, the Big Four have passed on ownership from generation to generation of partners over their long existence. Profits of the firm are divided among the partners on the basis of the partnership agreement, with a partner's share of profits typically determined by the partner's tenure and performance (Greenwood & Empson, 2003; Morris & Pinnington, 1998).

Partnerships were the predominant form of business organization in Western countries until the emergence of the public corporation in the 19th century. While most businesses moved to the corporate form, professional service firms by and large retained the partnership form, particularly in the legal and accounting professions (Greenwood & Empson, 2003). Three important characteristics of professional service firms may have contributed to this phenomenon: knowledge intensity, low capital intensity, and a professionalized workforce (von Nordenflycht, 2010).

3.1.3.1. Knowledge Intensity

Von Nordenflycht (2010) observes that professional service firms rely on an intellectually skilled workforce. Intellectually skilled workers are difficult to retain, because their high skills put them in a strong bargaining position with the firm. Highly skilled individuals are also notoriously difficult to manage, with strong preferences for autonomy and disdain for formal organizational processes (Greenwood & Empson, 2003; Lorsch & Tierney, 2002). The management of knowledge-intensive businesses has often been described as "herding cats" (Lowendahl, 2000; von Nordenflycht, 2010).

3.1.3.2. Low Capital Intensity

The low capital intensity of professional services firms has allowed the firms to prosper despite being unable to access capital markets due to restrictions on their ownership. However, the low capital requirements of professional service firms also increase employee bargaining power because it is easier for employees to leave and start their own firms. Von Nordenflycht (2010) observes that if knowledge intensity creates the cat herding problem, adding low capital intensity turns it into a situation where the cats go down the elevator each night, and the firm cannot control whether they come back. Greenwood and Empson (2003) argue from tournament theory and property rights theory that partnerships are unusually well suited to the management of knowledge workers because of the superior incentive systems they offer. The promise of partnership, the participation in management and governance, the up or out nature of most partnerships, and the flexibility in compensation offered by the partnership structure all appeal to knowledge workers (Burke, 1996; von Nordenflycht, 2010).

3.1.3.3. Professionalized Workforce

Professionals have become increasingly important to modern institutions. Scott (2008, p. 99) observes: "They have displaced the seers and wise men of earlier times to serve in a variety of capacities as institutional agents." According to Greenwood, Hinings, and Brown (1990, p. 731), "the dominant characteristic of the primary task of a professional partnership is that the work is done almost entirely by professionals." Through an expansive review of literature, Torres (1991) identified three characteristics of professionals: a knowledge base, regulation and control, and an ideology. The knowledge base relates to the knowledge intensity of partnerships. The professions are generally subject to tight regulatory control, a bargain the profession reached with the state to obtain closure of the occupation (Chua & Poullaos, 1998; Lee, 1990; Murphy, 1984). Ideology is a key component of professionalism. The conception that professionals have a responsibility to protect the interests of clients and/or society in general is the foundation of this ideology. Professionals consider themselves called to a profession, and perceive this calling as greater than the firm. This contributes to the demand for autonomy that is characteristic of professionals. Suddaby and Greenwood (2005) describe this calling as the trustee model of professionalism, which places the public interest ahead of mercantile elements. The Big Four brings this ideology to China; an ideology that indigenous accounting firms would ultimately accept as well, forming the foundation for the establishment of Big Four hegemony.

The partnership form has endured significant change in the 150+ years since partnership accounting firms first emerged in England in the mid-1800s. The Big Four firms have increased exponentially in size to include thousands of partners and in geographic scale to include operations in nearly every country on the planet. Even where superior forms of organization were adopted, such as vehicles that limited the liability of partners (limited liability companies and limited liability partnerships), the firms have retained the unique features of partnerships to the extent possible. IBM, a decade after purchasing PricewaterhouseCoopers' consulting practice, continues to use the title "partner" for the senior executives in that business despite not using the partnership legal form (IBM, 2010). The concept of partnership has evolved to mean more than a legal form of organization and now reflects a strategic orientation to managing a professional services firm. The Big Four partnerships resemble smaller accounting firm partnerships in form only; they have become commercialized entities less tied to the traditional values of accounting firms (Malsch & Gendron, 2013; Suddaby, Gendron, & Lam, 2009).

3.1.4. Strategic Challenges of Partnerships

The Big Four partnerships face a number of strategic challenges made more complex by the characteristics of the partnership organizational form. These challenges have particular significance to the ability of these firms to expand into new markets. Ferner, Edwards, and Sisson (1995, p. 357) observed that the partnership form of organization was so fraught with difficulties that "the wonder is not that partnerships function badly, but that they function at all." Ferner and his coauthors acknowledged that the firms appear to be markedly profitable, so they must be highly successful at operating with the ambiguity created by the partnership form of organization. However, as Greenwood and Empson (2003, p. 916) conclude:

> There are other reasons for expecting the partnership and the private corporation to be more successful than the public corporation in the management of professionals. They use more appropriate control processes, which provide incentives for sharing proprietary knowledge, and they deploy unique human resource practices that produce exceptional productivity.

The key strategic challenges that create the greatest obstacles for global expansion of the Big Four include: organizational size and complexity, organizational homogeneity, and capital availability and deployment.

3.1.4.1. Organizational Size and Complexity

Big Four firms have typically had three general levels of professional staffing. At the apex are partners/owners who were typically admitted to the partnership after about a dozen years of practice. In the middle are managers, usually divided into several subgroups (seniors, managers, senior managers, directors) depending on experience and who typically have between 3 and 12 years of experience. At the bottom level are staff accountants, most of whom are recent university graduates beginning their professional careers (Hinings, Brown, & Greenwood, 2007; Maister, 1982). The professional ranks have long operated under an "up or out" philosophy, where continued employment is conditional upon continued advancement (Carter & Spence, 2013; Greenwood & Empson, 2003; Mueller, Carter, & Ross-Smith, 2011; von Nordenflycht, 2010). Firms also have significant numbers of administrative staff, often sharing similar titles with professional staff.[1] Administrative staff tend not to be subject to the "up or out" philosophy.

The firms tend to select management from the professional staff ranks, although firms increasingly hire specialists for administrative management positions in marketing, finance, and human resources. Partnerships have traditionally had informal management processes, with few formal rules, little strategic planning or market analysis, and weak performance accountability (Greenwood et al., 1990; Hinings, Greenwood, & Cooper, 1999; von Nordenflycht, 2010). A key feature of partnerships has been collegial decision making. When Samuel Price and Edwin Waterhouse joined forces in 1865, decision making was likely easily concluded over lunch, but as the partnership grew to hundreds and then thousands of partners, a more efficient management structure was required. Ferner et al. (1995, p. 356) observed that

> ... growth, internationalization and diversification have encouraged a bureaucratization of structures of control that sit uneasily with the ethos of professionalism in partnership-based service firms.

The internationalization challenge is significant. Partnerships were initially used to serve local markets, but soon they no longer served only local clients, "but transnationally integrated global clients expecting coherent and coordinated international services" (Ferner et al., 1995, p. 356). Hinings, Brown, and Greenwood (1991, p. 390) observed the weakness of the partnership structure in developing and implementing long-term strategies:

> In a partnership the professional system of authority is institutionalized in the ownership structure producing a juxtaposition of individualized, autonomous day-to-day activities with collegial, group based policy decision-making. This makes the authority system fragile for dealing with long-term, strategic change because of the lack of an organizationally prescribed, hierarchical system of decision-making, which can be mobilized when necessary.

Through the 1990s, and early into the 21st century, the firms developed new systems of control that Greenwood, Morris, Fairclough, and Boussebaa (2010, p. 180) refer to as a multiplex organizational form:

> The multiplex form balances the need to maintain and enhance several axes of deep specialization: professional expertise (achieved through lines of service in which staff can build their careers), client expertise (achieved through industry and market analysis), and jurisdictional expertise (achieved through a distributed network of local offices in national firms).

The multiplex form is management by means of a matrix, with each partner and staff member typically assigned to a line of service, industry or market specialization, and a geographic location. Because each staff has multiple affiliations within the organization (line of service/industry/geography), the form encourages cooperation and discourages isolating behaviors. In practice, Greenwood et al. (2010, p. 175) found that the multiplex form created several tensions:

> One tension that stood out was securing an appropriate balance between national and international considerations. On the one hand, the historical center of gravity consists of the "national firms," partly because they are the original building blocks of today's international network, partly because they are still the "home base" of professionals who need to be located near "their" clients, and partly to contain risks of legislation. On the other hand, the strategic emphasis of the evolving firms was, and remains, transnational: they seek to provide cutting-edge services to global, as well as national and local clients, and to deliver those services in an apparently seamless way with consistent standards of service quality.

3.1.4.2. Organizational Homogeneity

Early professional services firms were relatively homogeneous. Partners were engaged in very similar kinds of work and had experienced similar training and career paths. Partners usually came from similar geographic and ethnic backgrounds and were further socialized into conforming behaviors through an internal process of cloning (Covaleski, Dirsmith, Heian, & Samuel, 1998).

As the firms grew, they became more heterogeneous, mixing in new service lines and geographies. The new service lines brought people with different educational backgrounds and differing career expectations. Geographic expansion introduced new cultures, languages, and ethnicity. Heterogeneity created new challenges for firm management, with implications for organizational form, team-working, and pricing systems (Malhotra & Morris, 2009). Greenwood and Empson (2003, p. 923) observed "heterogeneity strains collegiality and the willingness to cooperate."

The firms responded to the challenge of disciplinary heterogeneity by creating a new business form – the multiplex organizational form identified by Greenwood et al. (2010). By managing through a matrix of service line, industry, and geography, the firms found a means of addressing the challenges of heterogeneity.

3.1.4.3. Degree of Capital Intensity

Accounting firm partnerships do not typically require significant capital, since most of their value is related to their people and client relationships (human and relationship capital) and not to tangible assets (Hitt, Bierman, Uhlenbruck, & Shimizu, 2006). Nevertheless, firms require working capital and a sizable investment in information technology and office fit-outs. It is fortunate that capital requirements for professional service firms are not significant, because access to investment capital for accounting partnerships is typically limited. A partnership's capital base is limited to the wealth of its partners (Wilhelm & Downing, 2001).

New partners typically contribute capital upon admission to the partnership, and the capital requirements typically increase as the partner's share of the partnership profits increases. Morrison and Wilhelm (2004) observe that partner capital is illiquid, and the prospect of repayment is dependent on existing partner's skills in mentoring new partner candidates who can be admitted and provide the capital necessary to pay retiring partners.

Because partners typically are only returned their original capital upon withdrawal or retirement, intergenerational issues exist. Often, those responsible for managing the firm are older partners who may resist longer-term investments because the returns are not immediately received and do not advantage those approaching retirement (Wilhelm & Downing, 2001). Some of the firms have retirement programs that give partners a continued interest in the firm and a certain incentive to ensure its long-term success. Others rely on a partnership culture that focuses on the long-term viability of the firm. A Big Four partner remarked: "When I became a partner in (a Big Four firm), I was told that I was a trustee for future generations of partners; I was responsible for leaving the firm better than I found it. Building a practice in China was part of that responsibility."

The vulnerability of partners to the risks of litigation has been a defining characteristic of Big Four partnerships (Talley, 2006). The firms have attempted to mitigate this risk in three ways. First, firms have become more selective about the clients that they accept and have improved internal quality processes (Bockus & Gigler, 1998; Shu, 2000; Smith, 2008). Second, where possible, firms have adopted limited liability partnerships or have incorporated to limit the liability of partners to the assets of the firm (Ribstein, 2003). Third, the firms are careful in their international structuring to prevent situations that could result in spillover liability from one jurisdiction (and partnership) to another.

The focal point for capital investment in the Big Four is the national firm. Partners are admitted to a national firm, rather than the global firm, and contribute their capital to that firm. This historical relic has been retained in large part because of its efficacy in "ring fencing" exposure to litigation. When AA failed in 2002, only the US firm failed outright, despite AA being considered the most integrated of the Big Five. The national firms of AA outside the United States generally survived to merge with another of the Big Four (McBride, 2002).

The national firm structure creates significant barriers to seamless global operations for the Big Four firms. Because profits are determined and distributed primarily based on national results, the legal structure has the potential to create tensions between member firms. The allocation of fees on global audit clients among the various firms participating in the audit is a continual source of conflict. The firms have put in place global sharing arrangements and regional groupings of firms to help to mitigate the problem, and they attempt to become as close to a global entity as they can be without allowing the spillover of legal problems from one territory to another.

The existence of separate capital and profit pools has been a major challenge for the international expansion of firms to new markets. In addition to the expected dialogue about the viability of entering a new country, the firms must resolve who would invest the funds necessary, who would own the resulting firms, and who would share in its eventual success.

3.2. GLOBALIZATION OF THE BIG FOUR

Globalization creates both risks and opportunities for the major firms. Converging international accounting and auditing standards create the opportunity for significant cost savings for the international firms, allowing them to share technical, training, and quality practices globally. Perera, Rahman, and Cahan (2008) pointed out the risk to reputation created by the increased visibility of globalization. Because globalizing firms are exposed to more regulators and higher public expectations, problems in one part of the world can easily affect the brand globally.

Perera et al. (2008) highlight the pressure that globalization puts on the traditional ownership structures of international accounting firms. The traditional partnership form of organization may result in slow decision making and lead to an overly conservative entity. The partnership form can also be divisive because of regional and national differences. Perera and his coauthors predict that the Big Four in the future may become alliances of relatively autonomous sub-entities held together by a strong central core. Under their vision, each sub-entity would focus on a functional specialty or geographic region, and each would have a unique ownership and organizational structure depending on its market and risks.

Daniels, Thrift, and Leyshon (1989) identify two distinct periods of expansion of the major accounting firms. The first period began in the 1890s and lasted until World War II (as typified by the case of Price Waterhouse discussed earlier in this chapter). The second period started in 1945 and led to more structured international partnerships. I argue that this period ended in the late 1970s as the firms substantially filled out their global networks (Baskerville & Hay, 2010; Lewis, 2005; Wallerstedt, 2001; Way & Nield, 2002). Annisette (2000) observes that the accountancy internationalization movement of the 1970s was part of a wider process of building informal empire for it served to facilitate a smoother incorporation of overseas economies into the expanding world economy, oriented around the United States.

I argue that a third period commenced with the opening of the accountancy market in the former Communist states of the Soviet Union and China (Cooper et al., 1998; Hilmy, 1999; King, Beattie, Cristescu, & Weetman, 2001; Kirsch, Laird, & Evans, 2000; Mennicken, 2010; Samsonova, 2009; Seal, Sucher, & Zelenka, 1996; Tang, 2000). The opening of these markets was concurrent with major structural changes in the economies where market-oriented systems replaced communist ideologies. This third period is the focus of this study.

3.2.1. Structure of International Accounting Firm Networks

The management strategy literature pays considerable attention to the structuring of the multinational firm (Bartlett, Ghoshal, & Birkinshaw, 1995; Daniels, Pitts, & Tretter, 1984; Ghoshal & Bartlett, 1990). This research is of limited application to the Big Four. While the Big Four are among the largest of multinationals, their structure is very different. Rather than employing the typical MNC structure of a parent company with subsidiaries around the world, accounting firms are structured as associations of independently owned firms.

As accounting firms expanded internationally or began to serve clients with a need for global services, a structure to organize the firms was required. Lenz and James (2007, p. 369) observe that: "in most countries the right to practice as a certified audit firm is granted only to national firms in which locally qualified professionals have majority or full ownership." As a result, the typical corporate multinational solution of using controlled subsidiaries or branches was not available and instead the firms organized through network arrangements. This creates unique strategic challenges that are particularly evident as the firms attempted to expand into developing markets.

The characteristics of international accounting firm networks are important to understanding the development of the accounting market in China. The nature of the international networks of the firms shaped the manner in which the firms entered and expanded in China.

3.2.1.1. Network Typology

Lenz and James (2007) proposed a two-category typology for international accounting firm networks: correspondence contracts and cooperation contracts.

Correspondence contracts: Many small- or medium-sized networks use correspondence contracts particularly where firms have a small number of internationally oriented clients. The correspondence contracts typically serve to facilitate the mutual referrals of clients. The arrangements may be on an exclusive or nonexclusive basis and there is no exchange of personnel or continuous quality controls. Firms may use a common international name for branding purposes but typically use a local name when providing services. Accounting networks such as Nexia or The Leading Edge Alliance (both with China affiliates) are typical of this form (2010 annual directory of CPA firm associations and networks, 2010; Koza & Lewin, 1999).

Cooperation contracts: Larger international firms require a stronger institutionalized structure due to the need for greater control over quality and standards, and greater coordination of services. Lenz and James (2007, p. 376) state:

> We define a contractual cooperation between legally and economically autonomous national audit firms, which are organized based on partnership principles under the strategic leadership of one or more member firms for the joint fulfillment of international client needs as a strategic audit networks.

These cooperation contracts typically specify the following rights and obligations of member firms (Lenz & James, 2007, p. 378).

Rights of member firms:

1. Use the international name.
2. Use joint resources (audit technologies, training materials, etc.).
3. Exclusive service rights in local market.
4. Local decision making for local market.

Obligations of member firms:

1. Follow worldwide quality standards.
2. Maintain a consistent global identity and branding.
3. Refer foreign work to other member firms.
4. Use best efforts to convince clients to use member firms for foreign work.
5. Contribute to network costs.

A study by the Fédération des Experts Comptables Européens (FEE) (2008) examined the structure of international accounting firms operating in Europe. This study surveyed the top 20 international accounting organizations based on European revenue and 10 other groups outside the top 20. While this study was focused on Europe, each of the groups surveyed in China.

The FEE study found that international accounting firms could use three distinct models of transnational organization and practice: (1) an international association of independent firms coordinated by a separate legal entity; (2) an integrated international partnership; and (3) a national practice with subsidiaries in other jurisdictions. The first model, the international association of independent firms, is used by the Big Four and the other largest and most commonly known accounting practices (Fédération des Experts Comptables Européens, 2008, p. 26; Post, 1996). Legal liability risks, local statutory requirements, and the expectations of local partners have precluded broad use of the other two models by the largest international firms.

Within the commonly used international association model, the FEE study identified three discernable categories of associations:

a. Category A – First level of transnational interaction and coordination.
b. Category B – Increasing and evolving level of transnational interaction but in some respects a still modest degree of transnational coordination.
c. Category C – Considerable to high degree of transnational interaction and coordination and to some degree integrated transnational functioning.

The majority of associations in the FEE study were either Category A or Category B organizations (Fédération des Experts Comptables Européens, 2008, p. 26). At the lowest level, Category A associations operate as essentially as directories to facilitate the referral of work, and require modest membership fees (Fédération des Experts Comptables Européens, 2008, p. 45). Category C organizations require substantial commitments to common operating practices and the sharing of substantial central operating costs. Category C organizations include the Big Four and some organizations outside the Big Four.

Each of the Big Four currently has a nonpracticing governance entity[2] in which individual firms become members. The governance entity coordinates the activities of firms, promotes the brand, and establishes and enforces quality standards. The member firms are established under the laws of the countries in which they operate and are owned by individual partners. Most member firms use the partnership structure, although corporations and other forms of ownership are used depending on local laws and customs. Many member firms operate within a single country; some combine operations of several countries or related markets.

As discussed more thoroughly in later chapters, the Big Eight initially entered China with representative offices owned by an entity related to the international coordinating entity. Over time, they have evolved into separate legal entities that are members of an international association of firms coordinated by a separate legal entity. There are elements of an integrated international partnership present as well. Each Big Four firm currently operates in China, Hong Kong, and Macau as a single business unit. PricewaterhouseCoopers also includes Singapore in this combination from 2008 and Taiwan from 2010 (PricewaterhouseCoopers, 2011). E&Y combines 15 countries in Asia into a single business unit (Tydd, 2008).

3.2.1.2. Network Expansion

As the Big Four expanded around the world, the typical means of doing so was through alignment with a local firm in the new location. This provided immediate access to local expertise and resources and provided the local firm with access to international clients. Often the local firm had maintained a long correspondent relationship with the international firm before formally joining the network (Way & Nield, 2002). Where a suitable local firm was not available, firms could establish a new firm. Brown, Cooper, Greenwood, and Hinings (1996, p. 62) observed:

> Once they become viable, the firm operates as a separate profit center, like any other national firm, rather than as a mere branch of the parent firm sending profits back to the head office.

There are several good examples in the literature that describe the how the process of network expansion has typically operated. These examples are from New Zealand, Spain, and Sweden.

New Zealand. Baskerville and Hay (2010) describe the entry of the Big Eight into New Zealand. The major New Zealand firms were established in the 1930s or earlier. By the late 1960s, all of the Big Eight had affiliations with New Zealand firms, which, with the exception of Price Waterhouse (which had special dispensation due to its early arrival), were not permitted to use the international firm names. In 1982, the rules were changed to permit firms to adopt international names, and a major restructuring of the profession commenced. Major firms that were unable to affiliate with a Big Eight firm generally broke up and became a series of smaller firms. By the mid-1990s, the large international firms dominated the New Zealand market, which had a Herfindahl–Hirschman Index (HHI) in excess of 2000 (Baskerville & Hay, 2006).

Spain. Price Waterhouse entered Spain in 1929, and by the 1960s, all of the Big Eight had offices in Spain. A 1988 Audit Law made audits compulsory for all medium and large companies. After the law was enacted the large multinational audit firms became a dominant force in the Spanish audit market and, by the mid-1990s, had a 64% market share (Moizer, Benau, Humphrey, & Martinez, 2004). Mozier et al. examined the images of the Big Six and non-Big Six firms in Spain. They found:

> Hence the Big Six audit firms were seen as more American, more oriented towards Madrid, more modern, stronger internationally, more successful, better organized, more energetic, more well known and with more famous clients. They were also thought of as having better coverage of Spain, in accordance with the existence of few, large Spanish national audit firms. The Big Six firms were also seen to have some different attitudinal characteristics: being perceived as more arrogant, more informal, more ruthless, more unfriendly, more private school biased and more female oriented. They were also regarded as being more overpriced and more overrated. (p. 566)

Sweden. Wallerstedt (2001) examined the development of the accounting profession in Sweden from 1912 to 1999, focusing on the emergence of the Big Five. Three Big Five firms that employed 55% of the public accountants in the country dominated the audit market in Sweden in 1999. Yet, sole practitioner firms made up 81% of the number of firms.

Price Waterhouse entered Sweden in 1932 directly after being called in from London to handle a major accounting scandal. The other members of the Big Five entered by aligning with significant local firms in the 1960s, and by the 1990s, all of the affiliated local firms had changed their name to that of the international firm. A major motivation for the alignment with Big Five firms was the need to serve Swedish companies internationally.

PricewaterhouseCoopers and E&Y pursued an aggressive strategy of acquisitions to grow market share in Sweden. KPMG relied more on organic growth. These three firms dominated the market in Sweden in 1999, with Deloitte Touche and AA holding lesser positions.

3.2.2. Organizing International Activities

There were no accounting firms in China when the Big Eight first entered that market in the early 1980s. Consequently, the traditional approach of aligning with an established local firm was not available. Local firms were established under state control at the same time as the Big Eight entered China and the international firms later allied with local partners in joint ventures. The local firms allied with the Big Four eventually separated from the State and were effectively absorbed by the international firms. Rather than becoming independent member firms, they were absorbed into the Hong Kong member firms.

Brown et al. (1996, p. 62) identified seven major types of arrangements used by the Big Six to organize international activities:

1. The firm operates under its international name.
2. A combined name is used where an international firm affiliates with a local firm.
3. A local name is used where an international firm is totally affiliated with a local firm.
4. An association or federation may be relied on to coordinate activity among member firms.
5. Correspondents may be used if an international firm does not have an office in a locale and exclusively refers clients to a single local firm.
6. On rare occasions, a local firm may have multiple affiliations with several international firms.
7. A final case is when two or more names occur – where an international firm practices under two or more national firm names.

Brown observes that the first alternative is the one usually preferred by the Big Six. Although the international firms tend to practice in each country using the same name, each country is typically a separate firm owned by the partners in that country. The key organizing principle, according to Lenz and James (2007), is that the firms retain legal and economic autonomy.

Writing in 1996, Brown et al. noted:

> Furthermore, each of the national firms has developed to the point where it maintains a high degree of independence. With the single exception of Arthur Andersen, which is centrally directed worldwide, the Big-Six national firms direct their own affairs, allocate profits on a national basis, and independently decide on promotion to partnership.

As Brown et al. indicate, the exception to the independence of national firms was AA, which entered international markets only after the death of founder Arthur E. Andersen in 1947.[3] AA's late arrival in international markets allowed it to develop a more integrated international partnership. AA member firms shared a common global profit pool, although they remained structured as national legal partnerships for liability and local regulatory purposes (Caso, 2002). Lenz and James (2007) assert that the restriction imposed by liability concerns and local regulation hindered cross-border exchanges of audit services. Absent these restrictions the firms would have likely evolved into more integrated organizations with lower organizational and control costs and better funding options (Lenz & James, 2007, p. 375). Consulting firms, such as Accenture and IBM Consulting (both with Big Four roots), are examples of integrated consulting companies that were able to organize without audit-related regulatory restrictions. Accenture is a public company organized like a traditional MNC with a parent company in Ireland and subsidiaries around the world. IBM Consulting is a subsidiary of IBM.

Ferner et al. (1995, p. 355) observes: "International accounting firms are built on an essentially devolved and fragmented federal structure, more akin to a franchise than to a corporate multinational." Franchises, however, typically serve local markets, while the principal clients of the international accounting firms were multinational corporations looking for consistent quality and seamless service on a global basis. Ferner et al. (1995, p. 356) noted:

> At a more practical level, the growing tension, between a structure of federated quasi-autonomous firms and a strategy of providing integrated global business services, raises a series of choices for strategic decision makers in such firms.

The firms responded to this strategic challenge by developing structures to organize their far-flung international operations. These structures must provide for the construction of social, relational spaces, and communities in order to facilitate managerial coordination and control. The nature of professional services required these structures to flexibly facilitate both decentralization and integration (Morgan, 2001). Boussebaa (2009, p. 832) states:

> The raison d'etre of these umbrella structures is not to command and control the partnerships, but simply to bring them together to practice under common brands, methodologies and other professional guidelines. The partnerships themselves remain independent firms owned and managed on a local basis.

3.2.3. Relationships between Member Firms

Structure alone did not lead to the globalization of the major accounting firms. Internal processes are also important for ensuring the global consistency of service demanded by MNC clients. Because of market expectations and the risk of spillover of liability, the firms needed consistent quality and risk management processes. Barrett, Cooper, and Jamal (Boussebaa, 2009) found that the mechanisms deployed by the Big Four to manage these processes were standardized audit methodologies and interoffice instructions. The inter-office instructions linked the local and global in a dialectical manner.

Boussebaa (2005) observed that partners are reluctant to share staff with different profit pools because metrics and profit sharing were determined on a national basis. The ways in which the firms measure and pay subunits creates reward and recognition systems that implicitly favor competition over cooperation. He said that firms would have already solved the problem if it required only modification of the reward and recognition systems. Instead, he pointed to the American system of management that focuses on short-term results and the vast differences in global consulting markets. This situation is accentuated in the Big Four, where developing and smaller country markets are significantly different from the major markets in the United States and the United Kingdom. There are wide differences in partner compensation between these large markets and smaller markets, which reflect differences in market opportunities and cost structures. Because a substantial portion of the work of the Big Four is serving multinational clients, the internal market for sharing work and resources is an important dynamic for these firms.

3.3. THE BIG FOUR IN EMERGING MARKETS

The literature with the Big Four as a research subject and developing markets as a research site is limited. In a broad survey, McKee and Garner

(1997) examined the role of the Big Six in markets of the Pacific Basin. They concluded that while the Big Six are not central to the economic potential of these nations, they are important institutions for international linkage and the functioning of capital markets. Reviewed here are studies that are instructive as to issues found in China.

3.3.1. Big Four Market Strategies in Emerging Markets

Kirsch et al. (2000) examined the strategic marketing approaches of the Big Six when entering the emerging markets of China, Central Europe, and the Commonwealth of Independent States. They conducted the study using a 44-question survey completed by each of the Big Six. The surveys were completed in the fall of 1996 and the spring of 1997, an early point in the development of these markets. Respondents reported opening offices in 6 of the 11 member states of the CIS, 3 of 4 former republics, and all 7 of the former Eastern European Satellites. Each had multiple offices in China. The most commonly mentioned factors for opening offices were the size of the potential market and the political stability of the country. The leading reasons to enter were explained as (1) market analysis of potential, (2) political stability, and (3) availability of workforce. Four of the six firms said they priced their services in developing markets the same as the rest of the world.

The survey instrument was weak because it is clear that the authors did not understand the nature of the firm's operations or intent in these markets. Since it appears that the authors sent a single survey to the global office of each firm, there is no way of gauging whether the persons who completed the survey were knowledgeable about the operations in each jurisdiction. Based on my personal experience, I believe that the information the authors sought was widely diffused at PW at the time of the survey, and that no single individual could accurately complete the survey. The weakness of the survey is illustrated on one question where the authors interpreted answers that suggested that the firms were reinvesting profits to mean that the firms were not merely interested in a quick profit and exit but rather, that the firms were in it for the long term. I had access to the largest firm's data at that time and the reality was that they did not have any profits in emerging markets to reinvest, a fact further documented on another firm by Cooper et al. (1998). Rather, the firms were investing heavily (through funding operating losses) to develop practices in those markets. It is also apparent from the article that the authors were unaware of the organizational complexity of the Big Six, since they take an

American-centric approach. An example of this approach is a survey question that asked whether the firms staff their offices with US nationals. This question fails to recognize the global nature of these firms and the significant involvement of the Hong Kong member firms in China.

3.3.1.1. Greece and the Role of National Politics

The development of Greece's accounting profession has some interesting application to China because it helps to explain the interconnectedness of national politics with regional and global forces and the implications of this interaction for the regulation of the accounting profession. In particular, the struggle between indigenous and international auditing firms was a key theme in the development of Greece's auditing markets (Ballas, 1998, 1999; Caramanis, 1997, 1998, 1999, 2005; Citron & Manalis, 2001).

The Greek government brought in British auditors to support the work of American agencies involved in post-World War II reconstruction. Ballas (1998) said the role of the British auditors was to facilitate government control. In 1955, legislation created an indigenous auditing profession. The State opted for a State-sponsored profession based on the view that only State employees are trustworthy. The profession was under the Body of Sworn-in Accountants (*Soma Orkoton Logiston*, hereafter SOL), which acted both as a professional body and a practicing firm. SOL held a monopoly on statutory audits until it was abolished in the early 1990s, and the profession was opened to competition. SOL audits were not accepted outside of Greece, and international firms typically did any work that was used outside of Greece. SELE (*Syllogos Eghekrimenos Loghiston Elegton*), formed in 1979 by partners of the international auditing firms, argued for opening up the statutory audit market to the international firms (1998). It was not until 1992 that SOL terminated and the auditing market was opened up. Ballas (1999) argues three factors led to the abolishment of SOL in 1992. First, the European Eighth Directive created pressure to harmonize auditing practices throughout Europe. Second, political conditions had changed to disfavor State intervention. Third, regulators faced the practical problem of privatizing State-owned firms whose financial statements, audited by SOL, were not accepted in the international markets.

Political changes in Greece resulted in an attempt to reverse the 1992 reforms that had opened up the statutory audit market to international firms and to return it to local firms. The local firms suffered a humiliating defeat, which Caramanis largely attributes to lobbying efforts of transnational institutions such as FEE, IFAC, OECD, and EU Commission (Ballas, 1999).

Caramanis argues that the key reason that the international firms were successful in this effort was that they were influential enough within another major nation-state to mobilize the resources of that state in their attempt to expand internationally and compete with indigenous firms and other businesses. Caramanis observes that only one of the Big Five (AA) is considered to be American, yet these firms are thought to be very influential in the United States, as well as other countries in the Anglo-American world (United Kingdom, Canada, Australia, etc.). The international firms, despite their ambiguous nationality, proved capable of enlisting various states and transnational institutions to fight market access battles. Caramanis (2002) suggests that local professions must integrate globally in order to compete:

> However, in order to be successful in this new age, aspiring occupational groups will have to diversify political resources from the local to the international domain. Thus, professional politics at the level of the nation-state are to be reshaped to take into account changes in the international governance system, although the exact configuration will vary to reflect the relative power of the local and the international. Inward looking occupational groups, particularly in weaker nation-states, that by some historical accident or by some mistaken policy have failed to integrate within the dominant global system will find it increasingly difficult to compete with rival groups that have been properly linked to the international system and enjcy the active support of potent international actors.

3.3.1.2. Malaysia and Local Firm Competition

Research with Malaysia as the setting is instructive in two ways. This research emphasizes the importance of localization for political advantage (in Malaysia this involved including Bumiputras (indigenous Malays) in a profession dominated by ethnic Chinese). It also highlights the challenges faced by local firms when faced with competition from international firms.

The Big Four dominate the Malaysian market for audit services for public companies. As early as 1991, the Big Six audited 75.9% of the Bursa Malaysia (Main Board) listed companies (Che-Ahmad, Houghton, & Derashid, 1996; Che-Ahmad, Houghton, & Yusof, 2006). While ethnic Chinese dominate the profession, Che-Ahmad et al. (2006) discovered that the Big Six employed over 90% of Bumiputra and Indian auditors. Because the Bumiputra hold significant political power in Malaysia, the hiring of most Bumiputra auditors may have helped the Big Six to dominate the market. The Big Four in China might draw from this experience the importance of Communist Party membership by their local partners and staff in order to secure access to political power.

Salleh, Rose, Kumar, and Peng (2007) surveyed Malaysian auditing firms to determine their readiness for the challenges of globalization. They found that only 28 of 573 members of the Malaysian Institute of Accountants had international affiliations. They found that firms without international affiliation were poorly prepared to meet globalization challenges, and that size was a critical criterion for competing in the international market.

3.3.1.3. The Big Four in Former Soviet Block Countries

The Union of Soviet Socialist Republics (USSR) was the first modern centrally planned economy developed under socialist principles. Accounting in the USSR was designed to provide statistical information to different levels of government to facilitate management of the centrally planned, command economy (Salleh et al., 2007).

The former countries of the Soviet Union in Eastern Europe won freedom from the USSR in the 1980s, ultimately leading to the collapse of the Soviet Union in 1991. This political process was accompanied by a transition from a state controlled to a market economy (Gaidar & Gaidar, 2003; Radebaugh, Krylova, & Rahman, 1994). Bailey (1995) theorizes that this transition raises a number of questions about how the accounting profession will develop in transition economies:

> In what circumstances does accounting cease to be merely legally obligatory (and commercially and economically irrelevant) and become commercially and economically relevant?
>
> How does accounting, shaped by a political perspective, become responsive to a commercial or economic (i.e., market induced) imperative?
>
> How does accounting, instead of being politically driven (i.e., designed so as to promote the realization of certain political objectives) come to be market driven?
>
> Or, how does accounting cease to be state directed and become state regulated?

Literature addressing the development of the accounting profession in Russia is particularly applicable to this study. The USSR had significant influence on the development of Communist ideology and institutional practices in China. Both countries transitioned from a centrally planned economy to one based on market principles at about the same time. While China's scale was greater, the issues faced by Russia and other former members of the Soviet Union in the transition to a market economy were similar.

Russia's transition economy. The tension between national and international considerations is highlighted by Cooper et al. (1998, p. 603) in their detailed case study of how one of the Big Six firms invested in the former Soviet Union. Bychkova (1996) predicted that new audit reforms in 1994–1995 would most certainly result in a market dominated by the big international accounting firms. Cooper et al. identified two themes: tensions between nationalism and globalization, and the limits of rational investment and strategic decision making in complex organizations.

Cooper et al. (1998) found that the firm that they studied liked to state that their motivation for entering new markets was to meet client needs, and they found evidence to support that assertion. They also found an expansionist desire of the firm to develop local markets around the world. This was accompanied by a strong sense of national spheres of interest within the Big Six firm they studied, indicating that the German firm has an "historic place" in Eastern Europe or the British firm a "special connection" with Britain's former colonies. I see ample evidence of all of these factors in China. The firms that substantially funded the investment in China for the Big Four (generally the US and UK member firms) had a keen interest in serving their existing clients who were coming to China, and to develop new markets for that purpose alone. The Hong Kong firms viewed that they had a special connection with China and some of the Hong Kong firms of the Big Four previously had an historic role in China before the 1949 revolution.

Cooper et al. (1998) describe the complex negotiations between various member firms that were interested in developing the new markets. In the firm that they examined, the global board and its International Executive Committee had overall responsibility for this project, yet the funding and operational decisions were made by individual member firms with a keen interest in these markets. The relevant member firm was sometimes a geographically adjacent firm (i.e., Austria to Hungary) or more commonly was one or more of the larger member firms (United States, United Kingdom, Germany). In the case of the Russian market, the initial firms involved were from Germany and the United Kingdom. The Russian authorities wanted a more international (and less European centric), investment, and asked if the Americans could join. The Canadian firm, seeing an opportunity, pushed their way into the deal despite the resistance of the others.

However, as the new venture came into operation, the American and Canadian firms withdrew support, finding the required investments were too high in face of the need to maintain partner incomes at home. The result was a poor performance of the firm in Russia, where it became one of the smallest of the Big Six. This case illustrates how the international firms cooperate while operating in their own self-interest. While the international CPA firms like to position themselves as seamless global firms, the national identities and economic interests of the firms significantly guide their behavior.

Mennicken (2010) examined the development of auditing in Russia as it transitioned from state-led inspections to market-oriented auditing from 1985 to 2005. Mennicken used a linked ecologies approach derived from Abbott (1999), explaining that this means that "audits and markets, and the boundaries that come to be formed around them, only exist in relation to other arenas of economic, political and social activity" (p. 355). The emphasis in this approach was on how arenas and fields came to be interlinked and reworked. Mennicken found that audit reforms were inextricably linked to Russia's wider transition from a planned to a market economy. Quoting Rose (1999, p. 150), Mennicken observes that auditing became involved in discourses aimed at transforming the Soviet ethos of government:

> ... From one of bureaucracy to one of business, from one of planning to one of competition, from one of command and control to one of choice, self-regulation and individual responsibility.

Mennicken observes that three key factors led to the realization that the old Soviet inspection system needed replacement by a privatized auditing profession. These factors were the activities of the Big Six in Russia, the opening up of the Soviet Union for foreign direct investment, and the introduction of new forms of private property. China experienced these same factors, with the added influence of significant capital markets.

The accounting profession in Russia developed differently than in China, with a number of large indigenous firms. PricewaterhouseCoopers is the only Big Four among the top 10 firms in Russia (although it is the largest and more than twice the size of its nearest competitor). Three firms affiliated with second-tier international firms (BDO International, PKF International, and RSM International) are in the top 10 in Russia (Mennicken, 2010). Mennicken reports that the rankings indicate that the indigenous firms are able to compete with the Big Six. The evidence is found in Russian attempts to establish a Russian alternative, a Russian Big Nine, or Big Ten. She reports that four groups of audit firms came to be identified – the Big Four, second-tier international audit networks, large- and medium-sized

Russian audit firms, and small firms and partnerships. Professional prestige accrued not to individual accountants or professional associations, but to particularly prestigious firms portraying themselves as enforcing high standards.

Mennicken (2010, p. 355) found that despite the fact that the Big Six did not dominate the Russian market, they were important role models:

> Their international standing and local presence reinforced beliefs that the foundation of commercial, market-oriented audit firms constituted the right response to inspection reform demands. The big firms came to be seen as entities that had successfully embraced market ideals, and that exhibited high standards of professionalism. They had a "trademark" that particularly larger Russian audit firms aspired to. The big firms were further important in the diffusion and local transfer of Western marketing and branding instruments.

The harmonization of Russian auditing processes with Western methods was studied by Samsonova (2009). Samsonova observed how Russian audit policy evolved through transnational communications between actors within and without Russia. The presence of Big Four firms in Russia encouraged the cross-border acceptance of international standards and uniform approaches to service delivery. She determined that Russia favored the Continental Europe tradition of greater state involvement in accounting as fulfilling its aspirations for an alternative mechanism for state control.

International firms in the Czech Republic. Seal et al. (1996) chronicle the development of the accounting profession in the Czech Republic. No accounting profession existed at the time of the Velvet Revolution that separated the Czech Republic from Russian influence. Most of the Big Six came to Czechoslovakia in 1990, immediately following the Velvet Revolution. In a pattern similar to that seen in China, the Big Six initially served MNC clients investing in the Czech Republic, and later expanded into providing services to newly privatized local Czech enterprises. The authors forecast that the Big Six audit the majority of large enterprises and smaller local audit firms provide services to small local Czech enterprises. They observe that Czech companies perceive a need for international standard audits and the Big Six dominates this market. However, the authors assert that the internationally based credibility of the Big Six raises the reputation of Czech accountants in general, regardless of whether the accountants are Big Six employees.

Entry of the Big Five into Slovakia. Daniel, Suranova, and De Beelde (2001) observed that the Big Five entered Slovakia after 1989 and increased their impact significantly between 1993 and 2000. The key factors driving this increase were increasing foreign investment and the privatization of the banking industry. At least 75% of Slovak banks used a Big Five firm as auditor. Many privatized banks used both a local and international auditor to increase acceptance in international markets. While many Slovak industrial companies choose to use the Big Five to enable access to international financial markets, the authors said that local audit firms remain dominant.

3.4. LAW FIRMS

The legal profession has many similarities to accounting, in particular including its use of the partnership structure (King et al., 2001). Similar to the trend in accounting, globalization has led many law firms to open overseas offices in order to serve international clients who are investing in those markets and local clients with needs for international legal advice (Greenwood et al., 1990).

Morgan and Quack (2006) determined that US mega-law firms tended to follow the strategy of an exporting global law firm. A strong central headquarters that establishes overseas offices in a small number of world city centers or promising emerging markets by practicing domestic law abroad characterizes this model. The exception was Baker & McKenzie, which uses national partnerships similar to the Big Four. The managing partner of the foreign offices of law firms tended to be a senior US partner. Where rules permit the practice of local law by foreign law firms, the firms generally use separate teams of local lawyers within the firms. The spread of American style contract law has made US law firms powerful forces for the spread of American legal norms, techniques, and style abroad while skimming the most lucrative legal work in the market (Beaverstock, 2004; Silver, 2007).

British law firms developed internationally more along the lines of the Big Four, following "the integrative model of the global law firm" with national partnerships at the center of the governance structure and elements of the multiplex organizational form being used (Dezalay & Garth, 2002; Morgan & Quack, 2006, p. 419). Morgan and Quack observe that the international structures of law firms were converging, but not necessarily on the American model.

In China, high levels of foreign investment attracted many large law firms to open representative offices in China. As Chinese companies began to tap international capital markets and expand internationally, the client base of these firms expanded to include these companies. Law practice in China was far more restricted than accountancy, with foreign law firms not permitted to practice local law, hire local lawyers, or enter into joint ventures. Law firms are more subject to local regulations, norms, and cultural practices that restrict the ability of the firms to adopt globalizing strategies (Muzio & Faulconbridge, 2013). The sensitivity of legal practice, particularly with respect to civil and criminal litigation, and local concerns about foreign competition have prevented foreign law firms from enjoying similar market access as was afforded to accounting firms. As a result, foreign law firms presently practice in China using representative offices that are severely restricted in their scope of operations. Nevertheless, most major global law firms have a presence in China, albeit at levels far smaller than the Big Four; generally having only a handful of lawyers present in the country (Godwin, 2009).

NOTES

1. For example, Deloitte LLP in the United States reports that 8,762 of its total employees of 42,367 in 2009 were administrative staff, or about 20% of the total (www.deloitte.com).

2. PricewaterhouseCoopers International Limited is a UK membership based company. Ernst & Young Global Limited is a UK private company limited by guarantee. KPMG International is a Swiss cooperative. Deloitte Touche Tohmatsu is a Swiss Verein. Each of the Big Four has member firms in more than 140 countries worldwide. *Source*: Big Four websites.

3. Arthur E. Andersen had opposed expansion of his firm outside of the United States. His successor, Leonard Spacek, led AA's international expansion, expanding to 25 countries by his retirement in 1973 (Gant, 2005).

CHAPTER 4

BUILDING FOUNDATIONS

In China, you need to have friends in high places.
– Nellie Fong, Arthur Andersen, and PricewaterhouseCoopers

There are four broad segments in China's history that are important for purposes of understanding the involvement of accounting in Chinese society. The first is the dynastic period that begins with the Xia Dynasty about 2100 BCE and ends with the Qing Dynasty that fell in 1911. Accounting never achieved a prominent role in the dynastic period. Its function during that period was limited to keeping track of the emperor's wealth because the agricultural-based economy did not require sophisticated accounting practices. The formation of the Republic of China in 1912 begins the second period and marks the entry of China into the modern world. It was during this period that public accounting was first established in China. The third phase commences with the foundation of the People's Republic of China in 1949, which marked the introduction of communism to China. Over the following decade, private ownership of business ceased and the public accounting profession disappeared. Under China's centrally planned economy accounting became a bureaucratic function, heavily guided by Soviet practice. The fourth segment begins with Deng Xiaoping's decision to end China's long isolation from the West, marking the remarkable transition of China to a market-based economy, and giving it a major role in the world.

This chapter is the first of four that will explain the development of the certified public accountant (CPA) profession in China with a focus on the role played by the Big Four. It begins with a brief review of accounting in China from the dynastic period through the founding of the People's Republic in 1949 and the subsequent collapse of the accounting profession.

It then turns to the decision of Chinese leaders to open up to Western influence following the failure of the Cultural Revolution. As China opened up, foreign companies began to return to China. Chinese bureaucrats created a new indigenous accounting profession to help administer the new foreign investors, and the Big Eight firms followed their clients into China and began to consider what China might mean to their practices in the future. During the Big Eight's first decade in modern China in the 1980s, their principal focus was to build the relationships that would allow them to prosper as China developed. Prohibited from auditing, the Big Eight were limited to advising clients and planning for day when China would need their full range of services. The initial development of the profession, and this chapter, ends with the events in Tiananmen Square on the night of June 4, 1989.

4.1. ACCOUNTING PRACTICES IN EARLY CHINA

China is one of the earliest human civilizations, and for long periods of history, it has been among the most advanced. Accounting practices, particularly those related to governmental accounting became fairly sophisticated as early as the Western Zhou Dynasty, which existed from 1050 to 770 BC (Fu, 1974, p. 92; Gao, 1982a; Lu & Aiken, 2003). The primary purpose of accounting during the dynastic period was to keep track of the Emperor's wealth and state property (Chen, 1998). China's feudal and agrarian society had little need for a public accounting profession.

Following the collapse of the Roman Empire and until about 1700, China's culture was unrivaled by the West. The huge appetite of Europeans for Chinese silk, porcelain, and tea led to a robust trade with China during the 17th and 18th centuries. The Chinese did not reciprocate with an interest in European goods, resulting in a serious imbalance of trade. Only Guangzhou (Canton) was open to foreign trade, and foreigners were sequestered from the population lest they pollute the culture. While China was never colonized, Western nations began to have a significant influence on Chinese society (Ebrey, 1996).

The Opium Wars of 1840–1842 began a series of military encounters between China and Western powers that played out over the course of the 19th century. To address the significant balance of trade issues with China, Britain had begun to produce opium in India for export to China. Facing enormous social consequences from drug addiction and a draining of the national treasury, China sought to cut off the drug trade. Britain attacked, and the Chinese sued for peace. The resulting Treaty of Nanjing, concluded at gunpoint, resulted in the opening of five treaty ports: Guangzhou, Xiamen, Fuzhou, Ningbo, and Shanghai (Ebrey, 1996). By 1893, 28 additional places had been opened to foreign trade, and during 1894–1917, 59 more were established (Feuerwerker, 1976, p. 2). In treaty ports, foreign nationals could reside, own property, and engage in business. Sixteen foreign concessions were established under which entire areas were expropriated or leased in perpetuity to particular foreign powers. By 1903, there were an estimated 1,292 foreign firms established in China and an estimated 20,404 foreign residents. By 1918, these numbers increased to 6,930 foreign firms and 244,527 foreign residents. Japanese firms and residents made up 65% of both totals in 1918, followed by the British and Americans (Feuerwerker, 1976, p. 17). Among the Americans was Cornelius Vander Starr who formed an insurance agency in Shanghai in 1919. The company moved to New York in 1949, where its successor, AIG, collapsed in 2008 and threatened the collapse of global financial markets.

Similar to the situation occurring in America at the same time, the need for independent verification of far-flung investments led to foreign accountants, principally British, opening offices in China. One of the earliest accounting firms in China, Gibb, Livingston & Co. was formed in Guangzhou in 1836 by two Scots associated with the East India Company (Way & Nield, 2002, p. 11). Early in the 20th century there were several new firms opening practices in Hong Kong and Shanghai. Twenty-nine year old Arthur Rylands Lowe opened a practice in Hong Kong in 1902 and established an office in Shanghai in 1906 (Way & Nield, 2002). The firm, then named Lowe & Bingham, ultimately became the PwC member firm in China and China's largest CPA firm in 2012. Haskins and Sells, a predecessor of DTT, arrived in Shanghai in 1917 with three American CPAs keeping the books of US clients (Way & Nield, 2002, p. 98).

The foreign accountants formed a trade association at 59 Hong Kong Road in Shanghai. The association, named the Shanghai Public Accountants Association, issued no professional standards. Since the majority of foreign businesses in Shanghai was incorporated in Hong Kong to take advantage of the more developed legal system in the Crown Colony, most practitioners tended to follow Hong Kong practices, which were based on the British system (Way & Nield, 2002, p. 86). Despite the fact that Japanese business made up the majority of foreign investment in Shanghai in the 1920s, there is no record of Japanese CPA firms in China at this time, perhaps because the profession was only beginning in Japan at this time.

In May 1921, the Japanese Society of Accountants was formed in Japan with a very limited number of members (Watanabe, 1939). Accordingly, Japan had little influence on the new Chinese profession since its profession was in a similar state of development.

4.1.1. Introduction of Western Accounting

The influx of foreign business after the Opium War brought with it the Western system of debit–credit accounting. Some Chinese accountants began to understand that the traditional Chinese methods of accounting were inadequate for their increasingly complex economy and people began to consider Western accounting as an alternative (Chen, 1998; Gardella, 1992; Lin, 1992; Liu & Wang, 1994). In 1905, Xi Yong Cai, an accountant who had once studied in Japan,[1] wrote *Interlocking Bookkeeping* (*LianHuan Zhang Bu*) which was the first such book in Chinese which attempted to incorporate the debit–credit system into traditional Chinese receipt/payment-based accounting (Lin, 1998; Liu & Wang, 1994). Two years later, Xie Lin and Sen Meng published *Bank Bookkeeping*, which introduced double-entry bookkeeping and illustrated the application of the method to the banking industry. By 1916, the Bank of China followed this book to adopt the Western double-entry system. Gradually, the entire banking industry in China followed their example (Chen, 1998; Liu & Wang, 1994).

Throughout thousands of years of imperial rule, China never developed a domestic public accounting industry. After the collapse of the imperial system in 1912 and the formation of the Republic of China, and as Western accountants grew in prominence in China, some Chinese believed that China needed its own public accounting profession (Gao, 1988, pp. 422–423).

4.1.2. Recognition and Licensing of Public Accountants

Xie Lin, the double-entry advocate and banking expert, submitted a proposal to the Northern Warlord (*Beiyang*) government in June 1918 for the establishment of a public accounting profession and was granted the number one certificate as a public accountant. In September 1918, the Ministry of Agriculture and Commerce issued *Provisional Regulations on Accountants*. Under these regulations, it was established that an accountant must be at least 30 years old and a graduate of a Chinese or foreign university or specialized accounting school. Alternatively, an accountant could have worked as a chief accountant for at least five years in a bank or firm with assets of at least 500,000 Yuan (Xu & Xu, 2003).

Xu and Xu (2003) report that the early indigenous profession in China was focused on Shanghai, the major commercial center at the time, and also the center of Western investment. Xu and Xu observed:

> In asserting their professional status and identity, Shanghai accountants not only had to win over the Chinese public, they also had to contend with the dominance of foreign interests in Shanghai that presented both a model and source of competition. (p. 141)

Chinese and foreign accountants competed for clients in Shanghai. Chinese accountants had selected the Chinese term "*kuaijishi*"[2] as the title for licensed public accountants. In English, they used the term "chartered accountant," prompting the British Embassy in April 1925 to send a note to the Chinese Ministry of Foreign Affairs complaining that the use of the term "chartered accountant" was confusing and inappropriate because British accountants were called chartered accountants and strict standards applied to the designation (Xu & Xu, 2003). Chinese accountants successfully refuted the British complaint, arguing that British laws had no force in China. They pointed out that British accountants called themselves *kuaijishi* in Chinese, and that "chartered accountant" was the best translation of the term because they also had strict standards for use of the title. Besides, if they were to use the term "certified public accountant" they would likely receive the same complaint from the Americans. Chinese accountants organized the Institute of Chartered Accountants of the Chinese Republic in 1925, which later changed its name to the Institute of Chartered Accountants of Shanghai.

Xie Lin started a firm, named Zhengze, with headquarters in Beijing and an office in Tianjin. Another strong advocate of double-entry accounting, US educated Shu Lun Pan, had organized the first indigenous accounting firm in 1917. His firm, later renamed Li Xin, became a major firm. In 1986, the original name was recovered and today Shu Lun Pan is the member firm of BDO in China. Shu Lun Pan favored completely replacing Chinese bookkeeping methods with Western methods (Chen, 1998). In 1921, Xu Yongzuo built the Xuyongzhou accounting firm, later renamed Zhengming. Xu Yongzuo was considered the chief advocate of the reformist school, which advocated retaining some traditional Chinese booking methods with Western adaptations (Chen, 1998). Gongping accounting firm, later called Gongxin, was organized in 1927. These four accounting firms, Zhengze, Zhengming, Lixin, and Gongxin were called the "Big Four" in China before the revolution.

4.1.3. Competition between Foreign and Domestic Accounting Firms

The rules set up for foreign concessions established a principle of extraterritoriality, which meant that foreigners were not subject to Chinese law but rather the laws of their home countries. This meant that foreign accountants practicing in China were not subject to the new accounting regulations in China. While foreigners had set up their own professional association, the Shanghai Public Accountants Association, this group did not regulate the foreign profession, nor did it issue any accounting or auditing standards. Accountants were certified or chartered in foreign jurisdictions – principally England, Scotland, or America.

The foreign concessions were the hub of economic activity, and had a concentration of foreign and Chinese businesses. Xu and Xu (2003, p. 144) indicate:

> Since foreign accountants resided and operated in the concessions long before the emergence of the Chinese accounting profession, they were able to take and hold the market of auditing not only foreign but also Chinese businesses there. In addition, because the Mixed Court of the International Settlement was under foreign control, British accountants monopolized the position of Forensic Auditor for the Court, a situation Shanghai accountants wanted, above all, to change.

Chinese accountants began to lobby the Chinese government to exclude foreign accountants from serving Chinese businesses. The Ministry of Foreign Affairs advised there was no way to prohibit foreign accountants from practicing in the foreign concessions. However, since foreigners could not work for Chinese businesses outside the concessions, the Chinese government could prevent them from serving Chinese clients outside the concessions. In 1927, the Ministry of Agriculture and Commerce ordered that Chinese firms not hire foreign accountants (Xu & Xu, 2003). In 1933, the Shanghai Municipal Council, facing political pressure from local firms, appointed joint auditors. Thomson & Co., one of the larger international firms with seven partners and offices in Shanghai, Tianjin, Beijing, Harbin, and Hankow,[3] served jointly with Shu Lun Pan (Way & Nield, 2002, p. 100).

The indigenous profession developed at a slow pace and the profession was almost nonexistent outside of the major business centers of Beijing, Shanghai, Guangzhou, Tianjin, Wuhan, and Chongqing where associations of licensed public accountants were also set up (Hao, 1999; Lin, 1998). In 1926, the total number of licensed accountants in China totaled 183, of which 54 worked in Shanghai (Annual Bulletin of the Institute of Chartered

Accountants of Shanghai, as cited in Xu & Xu, 2003). By 1947, the numbers had peaked at 3,355 licensed accountants (Li & Wang, 1989, p. 144).

4.1.4. Implications to Current Practice

There are many remarkable similarities between the development of the accounting profession in China in the early 20th century and its redevelopment in the late part of that century. Foreign accountants arrived in China in the early 20th century to serve foreign direct investment. They brought with them superior technologies and ideologies. Local firms emerged as a response to the presence of the international firms and used them as role models for development. Local accountants embraced the new accounting technologies that foreign accountants brought to China, including double-entry accounting.

Local firms and foreign firms were different classes, and if they had divided the market between foreign and domestic clients, they would likely have coexisted peacefully. Foreign firms, however, did not confine themselves to foreign clients. They began to serve Chinese clients located in the concessions and were routinely appointed as experts in commercial litigation between Chinese and foreign companies. Here we see the impact of transnational institutions on the regulation of accountants. While China had taken steps to regulate its emerging accounting profession, the indigenous profession was unsuccessful at reaching closure because of the state's limited jurisdiction over foreign concessions. The foreign accountants operated without local regulation and presumably with scant regulation from afar. Transnational institutions, such as the Mixed Court of International Settlement, which favored the appointment of foreign accountants in sorting out commercial disputes, helped the foreign accountants dominate the indigenous firms.

It appears that foreign firms succeeded in establishing hegemony over indigenous firms in the early 20th century. The situation was different than in modern times. In the present period, indigenous and foreign firms appeared in China at the same time. In the early period, the foreign firms came first, and their success attracted local accountants to mimic their behavior. Nevertheless, the situation ends up the same, with foreign firms dominating their indigenous counterparts. There is an interesting twist here. The indigenous firms appear to have created a local market by abandoning traditional Chinese accounting practices in favor of the new Western approaches used by the foreign firms. This is an example of the operation of the hegemony of consent wherein the subordinate class accepts the ideology of the dominant group as superior. In this case, however, the consent of the local accountants appears to be conscious, and deliberate. Consent to the ideological hegemony of the foreign firms created the opportunity for the formation of indigenous firms.

Indigenous accountants in the early period also appear to have followed the long march through the institutions in their attempt to break the hegemony of the foreign firms. The first step in the long march was to accept the Western accounting technologies of double-entry accounting and to convince Chinese society of its merits. The profession then needed to seek legitimacy, which it did by obtaining recognition from the state and forming the Institute of Chartered Accountants of the Chinese Republic. These factors were insufficient to break the hegemony of the foreign firms, so the indigenous firms appealed to the state on nationalistic grounds for support. This was partially successful, since they succeeded in obtaining a ban on foreign firms serving Chinese clients outside the concessions. The concessions, however, were a form of transnational institution that had subsumed the power of the Chinese state. This case, however, is not a situation where the foreign firms deliberately sought the power of transnational institutions to establish hegemony. The transnational institutions had enabled the presence of the foreign firms.

We can speculate as to how the Chinese accounting profession might have developed had the subsequent war and revolution not occurred. Would it have followed the pathway of former British colonies like Hong Kong and Singapore, where foreign domination continued despite localization of the state and moderation of foreign influence? Alternatively, would it have largely localized, perhaps resulting in large local firms that ultimately aligned with the Big Four? Alternatively, would the world's accounting markets be different today? If China had become a major economic power following World War II, would a major Chinese firm have emerged that would have competed against the Big Four, particularly in Asia?

4.2. WAR AND REVOLUTION

China's imperial system collapsed in 1912 and a period of instability began as competing ideologies sought to shape the new China. The Nationalist government was formed in 1928. Foreign powers consented to reductions in their special privileges. The number of foreign concessions was reduced from 33 to 13, and extraterritoriality was eliminated for some countries (Ebrey, 1996, p. 276). Communists took advantage of the widespread corruption of the Nationalists, which together with spiraling inflation and widespread poverty gave fertile ground for recruitment of peasants to the Communist cause. Conflict between the Nationalists and Communists, coupled with increasing Japanese aggression, made business conditions difficult, leading to a decline in foreign investment. The Great Depression, which commenced in 1929, worsened an already difficult situation.

Full-scale war broke out with Japan in 1937. Some foreign accountants remained in China to do liquidation work, only to be sent to internment camps in 1942 (Way & Nield, 2002, p. 113). The end of the war saw some of the foreign accounting firms commence operations again, although the flight of capital resulted in bleak business conditions.

The Communists formed the People's Republic of China in 1949, which initiated a transition from private ownership to state ownership and a centrally planned economy. Foreign investments were confiscated and Alan Forsyth, the last employee of Lowe, Bingham, and Thomas, left Shanghai on September 26, 1956 and relocated to Japan. Lowe, Bingham, and Thomas later became the Japanese affiliate of Price Waterhouse (PW), while Lowe, Bingham, and Matthews (LBM) in Hong Kong became PW's member firm in the Crown Colony (Way & Nield, 2002, p. 151).

The transition to public ownership accelerated during the Great Leap Forward in the late 1950s, resulting in only two types of businesses: state-owned and collectively owned (Hao, 1999; Huang & Ma, 2001). The Communists fully nationalized the economy by 1962 and abolished auditing by public accountants. The profession did not exist in China for the next 18 years.

4.3. CHINA OPENS TO THE WORLD

China was isolated from the West following the revolution in 1949. The failed programs of the Great Leap Forward and the Cultural Revolution brought great hardship to the Chinese people. In July 1968, Mao Zedong dismantled the Red Guards, marking the beginning of a period of moderation in Chinese political ideology. Zhou Enlai, a leading moderate, began to see the benefits in increasing relations with the West to counter the influence of the Soviet Union. At a table tennis competition in Japan, a practice session between a Chinese and American player led to an invitation approved by Mao Zedong for the American team to visit China, marking a warming of US and Chinese relations. Richard Nixon's visit to China in 1972 stimulated Western interest in the possibilities of the Chinese market and the international accounting firms began to seek opportunities to establish contacts on the mainland (Lewis, 2005, p. 125). Early visits resulted in reports that development of the China market would take considerable time.

4.3.1. Reestablishment of the Domestic Accounting Profession

In December 1978, Deng Xiaoping launched China on a program of economic reforms called the "Four Modernizations" that was intended to transform China into an economic power by the early 21st century. The cornerstone of the reforms was the transformation of the economy from a centrally planned system to "socialism with Chinese characteristics" – a market-driven system (Mackerras, Taneja, & Young, 1994). A part of these reforms was to open China's economy to foreign participation. While there was concern that allowing foreign investment would introduce too many elements of capitalism to China, Deng Xiaoping took the view that China could learn advanced methods of operations and management that could be incorporated into a socialist economy.

Foreign investment began to flow into China in 1979, and laws were needed to define the rights and responsibilities of the parties to new joint ventures. *The Law of the People's Republic of China on Sino-Foreign Equity Joint Ventures* was enacted on July 1, 1979 (Huang & Ma, 2001). The National People's Congress enacted *The Income Tax Law for Sino-Foreign Joint Ventures* in September 1980, which created the need for an accounting profession. Detailed implementation rules issued on December 14, 1980 required that tax returns be accompanied by an auditor's report signed by a Chinese CPA. The absence of any CPA firms in China to provide those reports was addressed nine days later with the issuance of *Provisional Regulations Concerning the Establishment of Accounting Consultancies.* These regulations firmly placed the profession under the control of the state. The regulations provided rules for the qualification of CPAs and firms and placed their administration under finance bureaus at the provincial level. Notably, the new rules establishing a CPA profession did not allow foreigners to practice.

Hao (1999, p. 292) states that the beginning of the CPA profession was "... just one step away from a planned economy and was of the nature of a very careful trial" since the profession initially served only foreign joint ventures. The new accounting firms were required to affiliate with existing government or educational institutions because socioeconomic and political factors would have made the establishment of independent accounting firms very difficult (Dai et al., 2000). There were practical reasons for the affiliation program as well. Because the only clients of the new firms were foreign joint ventures, accountants needed foreign language skills. People who possessed the required combination of accounting and language skills tended be assigned under the communist system to government finance offices or universities (Dai et al., 2000). Convincing these employees to leave secure and prestigious positions to join speculative new accounting firms would have been difficult. Under China's "iron rice bowl" system of lifetime employment, it was necessary to second employees to the new accounting firms, giving them a lifeline back to their work units and access to employee benefits such as housing, medical care, and pensions. This system, however, significantly undermined the independence of the new profession, since it gave the seconding organization extraordinary influence over the new CPAs.

Other factors made the affiliation program necessary at this stage of China's development. The new CPAs were unable to raise the necessary capital to form the new firms. Even if they had been able to do so, they would likely have had difficulty obtaining a CPA certificate since certification was initially done on a subjective basis by the Ministry of Finance based on recommendations from provincial governments (Dai et al., 2000).

Shanghai CPAs, formed on January 1, 1981, became the first modern Chinese accounting firm. Like other accounting firms to follow, it was a state-owned enterprise, affiliated with the Finance Bureau of Shanghai. More firms were established in other locations over the succeeding years (Hao, 1999). In Shanghai, for example, some the largest firms were affiliated with the Finance Bureau, the Shanghai University of Finance and Economics (SUFE), and the Taxation Bureau (Dai et al., 2000, p. 23). Dai et al. (2000) observe that, although not openly stated, tax returns prepared and certified by firms affiliated with the Taxation Bureau tended to avoid audit.

4.3.2. Foreign Firms in China: The Representative Office Period from 1979 to 1990

I found no record of any involvement of the Big Eight in China during China's long isolation after 1949. The year following Nixon's groundbreaking

1972 trip, KPMG attempted to secure an invitation to visit China through contacts at the Bank of China in London, but concluded that probably only consulting work was possible at that time, and that any approach would need to be low key. In 1975, Rick Willens, an American management consultant with Peat Marwick in Hong Kong visited the Canton Trade Fair, meeting with two representatives of the Machinery Export and Import Corporation to talk about computer systems (Lewis, 2005, p. 125). By 1980, other representatives of the then Big Eight had begun to travel into China to explore the possibilities of that market.

4.3.2.1. Developing Relationships

Interpersonal networks are central to Chinese culture, and the establishment and maintenance of these networks was critical to the ability of the Big Four to gain practice rights and to build practices in China. The ambiguity of Chinese laws and policies meant that the capability to solve problems faced by the firms and their clients was dependent on the firm's ability to access the power of the state through the reciprocal obligations of officials under the concept of *guanxi*. This theme permeates the development of the profession, and is expressed in how market access was obtained, how clients were won and served, and how conflict was resolved.

The concept of guanxi. Guanxi is loosely translated as connections, and describes the centrality of personal networks in Chinese life. The practice of *guanxi* is derived from Confucianism, which gave rise to the broad cultural aspects of collectivism manifested in the importance of networks of interpersonal relations (Park & Luo, 2001). As Jacobs (1979) indicates, the modern practice of *guanxi* is grounded in particularistic ties. Common traits such as kinship, native place, and ethnicity give rise to these ties. The ties are also based on acquired characteristics such as attending the same school, sharing similar experiences, or doing business together. Marx (1867), likely unaware of the concept of *guanxi*, appears to describe this phenomenon as emergent class consciousness in the industrial proletariat. Thrown together in a common situation, workers learn to identify with each other and support each other's initiatives. *Guanxi* is a special kind of relationship, marked by implicit rules of obligation and reciprocity (Hwang, 1987).

In Chinese business, people often consciously seek to establish or "manufacture" *guanxi* by establishing a relationship either directly or through intermediaries (Gold, Guthrie, & Wank, 2002). Even where the bases for *guanxi* naturally occur because of birth relationships or life experiences, *guanxi* must be consciously produced, cultivated, and maintained over time (Yang, 1994). However, as Kiong and Kee (1998, p. 77) indicate:

> The existence of a shared *guanxi* base does not imply the existence of a *guanxi*. A *guanxi* base, whether it is ascriptive, as one based on kinship, or achieved via shared experience, only facilitates the development of a *guanxi* relation but does not pre-determine it.

Guanxi-based relationships can grow into highly complex networks constituting a "highly differentiated intricate system of overt or covert, as well as formal and informal social subsets governed by the unwritten law of reciprocity" (Wilpert & Scharpf, 1990). *Guanxi* relationships are the foundation of much of the business that is conducted in China (Buttery & Wong, 1999). Once *guanxi* is developed between two people, each can ask a favor of the other with an understanding that the receipt of the favor creates an obligation to reciprocate at some time in the future (Yang, 1994). The concept of reciprocal obligation is central to the concept of *guanxi* (Gold et al., 2002). *Guanxi* is more than an issue of social connections and the good manners of reciprocity; it is a system of gifts and favors that manufactures obligation and indebtedness (Yang, 1994).

Ganqing and guanxi. Another important component of *guanxi*, which distinguishes it from Western concepts of reciprocity, is the inter-linkage with emotion. The Western ideal is to separate emotion from business, yet such a concept is strange to the Chinese. The Chinese word *ganqing* – human feelings or affection, is an important part of *guanxi*. Kiong and Kee (1998, p. 80) observe:

> Whilst the presence of *guanxi* depends upon the existence of a *guanxi* base, the value of a *guanxi* – how close the *guanxi* is – depends upon the element of *ganqing* or affection. Thus, if *ganqing* can be developed, the *guanxi* becomes closer, more dependable, and valuable. Without *ganqing*, *guanxi* is more distant and less reliable.

Kipnis (2002, p. 28) considers it idealistic to think that *guanxi* always involves *ganqing*, "… more accurate would be the statement that practices of *guanxi* rely on strategic and more and less successful attempts to generate *ganqing* and manipulate obligations." The generation of *ganqing* is what makes *guanxi* so powerful in Chinese society. The *ganqing* component of *guanxi* is reflective of the rule-of-man characteristic of most of China's existence. As China tries to move in the direction of a rule-of-law, *ganqing* avoiding practices such as enforceable contracts moderate the usage of *guanxi*. *Guanxi* creates moral hazard, because the reciprocal obligations created are almost impossible to refuse (Tsang, 1998). Gift giving and entertaining may be a means of establishing and maintaining *guanxi*, but these activities are not equivalent to corruption. Bribery may get business transactions done on a one-off basis, but it cannot produce *ganqing* (Tsang, 1998). Nevertheless, the compulsory nature of *guanxi* obligations creates tension when the resources of a third party, such as an employer, are used to fulfill a *guanxi* obligation. This is particularly difficult because *guanxi* obligations have no expiration date, and the fulfillment of an obligation may have nothing to do with a benefit received by the present employer. *Guanxi* is dyadic, not inter-organizational, and accordingly is personal to the human participants even when it is used to the benefit of an organization.

Guanxi and the Big Four. As China opened up, the Big Four accounting firms assigned ethnic Chinese employees from America and Hong Kong to develop relationships within China. These employees appear to have been selected primarily based on their perceived linguistic skills, which were commonly absent because they spoke Cantonese rather than Mandarin. Despite their shortcomings in language, these employees understood Chinese culture, and they were cognizant that success in China would require the development of *guanxi* networks with government officials in order to assist their firms in gaining market access, winning clients, and solving client problems. While many people were among the pioneers who opened China for the international accounting firms and played key roles in developing the relationships that would open the Chinese market to foreign accountants, I have identified five people who played outsized roles.

Opening the door: David Ma of Ernst & Whinney. David Ma was born in Wenzhou, China in 1919. He was a student at the University of Wisconsin when World War II broke out and he was unable to return to China. He joined S.D. Leidesdorf in New York in 1953, an accounting firm later acquired by Ernst & Ernst, which became Ernst & Whinney in 1979. He met his wife, Teresa, in New York. Teresa, originally from Beijing, was a nurse at the Woman's Hospital.

At the twilight of his career as a partner he was assigned to Ernst & Whinney's international office from which he directed the firm's entry into China starting early in 1979. He tracked down many of his former Chinese classmates and found that some had achieved positions in the government. He took a group of four people from China to New York in 1979 to visit the Ernst & Whinney offices. One of those people later became the Deputy Secretary of Finance for China, two others were university professors, and the fourth, Ge Ming, in 1985 joined CCFM – E&Y Management Services, a joint venture between E&Y and MOF in Hong Kong that served as MOF's window to the outside world. Ge Ming later became the managing partner of Hua Ming, the MOF-owned CPA firm that became E&Y's joint venture partner in 1992 (Ward, 1992).

Ma opened an office in a hotel room at the Beijing Hotel in 1980 and worked alone with his wife. Ernst & Whinney did not receive permission to open a representative office until the following year, but Ma recognized that they needed to be there immediately. The first client to visit was Coca-Cola, a major Ernst & Whinney account and the first American company to distribute its products in China after it opened up under Deng Xiaoping. Ma stayed in Beijing only until 1982, when he returned to the United States to retire, but the door to China for accounting firms was open (Ann Ma, Personal Communication, November 21, 2008).

Building bridges: Margaret Jack of Price Waterhouse. Among the early travelers to China was Margaret (Sun) Jack, born in Hong Kong in November 1951, and sent to boarding school in Australia. After studying accounting at the University of New South Wales she and her new husband, Australian Graeme Jack, joined PW in Sydney. In 1976, Graeme transferred to the Hong Kong office of PW and Margaret joined Touche Ross. As China began to open up in 1978, Margaret took on the task of developing relationships with China. In 1980, she left Touche Ross to join her husband at PW Hong Kong (Way & Nield, 2002). Working through family contacts, she got in contact with the newly formed Chinese Accounting Association, a branch of the Ministry of Finance, and asked what role an international accounting firm might play in China's development. She learned that China needed advice in the area of auditing. A series of seminars followed, including a seminar on *The Role of International Accounting Firms in China* that was presented in November 1980 by partners of the UK and US firms of PW. The PW partners came away from the meeting realizing that the process of registering a representative office in China would be "complicated" (Way & Nield, 2002, pp. 214–215).

The foreign accountants learned that they needed *guanxi* with individuals in the Chinese government in order to serve their clients. They soon found that an easy way to obtain access to important individuals in government bureaus was to provide them with training (Lewis, 2005). Contacts made with people in the course of this training helped create *guanxi*, which the foreign accountants used to ask favors to solve client problems. The firms provided seminars on a broad range of topics, from industry focused lectures in petroleum and banking to targeted programs on the role of accounting firms in the economy. What began initially as casually arranged seminars in government offices evolved into overseas jaunts to visit offices of accounting firms and client companies. A substantial portion of the travel was for sightseeing, with Las Vegas being a popular stop. The accounting firms typically funded these trips and usually sent a senior staff member to accompany the group for building deep personal relationships. The Hong Kong partners who typically led these events understood the important *guanxi* creation nature of these commitments, disregarding the concerns of Western colleagues who sometimes questioned the appropriateness of the expenditures. This practice was widespread in many industries, ultimately resulting in high-profile criminal prosecutions against several US companies under the Foreign Corrupt Practices Act, but to date there have been no prosecutions against any of the Big Six (Warin, Diamant, & Pfenning, 2010). Chinese regulators also became concerned about this behavior. Ding Pingzhun, CIPCA director-general said in 1998 that any of the international firms that "use improper or illegal measures, for example to bribe the relevant officials, are to be severely punished" (Ding, 2006b, p. 92).

Part of the process of building *guanxi* involved providing favors for government officials. Often these favors included providing employment, either in China or abroad, for the family of officials including the following more notable examples. Coopers and Lybrand employed Qian Ning, the American educated son of Foreign Minister Qian Qichen. PW arranged a job for the son of Ding Pingzhun, the head of the CICPA, at the firm's offices in California. Zhu Rongji's son, Zhu Yunlai, was educated in the United States and worked for Arthur Andersen (AA) in Chicago for a time before returning to take up a senior post with an SOE in China (Wang & Zweig, 2008). Zhu Rongji sent Minister of Finance Xiang Huaicheng (whose daughter became an AA partner[4]) to AA's famed training center in St. Charles, Illinois. St. Charles, as the center was known, became the blueprint for China's National Accounting Institutes (Suzuki, Yan, & Chen, 2007). The intertwining of official's families and the Big Four firms gave the firms access to high levels of government.

Moving in: Dominic Ho of KPMG. Dominic Ho was born in Guangzhou and raised in Hong Kong. He went to the United States for education and joined PMM in Houston where he focused on oil and gas companies. He married a woman from Taiwan and learned to speak Mandarin. In 1978, when the awakening of China caught his interest, he wrote to Stan Klion, the Secretary-General of PMM International asking what plans the firm had for China. Two years later, Klion asked Ho to become involved with oil and gas consulting in China and he began to make regular visits to China to give lectures to the China National Offshore Oil Company (CNOOC) and the Ministries of Petroleum and Finance.

Ho moved to Beijing in September 1984, becoming a partner in the US partnership of PMM the following year. Klion, to whom Ho reported, told him "Your number one priority is to obtain the right for PMM to sign audit reports in China" (Lewis, 2005, p. 155). After a few years, Ho became concerned that his career with the US firm might be compromised if he stayed longer. The Hong Kong firm, concerned about losing the *guanxi* that Ho had developed in China, convinced him to join the Hong Kong partnership of KPMG[5] in 1989. Ho relocated to Hong Kong for a decade, returning to the mainland when the global firm of KPMG turned over management of their China member firm to the Hong Kong firm in 2000. Ho remained engaged with China during his Hong Kong tenure, playing a key role in the development of the H-share market.

Dominic Ho was the first international partner of any professional services firm to live in China full time. Even as a young partner, Ho was likely the most senior foreign businessman living in China at the time and he developed broad relationships, sitting "up in dimly lit offices or hotel rooms until the early hours talking to middle ranking ministry and state company managers on a variety of subjects" (Lewis, 2005, p. 153). He also developed contacts at the highest levels of the Chinese government and with their children. Senior Chinese officials invited Ho to sit in the dais with them during China's National Day military parades, Ho enjoyed access at the highest levels of government. Ho's deepest relationships were within the Ministry of Finance and in particular with those responsible for the development of the accounting profession.

Friends in high places: Nellie Fong of AA. Nellie Fong was born and raised in Hong Kong and educated in the United Kingdom. She joined AA after her return to Hong Kong in 1973 and worked as a tax accountant. She became a partner in AA in 1981, just as the China market was opening up. Although she spoke only Cantonese and English at the time, she was enthusiastic about getting involved in China, and began developing relationships despite her struggles with Mandarin:

> When I started, I couldn't understand what other people are talking about and I think people don't understand. So I just didn't care. I just went along being happy. Most of the time you can catch people anyway a little bit. So people are making so much fun about me about my pronunciation being wrong. So the entire dinner conversation was correcting my Mandarin. People find it so fun that they could correct me. (Nellie Fong, personal correspondence, August 2009)

Fong remained in a leadership position with AA until its demise. She then joined PwC, which acquired substantially all of AA's China and Hong

Kong practices in 2002. Her husband was a partner with PwC and together they facilitated the negotiations for the acquisition. She retired in 2007, yet remained active as an advisor to the firm. She has redirected her efforts to philanthropy. Fong heads up Lifeline Express, a hospital eye surgery train which travels to remote areas of China to perform cataract surgery. She was recognized for these activities by the Clinton Global Initiative and the Chinese Ministry of Civil Affairs (Loong, 2001).

Fong's relationship with Zhu Rongji gave her a major role in the development of the accounting profession in China. Zhu was twice purged from the Communist Party for his rightist views. Deng Xiaoping formally rehabilitated Zhu when he sought him out for his like-minded economic views. Zhu headed the State Economic Commission until 1989 when he became the Mayor of Shanghai. He became vice-premier of China in 1991 and premier from 1998 to 2003. Zhu is widely acclaimed as the person who drove China's rapid economic development (Brahm, 2003).

Nellie Fong entered Hong Kong politics in 1983 with appointments to several local government boards. In 1988, she accepted appointment to the Legislative Council of Hong Kong. In June of 1989, the Tiananmen incident roiled Hong Kong with protests that continued for several days. Only five years earlier, on December 19, 1984, Margaret Thatcher and Zhao Ziyang had signed the Sino-British Joint Declaration setting forth the terms under which Hong Kong was to return to Chinese sovereignty. While many in the business community were concerned about the pending handover, Nellie Fong was a contrarian voice arguing: "The real economic success of Hong Kong will come after 1997 when we become much closer to China" (Kraar & McGowan, 1995). In September 1989, Zhu Rongji was the first Chinese official to venture into Hong Kong after Tiananmen and faced widespread protests. Fong was among the few who spoke out in favor of Mainland China. No other Big Six partners spoke out in favor of China. AA's insignificant market share in Hong Kong at the time (see Table 4.1) meant the firm had little to lose by having one of its partners stand up to the Hong Kong establishment.

Fong went to London to challenge the incoming, and final, British governor, Chris Patten. She told Patten that he needed to meet with and provide face to Lu Ping, the Chinese official responsible for Hong Kong, by visiting Beijing prior to his arrival in Hong Kong to discuss Hong Kong's proposed new airport. Patten (1998, p. 53) writes of this encounter in his memoirs:

> It was suggested to me, not least by an emissary from Lu (a ubiquitous Hong Kong businesswoman called Nelly (sic) Fong, whose regular and self-advertised presence in what appeared to be the inner chambers of Chinese policy-making inevitably raised

questions about the seriousness and understanding of those in Peking who were helping to determine the future of the colony), that if I were to tell Lu what he wanted to hear about political development then he would give me good news about the airport. I pointed out to Ms. Fong that everyone talked to me about Chinese "face," but there was also a thing about British "face."

Fong's vocal support for Mainland China resulted in her losing all of her Hong Kong government appointments. These were soon replaced by an appointment to the Chinese government's Preparatory Committee on Hong Kong's Transfer of Sovereignty to China and, following the handover, to the HKSAR Executive Council and the 10th and 11th National Committees of the Chinese People's Political Consultative Congress.

Fong's relationship with Zhu Rongji developed while he was mayor of Shanghai. Fong wrote a paper about how Shanghai needed to change to catch up with the more rapidly developing Guangdong. Zhu was so delighted with her paper that he published it in the newspapers. Fong suggested to Zhu that bringing in an international viewpoint would help him in developing Shanghai. In 1988, Fong assisted Zhu in setting up the International Business Leaders Advisory Council for the Mayor of Shanghai, which more than 20 years later continues to connect Fortune 50 CEOs to Shanghai. Frustrated with high levels of incompetence and corruption in state-owned enterprises, Zhu turned to Fong for advice. Nellie Fong (personal correspondence, August 2009) recounts:

I said we're opening to the world. The foreign companies who came to China to run the business are the biggest, the healthiest, and the brightest. I said the old SOEs were old and had the burden. It's like a boxing ring. The foreigners who came in were able to fight, healthy and strong. We push in our old people carrying a bag, hands cuffed because of your policies, with an iron ball linked to their legs. I said you're sending them off to fight this battle. How can you ever expect to win? So he stopped and looked at me. I said: even if I helped you train them, you also blindfolded them because they don't know about the world. Even if I trained them, I open their blindfoldedness. I said before they die and don't know why, now they die knowing why. They still die. I said therefore you have to change policies to lessen their burdens and take away the cufflinks before they can go off and fight. I think I had this very major story. Anyhow he liked it. I think that's why there was a corporate state-owned emphasis to reform and I was engaged in that training.

Zhu engaged Fong to provide training for SOE managers, which included bringing in MNC company managers to talk about how they run their businesses. The training became mandatory for all SOE owners, and was still being conducting in 2009 for the 18th year, two sessions a year, with 1,500 participants at each session. Fong said: "If you go to a state owned enterprise and ask if they know me, if anyone says they don't know me, there are only two reasons: He's not an SOE or he's not a leader." AA positioned itself front of mind with all SOE managers, which helped them considerably as SOEs began to seek overseas listings.

Ding Pingzhun, CICPA director general, often found that Nellie Fong and AA outmaneuvered him:

> ... I started to ask whether Andersen is trustworthy or not. Later on, I was told that the advantage enjoyed by Andersen is not only its exploring spirit, but also the ability to directly communicate with the "upper class" (the high officials). In the past, I knew only that in the accounting firms the people working are all accountants who are honest and steadfast. Later I knew that the accounting firm is also a "merchant" who has to make money, which has nothing to do with titles in the accounting world but is really "something" in China and even in the world. I am just a "head" to administer the CPA profession in China who is only familiar with accounting principles and procedures but not with the strategies in dealing with politicians. (Ding, 2006b, p. 124)

AA effectively used its international connections to gain access to high-level officials and to establish its credibility with officials. Ding relates being particularly impressed with the skills of Edward Heath, the former British prime minister. One of Ding's early tasks was to write a welcoming speech for a visit by Heath in 1983, and Ding was surprised that the request came from AA. At a dinner in 1997, celebrating the fifth anniversary of AA's joint venture, Heath astonished Ding by saying that three issues he prided himself with were (1) meeting with Chairman Mao and establishing diplomatic relations with China, (2) working with Deng Xiaoping to solve the Hong Kong issue, and (3) helping Andersen to enter China to aid in the development of the economy (Ding, 2006b, p. 124).

Tan Man-Kou. Wong, Tan & Co commenced operations in Shanghai in 1936. The firm established a branch office in Hong Kong, where it relocated after the war. Founder Tan Jat Min's son, Tan Man-Kou succeeded him (Hutcheon, 1998). The firm merged with M. W. Kwan and Co. in 1976 to form Hong Kong's largest local firm, Kwan Wong Tan & Fong (KWTF). The firm continued to serve Chinese controlled entities in the decades after the 1949 revolution including the Bank of China and eight of its member banks, the Xinhua News Agency, China Travel Service, and China Resources. KWTF became a member firm of BDO and was the only non-Big Six firm to participate in the first initial public offerings in China. Senior partner Tan Man-Kou, who was appointed to the Chinese People's Political Consultative Congress, said in 1994 "The China link is helpful for us to understand the Chinese situation and to communicate with them more effectively" (Chen, 1994b).

In 1997, KWTF merged with DTT in Hong Kong. In 1992, DTT had a 14.08% market share of revenue in Hong Kong and KWTF had an 8.04% share. Combined they became competitive with PW and KPMG. Tan Man-Kou, 61 years old at the time of the merger, retired in 2002. His effectiveness in China waned after the initial H-share offerings.

4.3.3. Approval of Representative Offices

The Big Eight lobbied for permission to open offices, arguing that their clients who were investing in China required their expertise, as did China itself. Coopers & Lybrand (C&L) won the first representative office approval on January 12, 1981, for an office in Shanghai followed that same year by Ernst & Ernst and PW with offices in Beijing. The C&L office was the first representative office of any foreign organization in Shanghai and only the 11th foreign organization registered in the PRC (Sir John Stuttard, personal communication, September 1, 2009). American Roderick McLeod, who opened the office, became the first foreign accountant registered in China since 1949. McLeod was the recently retired managing partner of C&L's Boston office and had been the coauthor of the ninth edition of legendary accounting text *Montgomery's Auditing*.

4.3.3.1. Expansion of Representative Offices

Within two years, most of the Big Eight had representative offices operating in China. Separate approval of a representative office was required if an accounting firm wished to register in additional cities and within a few years a total of 30 representative offices had been opened. The offices opened principally in the four major commercial centers of China: Beijing, Shanghai, Guangzhou, and Shenzhen, but also in some second-tier cities such as Dalian, Nanjing, and Chongqing (Brandenberg, 1987; Ding, 1996).

Increasing client enquiries about China led to a visit to Beijing in 1979 by PMM US senior partner Walter Hanson accompanied by Hong Kong senior partner Denys Connolly. Appalled by conditions in China, including in particular the condition of his hotel, Hanson concluded it would be many years before China could afford the firm's services. Nevertheless, at a PMM International (PMI) Advisory Board meeting in New York in March 1979, it was decided that a committee consisting of one partner from each of the US, UK, and Hong Kong firms would prepare a report "on how to best obtain business and in due course representation in China" (Lewis, 2005, p. 125). Tony Howitt, the partner-in-charge of PMM's management consulting practice in the United Kingdom, chaired the committee and visited China the following year as part of a UK delegation. By September 1980, PMM Hong Kong began to seek engagements that would take them into China and to look for accountants who could speak Mandarin. At the PMM International Advisory Committee meeting in Johannesburg in March 1981, Stan Klion agreed to prepare proposals for establishing an operation in China for a three-year period. C&L had received approval for a representative office two months earlier and, despite Hanson's pessimism about the opportunity, the PMM executives recognized they were falling behind the competition.

In 1982, the Hong Kong firm of PMM was invited by the Beijing Economic Development Corporation (BEDC) to give a series of lectures to Chinese accountants on modern accounting practices. BEDC in turn offered to sponsor PMM's application for a representative office in Beijing. David Gairns, the Hong Kong PMM partner assigned responsibility for China observed at the time "the overall view was that development of business with and within China would be a long-term activity with little immediate fee earning work, but that this should not cloud the long-term importance of the future potential" (Lewis, 2005, p. 126). BEDC failed to deliver on the representative office approval, and in 1984, the sponsorship was transferred to CNOOC with which Dominic Ho of the Houston office had developed a relationship. PMM's representative office opened on April 26, 1985, the last of the Big Six to establish an office, perhaps delayed in large part due to the lack of enthusiasm of Walter Hanson.

4.3.3.2. Operation of Representative Offices

Like most of the firms, PMM did not wait for approval of the office to begin working. The PMI Board, in 1983, approved an annual budget for China operations of $350,000 and selected Robert Kwauk, a Canadian manager based in Hong Kong, to manage it:

> By October of the same year, Kwauk was described as being very active, especially with tax advice, and even producing some billable work. The kind of work he did in the PRC often involved negotiating with the PRC authorities for clients in areas where the law was inadequate or non-existent. (Lewis, 2005, p. 126)

In newly opened China, office space was scarce and several of the firms set up operations in hotel rooms in the Beijing Hotel and in the Jianguo Hotel. These were the first hotels opened to foreigners in China, and served as the base for most MNCs venturing into the country. The space was cramped, even though the offices were staffed by only a handful of people on short-term assignments. Demand for their services was high, particularly for tax and market entry consulting services. Interviewees reported that clients often waited in the hallways of the hotel for the opportunity for a few minutes with the haggard consultants. Much of the work involved "negotiating with the PRC authorities for clients in areas where the law was inadequate or non-existent" (Lewis, 2005, p. 126). Many of the early practitioners were tax professionals, typically from Hong Kong, Canada, or the United States, and while they knew little more than their clients about the rapidly emerging market, one partner quipped: "in the land of the blind, the one-eyed man is king." A little experience and expertise was invaluable in dealing with the uncertainty facing investors in China.

Although PMM was the last to open a representative office, by 1987 they had offices in Beijing, Shanghai, and Guangzhou. PW and Ernst & Whinney both had offices in Beijing and Guangzhou, KMG (which would later merge with PMM to form KPMG) and Touche Ross (which would later merge with Deloitte) were both in Beijing, and Deloitte had opened in both Beijing and Shanghai (Brandenberg, 1987). The representative offices of the Big Eight were permitted to provide consulting services in defined areas, including accounting and auditing advice to foreign clients in China, international tax advice to prospective foreign investors, and business information to Chinese companies involved in international trade (Ding, 1996). Rules precluded representative offices from performing auditing services. While this was clearly understood to mean that the firms could not conduct statutory audits in China, firms generally took a more permissive view of the ability to perform audits or agreed-upon procedures for foreign clients. In the early years, however, these restrictions were not problematic, since foreign client investments tended to be small and demand for audit services was consequentially limited. There was, however, extensive demand for tax, market entry consulting, and due diligence work for foreign clients looking for Chinese joint venture partners (Jack, 1993b). Expatriate personnel on short-term assignments to Beijing from the Hong Kong offices of the firms typically provided these services.

For some time after opening up, the only foreign accounting firms that were allowed to establish a representative office were the Big Eight firms. The intent was to protect the nascent Chinese firms from competition by keeping out smaller firms from Hong Kong, Taiwan, and foreign countries. The Big Eight were seen as necessary to train local accountants and to serve multinational investment. Smaller international firms, particularly from Hong Kong and Taiwan, were viewed as potential competitors to the indigenous firms. Foreigners were not allowed to obtain CPA qualifications and the reports that they signed were invalid in China (Ding, 2006b).

4.3.4. The Role of Hong Kong

Hong Kong served as the principal gateway for foreigners looking to China until the late 1990s, when the infrastructure in China had developed sufficiently for foreign investors to base their operations in Mainland China. Geographic proximity, low taxes, and a well-developed infrastructure were Hong Kong's principal advantages, and actors in Hong Kong touted China know-how and cultural and language abilities as key advantages. As China opened up to foreign investment, there was a rapid movement of Hong Kong's manufacturing base to the neighboring Guangdong province. The close proximity and common language (both Hong Kong and Guangdong speak Cantonese) made it easy for Hong Kong companies to take advantage of the low labor costs in China. Service industries, including accounting, law, and investment banking were slower to make the move. This was in part because of the slower pace of opening up of these markets as compared to manufacturing, the difficulty in finding professional level employees, and because of the perceived superior lifestyle and low taxes in Hong Kong.

Hong Kong's claim to China expertise in cultural and language matters was tenuous. Most people in Hong Kong speak Cantonese, a language that is incomprehensible to the majority of Chinese who speak Mandarin. Studying Mandarin became popular in Hong Kong due to the business and employment opportunities it presented. Cultural convergence, however, was more difficult. Hong Kong managers had developed a unique set of managerial values that often diverged from both Western and Chinese value systems (Ralston, Gustafson, Cheung, & Terpstra, 1993). A regular theme in my interviews with Chinese nationals was a widespread distrust and dislike of people from Hong Kong.

The Hong Kong member firms of the Big Four played a critical, often conflict-filled role in the development of the Big Four practices in China. Ultimately all of the firms merged their Hong Kong and China practices. While this result might have seemed predestined, three complicating factors required resolution first. First, at the time that China's accounting markets were opening up, Hong Kong was preparing to end its 156 years as a British Crown Colony. The accounting profession, and in particular the two dominant firms in Hong Kong, PW and KPMG, were deeply entrenched as colonial institutions. Second, many Hong Kong people were ambivalent at best over the pending handover of Hong Kong to China. Third, the Hong Kong partners of the Big Eight firms in Hong Kong had different views about the future role of China in the firms than did their global leadership.

4.3.4.1. Hong Kong's Colonial Legacy

The accounting profession in Hong Kong was a product of its colonial history and two accounting firms dominated the market for much of its history. LBM, the predecessor firm of PW, had opened in 1902. Three partners survived the Japanese internment camps during the occupation during World War II, and the practice reopened in Hong Kong and Shanghai shortly after the war with a staff of 39, including 7 Chinese staff and 7 partners. The firm found work from the American military forces in Shanghai, which led to a relationship with PW that, on October 1, 1974, resulted in LBM becoming a licensed member firm of PW (Way & Nield, 2002). The Shanghai office closed in 1956, with some of the partners moving to Japan, but the Hong Kong firm continued.

KPMG traces its roots in Hong Kong to the 1920s, when Bernard Brown opened his practice as a sideline to his regular job as an accountant for a wool import/export company. By the time the war broke out, Brown's practice had signed up some major clients, including HSBC, and it had secured its position with LBM as one of the Big Two in Hong Kong. Brown left before the war and serviced HSBC in London, developing a relationship with PMM that had him return to Hong Kong in 1945 as the PMM affiliate, with the British firm of PMM holding a 50% interest. The early entry of both LBM and PMM would lead to their domination of the market in Hong Kong. The remaining Big Eight firms arrived in Hong Kong in the late 1960s and 1970s, but by 1988, PW and KPMG still had a 75.5% market share of the audit fees of publicly listed companies (Table 4.1).

KPMG Hong Kong's connection with the United Kingdom included a direct ownership by the UK firm. The British firm ownership had originated in 1945 when the firm associated with Brown upon his return to Hong Kong. The UK firm's interest was reduced over time as more partners were locally admitted. In 1987, it was agreed that the UK firm would give up its interest in the Hong Kong firm entirely by the handover in 1997 (Lewis, 2005, p. 143).

Decolonization efforts began in Hong Kong in the decade before the handover to China in 1997. These efforts were marked by increased localization and expanding global linkages (Chan, 1996). Localization had come

Table 4.1. Market Shares by Audit Fees of Publicly Listed Companies in Hong Kong, 1988–1992.

Firm	1988 (%)	1989 (%)	1990 (%)	1991 (%)	1992 (%)
PW	47.94	43.78	37.45	27.33	22.87
KPMG	27.57	28.55	27.73	33.90	36.64
DHS/DT	4.44	6.39	8.90	12.07	14.08
TR	0.03	0.03	–	–	–
EW/EY	4.04	4.09	9.21	11.27	11.02
AY	0.29	0.78	–	–	–
CL	1.05	1.28	1.08	1.23	2.14
AA	0.63	0.90	0.51	0.00	0.40
KWTF	6.76	6.99	7.85	8.11	8.04
Others	7.25	7.21	7.27	6.09	4.81
Total	100.00	100.00	100.00	100.00	100.00
CR4	86.71	85.71	83.29	84.57	84.61

Source: Lee (2005).

slowly to the leading international accounting firms in Hong Kong. The first Chinese chartered accountant to work for LBM, Wilson S.R. Poon, started work in January 1962, reversing a decision made in 1957 to not hire Chinese CAs. Alan F.S. Li became the first Chinese partner in 1969. PW had an expatriate senior partner until 2001 (Way & Nield, 2002). KPMG's first Chinese partner was admitted in 1974, with the first Chinese senior partner in 1996 (Lewis, 2005). Both firms were cornerstones of the colonial legacy of Hong Kong. By contrast, in Singapore, a former British colony that achieved independence from Britain in 1965, PW and PMM elected their first local senior partners in 1984 and 1987 respectively, more than a decade earlier than Hong Kong, but still long after Singapore became independent (personal correspondence with PW and KPMG Singapore, August 2009).

The partnerships of both PW and KPMG in Hong Kong had a substantial, but decreasing over time, percentage of British born partners. Most of these partners had come to Hong Kong as managers after having qualified as accountants in the United Kingdom, spawning a pejorative acronym for them – FILTH, failed in London, try Hong Kong. In reality, many were high performing and were attracted to Hong Kong by the high salaries, low taxes, and sense of adventure. As China opened up and the handover approached, there was a growing awareness within these firms that future opportunities would be in China and growing concern among British expatriates that their lack of Chinese language and cultural skills portended an uncertain future for them. The pace of localization increased as the handover loomed. While AA had been the first firm in Hong Kong to select an ethnic Chinese senior partner, its practice in Hong Kong was insignificant when compared to the other firms. KPMG was the first major firm to elect an ethic Chinese senior partner when it did so in 1996, a year before the handover. The new senior partner, Marvin Cheung, appears to have been an uncontroversial choice for the firm. The same could not be said for the next two firms to select new senior partners. Dermott Agnew of DTT was defeated in a reelection bid in June 1996, and was replaced by Patrick Cheung (Tabakoff, 1996). At PwC, British educated Silas S.S. Yang was elected the first Chinese senior partner in 2001, replacing Patrick Paul who returned to England to become a Commander of the Order of the British Empire. The election of Yang was hotly contested, and Yang's British opponent, as well as a number of other British partners, elected early retirement in the aftermath. Yang had spent several years running the Shanghai office of PW, beginning in 1992, and clearly had his focus on the mainland (Way & Nield, 2002). As the end of Marvin Cheung's term as senior partner at KPMG approached, he found the partners divided in their support for two candidates to replace him. American Dominic Ho had played a key role in the development of China. John Harrison had arrived as a secondee from the UK firm in 1982. Wanting to avoid a potentially divisive, racially tinged election like that recently experienced at PW, Cheung proposed, in January 2002, that the two become cochairman and the partners accepted this proposal. Ho retired in 2007 and was replaced as cochairman by Carlson Tong.

The change of leadership at the Big Four away from expatriates to local Chinese partners accelerated changes in the culture of these firms. The changes allowed the firms to argue to both their global firms and to Chinese regulators that they were Chinese and by virtue of ethnicity (and after handover nationality) rightfully should develop the Big Four practices in China. However, under China's "one country, two systems" approach to Hong Kong, the Special Administrative Region is treated in many ways as if it is a separate country, a system that will remain in place until 2047. The accounting professions in Hong Kong and in Mainland China are separate institutions governed by separate laws and separate regulators. Hong Kong accountants did not gain practice rights in Mainland China and are treated for most purposes like any other foreigner.

One thing that did not change with the localization of senior partners in Hong Kong was the strong focus on profitability. The firms had long focused on maximizing short-term profitability. Expatriate partners often chose to retire early and return to their homeland. As a result, they wanted to maximize the profitability of the firms during their tenure. The firms had no retirement benefits for partners so partners needed to accumulate sufficient funds during their tenure to provide for retirement security. At PW, partners were required to retire at age 55, yet many elected to leave before reaching that age. Chinese partners enthusiastically supported the efforts to maximize profitability, although they were less supportive of the early retirement age. After Silas Yang took over as senior partner of PwC, he increased the retirement age to 58.

Maintaining high and consistent levels of earnings was the principal strategic goal of PW and KPMG in Hong Kong. The firms were reluctant to invest for the future or to take risks on unproven new businesses. Jon Madonna, global senior partner of KPMG during the 1990s said: "… Hong Kong was the most short-term, profit-oriented firm in KPMG and was led at the time by someone who was extremely conservative in terms of growth" (personal correspondence, September 18, 2009). A UK partner of PW called their Hong Kong firm "the pariah of the firm" because of the difficulty of negotiating fee arrangements on shared clients and the Hong Kong firm's unwillingness to contribute to global initiatives (personal correspondence, July 5, 2008).

This intensive focus on profitability resulted in the Hong Kong firms reportedly having the highest partner earnings of any member firm in both PW and KPMG. The high partner earnings (and the low rate of tax in Hong Kong) created envy among other member firms. It also seeded resentment when members of the global firms perceived that the Hong Kong member firms were resisting investments to build the global networks of the Big Four. Global partners of PW and KPMG were reluctant to support the Hong Kong firm's development of China, fearful that the Hong Kong firm would use any funding to increase partner earnings and not develop the China market. Consequently, the global organizations of these firms sought to control the operations on the mainland.

4.3.4.2. Ambivalence over China

Patrick Paul, former senior partner of PW in Hong Kong, said that Hong Kong was a community of refugees. Nearly every Chinese resident of Hong Kong, or at least their near ancestors, had fled China during the difficult times in the early- to mid-20th century. That experience had made them fearful about China, and fueled great concern about the consequences of the handover. Fearing the uncertainty created by the pending changes, several large corporations, including HSBC and Jardine Matheson, moved their corporate headquarters out of Hong Kong. Many of the British colonialists made plans to return home. About 20,000 Hong Kong Chinese emigrants also began to leave every year beginning in the early 1980s, a total that reached 62,000 in 1990 (Murphy, 1991). Professionals were especially prone to emigration because they could often find employment in a new country. A survey conducted by the Hong Kong Society of Accountants late in 1989 found that 80% of Hong Kong accountants planned to leave the territory before the handover in 1997 and that over two-thirds of them had already applied for foreign passports (To, 1989). The resulting "brain drain" in Hong Kong slowed as the handover came to be viewed as less threatening, and reversed as some of those who had emigrated returned to seek opportunities in the rapidly expanding Chinese market.

As China opened up there was increasing demand for the firms to send staff to work and live in Mainland China. Living conditions were primitive when compared to Hong Kong. Foreigners were a rare sight in the early years of opening up and foreign accountants were commonly stared at whenever they were out in public. While ethnic Chinese were spared that ignominy, they too suffered from the poor quality of food and accommodations. Often the work was in remote locations requiring long travel on old trains. It became necessary for the firms to pay significant premiums to incentivize staff to go even on short-term assignments. Finding people willing to go on long-term assignments was more difficult, even with significant financial incentives. Consequently, the firms were forced to accept those who were willing to go, rather than those best qualified. For many who accepted the opportunity, China was possibly their last chance with the firm. One partner observed that their China firm was built by the firm's rejects and discards.

4.3.4.3. Strategic Orientation of the Hong Kong Firms

As China began to open up, the Big Eight naturally turned to their Hong Kong member firms. The Hong Kong firms, other than PW and KPMG, were very small in Hong Kong and not well positioned for the challenge of opening such a potentially large market. PW and KPMG, while of significant size, were burdened by their colonial heritage and focus on short-term profitability. None of the Hong Kong member firms of the Big Eight would be capable of developing China on their own. Consequentially, the investments required to build the practice in China would need to come from the global coordinating entities of the international firms, paid for by member firm contributions from around the world. Peter Bowie, China managing partner of DTT explained that the reason why member firms would contribute to the development of a practice they might not ultimately participate in: "If we are not a large, significant firm in China by the end of the decade, we can't really be a strong global firm – so we have to be significant in China" (Zhao, 2005a).

As the Big Eight began to open offices in China, they did so with the funding of their global networks. Hong Kong personnel typically staffed the offices, supplemented with some foreign partners and managers from other member firms. In some firms, most notably PW and KPMG, tension arose between the global network and the Hong Kong firm over whether the Hong Kong firm was sufficiently committed to developing the China market or was simply using the global firm contributions as another source of revenue. In 1991, the global firm of PW took back management of China from Hong Kong and ran it as an independent practice until 2001, when the practices were combined.

The global networks and the Hong Kong firm had differing objectives with respect to China. The global networks were most interested in making certain that their global MNC clients were adequately served in China. This required sizable local practices in each of the major cities of China, the recruiting and development of bilingual staff, and adoption of global standards and processes. Building the capability to serve MNCs was expensive, and mostly required on the ground resources in China. The Hong Kong firms were less interested in the MNC market, and by the early 1990s became focused on the emerging market for IPO services. They were particularly well positioned for this work, since listings in Hong Kong required the use of a Hong Kong based auditor. IPO work could be done on a fly-in basis, alleviating the difficulty of convincing partners and staff to relocate to the mainland. As a result, the Big Four often operated in China as two separate firms – the Mainland China firm, controlled by the global organization and mainly serving MNCs, and the Hong Kong firm that mainly served Chinese companies seeking listings in Hong Kong. This division was apparent to the regulators. Ding Pingzhun, Director General of the CICPA was particularly troubled by the behavior of the Hong Kong partners and saw them as wanting to compete with local CPAs:

> And the Hong Kong partners are greedy; they are fishing in troubled waters. They are different from the real westerners whose first job is to serve their international clients; the Hong Kong people want to take up the market in China. (2006b, p. 341)

Within the same networks, conflicts between the Hong Kong firm and the firm in Mainland China were common, and the firms sometimes competed for the same work. Chinese regulators were unhappy with the encroachment of the Hong Kong Big Six into China because they thought they had only allowed the international firms to enter. Ding Pingzhun complained in 1988 that the Big Six are not the "real foreign ones but instead are the Big Six from Hong Kong who took up practice in the mainland in the name of the international firm and squeezed out other real international firms in the name of China" (Ding, 2006b, p. 92).

As the China market expanded, some firms even found other firms in their network establishing operations on the mainland, such as the Taiwanese and Japanese member firms following their clients into China, or the US member firm setting up expatriate tax services for American clients. Partners with the official Chinese member firm viewed activities as "poaching" in violation of poorly defined territorial rights, and regularization of these activities often required considerable management time.

The degree to which the Hong Kong firms operated independently of the China firms during the 1990s varied by firm. At one extreme was PW, whose China practice operated independently from Hong Kong and was managed by an American team that was often in open conflict with their Hong Kong counterparts. At the other extreme was AA.

AA had been one of the last firms to come to Hong Kong. When the accounting market in China began to take off in 1992, AA held only a 0.4% market share in Hong Kong (Table 4.1). AA was the most globally integrated firm at the time and their weak position in Hong Kong, coupled with their tight global integration, would enable them to avoid the internal conflict experienced by their competitors. AA quickly saw that China would afford them the opportunity to rectify their weak position in Hong Kong, and focused on developing the resources that rapidly led them to market leadership in China.

The rapidly growing offices of the international firms in China required substantial capital. By 1998, the Big Six had invested over US$200 million.[6] The investment was necessary to help provide working capital, office build-outs, and technology acquisitions as well as to fund operating losses arising from high training costs and low fee levels. As profitable as the Hong Kong partnerships were, they did not have the capacity or the willingness to invest at these levels in China, necessitating the involvement of their global firms. Around the turn of the millennium, however, the profitability of the China firms had risen to the point where the two largest Hong Kong firms, PwC and KPMG, became interested in acquiring the China practices from the global firms. The negotiations were contentious, particularly in the case of PwC, and after the Hong Kong firm took over, Hong Kong partners replaced the mostly American leadership of the China practice.

The merger of the China and Hong Kong member firms of the Big Four was often accompanied by closer integration of the combined Hong Kong and China firms with the global organization. In some cases the firms in other Asian countries and territories (such as Singapore and Taiwan in the case of PwC) combined with the Hong Kong and China firms to create a regional firm.

4.4. TIANANMEN SQUARE

The first decade in China for the Big Eight came to a dramatic close when tanks entered Tiananmen Square on the night of June 3 into June 4, 1989 to crush protests calling for political reform. The incident outraged Western nations, and many international companies left China, at least temporarily. Foreign loans by the World Bank and the Asian Development Bank were suspended (Thakur, Burton, & Srivastava, 1997). Several of the Big Eight suspended operations because of the rising conflict. The Big Eight offices were very small at the time and were operated out of hotel rooms that were staffed by expatriate staff who retreated to Hong Kong when violence escalated (Brandenberg, 1987). The firms were reluctant to abandon China after the years they had invested in opening the market. Rick Murray of Touche Ross summed up the attitude of the profession:

> I do not believe anyone has the capacity to anticipate what the political or business environment will be in China in the near future. It is sensible for any profession with a foothold in China to maintain a presence, but subject to the security of its people. (*Accountancy Age*, 1989)

The first decade of the modern accounting profession in China was preparatory for the major changes yet to come. The Big Eight developed relationships through which they helped Chinese bureaucrats to understand the changes required under Deng Xiaoping's new ideology of socialism with Chinese characteristics. They had also played a key role as an intermediary between foreign investors and Chinese regulators. They opened the eyes of Chinese regulators to the problems of foreign investors, and helped their clients understand the often-unfathomable Chinese bureaucracy.

The events at Tiananmen Square in 1989 chilled foreign investment and gave voice to some in the Communist Party who wanted to slow or change the direction of Deng Xiaoping's policy of opening up. At the same time, however, the collapse of the Soviet Union convinced Deng of the need to drive ahead. Deng made his famous trip to Southern China in 1992 to advocate renewed reform and accelerated growth (Ash & Kueh, 1996). In the succeeding decade China followed Deng's call for faster reform and the economy rapidly transformed into a leading global force. This created ideal conditions for the Big Four to establish a dominant position in China, which is the focus of Chapter 5.

NOTES

1. Japan had adopted Western accounting methods earlier than China (Auyeung, 2002).
2. *Kuaijishi* translates as "accounting master." The term was also used for licensed public accountants when the profession was resurrected in 1980, but the English translation changed from "chartered accountant" to "certified public accountant."
3. Hankow is called Wuhan today.
4. Xiang Sisi, daughter of Xiang Huaicheng, became a tax partner at AA. She joined PwC when it acquired the China operations of AA, and later left PwC to join E&Y, later returning once again to PwC.
5. Peat Marwick Mitchell merged with Klynveld Main Goerdeler to form KPMG in 1987.
6. Response from the Big Five firms to the letter dated August 10, 1998 from Tania Friedrichs of DG1 of the European Commission obtained from Sir John Stuttard, former Coopers & Lybrand partner.

CHAPTER 5

FOREIGN DIRECT INVESTMENT AND CAPITAL MARKETS AS HEGEMONIC PROJECTS

> In order to do things the way they're done in market economy countries, we will need a complete system of accountant firms and accounting companies. China must train a group of accountants up to international standards, rely on them to establish a batch of accounting firms, and let them go check.
>
> – Zhu Rongi, July 23, 1993 (Zhu, 2013, p. 163).

The previous chapter discussed the emergence of a modern accounting profession in China. The political events that culminated in Tiananmen Square on June 4, 1989 marked the end of China's first decade of experimentation with opening up. After a period of introspection, Deng Xiaoping convinced Chinese society to move forward with reforms. This chapter will discuss how the Big Four accounting firms established a dominant position in the accounting profession as these reforms took place. I do this by evaluating two hegemonic projects that led to Big Four domination. The first hegemonic project relates to the massive amounts of foreign direct investment (FDI) that flowed into China after it opened up to the West in 1978. The second project relates to the reform of state-owned enterprises (SOEs), and particularly to the development of capital markets within China and the accessing of foreign capital markets by Chinese companies. Both of these hegemonic projects are related to the broader hegemonic project of globalization, under which a neoliberal ideology was increasingly accepted in China (Piehwe, Walpen, & Neunhoffer, 2007).

I follow Gilbert's (1999) definition of a hegemonic project:

> A hegemonic project is what you get when one group in society manages to convince a number of other groups that their interests will be well served by entering into a social coalition in which the hegemonic group is the leading partner.

This chapter explains how other groups – Chinese bureaucrats, investors, international regulators, and Chinese enterprises – came to believe that a Chinese auditing profession dominated by the Big Four best served their interests.

This chapter will also discuss the joint venture accounting firms that provided the Big Four access to the Chinese auditing market. The Big Four were successful at seizing near complete control over the joint venture firms, thereby excluding indigenous firms from participation in the hegemonic projects of FDI and capital markets.

Following the incident in Tiananmen Square, hardliners within the Communist Party seized greater power. General Secretary Zhao Ziyang, who supported the protestors, was placed under house arrest. Deng Xiaoping was forced to make accommodations to antireform communists, giving up his last position, chairman of the Central Military Commission. The hardliners, led by Li Peng, favored a return to a planned economy, an approach that emphasized Marxist ideology (Zhao, 1993).

The Soviet Union disintegrated in 1990 and 1991 leaving Deng Xiaoping convinced that China faced a similar fate if it did not proceed with reforms. On January 17, 1992, Deng left Beijing with his daughter and son by train. He arrived in Shenzhen on January 19, 1992, and continued on to Zhuhai and the surrounding municipalities (Ash & Kueh, 1996). Throughout his trip he boasted of the accomplishments of the economic reform program and attacked those who had opposed reforms in the period following the events in Tiananmen Square. Favorable media coverage of Deng's Southern Tour shifted public opinion away from the hardliners. Zhao (1993, p. 755) argues that the southern trip irrefutably proved that Deng was still the most powerful man in China, yet his ability to maneuver politically had suffered under Tiananmen. Nevertheless, he was successful at steering Li Peng and Jiang Zemin back toward a reform agenda.

5.1. FOREIGN DIRECT INVESTMENT

Following Deng's Southern Tour in 1992, the pace of opening up accelerated. Foreign investment was a key component of Deng's strategy to reform the economy (Fung, Iizaka, & Tong, 2004). Growth in FDI had slowed after the events at Tiananmen Square in 1989, but surged beginning in 1992. FDI inflows to China rose to $46.9 billion annually by 2001, making China the second largest destination for FDI (behind the United States).

FDI statistics tend to overstate the actual level of foreign investment because many Chinese companies have followed a practice known as *round tripping*, where capital leaves China to Hong Kong and returns as FDI (Xiao, 2004). Round tripping allowed Chinese companies take advantage of the special tax and operational incentives provided to foreign invested enterprises. Xiao (2004) indicates that it is impossible to accurately determine what portion of FDI is related to round tripping, but estimates that 30–50% of total FDI may be of this nature.

Increasing levels of foreign investment led to the approval of more than 450,000 foreign-invested companies by 2003 (Chen, 2004). By 2008, 480 of the Fortune 500 had invested in China (*China Daily*, 2008). For some, like mobile phone manufacturer Nokia Corporation, China became their largest global market (Nokia Corporation, 2009). By 2001, foreign-invested enterprises had a 31.2% share of Chinese industrial outputs, a share that dropped slightly to 29.5% by 2008 (Tang, Metwalli, & Marie Smith, 2010). The significant share of China's economy held by foreign investors was an important force in the development of international accounting firms in China.

Rose and Hinings (1999) observed that MNC clients view themselves as global entities and expect their professional service firms to be able to respond in a global way. Consequentially, most large corporations tend to use the same accounting firm for all of their global operations and they preferred to use the same firm in China that they use elsewhere in the world. Accounting firms tend to reinforce this tendency, resisting requests to rely on the work of other accounting firms and insisting that their member firm in a particular location perform the local work. Exceptions exist, but they tend to be for small, inconsequential operations that are immaterial to the consolidated financial statements. Consequently, it is difficult for local accounting firms to compete for the local audits of MNCs, even when they offer substantial fee savings. With foreign investment constituting such a large portion of China's economy, the Big Four were destined to have large practices in China even if they failed to gain inroads to the domestic market.

During the 1980s, the level of foreign investment was modest and the indigenous state-controlled accounting profession was successful at keeping the Big Eight firms out of the audit market in China. As foreign investment grew rapidly in the early 1990s, the closure of the market to the Big Eight came under great pressure.

The sudden increase in demand for their services found the Big Four poorly positioned to respond. The terms of their representative office status prohibited them from performing audits, although they could, and did, perform agreed-upon procedures for their overseas affiliates. Each of the new foreign investments required statutory audits by certified public accountants (CPAs), and local regulations blocked the Big Six from this market, to the benefit of government-affiliated local accounting firms. While clients were required to use local accounting firms for this work (and some continue to do so today for cost reasons), they often preferred that a familiar firm, and one that could communicate with them in English, do the work.

Representative office rules prohibited the Big Six accounting firms from directly recruiting and hiring employees. Instead, they were required to use government entities such as the Foreign Enterprise Human Resource Services Company (FESCO) to provide local employees. FESCO hired employees, maintained the all-important personnel file that existed on every Chinese national, and took responsibility for paying the required benefit fund contributions and maintaining party membership where applicable. Firms could not hire new staff on university campuses, as was their standard recruitment model elsewhere in the world. Because of these restrictions, there was a significant shortage of staffing resources.

Because of the increasing demand for their services and their inability to operate under existing rules, the firms began to press more urgently for practice rights. They needed both the right to perform statutory audits for international clients and the ability to directly employ staff. The representative office vehicle that the international accounting firms were using in China prohibited both.

5.2. JOINT VENTURE ACCOUNTING FIRMS

Until 1997, the joint venture form was the most common vehicle for foreign investment into China. The wholly foreign-owned enterprise (WFOE) became the predominant form by 1999 (Deng, 2001). When the Big Six began to push for greater practice rights, they suggested the use of joint venture form because the firms understood that there was no appetite to allow full foreign ownership of accounting firms and the joint venture form had already gained wide acceptance within China (Dominic Ho, personal correspondence, August 10, 2009). In the months following the Tiananmen

Square incident, Dominic Ho of KPMG approached his contacts in the Ministry of Finance (MOF), suggested that they should try an experiment to allow an international accounting firm to form a joint venture with the MOF, and suggested that the international firm for the joint venture should be KPMG.

As this proposal gained acceptance within the Chinese bureaucracy, Nellie Fong, a young partner with Arthur Andersen (AA) in Hong Kong, leaned on Zhu Rongji, the reform-minded mayor of Shanghai who later became premier, to include AA in the experiment (Nellie Fong, personal communication, August 30, 2009). AA's high-level connections ensured they were on the forefront of any new development.

Ernst & Young (E&Y) had also developed a close relationship with the MOF and had joint ventured with the MOF on a consulting firm in Hong Kong. The consulting firm, CCFM, provided the MOF with a presence outside of China. Ge Ming, an MOF official who headed one of China's state-owned accounting firms, had gone to the United States for training with E&Y years before and had been involved in CCFM. All three firms (KPMG, AA, and E&Y) obtained permission to form joint ventures with the MOF in the summer of 1992. The remaining Big Six firms formed joint ventures in the months that followed, selecting different joint venture partners. All of the joint venture partners of the Big Six were state-controlled entities. Deloitte Touche Tohmatsu (DTT) selected Shanghai CPAs (an MOF controlled firm) as its partner. Price Waterhouse (PW) affiliated with Da Hua, a firm associated with the Shanghai University of Finance and Economics (SUFE). Coopers & Lybrand (C&L) joined with CIEC, a branch of the powerful China International Trade and Investment Corporation (CITIC). The largest local Hong Kong firm, politically connected BDO member firm KWTF,[1] was also allowed to establish a joint venture in Shenzhen (Fisher, 1994). Eoghan McMillan of AA observed: "The door has been opened and this is the model basically that China has chosen for letting foreign CPA firms operate in China" (Ward, 1992).

5.2.1. Limiting the Number of Joint Ventures

Only seven firms (the Big Six plus KWTF) were allowed to form joint ventures. Chi Haibin, honorary president of the CICPA in 1996 summed up the policy of Chinese regulators "Open the door widely, and make the doorsill tall" (Ding, 2006b, p. 103). This policy excluded the second-tier global firms with the exception of BDO member firm KWTF. Other firms were given the opportunity to apply for a temporary license that conferred neither the right to sign statutory audit opinions in China nor permission to open an official office. These restrictions helped to mitigate the fear that a wider market opening would result in the entry of a greater number of Hong Kong and Taiwan-based firms that would become competitors of the local firms. Over 200 small and middle-sized firms, mainly from Hong Kong and Taiwan, obtained temporary licenses (Ding, 2006b, p. 111).

After a year of operation Ding Pingzhun, director general of the CICPA, reported to MOF leaders that the reputation and popularity of the joint ventures was creating pressure on domestic firms. Fearful that negotiations underway for China to join the General Agreement on Tariffs and Trade (later known as the World Trade Organization (WTO)) would bring pressure to open the market to more than the current seven firms, Ding cautioned MOF leaders to "watch our mouths" in the negotiations (Ding, 1998a, p. 290). China initially proposed to trade negotiators that only firms with annual income of US$1 billion and 10,000 professional staff (labeled the *two-one*) could form joint ventures. Regulators intended for the threshold to limit market access to the Big Six only.[2] In the early WTO negotiations many countries, principally those from Europe as well as Japan, objected to this threshold on the basis that it was too high. China proposed instead a threshold called the *two-five*, $500 million of income and 5,000 professionals, which they intended to restrict the field to the top 16 firms. Finally, China accepted its bottom line position of *two-two*, $200 million of income and 2,000 professionals. Ding (1998a, p. 324) reported: "This is the final limit, otherwise we could face thousands of firms." Beginning in 1994, China announced it allowed up to 15 firms to enter into joint ventures, including the seven already approved (Chen, 1994a). Ding (2006b, p. 106) considered that "The entering of these smaller ones might do some help in preventing the monopoly of the big firms." While these more liberal policies opened the door for second-tier firms, only nine joint venture firms were ultimately established and the three non-Big Six joint ventures were later terminated.

5.2.2. Regulating the Joint Ventures

On August 4, 1995, China Securities Regulatory Commission (CSRC) Chief Accountant Wang Jianxi suggested to CICPA Director General Ding Pingzhun that the time was right to regulate the Big Six. His view was that the Big Six did not have too much business to handle at the time, so they could not resist too much even if they were to be controlled or regulated more strictly (Ding, 2006b, p. 91). The CICPA responded with three proposed regulations:

i. Provisional rules on management of representative offices of overseas public accountants firms (January 4, 1996)
ii. Notice concerning permission for foreign accounting firms to identify member firms in China (January 22, 1996)
iii. Administration of Sino-foreign cooperative accounting firms tentative procedures (March 28, 1996)

Ding observes that they issued the rules in the order of difficulty, with the easiest rules first. Ding sent the draft regulations to the Big Six (plus BDO member firm KWTF) for comments. He met with each of the firms and was pleased when they said the documents fit the international situation quite well and were appropriate for China. Nellie Fong of AA provided some written suggestions that Ding adopted in the final drafts. One of the reasons for the warm reception to the rules was the notice regarding the ability to have member firms in China. This opened an intriguing new door that the Big Six later attempted to exploit.

5.2.3. Operation of Joint Ventures

The establishment of joint ventures provided significant benefits to the international firms. Most importantly, they obtained the right to sign statutory audit reports in China. This allowed them to serve their international clients with investments in China, and to begin to pursue work for local companies, in particular those preparing for listings in China or overseas.

The formation of joint ventures gave the international firms a license to audit in China and put them into direct competition with local firms for the first time. Meocre Li of AA observed:

> Once we have become a joint venture … there is nothing to prevent us from doing the accounts of A-share companies that are seeking listings. There is no business yet, but the People's Bank in Beijing has already asked the major Hong Kong firms to evaluate some A-share companies that are seeking listings. (Parker, 1992)

Li's comments reflect the attitude of Big Six accountants at the time. While the joint venture form gave them the immediate opportunity to serve their multinational clients, all eyes were on the imminent opening up of the capital markets.

Rules permitted the joint ventures to operate in only one city, yet the firms had clients with investments in many locations across the country. The firms had established representative offices in the four key *tier-one* cities in China: Beijing, Shanghai, Guangzhou, and Shenzhen, and some had offices in selected *tier-two* cities like Nanjing, Chongqing, Tianjin, and Dalian. After establishing the joint ventures, the firms kept their representative offices in the other cities, and even opened new ones, but these representative offices remained banned from performing audits. The firms found a way around that obstacle. Although the joint ventures rules allowed for branches, the CIPCA generally turned down applications for new branches arguing that the joint ventures were not well enough developed and should be turned into member firms anyway (by 2000, only two branches in total were approved for accounting joint ventures (Ding, 2006b, p. 97)). The Big Six firms decided to treat the representative offices as if they were branches of the joint venture. They hired staff in the name of the joint venture, yet the foreign firm, as "support to the cooperative firm," paid them. CICPA examiners took issue with this approach:

> Actually, the staff are like mercenaries, they work for both the overseas firm and the representative office; they are paid according to their working hours when they work for cooperative firms, in essence, they still work for the foreign side and it takes a huge share of the income, so this is not a support for the cooperative firm at all. (Luo & Liu, 1996, p. 420)

Ding fought against the representative offices throughout his tenure at CICPA (until early 1999), insisting that firms close the representative offices in the city where the joint venture existed, and directing a series of inspections of each firm's activities. Chinese employees of representative offices or WFOEs of the international firms could not register as CPAs. KPMG complained about this rule by mimicking Ding's nationalistic tone, arguing that the policies prohibiting employees to be registered as CPAs in other locations "have greatly restricted the career development of Chinese citizens" (Ding, 2006b, p. 358). Nonetheless, Ding, when discussing PW's activities in Beijing, concluded that these types of arrangements were legal under current law, although they were hard to maintain. PW's representative office in Beijing employed over 200 accountants. Auditing was done under the name of PW Da Hua, the joint venture which had a license to audit, by staff employed by the representative office which was prohibited from auditing (Ding, 2006b, p. 133). PW believed they had "head nod" approval for these practices (Kent Watson, personal correspondence, March 21, 2009).

The firms also decided that they could keep H-share and B-share audits out of the joint venture. Representative office staff and overseas staff did the work and the report was signed on the letterhead of either the Hong Kong office or some overseas entity that might not even have an office. Confronted with the question of why the firms were not issuing H-share and B-share audits under the joint ventures, the firms gave three justifications. First, the CSRC did not stress that the joint ventures needed to do the audits. Second, clients and investment bankers asked that the foreign offices issue the reports. Finally, there were no written rules dealing with the situation. CICPA examiners Luo and Liu (1996, p. 419) reported their frustration with the situation:

> … CICPA is out of the security business and has no control power, so it is hard to prohibit the foreign side to do the audit operations directly. If we cannot take control of it in the future, the current sanctions seem short-term and powerless. So, we need to study and make supplementary measures collaboratively with the China Securities Regulatory Commission.

Luo and Liu (1996, p. 419) found that the overseas business done by PW totaled over RMB 100 million in 1995, yet the PW Da Hua joint venture had received only RMB 5 million of those fees. They were surprised that even when all the overseas business was included, PW still incurred a loss, which the examiners blamed on excessive salary costs.

There were advantages to recording revenues outside the joint venture, even when the joint ventures were unprofitable. By billing overseas and in foreign currency, the firms acquired foreign currency that they used to pay expatriate personnel who expected payment in hard currency. Billing outside of China also avoided business taxes and CICPA fees in China, and minimized the risk that joint venture partners might lay claim to the fees. The CICPA charged firms a membership fee of 2% of revenues. The fee applied only to accounting firms such as the joint ventures and not to representative offices or WFOEs, so there was an incentive for foreign firms to perform and bill work outside of the joint venture, and an incentive for the CICPA to put a stop to the practice.

5.2.3.1. Arthur Andersen's Wholly Foreign-Owned Enterprise

AA tried a more radical approach of using a WFOE to conduct certain business activities in China. The *Law of the People's Republic of China on Wholly Foreign Enterprises* was enacted in April 1986, although implementing rules were not available until 1990 (He, 2003). Frustrated with the performance of joint ventures, foreign investors rapidly migrated to the WFOE form which provided them with greater control and less risk.

In 1991, Andersen Consulting formed the first foreign invested consulting company as a WFOE organized in Shanghai. In 2001 Andersen Consulting separated from AA to become Accenture. Following the lead of Andersen Consulting, the other Big Six firms also established consulting WFOEs in succeeding years. The WFOE form had the advantage of allowing the consulting business to directly engage staff, a practice not permitted in the representative office.

AA formed a second WFOE in Shenzhen in 1992, the same year that they established their joint venture. The accounting practice of AA controlled this WFOE, and AA's first WFOE became part of Accenture when the consulting division separated from AA. AA's new WFOE began to conduct audit work for foreign clients where no statutory report was required. This practice soon outraged the other international firms who did not believe that a WFOE could legally engage in auditing. The other firms complained to the CICPA about AA's behavior, and the CICPA wrote to AA's headquarters in Chicago about the matter. The CICPA's position was that, following Chinese law and international convention, only CPA firms are permitted to conduct an auditing business. AA's worldwide CEO came to China to meet with Ding Pingzhun (2006b, p. 125) on September 4, 1993, expressing his regret and promising to remedy the situation.

WFOEs have become popular vehicles for the Big Four to operate non-audit businesses. A review of the websites for the Big Four in China indicates that most firms have more than one WFOE for various non-audit businesses in China.

5.2.3.2. Rectification

If AA changed its practices following the meeting between AA's worldwide CEO and Ding Pingzhun it was not apparent to the CICPA. In 1994, the CICPA launched an examination of the international accounting firm's practices in China, which extended into additional examinations in 1997 and 1998. The examination process was called *rectification.*

The rectification process did not go well. Ding (2006b, p. 127) writes of his discussion with AA:

> ... During the inspection in 1994, Andersen did not cooperate, the Miss from Hong Kong was quite aggressive, and your accounts book was unacceptable – written with pencil, full of marks, and sign of eraser.

At least AA had accounts books. E&Y apparently did not have any books in China. They simply reported to Hong Kong and operated in China through an imprest system – a situation that inspectors considered ripe for license revocation (Ding, 2006b, p. 413). When the global chairman of E&Y learned of the CICPA's inspection, he had a representative call Ding from New York on August 5, 1997. The representative told Ding that the global firm would come to run China. According to Ding:

> … the partner from Hong Kong E&Y got quite angry, for they have worked here for a decade or more and have accumulated some fruits, but the international side wants to take it away; there is not any free meal in the world. (Ding, 2006b, p. 117)

Interviews with some of the partners from this period lead to the conclusion that there was no malice on the part of the Big Six firms in these matters. It appears to be a case akin to the legend of the shoemaker's kids, who go shoeless because their father is too busy with customers. The firms were growing so rapidly that they failed to put in place the appropriate systems needed to manage the business.

The CICPA asserted that the all of the Big Six firms were evading taxes, pointing out that the audit fees reported by public companies exceeded the fee income that the firms were reporting, and that the firms obviously had much more business than just public companies. BDO had not even reported income for three years. The examiners also accused the firms of evading individual income taxes. The examination process was made more difficult by the poor state of accounting records for the firms in China. The CICPA established a policy to "be strict in the inspection, but lenient in punishing; merciful to the wrong doings in the past, but strict with the doing in the future" (Ding, 2006b, p. 99). As a result of the 1997 inspection the Big Six firms paid a total of RMB170 million (US$20 million) in settlement of past tax liabilities (Ding, 2006b, p. 104).

Regulators singled out AA for harsh treatment. Despite their earlier admonition, they were caught again using their WFOE for auditing. While Ding believed that all of the firms were doing illegal auditing through their representative offices, he considered AA's behavior the most egregious. In the situation that most concerned Ding, AA had done an audit in Hunan Province using staff employed by their WFOE. The Hunan Institute of CPAs sought the maximum statutory penalty, which included forfeiture of the fees collected and a fine equal to five times the fees. AA used its strong political connections in China to substantially reduce the fine and retain the right to practice (Ding, 2006b, p. 129).

5.2.3.3. Management Challenges

The problems of international joint ventures, and in particular those in China, have been well documented (Calantone & Zhao, 2001; Li, Xin,

Tsui, & Hambrick, 1999; Park & Russo, 1996; Yan & Zeng, 1999). Joint ventures often underperform because the partners do not share the same objectives and institutional loyalties often undermine management teams. It quickly became apparent to the firms and to their Chinese partner that they did not share objectives for the joint venture, or as the Chinese idiom says: *tong chuang, yi meng* – same bed, different dreams. The international accounting firms wished to expand the businesses rapidly, and expected to incur losses for some period while doing so. The Chinese appear to have expected that the joint ventures served to transfer technology to the Chinese that allowed them to create their own auditing industry. Ding (1998b, p. 441) came to recognize that it was reputation, not technology, which was important in the accounting profession:

> For the management of the foreign-related accounting institutions in the Mainland, we did not implement the principle of "rules first, games next," but were invaded by the Big Six in a civilized way. We failed to get the technology and lost our market. While, to be frank, there is nothing concerning technology: the truth is that international society does not recognize the Chinese firms, only the Big Six.

Initially, the management issues in the joint venture firms manifested themselves in conflicts between the Big Six firms and the Chinese representatives appointed to the joint ventures. Ding (2006b, p. 117) observed that the MOF did not carefully consider the appropriateness of the Chinese representatives selected for the joint venture:

> The representatives sent there are of quite high rank, more than 70 years old and actually could not do anything. Their state-owned partners were unable or unwilling to commit additional capital, yet wanted to preserve an equal say in all matters.

Squabbles arose over strategy and tactics. Most commonly, the arguments were over spending decisions. The Chinese representatives wanted to strictly control costs so that the ventures could be immediately profitable. The Big Six had a longer period in mind, and believed that significant investments would be required to build large enough firms to serve the market. Nellie Fong (personal communication, August 30, 2009) recounts:

> Arthur Andersen at that time, the joint venture was very difficult because they won't let you spend money. They won't let you spend money because they were the chairmen and you were the co-chairman. In everything, they interfere because they don't understand. I was the representative and had to work with the chairman. Again, I call on him every week, make him tea, and be nice to him in order to get him to agree to what I want to do. We underwrite all the losses. We spent a lot of money training, recruiting, had a lot of cars, let people travel, come to Hong Kong. We would underwrite all of those so that he won't lose any more money. Because he had to make money from the

practice. So, I said, ok, we'll give you 5%. Of all the money I spend, I give you 5%, as a profit, we agreed. We were able to negotiate it to get full control of the joint venture with their people participating in it.

The solution was to convert the Chinese partner into a silent partner in the venture. The rest of the Big Six (with the exception of Coopers and Lybrand) negotiated similar agreements to varying degrees. Ding's (2006b, p. 109) report is consistent with other sources:

Among China's firms that are cooperating with the international firms, the "three hua" (KPMG Huazhen, Arthur Andersen Huaqiang and Ernst and Young Huaming) should be the strongest, for their supporter is the MOF. However, it seems that the three are the worst. The MOF is so busy that it has no time to take care of the small firms. China's side in the three joint ventures does not possess enough speaking right – the Hong Kong side eats them up. The "three hua" are actually hollow frames. Hardly did anyone care about the working performance of these managing directors who could not represent anybody and just fight in isolation with the international firms without getting any result. Therefore, the Chinese representatives at the time strongly expected that the CICPA could support them. The one who did better at that time was Zhongxin-Coopers & Lybrand, in which China's side – Zhongxin did get equal control of the firm, but the managing director, Zhang Ke, was also trapped into trouble which was termed by him the "civilized invasion by the gentleman."

As Ding observed, the C&L situation was different. First, C&L had chosen the accounting firm of CITIC for their joint venture partner. CITIC was a powerful organization in China and the most commercial of any of the joint venture partners of the Big Four. The Chinese manager of the joint venture was Zhang Ke, widely recognized as one of the most talented of Chinese CPAs. Kent Watson (personal correspondence, March 21, 2009), chairman of PricewaterhouseCoopers (PwCs) in China said: "...of all those joint ventures, that was the only one where they brought in a real CPA firm and tried to upgrade." Zhang Ke separated from C&L when it merged with PwC and formed Shinewing, one of China's leading local accounting firms (Chan, 2008; Dugdale, 2011; Jones & Rabinovitch, 2013; Luk, 2010a).

In 1994, Ding Pingzhun spoke at a meeting of the Chinese representatives in the joint venture firms and admonished them to resolve the emerging difficulties in the firms: "Now that they are 'married' they should live happily and harmoniously. The conflicts and problems are to be solved as soon as possible." Ding however, acknowledged:

In some of the current joint venture firms the two sides want to "divorce." We hope that they could live happily together since they have "married." But if they are really unhappy, it is better to divorce and we will agree. (Ding, 2006b, p. 113)

In 1994, BDO was the first second-tier firm to form a joint venture with Chinese firm Xinde. Unlike the Big Six joint ventures, the Chinese partner got control of the joint venture. The Hong Kong partners and Xinde began fighting immediately, and the warring partners were granted their "divorce" on June 2, 1997 (Ding, 2006b, p. 114).

All of the non-Big Six joint ventures terminated; the Big Six ventures all continued despite their difficulties. The Chinese representatives to the joint ventures were in a difficult position. Ding observed: "The Chinese side in a joint venture is only an affiliate, in reality, only several people are fighting with the Big Six which is so big that we cannot compete with them" (Ding, 1998b). Ding (2006b, p. 117) reports that the Chinese representative to the E&Y joint venture told him: "they are just like orphans, for foreigners, the MOF and CICPA don't care about them."

Lacking power within their firms, the Chinese representatives began to seek support from each other. Ding (2006b, p. 114) reports:

> Roughly from 1995, the Chinese representatives in the joint venture firms located in Beijing starting organizing a meeting once a month. Most of the times, I was invited. They expressed their anger with the MOF, CICPA, me, and of course, more often than not, with the foreignershinese representatives in the joint ... Regrettably, this meeting stopped two or three years later.

The foreign leaders of the Big Six firms had similar meetings organized by Sir John Stuttard, chairman of C&L in China.[3] Stuttard (personal correspondence September 1, 2009) recalled:

> Faced with these difficulties, I contacted each of the other Big Six firms in China to see if we had interests in common, which we could share and then present on a united front. Meetings were held in China and Hong Kong of the key players and our discussions were confined to how we could:
>
> a) Meet the ever changing regulations and demands;
> b) Seek to influence the regulatory environment so that we could succeed in China;
> c) Plan for the WTO discussions, following the announcement by the new Premier Zhu Rongji that he wished to negotiate seriously for membership.
>
> I should emphasize that in no way did we come together as a cartel. There was no discussion of clients, tenders, or anything like that. It was simply oriented towards how we could best operate and succeed with a tight regime and how we could persuade that regime to change in the interest of both the Big Six and in the interest of developing a successful accountancy profession in China. Believe it or not, there was a strong altruistic intent, mirroring the historical attitude of accountancy firms throughout the world.

5.3. DEVELOPMENT OF CAPITAL MARKETS

The development of the capital markets was the most significant factor in the growth of the Big Four firms in China and an important factor that led to their domination of the accounting profession. From a base of no public companies in 1990, China became a leading player in global capital markets early in the 21st century. China has had three out of the top ten IPOs in world history. The Industrial and Commercial Bank of China (ICBC), which raised $22 billion dollars in 2006 from a concurrent listing in Hong Kong and Shanghai was the largest IPO in world history until it was eclipsed by General Motors IPO in by the US government in 2010 (Reeves, 2012). Seven of the top ten IPOs in the world in 2009 were from China (PwCs, 2010a). Following its listing in Shanghai in 2007, PetroChina Company Limited (popularly known as PetroChina), for part of a day (until the New York markets opened and brought the stock back to earth), became the world's first trillion dollar company by market value, surpassing Exxon Mobile and General Electric, the world's next two most valuable companies (Greenlees, 2007). In 2009, Hong Kong and Shanghai took the first and second place on the league table of IPO funds raised on worldwide stock exchanges, with Shenzhen coming in the sixth place. Companies raised $58.8 billion on the three Chinese exchanges in 2009, more than double the amount raised on the two leading American exchanges (Table 5.1).

By the middle of the first decade of the 21st century, China's three stock markets in Shanghai, Hong Kong, and Shenzhen ranked among the largest

Table 5.1. IPO Funds Raised in the World in 2009.

Rank	Exchange	Funds Raised (US$ Billion)
1	Hong Kong	31.3
2	Shanghai	18.3
3	NYSE	17.5
4	Bovespa Brazil	12.2
5	Shenzhen	9.2
6	NASDAQ	7.6
7	Australia	4.8
8	Bursa Malaysia	3.5
9	India	3.1
10	Warsaw	2.4

Source: World Federation of Exchanges monthly statistics (US$ billions).

Table 5.2. Global Stock Market Capitalization.

Stock Exchange	2006	2007	2008	2009
NYSE	15,421	15,651	9,209	11,838
NASDAQ	3,865	4,014	2,396	3,239
London	3,794	3,852	1,868	2,796
Shanghai	918	3,694	1,425	2,705
Hong Kong	1,715	2,654	1,329	2,305
Mumbai	819	1,819	647	1,307
Shenzhen	228	785	353	868
Korea	834	1,123	471	835
Singapore	384	539	265	481

Source: World Federation of Exchanges (US$ billions).

stock markets in the world, and combined only to be exceeded by the New York Stock Exchange (Table 5.2).

The development of capital markets was a result of major ideological shifts within China. Chinese leaders, most significantly Premier Zhu Rongji, considered these shifts necessary in order to reform the economy. Capital markets facilitated the reform of SOEs, and encouraged the growth of private businesses.

5.3.1. Ideological Shifts: Socialism with Chinese Characteristics

The People's Republic of China was founded under the principles of Marxism and Leninism, as interpreted by Mao Zedong (*Mao Zedong Thought*). Under this ideology, capitalism and private property ownership were counterrevolutionary. Those associated with those concepts were labeled "rightists" and "capitalist roaders"[4] and they, together with their families, suffered cruel persecution during the Cultural Revolution (Li, 1997). Deng Xiaoping, through a political and economic philosophy known as *Deng Xiaoping Theory*, introduced significant ideological changes in China that transformed the country into a socialist market economy. China's new socialist market economy was the politically acceptable term for a form of capitalism that transformed China, and changed the world (Redding & Witt, 2007). Zhu Rongji, who later became the premier of China, said in 1992:

> Deng Xiaoping's talks caused us to suddenly see the light. In these matters we have to boldly experiment, boldly forge ahead, and graft the good things from capitalist countries onto our socialist system. (Zhu, 2013, p. 59)

The sweeping economic reforms that proceeded from the Third Plenum of the Fourteenth Party Congress (1993) and the Fifteenth Party Congress (1997) established a new goal of separating enterprises from the government (Lau, 1999). The slogan "grasping the large (SOEs), letting go the small (SOEs)," captures the essence of the policy (*Zhua Da Fang Xiao*). Large SOEs were to remain under central state government control and smaller SOEs were to be privatized. A large-scale privatization of small SOEs took place in 1995, and by the end of 1996, over half of all small SOEs were private. Only about 1,000 SOEs were large enough to remain state owned (Lau, 1999).

5.3.2. Reform of State-Owned Enterprises

In the early 1980s, central government ministries or bureaus of local governments at various levels administered SOEs. From 1981 to 1995, China used the Contractual Management System (*chengbaozhi*) to administer SOEs. Under this system, SOEs agreed to remit specified quotas of profits to the administering central or local government. As the pace of development of the economy accelerated, discussions began about the need to separate SOEs from the Communist Party and government organizations. The objective was to separate policy from economic activity. Too many SOEs had become instruments of social policy and were used to provide a wide range of social services. To become efficient and competitive, leaders recognized that the companies needed to operate as businesses.

5.3.2.1. Corporatization

While there had been prior experiments with corporatization, the Third Plenum reforms in 1993 and 1997 launched a massive restructuring of China's SOEs. The objective was to make SOEs operate more efficiently by subjecting them to a new and different set of rules. The new rules followed those used by companies operating in more economically advanced jurisdictions.

There were two purposes for the corporatization policy. First, conversion to the corporate form moved the SOEs out from under government bureaucracies governed by bureaucratic rule and placed them in a company governed by company laws. This change arguably separated ownership from management and reduce the meddling by bureaucrats. Bureaucrats had differing, often conflicting objectives for SOEs. Some bureaucrats focused on labor, others production, others management, and it was difficult for anyone to decide between the often conflicting objectives. It was believed that centralization of the decision-making process around equity solved the problem of competing bureaucratic objectives and led to more efficient and profitable operations.

Second, the new corporate form facilitated the raising of equity capital necessary for the modernization of these enterprises. Before corporatization, SOEs had only the state and its institutions as a source of capital. Corporatization facilitated raising capital independently.

A third consideration was to promote the emergence of a non-state sector by creating new organizational forms for this purpose. Private business had disappeared during the Great Leap Forward, and there were no forms available for its reconstruction.

5.3.2.2. Privatization

The primary objective of corporatization is to separate management from ownership, but corporatization by itself was ineffective at reforming SOEs. Management was separated from ownership in the SOE system, and the removal of bureaucratic rule simply made management less accountable. The state remained the sole owner, and while decision making shifted to the corporation and its board, appointments to the board and management remained under the control of the state. While corporatization put in place the structure for improved corporate governance, the introduction of non-state actors, whose interests would not necessarily align with the bureaucrats, would be necessary to alter historical practices. Leaders decided that public offerings would lead to an increased focus on efficiency and profitability over other social objectives prioritized by bureaucrats (Clarke, 2003; Zhang, 2004; Zhu, 1999).

The concept of allowing private ownership was a major ideological shift that had started under reform-minded Premier Zhao Ziyang. The incident at Tiananmen Square led to the purge of Zhao Ziyang and his replacement by the conservative Li Peng, who slowed the pace of reform. Zhu Rongji, who is credited for leading China's economic transition in the succeeding years, later replaced Li Peng as premier, opening the way for accelerated reforms. As is the case with many reforms in China, privatization started at the local level and was later sanctioned by the central government (Garnaut, Song, Tenev, & Yao, 2005).

The first cases of private shareholding were three Guangzhou SOEs in 1986, when employees bought 30% of the shares of each firm. The first large SOE to be incorporated was the Shenyang Motor Corporation, which became Shenyang Jinbei Motors when it issued shares to the public in

August, 1988 (Garnaut et al., 2005). On October 8, 1992, the company listed part of its business on the New York Stock Exchange as Brilliance China Automotive Holdings, becoming the first international listing of a Chinese company. Fifteen times oversubscribed, the NYSE offering was the second most actively traded stock on its opening day. The company became BMWs joint venture partner in China and struggled with profitability, ultimately delisting from the NYSE in 2007 (Brilliance China, 2007).

5.3.2.3. Public Listing

China's capital markets date back to the late-19th century, when the first stock market opened in Shanghai in 1891. By the 1930s, Shanghai had become the financial capital of the East. Before the revolution, China had stock exchanges in Beijing, Shanghai, and Tianjin. The Shanghai Stock Exchange shut down in 1941 during the Japanese occupation, resumed operations again in 1946, and closed in 1949 due to the communist revolution. The Tianjin Exchange was the last to close in mid-1952 as private ownership and capitalism were erased from China (Thomas, 2001).

The opening up that began in 1978 resulted in experiments with corporatization. In 1984, a few Chinese companies began to issue shares, and in 1986, the government permitted some companies to issue shares to employees and the public. Formal over-the-counter trading in securities began in August 1986 in Shenyang followed rapidly in Shanghai and Shenzhen. The rise of stock markets generated significant ideological debate within China, and the state stepped in to regulate their development (Karmel, 1994).

On November 26, 1990, the Shanghai Stock Exchange reopened. The State Council authorized the Shanghai Stock Exchange as part of the plans to develop the Pudong area of Shanghai into a major financial center. Not to be left behind, Shenzhen also opened the Shenzhen Stock Exchange on December 1, 1990. In 2013, the Shanghai and Shenzhen stock exchanges remain Mainland China's two stock markets.

5.3.3. Stock Markets for Chinese Companies

Chinese equity markets are multifarious. Ideological shifts and the gradual development of the markets led to a wide range of approaches to raising capital. Significant to China was the extensive involvement of foreign stock exchanges. Use of a Big Four auditor became the accepted approach for companies seeking to raise international capital, and this led to Big Four domination of the market for listed Chinese companies.

5.3.3.1. A- and B-Shares

Two classes of shares are traded on the Shanghai and Shenzhen stock exchanges: A-shares, denominated in renminbi, that could be sold only to PRC nationals and PRC companies, and B-shares, denominated in renminbi but settled in US dollars or Hong Kong dollars, that were initially sold only to foreigners. After 2001, the B-share market opened to local investors. The B-share market was not successful, with shares usually trading at a discount to A-shares. By 2013, many companies had given up B-share listings in favor of H-share listings in Hong Kong (Noble, 2013). In 2004, a second board opened on the Shenzhen Stock Exchange for small and medium-sized enterprises (SMEs) followed by a ChiNext, a board that was also in Shenzhen, which facilitated fund raising for SMEs and growing venture enterprises (Zhao, 2009). When the A-share market opened in 1990, listed companies needed to use domestic state-owned accounting firms because foreign firms did not have a license to audit. Once the Big Five formed joint ventures they were permitted to audit domestic public companies but found few takers for their expensive, and for many, too rigorous audits.

The B-share market was a different matter. Because these shares sold overseas, the investment bankers involved insisted that international accounting firms (any recognized firm was eligible but it was typically one of the Big Five) serve as auditors. B-share financial reports used International Accounting Standards (IAS)[5] while A-share financial reports used Chinese generally accepted accounting principles (GAAP). Companies that issued both A and B shares were required to prepare sets of accounts under both IAS and Chinese GAAP (Peng, Tondkar, van der Laan Smith, & Harless, 2008).

Shanghai Vacuum issued the first B-share in 1991, audited by AA. AA won 7 of the first 9 B-share listings in Shanghai and 5 of the 11 listings in Shenzhen (Tong, 1992b). The conversion of Chinese GAAP accounts to international standards was a difficult process that often yielded startling results. Common adjustments included consolidating subsidiaries, using swap rates for foreign currency exchange and making provisions for bad debts. Shanghai Chlor-Alkali saw its profit drop from 69.7 million renminbi to 3.3 million renminbi after conversion. China Textile Machinery experienced an increase from 1.5 million renminbi to 12.8 million renminbi. While the Big Five did all of the B-share listings, local firms served the larger A-share market until dual listings in Hong Kong arose.

5.3.3.2. Audit Market Concentration on Chinese Stock Exchanges

Table 5.3 shows the 2012 market shares of accounting firms for audits of companies listed on Chinese stock exchanges. The Big Four has a 48% share of audit fees in this market while auditing only 6% of listed companies. This illustrates that the Big Four dominate the auditing of large companies, most of which are also listed outside of Mainland China. The market has a low level of concentration, with a Herfindahl–Hirschman Index (HHI) of 908 that indicates a competitive market.

In 2009, there were only nine A-share IPOs in Shanghai (raising RMB125 billion), of which the Big Four audited three. Shenzhen's SME Board, with 54 IPOs (raising RMB42 billion) and Shenzhen's ChiNext Board, with 36 IPOs (raising RMB20 billion) were more active albeit with smaller listings. The Big Four handled only one of the SME and ChiNext Board listings (*source*: PricewaterhouseCoopers). If the Big Four fails to improve its participation in the SME and ChiNext listings, or to obtain these companies as clients following their IPO, it is likely their market share will decline.

Table 5.3. Accounting Firm Market Shares on Chinese Stock Exchanges – 2012.

Firm	Auditor Remuneration	Number of Clients	Market Share/Fees	Market Share/Clients
PwC	809,044	56	21.16%	2.27%
E&Y	490,211	43	12.82%	1.75%
BDO	312,266	341	8.17%	13.83%
DTT	303,564	36	7.94%	1.46%
RSM	231,414	194	6.05%	7.87%
KPMG	230,173	20	6.02%	0.81%
Pan-China	216,084	257	5.65%	10.43%
Shinewing	146,806	149	3.84%	6.04%
Grant Thornton	124,621	110	3.26%	4.46%
Dahua	122,962	158	3.22%	6.41%
Others (38 firms)	835,883	1,101	21.87%	44.67%
Total	3,823,028	2,465	100.00%	100.00%
CR4	50.09%			
CR8	71.65%			
HHI	908			

Source: CSMAR Financial Database (RMB in thousands).

5.3.3.3. Regulation of Chinese Markets

The newly formed stock market was a rousing success as Chinese nationals came to believe that purchasing shares was a guaranteed way to make money. Beginning August 7, 1992, tens of thousands of people lined up outside offices of the People's Bank of China (PBOC) in Shenzhen to secure the opportunity to obtain subscription forms for an upcoming IPO. On August 10, the forms ran out in less than four hours. The crowd quickly surmised that the process was corrupt, and riots broke out that ran through the afternoon and into the evening. Additional forms were issued the following morning, yet the incident, now remembered in China as the *810* incident, led directly to the formation of the CSRC and central government control over the stock markets (Walter & Howie, 2001).

Zhu Rongji was the vice premier with responsibility for the economy, so reform of the markets fell to him. He turned to Liu Hongru, a vice minister at the Economic Reform Commission to investigate the 810 incident and to make recommendations. Lewis (2005) reports that an associate of Liu suggested he meet with Dominic Ho of Peat Marwick. Ho organized a meeting in Shenzhen of some of Hong Kong's leading investment bankers and lawyers to explain how stock markets work. They argued that the problem was not the markets, but the regulation of the markets. Four months later, the State Council Securities Commission and the CSRC were established. Liu became the first chairman of the CSRC. Zhu Rongji observed in 1992:

> At the moment, the securities market in our country are new things that only emerged in the past few years. We still don't have any experience in overseeing them and should borrow from and absorb the experiences of mature managerial systems that have proved effective in other countries, should integrate these with the practice in our country, and develop an oversight system that is appropriate for our nation's circumstances. (2013, p. 98)

The A-share market was plagued in its first decade by a series of scandals related to financial reporting. Frustration over widespread corruption in audit firms led to a crackdown on audits of listed companies that uncovered that companies had overstated profits by 18.9 billion yuan, or nearly 16% of the total profits recorded for 2001. Hundreds of accountants were arrested (Wu, 2003). Zhu Rongji said:

> The Ministry of Finance should refer to related laws in other countries and quickly come up with a method for managing accounting firms – this will be conducive to the smooth operations of pilot projections on the shareholding system and stock markets. (2013, p. 96)

The CSRC had previously decided to limit the number of accounting firms in China permitted to audit public companies. On December 5, 2000, the PBOC and the MOF announced that 68 accounting firms, including the Big Five, were granted licenses for securities related audits (Xu, 2000). The selected firms agreed to supervision by the CSRC. The number of accounting firms qualified for securities and futures work increased to 105 in 2002, but had been reduced to 54 by 2010, primarily as a result of the consolidation of accounting firms (Luk, 2010c).

The CSRC attempted to deal with rampant corruption and incompetence in domestic financial reporting by requiring companies to use international auditors. In 2001, the CSRC issued a regulation requiring all companies seeking an IPO or additional share listing to have a secondary audit by an international accounting firm (Yiu, 2001). Domestic firms, which held about a 90% share of the A-share market at that time, loudly protested. The CICPA took up their cause, arguing that the rules were discriminatory "They shrink domestic accounting firms' breathing space while expanding it for outsiders" said a CICPA representative (Hu, 2002). The state published *China Daily* even weighed in with an editorial, likening the CSRC to a really sick man who would turn to any doctor he can find. The editorial pointed out that AA, currently in the midst of its Enron travails, showed that the use of foreign firms did not necessary lead to quality. Instead they recommended that the CSRC needed to do its job and tighten its grip on the disreputable firms (Jiao, 2002). In the wake of this public outcry, the CSRC reissued the regulations omitting the requirement for foreign auditors.

5.3.4. Hong Kong Listings

The initial experience with public companies was generally positive from the perspective of Chinese bureaucrats and investors. However, China's capital markets were too small to raise the significant amounts of capital needed to modernize SOEs. While new public companies had implemented rudimentary corporate governance practices, China had no prior experience with corporate governance. Overseas listings could provide quick access to capital and would require overseas listed companies to follow established foreign governance practices (Green, 2004).

Dominic Ho of KPMG used his newly developed contacts with CSRC Chairman Liu Hongru to push to allow SOEs to list in Hong Kong. He proposed that the government identify a group of well-run companies in different industries as potential candidates for listing. In addition to raising foreign capital, Ho argued that the listings improved corporate governance and transparency, leading to improvement in management practices at SOEs. Ho realized, of course, that any company listing in Hong Kong required Hong Kong auditors. When Liu presented the idea to Zhu Rongji, Zhu approved it and a list of 35 candidates for listing was developed (Lewis, 2005, p. 184). While Lewis' (and Ho's) renderings of these events are KPMG centric, interviews with other actors indicate that other accountants were also involved in the deliberations; particularly Nellie Fong of AA and Tan Mankou of BDO affiliate KWTF.

Zhu saw the listings as an opportunity to introduce the rule of law and modern accounting practices to SOEs (Green, 2004). Hong Kong had a well-established securities law framework providing protection for shareholders and used accounting methods based largely on international standards. To help prepare for the listings, the Stock Exchange set up two committees to deal with these issues. Anthony Neoh chaired the legal subgroup. Clinton Chiu, the deputy chairman of the Hong Kong exchange's listing committee, headed the accounting subgroup. The key staff person for the committee was Estella Ng, recently recruited from Deloitte as the stock exchange's first accounting professional. The conclusion reached by the subcommittees was that PRC companies intending to list in Hong Kong needed to sign a listing agreement that required them to apply shareholder protection provisions equivalent to that available under Hong Kong law and that they must adopt either Hong Kong GAAP or IAS.

On July 17, 1992, representatives of the Big Six plus BDO affiliate KWTF were summoned to the PBOC in Beijing where they were informed that they had been selected to audit the first batch of 35 "cross-province" listings. The firms proposed that they each perform a "quick review" of one company in order to identify major problems before proceeding to the other 28 companies. Tommy Liu of E&Y quickly pointed out that only three firms, E&Y, AA, and KPMG had approved joint ventures in China (and licenses to audit) and that selecting the other firms might create legal problems (Tong, 1992a).

Chinese officials selected nine companies for the initial round of H-shares.[6] In preparation for the offerings each company needed to select auditors, lawyers, and investment bankers. Shanghai Petrochemical was earmarked as the first of the listings, to be followed by Tsingtao Brewery, Beijing Renmin Manufacturing, and Guangzhou Shipyard. Three of the 9 companies selected were among the 30 largest industrial companies in China. They were Shanghai Petrochemical Complex, Yizheng Joint

Corporation of Chemical Fibre, and Ma'anshan Iron and Steel Co. All of the companies proposed for listing were significantly larger than those that had previously issued B-shares (Tong, 1992b).

A request by HKSE Chairman Charles Lee that the accounting firms not approach the proposed H-share listings but rather wait for the Chinese companies to make a selection was ignored by the firms (*South China Morning Post*, 1992). The companies were slow in selecting firms and the process played out behind closed doors. On November 27, 1992, a closed-door meeting between the accountants and CRSC chairman Liu Hongru was motivated, in part, by the leak, on November 10, 1992, that KPMG had been selected for Shanghai Petrochemical (Tong, 1992c). One accountant reported of the meeting:

> We have taken frequent trips to China, but a decision has yet to be made. We felt very frustrated. So, in the meeting we all urged Mr. Liu to set a deadline to make the decision. (Chu, 1992)

Liu agreed and also told the firms that no firm could gain more than one of the listings, despite the fact there were nine companies and only seven firms (Chu, 1992). The decisions came down two weeks later. KPMG won three engagements, Shanghai Petrochemical, Yizheng Joint Corporation of Chemical Fibre, and Tianjin Bohai Chemical Industrial Group, making it the clear winner in the process. BDO affiliate KWTF's deep political connections helped it to win two engagements, Beijing Renmin Machinery and Steel Company and Dongfang Electric. E&Y won large steelmaker Ma'anshan Iron and Steel Company. DTT won Kunming Machine Tool Plant. C&L won large shipbuilder Guangzhou Shipyard Plant. PW initially won none, but was assigned Tianjin Bohai Chemical Industrial Group when it was decided that KPMG, which had won three, had too many. AA, despite its strong political connections, won only Tsingtao Brewery.

The biggest prize was Shanghai Petrochemical, the largest company on the list. Today the company is known as Sinopec and is the fourth largest company in the 2012 Fortune Global 500. It is currently listed on the Shanghai, Hong Kong, and New York Stock Exchanges. Due to Nellie Fong's close contacts with Shanghai Mayor Zhu Rongji, the audit of Shanghai Petrochemical was initially offered to AA. Fong returned to Hong Kong and was shocked when managing partner Eoghan McMillan told her that they would need to decline the opportunity. AA was the smallest firm in Hong Kong and McMillan felt they did not have the staffing resources to audit such a large company. He suggested instead that they take a more manageable assignment, such as Tsingtao Brewery. With AA out of the picture, Shanghai Petrochemical quickly selected KPMG. Partner Dominic Ho's China relationships and oil and gas expertise made KPMG the obvious second choice (Tong, 1992c). At this time, it is likely that only KPMG and PW were large enough in Hong Kong to handle an assignment of this size. It is remarkable that AA, the most globally unified of the Big Six at the time, did not find a way to deploy staff from other locations in order to win this significant prize. It appears to have been an error in judgment. McMillan left his post the following year, replaced by Meocre Li with Nellie Fong being appointed deputy-managing director (*South China Morning Post*, 1993).

The wins by both KPMG and KWTF illustrate the importance of political connections in this process. Second-tier and local Hong Kong firms had largely been excluded from the China accounting market in favor of the Big Six, but KTWF had succeed through its connections. In 1997, the larger KWTF merged with DTT in Hong Kong (Yiu, 1997) and the H-share market became a near exclusive province of the Big Six.

The poor performance of PW in the initial H-share listings reflected its weak political connections within China. At this time the China operations were under the control of the global firm and relations between the China practice and Hong Kong grew acrimonious. PW in Hong Kong was also viewed as being very British and allied with the colonial interests in Hong Kong. While KPMG was also viewed as British and colonial, Ho had succeeded in building deeper relationships in China.

Winning the H-share audits was one thing; actually doing the audits was a monumental task. The auditing process was slow and arduous. Eddy Fong of Coopers and Lybrand complained: "They have not been extensively audited by outsiders before, and have no idea what auditors want" (Chen, 1994b). Tommy Wong of KWTF said: "We had to spend a lot of time explaining. And I told them that we needed everything except the minutes of their Communist Party committee meetings" (Chen, 1994b).

Some of the companies had not been put into corporate form, which became one of the first steps in the process of listing (Tong, 1992b). Hong Kong listing requirements included audited financial statements for the most recent three fiscal years. For B-share listings only a current year audit and limited review of the two prior years was required.

Underwriters and clients pressured accountants to complete their work. The auditors claimed that the underwriters, and some of the companies, were willing to sacrifice accounting standards in order to keep the listings on schedule. "The information cannot be audited in six months," complained David Sun of E&Y, "The problem is that all these companies have December year-ends and that doesn't give us a whole lot of time. So, accountants must qualify some issues" (Naylor, 1993).

A major accounting issue arose with respect to exchange rates. China at the time had an official exchange rate, and an unofficial swap-center rate. Many of the companies proposed for listing had large foreign exchange incomes due to exports. Aloysius Tse, chairman of the Hong Kong Society of Accountants said: "The situation may arise in which accounts based on the swap center rate for overseas investors may reveal a profitable operation, while accounts based on the official rate suggesting (sic) losses" (Tong, 1993). Negotiations between the HKSA and Chinese authorities strung out for several months. HKSA representatives argued that IAS required the use of the swap-center rates, while Chinese authorities were concerned this would undermine China's foreign exchange policy. In the end, a compromise led to the use of both rates, with additional footnote disclosures in the international accounts to provide readers with adequate information.

Accounting firms were disappointed with the fees obtained for the initial H-share offerings. Despite their perceived naivety in such matters, the Chinese companies took advantage of the intensely competitive environment between the Big Six firms to negotiate low, fixed rate contracts. Raymond Woo of E&Y said at the time:

> In the past, accountants did not enjoy a very high status in China. So they thought our services too expensive because they didn't understand the importance of our services and were not used to paying such a high fee. Actually, what they paid was a small amount, considering the difficulties involved and what we had done. The fee was not a lot of money compared to the funds raised. (Chen, 1994b)

Six of the nine initial H-share offerings listed by early 1994. Observers were surprised by the quality of financial reporting, noting that the disclosures were more thorough than most companies listed in Hong Kong (Lai, 1994b).

Despite their frustrations with the low levels of remuneration for auditing the initial H-shares, the firms were anxious to obtain the audits for the second round of Hong Kong listings. Firms began to send in teams to do year-end inventory observations in the hope of snaring companies when they received permission to list. C&L partner Wong Kai-man predicted in 1994: "You will not see the firms battling each other for clients, but the competition will inevitably be very keen. If you don't take part, it would be very difficult to break into the business in future" (Chen, 1994b). Wong's prediction that the firms would not battle for clients was wishful thinking, but his prediction that competition would be very keen was prescient. The firms recognized that the China market was going to become very big, and that they must win these engagements at any cost. The losses incurred by the firms were substantial and the firms that obtained financial support from their global networks were better able to compete.

5.3.4.1. Further Listings in Hong Kong

The success of this initial experiment with nine companies led to additional listings. By August 2013, 151 main board listed H-shares had a total market capitalization of US$563 billion. Chinese companies also listed "Red Chips"[7] in Hong Kong. In addition to raising capital, establishing a Red Chip also allowed SOEs to take advantage of favorable tax and foreign exchange policies that were available to foreign invested enterprises in China (Xiao, 2004). By August 2013, there were 115 Red Chips on the main board with a market capitalization of US$584 billion. By August 2013, H-shares and Red Chips account for 41.6% of the market capitalization of the Hong Kong Stock Exchange (Hong Kong Exchanges and Clearing Limited, 2013). Dual listings also became common, with 61 of the companies listed in Hong Kong also listed in either Shenzhen or Shanghai. As of the end of 2009, 23 of the top 50 listed companies (by market capitalization) in Shanghai and 47 out the top 50 listed companies (by market capitalization) in Shenzhen had not issued H-shares.

Table 5.4 shows the Big Four market shares for the auditing market for both H-share and Red Chip listings in Hong Kong. The Big Four has a 95.4% share of H-share audits and a 96.8% share of Red Chip audits in 2009 measured by auditor remuneration. The HHI for the H-share and Red Chip market is 3239 and 2677. The Hong Kong audit market for all companies listed on the HKSE is highly concentrated with an HHI of 2390, yet the market for H-shares and Red Chips is even more concentrated. The Big Four have successfully closed the market for Chinese listings in Hong Kong and have largely succeeded in excluding local and second-tier firms from participation. The local firm with the largest market share, ShineWing (HK) CPA Limited, has only a 0.8% share of the combined H-share and Red Chip market. ShineWing (HK) Limited is the Hong Kong office of Mainland accounting firm ShineWing, which was the former joint venture partner of C&L in China and is headed by leading Chinese CPA Zhang Ke (Chan, 2008; Luk, 2010a).

Several factors aligned to ensure that the Big Four controlled the H-share and Red Chip markets. Their historic domination of the Hong Kong market

Table 5.4. Accounting Firm Market Shares on the Hong Kong Stock Exchange – 2009.

Firm	Total Auditor's Remuneration			
	H-Share	Red Chip	H and Red	All Listed
PwC	677	283	960	2,531
KPMG	445	129	574	2,082
E&Y	146	159	305	1,108
DTT	130	120	250	1,116
Shine Wing (HK) CPA Limited	17	1	18	78
Grant Thornton	5	5	10	119
Crowe Horwath	–	4	4	7
BDO	8	–	8	53
UHY Vocation HK CPA Limited	10	–	10	36
CCIF CPA Limited	3	2	5	48
Others	25	11	36	268
Total	1,466	714	2,180	7,446
Number of listed companies	149	94	243	1,323
Auditor remuneration per company	9.84	7.59	8.97	5.63
CR4	0.9540	0.9677		0.9182
CR8	0.9828	0.9903		0.9598
HHI	3239	2677		2390

Source: Hong Kong Stock Exchange (corporate governance reports) (HK$ millions).

meant that there were few firms other than the Big Four with the scale to take on the H-share and Red Chip listings. China's delays in allowing access to China's markets for Hong Kong and second-tier global accounting firms meant that these firms did not have the opportunity to build resources and capabilities on the Mainland. Hong Kong regulations that restricted the right to audit companies listed on its exchange to Hong Kong CPAs and to international firms legally precluded Mainland firms from pursuing this work. As of May 2010, only seven listed companies were authorized to use non-Hong Kong registered accountants, and in each case the auditor was a member firm of one of the Big Four (Legislative Council of Hong Kong, 2010). The requirement to use IAS or HKFRS was an additional barrier for Mainland firms that had no experience with these rules. The decision by Chinese regulators to allow the first international listings in Hong Kong ensured that the Big Four would come to dominate the CPA market in China.

PwC's leading position is partly because of its acquisition of the China and Hong Kong operations of AA in 2002. The strong positions of both

PwC and KPMG are likely a legacy of their long domination of the Hong Kong market, which gave them ample resources as the H-share and Red Chip markets opened up. DTT's relatively small market share is puzzling given the strong start by KWTF and suggests that the merger of KWTF did not have the expected result. Tan Man-Kou was 61 at the time of the merger, and already past the normal retirement age of Big Six partners in Hong Kong. The merger, in 1997, was probably five years too late for DTT.

5.3.4.2. IPOs of Large SOEs

By 1998, the early success with the Chinese stock exchanges and with H-share listings in Hong Kong had convinced regulators that the IPO process could help to reform China's larger SOEs. Chinese bureaucrats began to contemplate IPOs of major SOEs as "a propeller for the Mainland's painful State sector restructuring" which Zhu Rongji hoped would win the "heart and soul" of international investors back to China after the Asian Financial Crisis (Wang, 2000). China was on the threshold of entering the WTO. Diamond (2003) argues that a series of large IPOs of SOEs that began with PetroChina had a dual purpose; first to provide the increased resources necessary for the continued expansion of the Chinese economy, and also to defend the ability of its industries to compete, or at least hold their own, with foreign capital. While access to capital was certainly important, instilling modern corporate governance was also a key objective.

In 1997 Zhu Rongji talked about cleaning up the SOEs for listing:

> I'm thinking of inviting some comrades who are professionally very knowledgeable – including those who are knowledgeable about technology, business, and accounting, and also adding specialists from some major foreign accounting firms – to jointly draft a set of procedures, standards and methods for assessing SOEs. If we use software on the enterprises, then just by asking a few questions and checking some original books, we'll know if their seeming profits are actually losses, and whether their books are correct or falsified. We must strengthen the auditing of state-owned commercial banks and SOEs. (2013, p. 432)

In 1998, a group of 19 special inspectors was selected to evaluate larger SOEs in preparation for restructuring. Most of the special inspectors were senior level cadres whose positions are equivalent to ministers and they had formerly run departments or industries. AA was designated to assist these special inspectors in the investigation of 19 large SOEs that were considered likely candidates for public listings. The intent was that after this trial inspection of 19 SOEs the investigation would be extended to 500 SOEs that were to remain under state control under the "grasping the large, letting go the small" (*Zhua Da Fang Xiao*) policy (Ding, 2006b).

The award of this work to AA created a firestorm of opposition from local firms. A training session led by AA for the special inspectors was poorly received. Opponents of AA's participation appealed against AA's involvement using concerns over national security. Vice Minister Sun reported to the special inspectors on July 15, 1998 that local accounting firms replaced AA:

> Andersen asked to undertake the task and got the approval from my leaders to help special inspectors to inspect the accounts of these larger-scale SOEs, but we refused this. My major reason presented to my leaders is that we do such for the sake of the country's safety. Such batches of larger-scale SOEs are key enterprises that are important to people's livelihood. If they take part in this inspection of the enterprises, they will have a clear picture of China's business, economy, military, and safety. If there is any sign of disturbance, there will be a huge negative impact on our economy. (Ding, 2006b p. 456)

Two local CPA's deemed "socialist-minded" and "professional," and who were led by CICPA Director General Ding Pingzhun, replaced AA on each of the special inspection teams.

Following these special inspections, the Chinese government began restructuring large SOEs in key industries. The process included carving out key assets from SOEs to create world-class competitors in key industries such as petroleum, aluminum, and insurance. The resulting entities were then listed, typically in global IPOs on the New York, Hong Kong, and sometimes Shanghai stock exchanges. New York was included because of its prestige, as well as being the only market perceived to have the capacity to absorb IPOs of the scale of China's larger SOEs. Despite the perceived national security concerns that precluded AA's early involvement, international firms audited each of these listings (Table 5.5).

Noteworthy in Table 5.5 is the domination of the audit market for SOE's listed in the United States by PwC (49.5% by market capitalization) and KPMG (40.5% by market capitalization). The sole exception to this is CNOOC, audited by E&Y. E&Y obtained CNOOC as a client when its former auditor, AA was acquired by PwC which already audited petroleum giant PetroChina. PwC and KPMG have long dominated the Hong Kong market. While PwC did poorly in the initial round of H-share listings (as discussed above), they clearly have done better with larger SOEs. Some of PwC's clients in 2009 (China Unicom, Huaneng Power, and Guangzhen Railway) were formerly AA clients retained when PwC acquired AA in China.

Table 5.5. Major Chinese SOEs Listed on NYSE.

Company	IPO Date	Market Cap	Auditor
PetroChina	April 6, 2000	200,828	PwC
China Mobile	October 22, 1997	198,259	KMPG
China Life Insurance Company	December 17, 2003	122,857	PwC
CNOOC	February 1, 2001	76,014	E&Y
Sinopec	October 18, 2000	69,804	KPMG
China Telecom	October 31, 1998	38,783	KPMG
China Unicom	May 31, 1996	31,338	PwC
Aluminum Corp. of China	December 11, 2001	10,095	PwC
Huaneng Power	October 6, 1994	4,501	PwC
China Eastern Airlines	February 4, 1997	3,960	PwC
Guangshen Railway	May 13, 1996	2,874	PwC
China Southern Airlines	July 30, 1997	1,340	KPMG

Source: NYSE, Audit Analytics. Market capitalization in US$ millions on December 31, 2009.

5.3.4.3. New York Stock Exchange (NYSE EuroNext)

The capital needs of China's larger SOEs could not be met on Hong Kong's stock exchange in the late 1990s, so investment bankers advised that the companies should seek global listings both in Hong Kong and New York (Allen & Shen, 2010; Diamond, 2003). The first SOEs allowed to list in New York were the two China airlines, a power company, and a railroad, all of which needed more capital than would be available listing only in Hong Kong. China Mobile was the first large SOE to list. It required substantial capital to build what would become the world's largest cellular network serving 745 million customers as of July 31, 2013 (China Mobile Limited, 2013). Chinese bureaucrats then turned their attention to the petroleum industry.

In early 2000, a consortium of investment bankers led by Goldman Sachs launched an initial public offering of the common stock of the newly formed Chinese oil company, PetroChina. The offering raised $2.9 billion for a 10% stake in the company. The shares were offered on both the NYSE and HKSE, because it was viewed that neither the Shanghai nor Hong Kong exchanges could raise that level of capital at that time. PetroChina was formed out of China National Petroleum Company (CNPC), and only selected profitable assets and limited liabilities were contributed to the new company. Surplus employees and nonproductive assets were left with CNPC, together with operations in Sudan that could not be held under US laws.

Political conditions in the United States were considerably different from what had been experienced with the H-share listings in Hong Kong. The offering was highly politicized in the United States, where a coalition led by the AFL-CIO with significant support from conservative and religious groups plead with President Clinton to block it due to China's history of human rights violations. The offering went ahead, although in a size considerably lower than the hoped for $10 billion. Diamond (2003) argues that this introduced a new era in global capital markets, where the capital markets could no longer be seen as simply passive intermediaries but as inherently political because they impact social outcomes; in this case putting great pressure on China for labor and humans rights reform.

PetroChina selected PwCs as auditors. The China firm of PwC, which at the time of the listing was owned and operated by the global firm, rather than the Hong Kong firm that had done the H-share listings, won the engagement. An engagement of this size and complexity was beyond the capabilities of PwC's China practice, and it received considerable assistance from partners and staff from around the world, including US oil and gas partner Michael Cannon, who had spent a substantial portion of his career pursuing this engagement. The engagement set up a confrontation between the China and Hong Kong firms of PwC. Seeing its future market potentially falling out of its hands, two years later the Hong Kong firm persuaded the global firm to merge the China practice into its operations.

The PetroChina listing was a mixed success. It succeeded in restructuring a major SOE into a global competitor, and went forth despite considerable political opposition. Although it raised less capital than expected, it opened the door for the further listing of large SOEs. By 2008, 11 SOEs restructured and listed on the NYSE.

5.3.4.4. Private Companies and US Listings

Deng Xiaoping's reforms that began in 1978 allowed for the return of private enterprises to the Chinese economy. Private enterprises flourished in the decades to follow; some of these enterprises were the result of the efforts of entrepreneurs, others the complete or partial privatization of formerly SOEs. By 2002, the share of GDP produced in the non-state sector exceeded two-thirds, with the share produced by truly private activity comprising more than half (Asian Development Bank, 2002).

Entrepreneurs and businesspersons gained political legitimacy when President Jiang Zemin (2001), in an important speech commemorating the 80th anniversary of the Communist Party, declared that Marxism and Leninism, while remaining the foundational principles for China, needed to be interpreted based on modern times and needs. He recognized that private entrepreneurs were part of new social strata that:

> … contributed to the development of productive forces and other undertakings in the socialist society through honest labor and work or lawful business operations. They join workers, farmers, intellectuals, cadres and PLA officers and men in an effort to build socialism with Chinese characteristics. They, too, have contributed to this cause.

Jiang Zemin's speech set out the Principle of Three Representations (*San ge daibiao*) and led to the opening of Communist party membership to entrepreneurs and businessmen. By 2002, nearly 30% of China's entrepreneurs were party members (Kanamori & Zhao, 2004).

While Chinese society increasingly embraced private business, these new businesses had great difficulty accessing capital. The major institutions involved in providing capital to businesses, banks, and the stock exchanges remained under state control and were largely inaccessible to private enterprise. Shen, Shen, Xu, and Bai (2009) reported that 98% of the over 40 million SMEs in China could not obtain bank loans in 2006. China's private enterprises faced difficulty in raising capital on China's stock exchanges. By 2000, only 1% of the companies listed on China's stock exchanges were privately owned (Gregory, Tenev, & Wagle, 2000). Many of these companies sought capital in China's shadow banking system (Tsai, 2002). Table 5.6 shows the capital raised on Chinese stock exchanges by type of control at the time of the offering. From 1999 to 2007, private companies collected between 3% and 18% of the funds raised on these exchanges. A Small and Medium Enterprises (SME) Board opened in Shenzhen in 2004, supplemented in 2009 by a Growth Enterprises Board, more commonly known as ChiNext, that have created opportunities for private enterprises to list in China. ChiNext is touted as the NASDAQ of China (Li, 2011). The private company share of capital raised rose to 25% in 2008 and to 67% in 2009 indicating that the Chinese markets had become significantly more accessible to private companies. From 2010 to 2012 the private company share of capital raised averaged 60%.

Table 5.7 shows the market capitalization of China's stock exchanges by type of control. By 2012, privately controlled companies had only a 26% share of total market capitalization, despite the fact that many state controlled companies shifted to private control following the public offering.

Allen and Shen (2010) posit three reasons why private companies in China found access to capital difficult. First, the primary mission of the CSRC for the first 15 years of its existence was to support SOEs with additional capital. Second, the CSRC views its responsibility is to protect

Table 5.6. Capital Raised on Chinese Stock Exchanges by Type of Control.

Year	State Control	Private Control	Other Control	Total Raised	Private (%)
1999	102,285	4,089	14,383	120,756	3
2000	221,494	19,180	13,616	254,290	8
2001	135,235	15,679	11,921	162,836	10
2002	77,864	8,614	4,389	90,866	9
2003	69,586	16,528	3,897	90,011	18
2004	94,028	14,140	2,509	110,676	13
2005	28,750	3,524	160	32,434	11
2006	191,467	18,735	2,060	212,262	9
2007	684,419	78,557	8,097	771,073	10
2008	228,312	80,327	7,628	316,267	25
2009	394,243	859,926	31,971	1,286,140	67
2010	371,177	532,750	39,715	943,642	56
2011	267,836	430,177	33,143	731,156	59
2012	134,117	269,705	18,084	421,906	64
Total	3,000,813	2,351,931	191,573	5,544,315	42

Source: CCER. Other control includes foreign, collective, social group, employee and not determinable (RMB millions).

Table 5.7. Market Capitalization of Chinese Stock Exchanges by Type of Control.

Year	State Control	Private Control	Other Control	Total	Private (%)
1999	2,382,281	154,474	250,364	2,787,120	6
2000	4,224,558	371,533	416,549	5,012,640	7
2001	3,873,801	367,230	300,368	4,541,399	8
2002	3,398,324	429,153	209,942	4,037,419	11
2003	3,847,534	482,836	152,759	4,483,129	11
2004	3,327,991	476,879	123,493	3,928,363	12
2005	2,916,579	427,571	72,679	3,416,829	13
2006	9,213,389	952,441	144,141	10,309,972	9
2007	34,250,385	3,058,175	560,900	37,869,459	8
2008	10,730,055	1,342,209	228,707	12,300,971	11
2009	18,562,544	3,482,935	411,518	22,457,097	16
2010	14,716,302	6,676,555	5,223,019	26,615,876	25
2011	11,647,635	5,505,095	4,438.657	21,591,387	26
2012	12,003,396	6,092,102	4,943.765	23,039,263	26

Source: CCER database. Other control includes foreign, collective, social group, employee, and not determinable (RMB millions on December 31).

investors from risky investments, and from their perspective, private businesses were more risky than SOEs. Third, many entrepreneurs lacked political patrons and the denial of capital to them may reflect a lingering ideological bias against the generation of private wealth. Stringent listing requirements on size and profitability would have precluded many entrepreneurial companies from qualifying for listings even if regulators been more accommodating (Fung, Liu, & Yau, 2007).

Unable to access domestic sources of capital, Chinese entrepreneurs began to look to foreign sources. There were obstacles to doing so. The CSRC prohibited Chinese companies from listing overseas without permission. While there is no record of the CRSC denying a private company an overseas listing, that is probably because no one applied to do so, having anticipated a near certain denial. To avoid the CSRC restrictions, private companies began to incorporate holding companies in offshore jurisdictions, commonly including the Cayman Islands and the British Virgin Islands. These foreign holding companies are outside the jurisdiction of the CSRC. In 2005, Chinese regulators tried to control this avenue by requiring any Chinese person transferring property to an offshore company to receive prior approval from SAFE (Stender, She, & Jin, 2007).

While incorporating an offshore holding company was successful at avoiding CSRC regulation, it created new problems. China has restricted foreign investment in many industries in China and while China's entry into WTO began to open most of these, some sectors remained closed. Prominent among the closed sectors was the internet sector which was of keen interest to entrepreneurs and investors. The first private companies to list internationally would come from this sector.

SINA Corporation and Sohu.com were two of the early internet companies in China. Both were formed by Chinese nationals who returned from Silicon Valley to build internet startups during the dotcom boom. While they had established offshore companies that avoided Chinese securities laws, Chinese law did not permit a foreign company, nor a domestic company with foreign ownership, to hold an internet content providers (ICP) license. Because of these restrictions, the Chinese national founders of the companies formed a domestic company to hold the ICP license. Because Chinese nationals owned this domestic company, it complied with the restrictions against foreign ownership. However, in order to list the companies on NASDAQ, investment bankers said that the ICP license holding companies needed to be part of the listing group.

Both companies were audited by PwCs and the two American engagement partners, Kevan Bradshaw for Sohu.com and Michael Pfeiffer for

SINA, worked with international lawyers to find a way for the companies to include the ICP license holding companies in their consolidated financial statements. The solution was to create agreements between the listing entity and the ICP license holding entities and shareholders that would effectively transfer control of the ICP license holding entity to the listing entity. The agreements required the shareholders of the ICP license holding company to allow the listed company to make any management decision, to pay any dividends they received to the listing company and to transfer ownership of the ICP license holding company to the listing company should this ever be permitted under Chinese law. The accounting rules for consolidation under Accounting Research Bulletin (ARB) 51 had primarily looked at stock ownership, with greater than 50% ownership of the stock resulting in consolidation. Initially the ICP licensing company was not consolidated in the financial statements of the companies. Three years later, in 2003, the Financial Accounting Standards Board issued FASB Interpretation No. 46 (FIN 46) in response to perceived abuses by Enron and others related to off-balance sheet accounting. Although FIN 46 was drafted with the intent of curbing abuses of companies related to keeping financing operations off the balance sheet, it provided clear rules to allow companies like SINA and Sohu.com to include in their consolidated financials statements their "variable interest entities" (VIEs), as they were called in the interpretation (Gillis, 2011b). Absent this accounting treatment it is unlikely the offerings of SINA and Sohu.com would have been successful. The Big Four invented VIE structure for Chinese companies has been used by 97 Chinese companies listed on US exchanges (Gillis, 2011d).

The SINA offering closed on April 13, 2000 and sold 4 million shares at $17. Morgan Stanley served as underwriter. Sohu.com listed a few months later using Credit Suisse First Boston. Following these successful listings, NASDAQ became the preferred location for the listing of China-based technology companies. By December 31, 2009, 121 China-based companies had been listed on NASDAQ (Wei & Young, 2009). The VIE structure also became commonplace for Chinese private companies that chose to list on NASDAQ. Of the 121 China-based companies listed on NASDAQ as of December 31, 2009, 63 use the VIE structure (Gillis, 2011d). VIE use has been expanded beyond internet companies to include other industries where foreign investment is restricted, such as education and insurance brokerages. It has also been used in industries that have no restrictions on foreign investment, often as means of avoiding the attendant implications of an offshore transfer of shares in a Chinese company (Gillis, 2010a).

While privately held Chinese technology companies initially favored listing on NASDAQ, those in other industries, such as education and real estate, often sought listings on the New York Stock Exchange. Competition between the NYSE and NASDAQ for Chinese listings became fierce (Balfour, 2007). Some smaller Chinese companies were listed on the American Stock Exchange, and over 350 small companies listed on over-the-counter bulletin boards (OTCBBs) in the United States after reverse merger transactions (Alpert & Norton, 2010; Gillis, 2011c).

When SINA and Sohu.com prepared for two of the first IPOs of private companies, they sought out leading international investment bankers (Morgan Stanley and Credit Suisse First Boston), lawyers (Sullivan & Cromwell and Venture Law Group), and accountants (Pricewaterhouse-Coopers). The expertise of the accountants and lawyers at finding a means to avoid Chinese regulatory restrictions was critical to the success of these offerings. Unsurprisingly, the Big Four has dominated the market for audit services to Chinese companies listed on US exchanges. Because of the growing importance of this client base the firms have developed resources to serve this market, further enforcing their domination. For example, PwC's Global Capital Markets group in 2010 had three American partners based in China whose role is to advise engagement teams on US listings.

5.3.4.5. Audit Markets for US Listings

The major stock markets in the United States are the New York Stock Exchange and NASDAQ. Some small Chinese companies have also listed on the American Stock Exchange and the shares of others trade over-the-counter on informal markets known as the bulletin boards or pink sheets.

5.3.4.6. New York Stock Exchange

On December 31, 2012, there were 67 companies from China listed on the NYSE. They include many of China's largest state controlled corporations (PetroChina, China Telecom, China Life, etc.), as well as many companies with no government ownership (e.g. Xinyuan Real Estate, New Oriental Education, and RenRen).

The Big Four dominate the market for auditing Chinese companies listed on the NYSE Euronext (Table 5.6). The Big Four have a market share of 97.01% based on auditor revenue. The market is highly concentrated with an HHI of 2914. The auditing market for Chinese companies listed on the NYSE is more concentrated than the overall market for audits of public companies in the United States, which has an HHI of 2300

(Government Accountability Office, 2008). This is largely driven by the large SOEs such as Sinopec and China Life (Table 5.8).

5.3.4.7. NASDAQ

The Big Four dominate the auditing market for Chinese companies listed on NASDAQ with 81.27% of the market by auditor revenue in 2012 (Table 5.6). DTT and PwC, both of which have long had resident US specialists dedicated to these listings, lead the NASDAQ market with a combined share of 60% based on auditor remuneration. PwC, as previously discussed, was also the firm that played a major role in creating this market by finding accounting solutions that allow Chinese companies in regulated industries to access capital markets, and perhaps unsurprisingly, has been rewarded with the largest market share. The market is highly concentrated with an HHI of 2131. The market is not nearly as concentrated as the NYSE market, which has an HHI of 2914 and is less concentrated than the overall market for audits of public companies in the United States.

Many of the smaller Chinese companies that have listed in the United States have selected second-tier auditors or other small overseas accounting firms. The market for small US listed companies, including those traded

Table 5.8. Accounting Fees of Chinese Companies Listed on US Exchanges – 2012.

Firm	NYSE	NASDAQ	ASE	Total
PwC	47,190	27,161	–	74,351
KPMG	65,199	5,634	–	70,833
DTT	21,603	19,865	–	41,468
E&Y	20,083	11,038	–	31,121
Crowe Horwath	1,296	2,080	–	3,376
BDO	437	2,176	677	3,290
Friedman	900	2,251	–	3,151
Grant Thornton	1,158	1,964	–	3,122
Others	965	6,213	908	8,086
Total	158,831	78,382	1,585	238,798
Listed companies	67	109	8	184
Mean auditor fee	2,370	719	198	1,298
CR4	0.9701	0.8127	0.7800	0.9120
CR8	0.9913	0.8957	1.0	0.9661
HHI	2914	2131	2478	

Source: Audit Analytics (US$ in thousands).

over-the-counter, is served by small accounting firms mostly from the United States, but also from Hong Kong and Canada. Indigenous Chinese accounting firms do not have a significant presence in this market. Many small US listed companies have terminated their listings either by acquiring the shares of public shareholders and delisting, or by having their listings terminated for failure to make timely filings. Auditors of smaller companies have also been challenged by the PCAOB (2011) for the practice of outsourcing audit work to local Chinese accounting firms. Consequentially, many of these smaller US-based accounting firms have withdrawn from the market. Because most of the companies served by US-based accounting firms were traded in OTC markets, there has been increasing market concentration for the auditors of Chinese companies listed on NASDAQ, with CR4 increasing from 0.7154 in 2009 (Gillis, 2011a, p. 140) to 0.8127 in 2012.

5.3.4.8. Private Companies on Chinese Exchanges

The difficulty of raising capital domestically drove Chinese private foreign companies to foreign exchanges, and to foreign accounting firms. In 1994, an SME Board was opened on the Shenzhen Stock Exchange, and a Growth Enterprise Board (known as ChiNext) was opened in 2009 on the same exchange. The SME and ChiNext boards on the Shenzhen Stock Exchange have begun to attract a growing number of listings of companies that might formerly have listed on NASDAQ (Table 5.6). The higher valuations that were available on those boards when compared to NASDAQ have made them more attractive to companies seeking a listing. Chinese stock exchanges, like Hong Kong, generally require that companies present a track record of profitability before they are permitted to do an IPO. US exchanges do not have such a requirement. Because many early stage companies, particularly in the technology sector, often choose to do an IPO before establishing the required track record, they go to US markets. By June 2010, 437 companies had listed on the GEM and 90 on ChiNext (Allen & Shen, 2010). Indigenous accounting firms have won all but a few of these listings, and if this trend continues the Big Four domination of the non-state sector of public companies may be threatened.

Over half of Chinese companies that listed in China since 2009 were trading below offering price in August 2013 (Bloomberg Businessweek, 2013). The poor performance of Chinese stocks led regulators to suspend IPOs on Chinese exchanges in October 2012. Bain estimated that 600 companies in China awaited IPOs, creating a 3.9 year waiting list when regulators chose to resume IPOs (Bain, 2013).

5.4. ACCOUNTING FRAUDS AND SCANDALS

Early in 2010 certain research firms began to release reports on Chinese companies. On June 28, 2010, Muddy Waters Research, operated by Carson Block, issued its first report with a strong sell recommendation on Orient Paper, Inc., alleging accounting fraud (Muddy Waters Research, 2010). Orient Paper launched an investigation led by Deloitte, Loeb & Loeb, and TransAsia Lawyers that found no basis for the allegations. Nonetheless, the share price of Orient Paper, which collapsed by 60% following the allegation, failed to recover (Hobbs, 2011). Muddy Waters spawned an industry of short sellers targeting Chinese companies including Citron Research, Alfred Little, and Anonymous Analytics. The track record of the short sellers in successfully identifying fraudulent companies was mixed, but they were nearly always successful in depressing the share price of targeted companies (Steger, 2012). Darrough, Huang, and Zhao (2012) found that allegations against reverse mergers had a negative impact on the stock prices of all US listed Chinese companies. Short sellers themselves came under attack by companies upset with attacks on them (The Economist, 2012). Short sellers profit by selling borrowed shares and then later purchasing shares at lower prices to replace the borrowed shares.

Many of the early short seller attacks related to companies that had come to market through a transaction known as a reverse merger. The SEC (2011b) has defined reverse mergers as follows:

> In a reverse merger transaction, an existing public "shell company," which is a public reporting company with few or no operations, acquires a private operating company – usually one that is seeking access to funding in the U.S. capital markets. Typically, the shareholders of the private operating company exchange their shares for a large majority of the shares of the public company. Although the public shell company survives the merger, the private operating company's shareholders gain a controlling interest in the voting power and outstanding shares of stock of the public shell company. Also typically, the private operating company's management takes over the board of directors and management of the public shell company. The assets and business operations of the post-merger surviving public company are primarily, if not solely, those of the former private operating company.

5.4.1. Reverse Mergers

Reverse mergers result in a company becoming registered as a public company without having to go through the often-rigorous process of an IPO. IPO processes include an audit by a registered public accountant and

Securities and Exchange Commission (SEC) review of the filings before the IPO can become effective. In the case of a reverse merger, the audit does not have to be completed until the first post-merger filing that requires audited financial statements. SEC reviews, if any, would come after the post-merger filings are made.

Jindra, Voetmann, and Walking (2012) found that larger, more reputable Chinese firms are less likely to pursue reverse mergers. They also determined that those Chinese firms that do pursue reverse mergers significantly underperform those that conduct initial public offerings.

The PCAOB (2011) conducted a study of reverse merger transactions completed by Chinese companies. The study found 159 Chinese companies in the period beginning January 1, 2007 and ending March 31, 2010 that had obtained access to US capital markets by means of a reverse merger transaction. The Public Company Accounting Oversight Board (PCAOB) study was motivated by the large number of alleged frauds at Chinese companies that came to market through reverse mergers. PCAOB member Lewis Ferguson said in a speech at California State University that:

> "Beginning in the latter part of 2010, alleged financial frauds and serious accounting issues were revealed at a number of the smaller Chinese reverse merger companies," he said. "To date, 67 of these China-based issuers have had their auditor resign, and 126 issuers have either been delisted from U.S. securities exchanges or 'gone dark' – meaning that they are no longer filing current reports with the SEC. Billions of dollars of market capitalization of such companies have been lost in U.S. securities markets and it is fair to say that all of these smaller China-based companies listed on U.S. securities exchanges have suffered serious losses of both market value and investor confidence as a result of the problems of other companies." (Cohn, 2012b)

Most reverse mergers were audited by small US-based accounting firms. Table 5.9 lists the accounting firms that audited three or more reverse mergers in the PCAOB study. Notably, none of the Big Four are on the list. The main reasons for this are the small size of most reverse mergers, the high fees of the Big Four, the reluctance of the Big Four to take on clients perceived as risky, and the fact that the Big Four were exceptionally busy with IPOs at the time many of these companies came to market.

A reverse merger results in a company registered with the SEC, and thereby eligible to be listed on the major US stock exchanges, NASDAQ and NYSE. Such listing, however, is not automatic, and companies must meet the exchange's rules before being accepted for listing. In order to meet the exchange's rules, companies that had completed reverse mergers often sought to raise additional capital through a secondary offering or private placement. Companies that were unable to obtain a listing on NASDAQ or

Table 5.9. Number of Chinese Reverse Mergers by Audit Firms.

Firm	Clients
MaloneBailey, LLP	10
Bernstein & Pinchuk LLP	9
PKF	7
Paritz and Company	6
AGCA Inc.	5
Albert Wong & Co.	5
Frazer Frost, LLP	5
Goldman Kurland and Mohidin, LLP	5
Samuel H. Wong & Co., LLP	5
HKCMCPA Company Limited	5
Child, Van Wagoner & Bradshaw, PLLC	4
Friedman LLP	4
Kabani & Company, Inc.	4
Patrizio and Zhao, LLC	4
Sherb & Co., LLP	4
Weinberg & Company	4
Acquavella, Chiarelli, Shuster, Berkower & Co.	3
BDO Limited (Hong Kong SAR)	3
Dominic K.F. Chan & Co	3
Etania Audit Group P.C.	3
Kempisty & Company CPAs PC	3
Madsen & Associates CPA's, Inc.	3
MS Group CPA LLC	3
UHY Vocation HK CPA Limited	3
Others	47
Total	157

Source: PCAOB (2011).

the New York Stock Exchange typically traded in the OTCBB systems where they would find it difficult to attract investor interest. After the increase in alleged frauds associated with reverse merger companies, both NASDAQ and the NYSE adopted rules that required a seasoning period before a reverse merger company could upgrade its listing to the exchanges (SEC, 2011a). The new rules removed the timing advantage that reverse mergers had over IPOs and Chinese reverse mergers mostly stopped.

Table 5.10 shows that as of June 2011, 83 Chinese reverse mergers had succeeded in listing on the major US exchanges. The list excludes companies that had been delisted prior to June 2011.

Some of these companies used Big Four auditors. When the short selling attacks began in 2010, some companies that were using small accounting

Table 5.10. Chinese Reverse Mergers on US Exchanges.

Exchange	Number of Listings
NASDAQ	60
NYSE – Amex	21
NYSE	2
Total	83

Source: *Bloomberg News* (as of June 2011).

firms switched to Big Four firms (Aubin, 2011). In some cases, the Big Four firm was unable to complete an audit of the company and the company was eventually delisted (SEC, 2013). Pittsburgh Tribune reporter Lou Kilzer (2012) found 105 US listed Chinese companies that had been delisted, were the subject of fraud allegations, or had other serious problems.

In addition to the frauds uncovered in China that involved Big Four auditors, there were also cases in other markets. E&Y paid C$117 million to settle a class action lawsuit alleging shoddy audit work on Sino-Forest Corporation, which was listed on the Toronto Stock Exchange (Koven & Shecter, 2012). E&Y faces further charges from the Ontario Securities Commission on Sino-Forest, and on Zungui Haixi, another Chinese company listed on the Toronto Stock Exchange (McFarland, 2013). Deloitte resigned as auditors for Hong Kong listed Boshiwa International Holdings Limited after it was unable to complete its audit (Armstrong, 2012b).

Investors in companies that were accused of frauds often complained about the failure of auditors to identify the fraud. A short seller alleged that a Big Four firm had signed off on fraudulent accounts because of the involvement of "princelings" (family members of high officials) in the company:

> When given direct evidence of fraudulent accounts in the US filed by a large company with CPC family members as beneficiaries or management a big 4 audit firm will (possibly at the risk to their global franchise) sign the accounts knowing full well that they are fraudulent. The auditors (including and arguably especially the big four) are co-opted for the benefit of Chinese kleptocrats. (Hempton, 2012)

Oqvist (2013) examined auditors of US listed Chinese companies alleged to have committed fraud. He points out that there is considerable judgment applied to determine what constitutes a serious fraud accusation; his list totaled 158 companies (Table 5.11).

Table 5.11 evidences that the Big Four were not involved with most alleged Chinese frauds, but each firm had multiple occurrences. Deloitte

Table 5.11. Auditor of Alleged Frauds of US Listed Chinese Companies.

Firm	Instances	Share
Deloitte & Touche	17	10.8%
Frazier Frost	9	5.7%
Friedman	7	4.4%
Malone Bailey	7	4.4%
Kabani & Co.	6	3.8%
PwC	6	3.8%
E&Y	5	3.2%
Sherb & Co.	5	3.2%
Webb & Co.	5	3.2%
BDO Limited	5	3.2%
Goldman, Kurland and Mohidin LLP	4	2.5%
KPMG	4	2.5%
Marcum, Berstein & Pinchuk LLP	4	2.5%
PKF CPA	4	2.5%
UHY Vocation HK CPA Limited	4	2.5%
Zhong Yi CPA Company Limited	4	2.5%
Others	62	39.2%
Total	158	100.0%

Source: ChinaRai – Fredrik Oqvist.

had more alleged fraud situations than the other Big Four firms combined (Newquist, 2013; Pearson, 2012). Chaley Mah, Deloitte's Asia-Pacific chief executive, said the firm changed the work it did to test cash balances and introduced more-stringent tests to determine whether to take on potential clients. "We have a multilayer process, but if you have clients that are less than honest, it is not easy" Mah told *The Wall Street Journal* (Sanchanta & Mavin, 2013).

5.4.1.1. Auditing Standards for US Listings

On July 12, 2010, the PCAOB issued a Staff Audit Practice Alert (Practice Alert) that was prompted by observations that some US-based firms were issuing reports on financial statements of foreign companies listed in the United States that may not comply with the relevant PCAOB standards. The PCAOB found in a 27-month period, ending March 31, 2010, at least 40 US registered public accounting firms with fewer than 5 partners and fewer than 10 professional staff had issued audit reports on financial statements filed with the SEC by companies whose operations were substantially all in the China region (PCAOB, 2010). In some cases the PCAOB found that the US accounting firms had essentially engaged local firms in China to conduct the audit and had not done sufficient work to justify issuing a report. In one situation cited in the Practice Alert, a US firm retained the services of a consulting firm with Chinese speaking staff who planned the audit, communicated with management and completed a substantial portion of the audit. None of the US firm's partners or employees traveled to China. The work done by the US firm consisted primarily of reviewing certain work papers that had been translated into English, and reviewing the draft financial statements and lead schedules. The PCAOB staff determined that the firm had done insufficient work to justify their opinion.

The situation described above applies principally to smaller auditors and does not apply to the Big Four in China. However, the Practice Alert discusses language considerations that may have a broader effect. PCAOB auditing standards require that an auditor evaluate evidentiary material to determine whether specific audit objectives have been achieved (AU sec 326.25). The Practice Alert states that appropriately satisfying these requirements necessarily entails overcoming any language barriers:

> If the appropriate supervisory personnel of the principal auditor are not sufficiently fluent in the language in which the documentation of the other auditor is prepared, the principal auditor must take necessary actions to enable the principal auditor to fulfill its responsibilities in accordance with PCAOB standards. The principal auditor can neither omit the procedures described in AU sec 543 because of language differences, nor satisfy those requirements by reference to documents that the principal auditor does not understand. (PCAOB, 2010)

While the Practice Alert is directed to situations where the auditor uses the work and reports of other independent auditors it raises the issue of the language skills of supervisory personnel. The majority of partners in Big Four accounting firms are not PRC nationals (Table 5.11). Many of these partners are ethnic Chinese (often from Hong Kong, Singapore or Taiwan, or Mainland Chinese whose families had immigrated to foreign countries in earlier years). The ethnic Chinese partners typically, but not uniformly, can speak and read Mandarin fluently. The spoken language of Hong Kong is Cantonese, which is mutually incomprehensible to a Mandarin speaker. Most Hong Kong accountants assigned to China have developed a high level of proficiency in Mandarin. The written languages are slightly different, with Hong Kong using traditional Chinese characters and the Mainland using simplified Chinese characters, but Hong Kong accountants appear to have little difficulty adapting to the simplified characters.

The question raised by the Practice Alert applies to foreigners in audit supervisory positions who cannot fluently read and speak Chinese. While there are exceptions, most nonethnic Chinese foreigners speak little Mandarin and can read even less. While the firms have scoured the earth looking for Chinese speaking partners and managers, the supply was simply insufficient for the demands of the rapidly expanding China market. In addition, certain clients, particularly the giant SOEs, required deep industry experience that often was not present in an available Chinese speaker. Consequently, many audit partners with the Big Four in China are not literate in Chinese.

Non-Chinese speaking partners and managers were often assigned to lead the engagements of multinational companies. American CPAs were often assigned to work on US listings where the reporting was done in US GAAP. Often the senior engagement partner on large SOEs did not speak Chinese. These non-Chinese speaking partners and managers were unable to evaluate source documents and engage in client discussions that were in the Chinese language. They would need to have source documents translated if they were to evaluate them, or to rely upon bilingual staff to explain them. While many firms initially kept working papers in English, the MOF later required that all working papers be kept in Chinese if the work was used to support the statutory Chinese filings. It is likely that the quality of decisions by audit supervisory personnel will be impaired by the inability to examine original source documentation and to directly engage with the client on accounting issues.

5.5. SECURITIES REGULATION

The listing of Chinese companies on US stock exchanges brought them under American securities regulations. Access to US markets has long been at the cost of increased disclosure requirements (Bailey, Karolyi, & Salva, 2006). In the case of some of the SOEs that sought US listings as part of their reform, the increased disclosures may have been the medicine that Premier Zhu Rongji was looking for (Green, 2004).

A series of corporate scandals in America, including those at Enron and Worldcom, led the US Congress to enact the Sarbanes–Oxley Act of 2002. By tightening auditor independence rules, articulating the professional and ethical responsibilities of auditors, directors and officers, and enhancing corporate disclosure requirements, Sarbanes–Oxley transformed corporate governance in the United States. In the wake of Sarbanes–Oxley, many foreign companies chose to delist their securities in the United States in order to avoid costly compliance with the law (Beaver, McNichols, & Price, 2007; Marosi & Massoud, 2008; Morse, 2005). This trend was not evident among Chinese firms, since many were listed after the effective date of Sarbanes–Oxley. Indeed, if one of the reasons for listing in the United States was to appropriate the higher corporate governance standards of that jurisdiction, Sarbanes–Oxley provided all the more reason for listing large SOEs in the United States. China introduced its own version of the internal control provisions of Sarbanes–Oxley in 2008 with *the Basic Standard for Enterprise Internal Control* (popularly called C-SOX). Chinese companies with both domestic and international listings were required to adopt C-SOX by January, 2011 with companies on the Shanghai and Shenzhen main boards following a year later (Bayron & Ng, 2010).

A study by McKinsey found that investors in US listed Chinese companies lost 72% of value from December 31, 2010 to December 31, 2012 (Cogman, 2013). The increasing number of accounting frauds connected with Chinese companies listed in the United States led the SEC to form a task force focused on the issue (Ackerman, 2011). In addition to pursuing companies and executives suspected of fraud, the task force also scrutinized the "gatekeepers" – the investment banks, consultants, financiers, auditors, and others who helped these businesses gain access to US capital markets. The FBI embedded an agent in the task force who also worked with federal prosecutors. Robert Khuzami, director of enforcement at the SEC said: "Not having proper accounting and reliable audit review for publicly traded companies with operations in China is just not acceptable. We have to find a path to resolution of this issue; It is … a big issue for us" (Shalia-Esa & Lynch, 2011).

5.5.1. SEC v. Deloitte

Longtop Financial Technologies Limited (Longtop) listed on the NYSE in 2007 in an IPO underwritten by Goldman Sachs and Deutsche Bank. It was audited by DTT's member firm in China. Longtop had been a darling of Wall Street; its IPO surged 85% on the first day and it consistently outperformed the technology-heavy NASDAQ composite index. In 2011, Longtop came under attack by Andrew Left of short selling research firm Citron Research (Left, 2011). Left alleged that Longtop's margins were too good to be true. Deloitte had signed off on the previous six audit reports of Longtop, but refused to sign off on the current year, citing a number of problems including evidence that the bank confirmation process had been compromised. Deloltte's resignation led the NYSE to delist the stock, and the SEC began an investigation (Norris, 2011).

The SEC demanded that Deloitte turn over its working papers. Deloitte refused, citing China's laws that prohibited disclosure of working papers to foreign regulators. The SEC then served Deloitte's US counsel with a subpoena with the working papers, which the lawyer, perhaps unwittingly, said he would accept. The SEC then brought action in Federal District Court in Washington, DC to enforce the subpoena. Deloitte argued that Chinese law prohibited them from turning over the working papers, and that Chinese regulators had warned them that doing so could lead to life imprisonment for the partners involved and to the firm being banned from China. The SEC (2011c) argued that American law controlled the situation and that Deloitte must comply.

The SEC's request for Deloitte to provide its working papers was not unusual. Audit working papers are useful documents for investigators. While it would be highly unusual for these working papers to contain any smoking guns that point to the root of the fraud, they document many assertions of fact by management and others associated with the company. With the benefit of hindsight, investigators can use the working papers to figure out who lied to the auditors. Early in a fraud investigation authorities often seek to look at audit working papers to help them better focus their own efforts (Schulzke, 2013).

The SEC engaged in discussions with Chinese regulators to obtain the working papers for Longtop and other companies. The SEC reports that it has made 21 requests in 16 different cases for documents from the CSRC, including three requests for audit working papers. The SEC says it received no meaning assistance from the CSRC. In April 2012, the CSRC indicated that it was willing to cooperate under certain conditions. First, the CSRC would not let the SEC use the information in any legal action without written permission from the CSRC. Second, the CSRC would make its own judgment on what documents to provide. Unsurprisingly, the SEC rejected those conditions (Arevalo, 2013; SEC, 2012b).

The SEC came to the view that the CSRC is not a viable gateway for the production of audit work papers and in May 2012 it charged Deloitte with violations of US securities laws for failure to turn over the audit working papers in another unnamed case (SEC, 2011c).

In July 2012, SEC Chairman Mary Schapiro visited Beijing and met with high-level Chinese officials to discuss the problem of accessing documents necessary for the SEC to enforce American securities laws. Schapiro was sufficiently encouraged by the prospect for agreement that the SEC went to court after she returned to Washington and asked the judge in the Deloitte case to stay his opinion for six months while they sought a negotiated settlement with Chinese regulators (Viswanatha & Aubin, 2012).

5.5.2. SEC v. Big Four

The SEC began to seek audit working papers from other members of the Big Four in connected with alleged accounting frauds. Each of these firms also refused to provide the working papers to the SEC following the arguments advanced by Deloitte – that doing so would violate Chinese law and subject the firm and its partners to punishment in China.

In October 2012, the CSRC informed SEC staff that the CSRC had come to the view that audit work papers could be shared with the SEC. But they still insisted on retaining veto power over their use. If the SEC did not agree to this condition, then they said that the request might take an indeterminate amount of time as the CSRC consulted with other government bureaus.

The CSRC was invited to come to Washington in November 2012 for meetings with the PCAOB. The CSRC asked to meet with the SEC on the same trip. The SEC told the CSRC that unless they were prepared to hand over the working papers, there was not much sense in talking about them and instead said they should discuss other regulatory matters. The SEC point person on the audit working papers did not attend the meeting that was held on November 26, yet the SEC informed the CSRC at that meeting that it was going to move ahead on the issue.

Chinese regulators signaled that they would like to deal. Tong Daochi, CSRC Director General International told a conference in Hong Kong on November 26 that "We have engaged with the SEC, SFC, and PCAOB on audit working papers and we are making progress and I think we should be able to work out a way to get them out" (Verghese, 2013).

The following Monday, December 3, 2012, the SEC filed administrative charges against the China affiliates of the Big Four accounting firms, Deloitte, E&Y, KPMG, and PwCs, as well as second-tier accounting firm BDO. The charges were based on the failure of the firms to comply with requests to supply audit working papers to the SEC, as is required by Sarbanes–Oxley (SEC, 2012a).

An SEC administrative trial judge will decide the case against the accounting firms. Under SEC rules, the judge has 300 days to make a decision. The judge may impose sanctions against the accounting firms. In the past, accounting firms that have gotten into trouble with the SEC have faced a range of penalties from admonishment to a ban on practice before the SEC. A ban on practice means the firm can no longer audit public companies. In a couple of prior cases in the United States, Big Four firms have faced a temporary ban on accepting new SEC clients. The penalty most expected in the present cases would be to ban the firms from auditing US listed Chinese companies. The ban could also include forbidding the firms from participating in the audits of any US listed company. This would create huge problems for US multinationals with China operations, and accordingly would seem to be an unlikely outcome.

If the audit firms are banned from auditing US listed Chinese companies these companies would be without an auditor. All US listed companies are required to be audited annually by an accounting firm registered with the PCOAB. Failure to have an auditor leads to the company being delisted from the stock exchanges, and the company will eventually lose its registration as a public company when it is unable to file an annual report with audited financial statements.

The SEC also recommenced the suspended case against Deloitte, advising the District Court judge that negotiations had failed. If the judge decided to uphold the subpoena, it appears likely that Deloitte would refuse to comply since they believe that to do so would break Chinese law. Refusing to turn over the working papers under court order likely would have led to the judge finding Deloitte in contempt of court, and the penalties for contempt might be even more severe, precluding Deloitte's China partners from visiting the United States for fear of arrest.

Under the SEC case, only the five firms that have been charged faced a current threat to their practice rights before the SEC. Should these firms be banned, their clients could select one of the other PCAOB registered firms to do their audit. Although there are 41 of such firms in China, it is unlikely that any other than the Big Four have the skills necessary to audit the larger US listed Chinese companies, some of which are among the largest companies in the world.

The SEC scheduled a public hearing on July 10, 2013. Shortly before the hearing, CSRC officials contacted the SEC to say that they were ready to turn over the working papers in the Longtop case. The SEC then advised the court in the Deloitte case that they had received notice from the CSRC that they intended to produce the working papers on Longtop Financial Technologies, Limited (Triedman, 2013). According to testimony by Alberto Arevalo of the SEC at the administrative trial of the Big Four, the

CSRC offered to send 20 boxes of working papers if the SEC first paid the shipping charges. Arevalo expressed his opinion that he does not believe that getting records through the CSRC is a viable option (Lynch & Yukhananov, 2013).

While each of these cases remain unresolved as of December 2013, it appears that Chinese regulators are likely to prevail at preventing the SEC from unfettered access to records in China. The provision of the Longtop working papers would seem to resolve the subpoena case against Deloitte. If the CSRC then releases the working papers related to the cases against the Big Four and BDO, it seems likely that these cases will be dismissed as well. The CSRC has placed themselves as gatekeepers to China for the SEC, and while the SEC finds that unacceptable, it may not be able to do much about it.

If the CSRC provides the working papers in all of the instances that led to the charges against the Big Four and BDO, it seems likely that the charges will be dismissed. From a technical standpoint, the charges are for the offense of not providing the working papers when requested, but it seems unlikely the SEC would continue the cases if they had the requested working papers.

5.5.3. SFC v. Ernst & Young

Standard Water Limited pursued an IPO in Hong Kong in 2009. Before the listing was completed, E&Y resigned as reporting accountants and auditors, citing the discovery of certain inconsistencies in documentation. The Securities and Futures Commission, Hong Kong's securities regulator, issued a formal notice to E&Y seeking its working papers related to Standard Water. When E&Y refused, SFC brought suit in the Court of First Instance (Securities and Futures Commission, 2012).

The suit was brought against E&Y's Hong Kong affiliate, since it was the reporting accountant. E&Y Hong Kong indicated it did not have the working papers, since it had outsourced the work to its Mainland affiliate, E&Y Hua Ming. E&Y Hua Ming refused to turn over the working papers citing the same reasons used in the SEC case (Yiu, 2013).

The suit brought to light a common practice for the Big Four in Hong Kong to lend their name to audit reports of Chinese companies listed in Hong Kong when they did not perform an audit but instead outsourced the work to their Mainland affiliate.

5.5.4. Public Company Accounting Oversight Board

The Sarbanes–Oxley Act established the PCAOB. The PCAOB was given the responsibility to regulate the auditors of public companies listed in the United States. The US SEC oversee the PCAOB. Its responsibilities include the authority to set auditing standards and independence rules. It also has the authority to inspect the compliance of auditors with the rules of the PCAOB and the SEC, and the authority to bring disciplinary action against individuals and firms found to be in violation of these rules (Giles, Venuti, & Jones, 2004). All auditors of US listed companies must register with the PCAOB (2013a) and be subject to its jurisdiction.

One of the key requirements of Sarbanes–Oxley is the requirement that accounting firms register with the PCAOB in order to become "Registered Independent Accountants" eligible to audit the financial statements of US registrants. Foreign firms that audit or play a substantial role in the audit of US issuers must register with the PCAOB. There are 914 accounting firms outside the United States that are registered with the PCAOB as of May 2012, including 45 in China and 51 in Hong Kong. Only 9 of the China registered firms and 17 of the Hong Kong registered firms actually issue reports on US listed companies (PCAOB, 2013g). The registered firms include the Chinese affiliates of the Big Four and other global accounting networks. Each member firm of accounting firm networks needs to separately register with the PCAOB if it issues reports or plays a significant role in audits of US listed companies. By comparison, Japan the 3rd largest global economy after the United States and China, has only 17 PCAOB registered accounting firms (PCAOB, 2013f).

5.5.5. PCAOB Inspections

PCAOB inspections are conducted annually for the nine US-based firms that audit more than 100 issuers. These annually inspected firms include the US affiliates of the Big Four (PCAOB, 2013b). All other registered firms that issue reports, including all of the nine firms in China that issue reports on US listed companies, are to be inspected every three years.

The PCAOB has been an active regulator since its formation in 2002. Inspection reports of the PCAOB are partially released to the public and have been highly critical of auditing practices. The Big Four have received particularly harsh criticism for lacking skepticism and for failing to obtain sufficient evidence to support their audit opinions. Many credit the PCAOB for overhauling the audit profession, changing long practiced ways of doing audits and increasing the quality of audits (Carcello, Hollingsworth, & Mastrolia, 2011; Center for Audit Quality, 2012; Gunny & Zhang, 2013).

The PCAOB (2013e) began conducting international inspections in 2005, and has conducted inspections in 38 countries through June 30, 2012. A number of countries, including China and much of Europe, objected to PCAOB inspections on grounds of data privacy or national sovereignty. China also forbid the PCAOB (2013c) from conducting inspections in Hong Kong to the extent that the audits to be examined included companies that have operations on the Mainland. While Hong Kong is generally treated as a separate territory in matters related to international regulation, China asserted its sovereignty over PCAOB inspections in Hong Kong that involved clients with Mainland operations, which included virtually all clients of the Hong Kong firms.

Under the PCAOB's rules, the initial inspections of foreign registered firms were to be completed by December 31, 2009. As that deadline approached, it became apparent that the obstacles to inspections put up by various countries meant the deadline would be missed. The PCAOB changed its rules to defer the deadline for inspections to December 31, 2012. The rules allowed the board to postpone, for up to three years, the first inspection of any non-US firm that the board is currently required to conduct by the end of 2009 and that is in a jurisdiction where the board has not conducted an inspection before 2009. In the meantime, the PCAOB published the names of accounting firms and issuers that have not been inspected. The list, dominated by Chinese firms and issuers, is available on the PCAOB (2013c) website.

Since 2009, the PCAOB has been actively concluding negotiations with many countries to obtain access to conduct inspections. Most of these negotiations sought arrangements for joint inspections, where PCAOB inspectors work side by side with local inspectors to review audit firms. Ten agreements have been reached since 2009, and James Doty, PCAOB chairman, announced in 2013 that a number of agreements were close to conclusion (Doty, 2013).

Negotiations with China have been underway since shortly after the PCAOB began international inspections in 2005. PCAOB member Charles Niemeier traveled to Beijing in March 2007 to meet with the MOF and CSRC about PCAOB inspections of Chinese firms registered with the PCAOB (2007), but no resolution was reached.

China's position is that foreign regulators enforcing foreign laws on Chinese soil against Chinese companies violate China's national sovereignty.

In a 2009 letter commenting on the PCAOB's proposed delay in the deadline for foreign inspections, the CSRC said "that under the current Chinese laws and regulations, PCAOB is not allowed to perform any kind of independent or joint on-site inspection in the Chinese territory" (Tong & Zhou, 2009). The CSRC set forth China's position to the SEC in a comment letter on proposed inspection rules:

> Our position remains unchanged, i.e. cross-border inspection must abide by the principles of respecting mutual sovereignty and cooperating as equals…To address the challenges of cross-border inspection which are brought up by listing of public companies in host jurisdictions, the SEC and the CSRC should work together as equals under the existing framework for regulatory cooperation. Therefore, the oversight of Chinese accounting firms should fully rely on the work of the CSRC…We are strongly opposed to PCAOB's inspection on any Chinese accounting firm before any consensus has been reached between China and the U.S. (CSRC, 2009)

The Chinese position was consistent with arrangements that China reached with Europe. In 2011, the European Union recognized the equivalence of the audit oversight systems in 10 third countries, including China. The third countries and EU member states can now mutually rely on each other's inspections of audits (Kleinman, Lin, & Palmon, 2013). Chinese regulators want the same regulatory equivalency treatment from the United States as they get from the EU.

CSRC's assertion that the PCAOB should fully rely on the work of the CSRC has significant flaws. First, the regulatory power of the CRSC extends only to Chinese accounting firms with securities licenses in China. Not all of the Chinese firms registered with the PCAOB have securities licenses in China and without such as license they are not subject to CSRC inspections, although they do remain under MOF jurisdiction. Hong Kong Accounting firms are not subject to the regulatory jurisdiction of either MOF or the CSRC, although they are subject to regulation by the Hong Kong Institute of CPAs (HKICPA). As a result, the CSRC is unable to fulfill the PCAOB's role with respect to all registered firms in China and Hong Kong. While all of the registered firms are subject to either MOF or HKICPA regulation, there are no processes in place that would require inspections of the nature required by the PCAOB. Second, CSRC inspections relate only to audits of issuers of securities on Chinese exchanges and accordingly would not include the many Chinese companies that, while listed on US exchanges, are not listed in China. MOF examiners focus on reports prepared under CAS and do not examine the audits of financial statements prepared for use outside of China. Third, CSRC, MOF, and HKICPA examiners are not expert in PCAOB auditing standards or US

GAAP and would be unable to assess compliance with these standards. It is highly doubtful that examiners from these agencies would be willing to enforce foreign rules that are stricter than local rules. It is also unlikely that employees of these agencies, already struggling with the implementation of IFRS, would devote the training resources to develop the necessary skills to evaluate the auditing of US public companies.

Apparently frustrated with the pace of negotiations over access to China in order to conduct inspections, the PCAOB, on October 7, 2010, announced new processes for foreign firms that wish to register with the PCAOB. New registrants will be required to certify that inspections will be permitted. If they cannot do so (such as in China) they can either ask that their application be held in suspension or ask that it be allowed to proceed. If the application proceeds, the PCAOB will schedule a hearing specifying as a proposed ground for disapproval of the application the obstacle to the board's ability to inspect the firm. The firm will be given the opportunity at the hearing to argue that the registration is in the interest of investors and the public. The new rules making it difficult for Chinese auditors to register with the PCAOB do not affect the 59 Chinese accounting firms that were already registered.

Politicians in the United States began to turn the heat up on the PCAOB to address the inability to conduct inspections in China. Senator Chuck Schumer of New York wrote to James Doty of the PCAOB on November 22, 2011, chastising the PCAOB for their failure to inspect Chinese audit firms, writing "In the case of Chinese audit firms, the board is failing to do its job" (Schumer, 2011). Schumer called for the PCAOB to exercise its enforcement authority against Chinese audit firms that have not submitted to independent regulatory review. PCAOB chairman James Doty claimed that the PCAOB was not subject to political pressure in a speech to Baruch College, but admitted that Congress or the White House could stop them:

> No jurisdiction should think that we will not act because the political consequences are too great. Congress can tell us that. The White House can tell us that. The one thing that the Supreme Court decision about FEF vs. PCAOB decided was that we are part of the executive branch and we're subject to oversight by the White House, like the Treasury Department, and they can tell us to stop or pause. (Cohn, 2012a)

Chinese authorities became concerned that the PCAOB might act unilaterally to deregister accounting firms, an action that led to the delisting of Chinese companies from US exchanges. In a diplomatic cable released by Wikileaks, it was said that China warned:

> ... that any unilateral sanctions by PCAOB against Chinese listed firms would be roblematic for our bilateral relationship ... Shang and Geithner agreed that each country

> faces legal limitations and urged each other to be creative, pragmatic, and flexible. Given that the CSRC is working with the Ministry of Finance to seek possible solutions, and he urged PCAOB to avoid imposing unilateral sanctions. Shang and Geithner agreed to enhance bilateral exchanges to resolve the issue in a mutually acceptable manner. (Wikileaks, 2009)

A promising breakthrough came in August 2012, when Chinese regulators agreed to allow PCAOB inspectors to observe a portion of the Chinese inspection of E&Y in China. The PCAOB was only allowed to observe the quality control portions of the inspection and was not allowed to inspect any audit working papers. PCAOB member Lew Ferguson indicated that the observations were a "trust-building" exercise and did not meet the requirements of inspections (Aubin, 2012a, 2012b; Ferguson, 2012).

Chinese regulators came to Washington the week of November 26, 2012 to meet with the PCAOB and the SEC. The SEC meetings did not lead to a breakthrough and the SEC brought charges against the Chinese accounting firms the following Monday.

The PCAOB presented a proposal to Chinese officials in the meetings during the week of November 26. That proposal was likely for joint inspections along the lines of the agreements that have been signed with many other countries. PCAOB Chairman James Doty told an auditing conference in New York "the current state is not sustainable. We are coming to a crossroads where we will have to make some important decisions about how to best protect investors" (Doty, 2013).

The extended inspection deadline of December 31, 2012 passed without action by the PCAOB, which was then out of compliance with its own rules. PCAOB member Lewis Ferguson told a Reuter's report "we've had periods before where we ran over deadlines while trying to get things done." Ferguson indicated that Chinese regulators were reviewing a PCAOB proposal they received in November and that "there is forward movement" and "the number of issues … has been narrowed significantly" (Byrnes & Lynch, 2012).

On May 7, 2013 the PCAOB, MOF, and CSRC signed a memorandum of understanding on enforcement cooperation (PCAOB, 2013d). The agreement provided that Chinese regulators would assist in providing documents to the PCAOB in connection with enforcement activities. Enforcement activities, however, are not a significant part of the PCAOB's workload. In 2012, only 11 sanctions were handed out by the PCAOB, three of which related to Chinese audits (PCAOB, 2013h). The primary function of the PCAOB is inspections, and the agreement did not provide for inspection access (Gillis, 2013a). PCAOB chairman James Doty told Reuters that the agreement was "a step in the right direction," but it did not replace the need for the PCAOB to inspect accounting firms in China (Aubin, 2013).

5.5.6. US–China Strategic and Economic Dialogue

In 2009 President Barack Obama and President Hu Jintao established a Strategic and Economic Dialogue (SED) to discuss important issues in the relationship of the two countries.[8] The SED is a high level meeting that includes the US Treasury Secretary, the Secretary of State, and other high level officials from the United States. Their Chinese counterparts have included the vice premier and high-level ministers (US Department of Treasury, 2013c).

The issue of PCAOB inspections was added to the agenda of the first meeting held in Washington, DC on July 28, 2009. Agreement was reached to continue talking about the issues:

> The United States and China welcome continued dialogue between the bilateral competent authorities on the oversight of accounting firms providing audit services for public companies in the two countries based on mutual respect for sovereignty and laws. (US Department of Treasury, 2009)

No discussion of accounting regulatory cooperation was included in the fact sheets for the second meeting of the SED held in Beijing on May 27, 2010 (US Department of Treasury, 2010). At the third meeting of the SED that was held in Washington on May 10, 2011, agreement was reached to make joint efforts to accelerate the process of reaching agreement on cross-border audit oversight (US Department of Treasury, 2011). On July 11–12, 2011 the Sino-US Symposium on Audit Oversight was held in Beijing. Board Member Lewis Ferguson of the PCAOB and SEC Deputy Chief Accountant Mike Starr led the US delegation, which met with CSRC Chairman Shang Fulin and other officials (SEC, 2011d). The symposium provided Chinese regulators with information on the PCOAB and its inspection process.

The fourth meeting of the SED was held on May 4, 2012 in Beijing. For the first time, PCAOB Chairman James Doty was included in the US delegation and he conducted meetings with Chinese regulators on the sidelines of the meeting. No mention of accounting regulation was included in the fact sheets (US Department of Treasury, 2012).

The fifth meeting of the SED was held on July 12 in Washington, DC. PCAOB Chairman James Doty was again included in the US delegation. No breakthrough on PCAOB inspections was reached. Instead, the joint fact sheet reported "Both parties commit to strengthen communication and cooperation on accounting and to share observations about accounting practices in their respective markets" (US Department of Treasury, 2013a). In his public remarks at the close of the SED, Treasury Secretary Jacob Lew said:

> China's securities regulator announced that it will begin providing certain requested audit work papers to our market regulators, an important step towards resolving a long-standing impasse on enforcement cooperation related to companies that are listed in the United States. (US Department of Treasury, 2013b)

Lew was referring to the announcement that the CSRC had offered to turn over the working papers on Longtop to the SEC. PCAOB spokesperson Colleen Brennan told Reuters that while the announcement of the release of working papers to the SEC was a positive step forward, the PCAOB wanted to strike a second agreement with the Chinese to allow for inspections (Lynch & Yukhananov, 2013).

NOTES

1. KWTF would merge with DTT in 1997.
2. At the time, none of the US member firms of the Big Six (the largest member firms in the Big Six networks) had revenue of US$1 billion, although the firms met this threshold on a global basis. China's two-one proposal failed to recognize the legal structure of the Big Six.
3. The author participated in some of these meetings. The meetings included a representative from each firm who was not necessarily the managing partner or chairman of the firm. Stuttard's representations concerning the meetings are consistent with the author's recollections.
4. Rightists and capitalist roaders were two of the seven categories of black elements (*hei qi lei*) that were the enemies of communism, together with landlords, rich peasants, counterrevolutionaries, bad elements, and reactionary academic authorities (Li, 1997).
5. IFRS supplanted IAS in 2001.
6. H-shares are shares issued by state-controlled mainland corporations that are listed on the Hong Kong Stock Exchange.
7. A red chip is an internationally organized company (typically Hong Kong or Cayman Islands) that owns a company based on the mainland.
8. The SED replaced similar meetings that had been held under the Bush Administration.

CHAPTER 6

MAINTAINING HEGEMONY

> Although the Big Six compete against one another, they are comrades in occupying China's market. Wolves are wolves anyhow.
>
> – Lin Xiaoren, January 6, 1997 (Ding, 2006b, p. 550)

Chapter 5 explained how foreign direct investment into China and the use of stock markets as a means to reform SOEs served as the key hegemonic projects that allowed the Big Four firms to establish dominance in the CPA profession in China. This chapter focuses on the period of time that followed Tiananmen Square until the early years of the 21st century. This chapter extends the history of the Big Four in China to the present.

Following the theory established by Hunt (1990) that was discussed in Chapter 2, the hegemonic class must address and incorporate some aspects of the aspirations, interests, and ideology of the subordinate class if it wishes to retain its dominant position. The Big Four came to dominate the accounting markets because they were not local. Local firms were viewed to lack the expertise, independence, and name recognition of international firms, attributes that were considered necessary in the early years of China's reform and opening up. As will be discussed in Chapter 8, local firms began to address their perceived shortcomings. In order to maintain their hegemony, the Big Four would need to engage in a compromise to incorporate some of the interests of the domestic firms.

This chapter explains that while the Big Four achieved dominance because they were not local, they then attempted to sustain their dominance by becoming local. Rather than holding themselves out as different than local firms, they tried to become local firms, hiring large numbers of local staff and seeking legal structures similar to local firms. They would have a mixed record of success, succeeding at significantly localizing the staffing of the firms but failing to completely turn the ownership over to local nationals.

The chapter begins with an exploration of the people dimension. The major effort of the Big Four to become more Chinese was accomplished by hiring more Chinese. The Big Four has hired and trained significant numbers of accountants in China, and in the process has populated its staff ranks primarily with local nationals. The demands for experienced talent, however, could not be met with local hires because there were no people in the market with the needed skills. As a result, the firms have used large numbers of expatriates, many of whom became partners in China and became vested in careers based in China.

The large number of foreign partners would frustrate efforts to fully localize the practices. As a result, the firms would seek out alternative operating structures that would permit the continued involvement of foreign partners. Ultimately, the Big Four would have to access the power of the World Trade Organization (WTO) to maintain the right for foreign partners to continue in China. China would ultimately win this fight when the terms for the joint ventures expired.

The chapter concludes by presenting findings on the present structure of the accounting profession in China.

6.1. THE PEOPLE DIMENSION

Finding and retaining adequate staffing resources has been a constant problem for the Big Four's throughout their presence in China. China may have 1.4 billion people, but not nearly enough of them are the trained accountants that are needed to serve the rapidly modernizing economy. In 2008, a representative of DTT said that the mainland needs 350,000 qualified accountants, but only 130,000 members of the CICPA were available (James, 2008).

6.1.1. Staff Headcounts

The Big Six were allowed to directly recruit and hire staff once they established joint ventures in 1992. Modest numbers of staff joined the joint venture firms from the state sponsored joint venture partner, but most staff were recruited directly or transferred from foreign offices of the Big Six. Ivan Chan, AA's managing partner for China said the recruits were highly skilled, but: "The only problem is the country's one-child per family rule[1] has created a pampered new generation with high expectations, making staff retention difficult" (Jack, 1993b).

The number of employees grew steadily though the 1990s as shown in Table 6.1, prepared from data included in a CICPA inspection report.

Data are not available on staffing levels from 1998 to 2003 for all firms. Data has been collected from the Big Four firms for later years. Some of the firms had retained limited data for years prior to 2004. By agreement between the researcher and the Big Four firms, only summary data are reported and only for years for which data are available for all firms. Staff levels for 2004–2008 are reported in Table 6.2.

In 2007, the Big Four accounting firms each announced plans to significantly increase staff numbers by 2010. At that time, PwC reported staff levels of about 8,000 and said it expected to increase to 13,000.

Table 6.1. Big Six Mainland China Staffing: 1993–1997.

Firm	1993	1994	1995	1996	1997
Arthur Andersen	52	100	208	246	279
KPMG	65	104	152	165	220
E & Y	13	42	67	95	137
Coopers & Lybrand	85	108	170	200	232
Deloitte Touche Tohmatsu	28	124	201	296	505
Price Waterhouse	40	180	279	338	435
Total	283	658	1,077	1,340	1,808
Growth rate		133%	64%	24%	35%

Source: Ding (2006b, p. 443).

Table 6.2. Big Four Mainland China Staffing: 2004–2008 – All Firms.

Staff Level	2004	2005	2006	2007	2008
Partners	278	364	467	604	731
Senior Mgr/director	356	462	638	842	970
Managers	707	855	1,136	1,625	2,081
Seniors	1,639	2,224	3,033	4,944	6,379
Staff/associates	3,626	4,676	6,895	8,156	9,849
Total professional staff	6,606	8,581	12,169	16,171	20,010
Support staff	1,065	1,311	1,802	2,334	2,839
Total staff	7,671	9,892	13,971	18,505	22,849
Growth rate		28%	41%	32%	23%

Source: Author survey.

KPMG planned to increase from 5,000 to 9,000; DTT from 6,000 to 10,000; and E&Y from 5,500 to 10,000 (*Nikkei Report*, 2007). In 2013, DTT said it had a new target of 15,000 people by 2015 (Cohn, 2013). Based on survey data the base numbers reported in the article were slightly overstated and in certain cases may have included Hong Kong personnel as well as those located on the mainland. Anecdotal evidence indicates that the global recession that began in 2008 led the Big Four to temporarily lower those targets.

Speculation began as to how quickly the China operations would become the largest in the Big Four's networks. James Turley, Global CEO of E&Y said: "The question is not whether we need 9,000 people or 10,000; the question is how do we get to 30,000? So that is the path we are on" (Chien, 2009). In 2008, James Quigley, global CEO of DTT said: "…if China sustains its current growth track, it will not take long before China becomes the largest operation for Deloitte, passing the U.S." (Yiu, 2008). David Wu of PwC observed:

> To put the potential for growth in perspective, consider that today China's GDP is more than half that of the US, while at the same time, the number of partners and staff in PwC China is only one-third that of the US firm. (*China Daily*, 2013)

A significant shortage of accountants in China resulted in pressures on salaries to rise. According to a Mercer Human Resource Consulting study the average salary for accountants at Big Four firms in China rose 30% to $9,000 in 2005 over the prior year (Proctor & Qui, 2006). PwC experienced an embarrassing public work action in 2004 by employees dissatisfied with compensation and high workloads. PwC had allowed compensation levels to drop below competitors after the acquisition of the Chinese operations of AA. PwC was perhaps seeking rents for its market leading position or perhaps it was paying lower salaries in an attempt to maintain partner income while working through issues related to its acquisition of AA. The dispute, extensively covered in local and international newspapers, was settled through significant pay and benefit increases (Chan, 2004a, 2004b; *Shanghai Daily*, 2004).

As the recession hit in late 2008, the rapid growth of the firms came to a quick stop. The firms responded with layoffs and unpaid leaves. The unpaid leaves were hoped to lead to the retention of staff who would be needed when the market rebounded (Nakamoto, 2009; Yiu, 2009). Anecdotal evidence says that as the economy recovered in China in 2010, the firms began to experience record levels of turnover, indicating that staff shortages will likely persist in China.

6.1.2. Campus Recruiting

The Big Four have globally had a long tradition of hiring mostly new college graduates. This practice has enabled the firms to instill their culture and professionalism before the recruits are influenced by experience in another organization. As the firms experienced rapid global growth in the 1980s and 1990s, experienced hires became more common, yet the ubiquitous presence of the Big Four on college campuses worldwide remains today (Wyatt, 2004).

Beginning in 1993, international accounting firms were permitted to recruit on campus after they had opened joint venture firms. They quickly established themselves as the leading recruiters on many campuses, offering starting salaries that, while modest by Western standards, typically exceeded the highest lifetime earnings of the student's parents and the salaries of their professors. Dave McCann of PwC said: "Hiring talented local graduates in significant numbers is essential. China has a lot of talent, and we have put a huge effort into on-campus recruitment" (Boland, 2006).

The firms targeted bilingual students from any field of study. The working language of the firms tended to be English, because most clients required reporting in English. Later MOF regulations would require that working papers be prepared in Chinese, but English capabilities would always be critical for accountants working in the Big Four in China. In the early years there were few accounting majors at Chinese universities, and even fewer with adequate English skills. As a result, the majority of hires had majored in subjects other than accounting. Peter Yu of KPMG observed: "The job market is very competitive. Students may choose to join other industries, like banking or other finance related fields. We have to spread our net really wide" (James, 2008). In 2008, the Big Four hired 5,787 new recruits who had graduated from or studied at college campuses in Mainland China. Thirty-two percent were accounting majors, 44% other business related majors, and 24% had majored in nonbusiness areas. The Big Four now recruits at over 100 universities in China, yet acquire half of their new hires from 20 schools, including China's elite universities: Peking University, Tsinghua University, and Fudan University. In 2008, the Big Four hired only 157 new graduates from foreign universities, 2.6% of total campus recruits. Few graduates of Hong Kong universities would be hired to work on the mainland (Tam, 2002). By the early 2000s, Hong Kong graduates were considered too expensive and without superior English skills for mainland assignments, although they had been used extensively in earlier years.

A survey of 46,080 Chinese students from 90 leading universities in China found the Big Four included in the top 100 most attractive employers by business majors. PwC was 14th, KPMG was 20th, DTT was 23rd, and E&Y was 44th. No local accounting firm made the top 100, although Chinese enterprises took 8 of the top 10 slots (Universum, 2011).

The Big Four brought their international recruiting practices to China, and local accounting firms were slow to react. Local firms were accustomed to the former state practice of assignment of graduates to work units, and were unprepared to compete for staff. Salaries offered by the Big Four were well above the levels existing in local firms. Consequently, local firms did not participate in the market for top talent at China's leading universities. Only recently have some of the larger indigenous firms begun to recruit at China's better universities. For top talent, the Big Four competed vigorously against other MNCs, and each other, but not with the local accounting firms. Over time, the difference in talent would create a significant advantage for the Big Four.

6.1.3. Experienced and Expatriate Hires

While there was a large supply of new university graduates available to the international accounting firms, there were virtually no experienced auditors in the market. Until the local staff could be developed, the firms needed to rely on expatriate staff. Kent Watson (personal correspondence, November 10, 2008) of PwC recounts: "We scoured the world looking for Chinese speaking staff to bring to China. The China firm was built with people who were willing to come to China, not necessarily by the best people available."

The firms could not find enough Chinese-speaking expatriates, particularly for positions requiring specific leadership skills or industry knowledge. Consequentially, they would often need to bring to China expatriates who could not speak or read Chinese. Expatriate personnel were very expensive, leading the firms to incur substantial losses in early years. Sir John Stuttard (personal correspondence, September 1, 2009) of C&L commented on the high cost of expatriates:

> It was expensive to employ partners and managers from other countries, sometimes with wives and families. In the mid-1990s, the PRC was considered to be a hardship posting and additional allowances had to be paid, including incentive bonuses, cars, chauffeurs, housing allowances etc.

In the years following China's accession to WTO, the boom in foreign investment coupled with increasing IPOs of Chinese companies tested the capacity of the Big Four to serve the market. One investment banker observed: "My impression is that the Big Four are stretched. I've seen cases where clients may have to delay a transaction because their auditors can't provide resources at short notice" (Jopson, 2006b). The Big Four firms acknowledged the problem. Steven Taylor of DTT said "We are having to turn work away because we just don't have enough people" (Jopson, 2006a). The firms would find a way to serve major opportunities, but smaller and riskier clients needed to use firms other than the Big Four. Francis Sui of KPMG said "The fact we don't have enough people doesn't stop us from taking a good client, but they have to be very tempting" (Jopson, 2006a). The staff shortages allowed the Big Four to increase prices and to finally achieve profitability after a long period of investment (Chan, 2005).

The ability of the Big Four to fund the considerable investments in expatriate workers gave them an insurmountable advantage over poorly capitalized local firms. In the first years of the 21st century the Big Four firms turned profitable, and the problem shifted from developing a rudimentary practice to meeting the demands of an increasingly large and complex market. The shortage of staff in the early years of the 2000s should have created an opening for local firms to gain market share. As can be seen from Table 6.12, this failed to happen and the Big Four continued to gain market share until 2007. There are several reasons for this result. First, the barriers to serving MNC clients and clients with foreign listings proved too high for local firms to surmount. Second, while local firms were growing at a rate slower than the Big Four, they were still growing at a remarkable rate, and likely faced the same challenges finding qualified staff, particularly with the Big Four dominating recruiting at universities. Paradoxically, the Big Four ultimately helped local firms to solve the staffing riddle. As the Big Four market slowed markedly following the 2008 global financial crisis, local firms succeeded in hiring well-trained accountants from the Big Four firms.

To meet the needs of the burgeoning market in the early 2000s, the Big Four firms began a worldwide search for Chinese-speaking accountants. Hong Kong had largely been tapped out. By 2005, two-thirds of Hong Kong accountants were already working on the mainland (Chan, 2005). Dave McCann (personal correspondence, June 16, 2009) recalled the PwC strategy to address this issue was to seek Chinese-speaking accountants in Southeast Asia:

> What we went on to do was a fairly explicit targeting of Southeast Asia: Malaysia and Singapore in particular. Obviously language was an issue; quality was strong typically

> out of Singapore. Singapore was particularly attractive, but they're expensive. Malaysia was more attractive because they were cheaper, but there was a bit of a language issue. Both however, were cheaper than Americans.

Singaporean accountants could expect a 40% salary increase by going to China (Lee, 2006). The increase for Malaysians was said to be even higher, and one Big Four partner wondered how Malaysian accounting firms could cope after having lost so many qualified accountants to China. PwC was not the only firm looking south for accountants. Joe Tsang of E&Y said in 2005:

> There is always talk in the market that the Big Four do not have sufficient manpower to serve such a dynamic market. We admit that is our current challenge...For example; we have been hiring people from Singapore, Malaysia, Australia, even Canada, and the UK. We have been targeting people who have the language skills to come to this region to work...We hire university graduates every year, but we are also making a lot of experienced hires from the market. (*International Accounting Bulletin*, 2005)

Overseas Chinese, particularly Singaporeans, did not always easily adjust to the Chinese working environment. Although they were ethnically Chinese, Singaporeans and other overseas Chinese have developed different value systems (Ralston et al., 1993). Many viewed their assignment to China as an opportunity to return to their homeland, but were shocked by what they found. An interviewee of Yeoh and Willis (2005, p. 275) aptly expresses this reaction: "Lucky that our ancestors left the place, or we'd be one of them!"

In 2007, PwC started a program to send recruiters to London, New York, Sydney for the purpose of recruiting graduates and experienced accountants with international experience and Chinese knowledge and language skills (*Nikkei Report*, 2007). The program was funded by the international organization of PwC.

Conflict between overseas Chinese and local staff was a consistent theme in the interviews conducted for this study. Some Western partners referred to overseas Chinese staff as "Hong Kong mercenaries," who came to China solely to collect the higher salaries available with no commitment to the development of a local practice. Local staff often complained of overseas Chinese, particularly those from Hong Kong, as coming to steal their birthright.

6.1.4. Poaching

Facing critical staff shortages that limited the ability of the firms to take on new clients, the Big Four firms began to recruit from one another. Through

2000, there had been little movement of people between Big Four firms. In one of the few exceptions, PW had recruited Charles Feng, the Chinese representative to AA's joint venture, and AA had bitterly protested this hiring to the CICPA. Self-restraint among the firms against poaching ended after the PwC/AA merger. Anthony Wu, Chairman of E&Y acknowledged in 2004 that they were undertaking the practice of poaching staff from other firms: "There is a significant shortage of accountants in China. We have no choice but to pay higher salaries to recruit experienced accountants from other Chinese accounting firms" (Yiu, 2004c). As Table 6.6 indicates, E&Y had gotten off to a slow start in China and needed to play catch-up. Failing to acquire AA in China had been a wake-up call for the global firm of E&Y. E&Y took advantage of merger turmoil at PwC to recruit approximately 10 former AA partners and a considerable number of managers and staff who were disenchanted with their new firm (*Birmingham Post*, 2007). The recruits included Albert Ng, the former managing partner of AA who was managing mainland operations for PwC. Ng became the Senior Partner of E&Y following a series of auditing scandals at E&Y in Hong Kong.

Local firms have begun to look for talent in the Big Four firms and other local firms. A partner in a second-tier firm said that they were having increased success at hiring managers from Big Four firms who were disillusioned with the limited promotion opportunities in the Big Four as the business began to slow after 2009. In 2012, about 350 staff and partners from PKF in China joined BDO China (Reed, 2012).

6.1.5. Localization

Increasing disillusionment by MNCs with the financial performance of their Chinese investments during the 1990s turned the attention of foreign business to the topic of localization (Heim, 1997). Poon and Rowley's (2007) content analysis of two leading human resource journals found increasing research interest in the topic of localization, with 26% and 13% of the China-related HR articles focused on this issue in the two journals respectively. Wong and Law (1999, p. 26) provide a useful working definition of localization:

> Localization refers to the development of job related skills within the local population and the delegation of decision-making authority to local employees, with the final objective of replacing expatriate managers with local employees.

Localization therefore has two major components: the process of developing local talent, and the replacement of expatriates by the developed local employees. Selmer (2003) summarizes the arguments for localization into four categories:

1. Localization probably reduces total compensation costs.
2. Localization facilitates overcoming language and cultural barriers.
3. Localization may improve the confidence of Chinese managers since it offers opportunities for growth and career prospects.
4. Government relations could also be improved by staff localization and localization may be viewed as a sign of commitment.

The typical method by which the Big Four entered new countries in the 20th century was to seek out an established local accounting firm and bring it into their network. Ding liked to refer to this process as localizing first, and then internationalizing. Ding saw that the process had been reversed in China. First, the practices would internationalize and then they would localize, and in his view they localized far too slowly (Ding, 2006b, p. 120). A consistent theme in interviews with Big Four partners found Big Four were enthusiastic about the concept of localization. This view is well summarized by Sir John Stuttard (personal correspondence, September 1, 2009):

> It was the view of the CICPA that the role of the international firms was to train PRC nationals and then leave the Chinese accountancy profession to run itself in the future. It was also the C&L view that the firm was trying to build a capability in China that would one day be owned, managed, and staffed by PRC nationals.

The Big Four firms were anxious to quickly localize in order to reduce costs and make their practices profitable. Sir John Stuttard (personal correspondence, September 1, 2009) reported: "At its peak, C&L China was losing US$15 million each year, mainly because of high expatriate employment costs, which had to be funded from the international network."

Dave McCann, who was the human resource partner for PricewaterhouseCoopers (PwC) in China from 1998 to 2010, was initially assigned to China with a specific mandate to promote localization:

> It was described to me that they wanted to localize the practice and they needed to develop some approaches and some ways in which we can actually make localization work. It was an explicit goal around localization, which at that time didn't mean a whole lot to me other than we need to promote the recruitment and development of PRC nationals because the practice at the time was dominated by expatriates, particularly Americans. (Dave McCann, personal correspondence, June 11, 2009)

MOF and CICPA pushed for more rapid localization of management positions. They wanted control of the Big Four firms in local hands. Kent Watson (personal correspondence, March 21, 2009) observed:

> And they thought that they could, with a little bit of training, as to process mostly, assume the role of the Big Four. So they thought that their partners were fully ready with a little training to become partners in the international firms, as well as their managers, as well as anyone else.

The Big Six firms would resist demands from the MOF and the CICPA for faster localization, saying that they were moving as fast as they could, but it would take considerable time to develop local partners. Ding (2006b, p. 352) berated an American WTO delegation from the Big Six on March 24, 1998:

> The biggest discrepancy between the two sides centers on their opinions on timetable. The Big Six hold that we are pressing too eagerly on the process of localization. This is because we are talking about different types of personnel. You refer to the just graduated students who need a long time to be trained and improved. But we refer to the personnel like Zhang Ke and Ge Ming, who have already done auditing for eight to ten years. We do not hurry the establishment of the member firm, but the problem is that there is not one "qualified graduate" after 10 or 20 years of teaching. This might be because the students are too stupid or teachers are rather incompetent.

Most Big Four partners interviewed for this study agreed with the observation by Fryxell, Butler, and Choi (2004, p. 269), that "localization too often follows its own schedule." The Big Four were anxious to obtain the cost savings provided by localization, but were reticent to cede control of the practices to locals they did not consider sufficiently experienced or loyal to the firms. Jerry Leamon, Deloitte's global managing partner of Clients & Markets pointed to the misunderstanding between regulators and many Chinese and the Big Four as to their objectives with respect to localization:

> One of the misunderstandings is that people think we are building a subsidiary operation here in China. We are not. We are building a great Chinese professional services firm that will be owned and run by Chinese professionals. (Zhao, 2005a)

The arguments between the Big Four and regulators were not over whether the firms should localize and become Chinese managed, but over that pace at which Leamon's vision would be achieved.

Cost was the major motivation for the Big Four to push the pace of localization. A report dated in 2003 that was shown to the researcher by one of the Big Four firms stated that the cost differential between a local and an expatriate is about two times and that prior to that time the cost difference had been much higher. The salary gaps had converged because local salaries had increased dramatically due to market demands (Proctor & Qui, 2006). Improved living conditions and the increased popularity of working in China had also reduced the premiums required to attract expatriate staff.

Table 6.3 shows the level of localization at various staff levels for the five-year period ending in 2008. By 2004, the entry-level position of staff accountant was nearly completely localized and remained so throughout the period examined. The lowest levels, staff and senior accountants, typically have fewer than five years of experience. These positions can be considered fully localized, since the few foreign nationals employed at these levels are typically participants seconded into China as part of the firm's global talent development programs. As positions become more senior, the level of localization drops; at the partner level only 27.2% of positions are localized by 2008. Big Four partners explained that the relatively slow pace of partner localization relates to the lengthy path to partner at the firms. Typically, it takes about 15 years for a newly recruited graduate to progress to partnership admission. Since the firms were only allowed to directly recruit personnel after they obtained joint venture licenses in 1992, substantial numbers of local partner candidates only began to appear in the mid-2000s when those recruited on campus more than a decade earlier were finally ready for admission. During the five-year period covered by Table 6.3, the total number of Big Four partners increased from 278 to 731. While the proportion of local partners increased during this period, large numbers of expatriate partners were also added.

Table 6.3. Big Four Localization by Staff Level.

Level	2004	2005	2006	2007	2008
Partners	18.0%	16.2%	20.1%	24.3%	27.2%
Senior managers	46.2%	48.9%	51.2%	52.0%	59.0%
Managers	75.6%	74.9%	72.8%	75.5%	81.0%
Seniors	94.5%	88.7%	89.3%	94.6%	95.9%
Staff	99.6%	99.3%	99.3%	99.1%	99.1%
Total	90.1%	89.0%	89.7%	90.1%	91.6%

Source: Big Four survey. Localization percentage is PRC national personnel/total personnel at each staff level. Hong Kong and Taiwan identity card holders are not considered PRC nationals in this calculation.

Partners interviewed said that they expect that the proportion of local partners will continue to increase because the local proportion of senior manager and managers (who are the future partner candidates) is higher than the current local proportion of partners. While it will likely be some time before local partners are in the majority at any of the Big Four firms in China, PwC appears to have been sufficiently concerned about a youthful revolt that in 2009 it amended its partnership agreement to reduce the voting rights of recently admitted partners.

6.2. MEMBER FIRMS IN CHINA

The joint venture structure for the Big Six in China was a disappointment to the Big Four because it limited their flexibility in developing the China market. They faced great difficulty with obtaining permission to open new offices, and while they had found ways that limit the involvement of the local partner, they still periodically found the local partner interfering with the practice.

By 1994, only two years into the program, Ding was also convinced that the joint venture experiment was flawed. He had discovered that the joint venture form was virtually unheard of in the long history of accountancy in the world and that the normative form for the Big Six was a member firm. He became captivated by the concept of member firms as a means to return control of the accounting profession to the Chinese. China approved one member firm – local firm Zhonghua Shenzhen was admitted as a member firm of Horwath International in 1994 (Lai, 1994a). The member firm route would become the normative path for second-tier global firms to enter China. In 1995, RSM International would admit Shanghai Zhong Chuang and Shenyang CPAs would join Moores Rowland International (*Accountancy Age*, 1995; Lu, 1995).

On April 6, 1995, Nellie Fong met with Zhang Youcai and suggested that the Big Six firms should be allowed to develop member firms in China. Zhang discussed the idea with Ding Pingzhun and they decided to support the idea. While many of the Big Six firms had pushed to be allowed to open branches of the joint ventures in order to serve a broader geographical area, Ding felt this would result in only a "more abnormal and immature form" (Ding, 2006b, p. 93). Ding (2006b, p. 331) had difficulty understanding why the Big Six wanted branches, since they all complained of losing money – "would they not lose more money if they had more branches?" Local firms, however, did not seem likely to prosper without an international affiliation. As Ding saw the situation, the problem that Chinese accounting firms were facing was that they were too small and too unsophisticated to be effective. He wrote: "if there were only one or two member firms in one province, then there would be 30 or 40 firms in the whole country, and the overall level of the national CPA industry would leap onto a higher step" (Ding, 2006b, p. 336). He thought that if some local firms were to become member firms of the Big Four they could train and develop their local staff and introduce modern management systems.

Ding wondered whether there was precedent for a firm to have more than one member in a country, since Fong had indicated that Andersen might be interested in developing several member firms as a means of gaining practice rights in additional cities. Discussions with the Big Six found broad support for the concept of multiple member firms. China's personnel assigned to the joint ventures were mostly opposed to the idea, fearing they would be left behind. Most of the local CPA institutes were in favor, seeing multiple Big Six member firms as an opportunity to further develop their local firms.

On January 22, 1996, MOF issued Notice Concerning Permission for International Firms to Identify Member Firms in China. Some of the key provisions included:

1. Member firms could keep their Chinese name and use the name of the international firm. This followed the practice in Hong Kong and Taiwan.
2. Firms that wished to become member firms needed to complete their internal reformation first, the most substantial requirement was that they needed to separate from their government sponsors.
3. Member firms must be structured as partnerships.
4. Firms could work with international firms as a correspondent or associated firm, or could operate under joint management.
5. The international firm (or partners of the international firm – the wording was unclear) could own up to one-third of the member firm for a five-year period. Ding considered this a special favor to the foreign partners who had entered China but had not become Chinese CPAs.
6. Foreigners who passed the Chinese CPA examination and became Chinese CPAs could become partners in the member firm.
7. International firms could have more than one member firm in China, but those member firms would be expected to integrate into a single firm within an undefined time limit.

A few months later a deadline was set requiring existing joint ventures to convert into member firms by 2000 (*Asian Wall Street Journal*, 1996). Alfred Shum of E&Y said "The general concept is something we can work with, not something impossible" (Lai, 1996). Johnny Chen of PW observed that it would be difficult because most Chinese firms were linked to government ministries and member firms would need to be independent (O'Neill, 1996).

Each of the Big Six firms set out in earnest to find new candidates for member firms. C&L had discussions with 25 local firms in the following year (Ding, 2006b, p. 342). C&L had established a target list of cities, namely Chengdu, Chongqing, Dalian, Hangzhou, Jiangsu, Tianjin, Xiamen, and Wuhan. Gordon Barrass, a retired British diplomat, and Ruby Chin, a Shanghainese woman who was C&L's *fixer*, visited various firms in each city. Eventually one firm was chosen in some of the key cities listed above, memorandums of understanding were signed, and training was arranged, including the secondment of staff to Coopers and Lybrand offices in China and abroad. The firms developed slowly and never developed into member firms. Sir John Stuttard, C&L chairman at the time, observed that:

> They had been formed, in most cases, from the local finance bureaus and had a culture that was heavily influenced by being part of local government and involved in auditing state-owned enterprises. Methods were slow to change. Eventually this strategy was terminated in 1998 on the merger between C&L and PW. (Sir John Stuttard, personal correspondence, September 1, 2009)

AA had the idea to find a way to convert their wholly foreign owned enterprises (WFOEs) in Shanghai and Shenzhen into member firms. They sought out local firms that could serve the purpose. In Shenzhen they found (or perhaps had a hand in creating) a local firm that had been in existence for only six months. When approval was requested from regulators, both Ding Pingzhun and the Shenzhen Institute of CPAs objected. They pointed out the firm had only completed 16 assignments since it had been set up, and 14 of those had problems. Ding accused AA of looking for "slaves," not professionals, in an attempt to take up the market, and admonished Nellie Fong to "take care of your brand" (Ding, 2006b, p. 129). AA later gave up on a Shenzhen member firm and shifted its efforts to Guangzhou where, in 1998, it requested approval for a member firm. The Guangdong Institute of CPAs asked for guidance from the CICPA on whether to approve the member firm arrangement. They reported to the CICPA that the arrangement involved AA providing financial support to the firm and that AA had demanded that the firm take on all of the AA staff in Guangzhou and Shenzhen. Ding reacted angrily, writing that the transaction was a power–money trade that "has blasphemed the holiness of the CPA career" (Ding, 2006b, p. 130). Rather than approving the member firm arrangement, Ding ordered that the local firm be included in a rectification exercise.

6.2.1. Price Waterhouse and the Zhang & Chen CPAs Experiment

The first member firm of the Big Six was Zhang & Chen CPAs, a firm that was formed out of the PW representative office in Beijing. Ding Pingzhun held great hopes that this member firm would set the model for the Big Six. Unanticipated regulatory problems in China delayed the spread of this model, and fast moving changes in the WTO negotiations ultimately shifted the Big Six in another direction.

Kent Watson was the American partner of PW who was in charge of the Beijing representative office. Watson was fluent in Chinese, having studied it at Brigham Young University before going on a Mormon mission to Taiwan from 1963 to 1966. He joined PW and advanced to become the managing partner of the Salt Lake City office when, in 1989, he took a three-year leave of absence to return to Taiwan to lead the church mission. After his return to the firm he moved to Beijing in 1993, where he remained until his retirement in 2003.

Watson saw the new member firm rules as an opportunity to form additional joint ventures to give PW practice rights in other cities, but quickly concluded that new joint ventures cast as member firms would not achieve their objectives:

> When we looked at it and actually did a survey of all the major local CPA firms in China, we came to the conclusion that we could not be partners in a true sense of partnership with any of them and that was because of the skill. (Yet) there's more than skill. It was not only skill. It was just the whole background and philosophy of what this was all about. You boil it down to competence in a lot of your conversations. But I don't really know if it was that. It was just that we were schooled in one system for 100 years and they were schooled in another system for 100 years and never the twain could meet there as far as an international CPA firm. (Kent Watson, personal correspondence, March 21, 2009)

Instead of looking for local firms to join PW, Watson turned his attention to find a way to work within the pending guidelines for member firms, while meeting PW's objectives of creating a firm that would share its culture and philosophy: "We were going to be able to build a firm the way we saw building the firm and that was from the ground up" (Kent Watson, personal correspondence, March 21, 2009).

Watson turned to a local manager in the Beijing representative office of PW. Kevin Zhang had been one of the people sent by the MOF to KPMG's joint venture. Johnny Chen, an American who had left KPMG in China to become a partner at PW, had recruited Zhang to PW. Zhang was the most senior of the local staff at PW, a member of the Communist Party, and the person Watson thought most suitable to help him build a new firm. Perhaps most importantly, Zhang was young and Watson believed he could control him.

On the day before the notice[2] was released granting permission for international firms to find member firms in China, Kevin Zhang called on Ding Pingzhun at the CICPA. Zhang and Ding had been colleagues at the MOF and, despite Ding's over 20-year age gap, were close friends.

Zhang told Ding that the Beijing office of PW was at a crossroads. The representative office had become too difficult to operate now that they had more than 200 staff. They needed a license to audit rather than sending all the accounts to the Shanghai joint venture for signing. He saw two options. The first was to open a branch of the Shanghai joint venture in Beijing. The second was to form an independent partnership and become a member firm in PW. He proposed forming a firm, to be called Zhang & Chen CPAs, with another PW manager named May Chen (*Chen Mei*) and a few local staff who had passed the CPA examination. Ding enthusiastically supported the second option saying this could be the first Big Six member firm approved (Ding, 2006b, p. 133).

Zhang and Ding discussed the strategy of establishing this firm. Ding (2006b, p. 134) had a question for Zhang:

> Firstly, are you competent enough? At least you should be able to administer the 200 people under you. And of course you still need help from the foreigners. If you and your team have reached the international level, you could be a boss yourself, why not? You should make an effort in this direction and the CICPA will support you.

Ding saw Zhang & Chen CPAs as an opportunity to begin the process of moving PW in China under local management. Ding (2006b, p. 133) writes "…in the joint venture, foreigners are 'boss', Chinese are employees. In the member firm, Chinese are 'boss', foreigners are employees." Ding hoped that Zhang's member firm would become the model adopted by the rest of the Big Six. Ding warned Zhang that there was opposition to this direction of reform and to expect some criticism. He told Zhang …"don't mind it and just follow your own road" (Ding, 2006b, p. 134).

In Shanghai, Da Hua, PW's joint venture partner, took a dim view of the idea. They feared competition from Zhang & Chen CPAs and preferred that they be allowed to set up a branch of the joint venture in Beijing. Zhou Zhongwei,[3] the Chinese representative of the joint venture, met with Ding Pingzhun on March 6, 1996. Ding ignored Zhou's concerns about competition and told Zhou he needed to separate the joint venture from the SUFE and "try to get some control power in PW Da Hua" (Ding, 2006b, p. 136).

On March 15, 1996, three American partners of PW[4] came to meet with Ding Pingzhun to discuss their options with respect to Beijing. Ding said that while the option of opening a branch of the joint venture in Beijing would be the quickest and simplest choice, he was not going to approve it. In his view, the joint ventures did not work and he was not going to continue to approve them. Instead, he told the Americans to separate their joint venture from SUFE and to turn it into a partnership.

The PW partners said they were considering finding a local firm in Beijing to turn into a member firm. Ding told them that the Beijing practice could not be structured as a joint venture, because China was not going to allow the creation of new joint ventures. If they picked a strange firm to become it member firm, Ding estimated it would take three to five years to get approval. Then Ding got to the point. Why not use Zhang & Chen CPAs? The only obstacle is capital, and certainly PW can help with that. Ding pointed out that Kent Watson could work as a senior consultant to Zhang & Chen and that this would be a great contribution from PW to the accounting profession in China. Ding told the PW partners that the decision was theirs, but ominously told them they had best get on with it: "The situation is rough and tumble." Ding (2006b, p. 138) said, "You must find a way out, because we are going to investigate and punish some offices after the issuing of the three foreign-related documents."

PW announced it was entering into an affiliation agreement with Zhang & Chen CPAs in September 1996 (*The Asian Wall Street Journal*, 1996). The member firm status was officially approved by CICPA in December 1996. Kevin Zhang told *The Asian Wall Street Journal* that the arrangement was a "takeover" (AWSJ, 1996). While Zhang and his local partners technically owned Zhang & Chen CPAs, they had signed a side agreement with PW that allowed PW to manage the firm and retain any profits. This approach to avoiding China's ownership restrictions in certain industries would become widespread.[5] Ding appears to have been unaware of the side agreement, and would likely have challenged it had he learned of it. Gaining control of Zhang & Chen was critical from PW's perspective. PW was making significant investments in China and needed control to ensure the practice would meet PW's objectives.

Zhang & Chen CPAs was a local Chinese partnership with no direct PW ownership and as such was subject to the Chinese laws that generally applied to domestic companies rather than the special rules for foreign-invested enterprises. Domestic enterprises were severely restricted in their ability to obtain and hold foreign currency, so Zhang & Chen CPAs was unable to open a foreign currency bank account. This meant they would be required to collect fees in local currency, and immediately convert foreign receipts to local currency. Because the firm had significant foreign currency expenses, most importantly the salaries for the large number of expatriate staff, it could not operate without access to foreign currency. The firm then discovered that the deduction for salaries for employees would be limited to approximately $100 per month per employee. While this rule applied to all domestic companies at the time (foreign-invested enterprises had no such limit) it created a serious problem for a firm where local employees were paid well above those limits and expatriate compensation often substantially exceeded US$100,000 per year. The firm was not profitable at the time, and the resulting tax expense (at the 33% rate for domestic companies instead of the 15% rate for foreign-invested enterprises) would quickly bankrupt it. Ding reported that the increased tax burden totaled 60 million Yuan (approximately US$7 million) (Ding, 2006b, p. 139). As a domestic firm, Zhang & Chen CPAs was also restricted in the fees it was allowed to charge, and the regulated level of fees for local firms was well below the fees charged by the joint venture accounting firms.

On May 27, 1997, Kevin Zhang went to see Ding Pingzhun to tell him they could not survive on this basis. Zhang & Chen CPAs needed to do its work at international standards, and that was not possible under the constraints put on local firms. Ding was sympathetic and promised to work with regulators to find a solution. Zhang said he would also do his best and not come back for help unless it was absolutely necessary (Ding, 2006b, p. 138).

On April 2, 1998, Zhang was back in Ding's office and reported they could not stand it; they were losing too much money. Ding had communicated with the People's Bank of China and the State Administration of Taxation, arguing that member firms should get the same treatment as foreign-invested firms. He complained that these institutions failed to understand the direction of reform. On April 15, 1998, Don Menovich, CEO of PW China, proposed to Ding that the international firm of PW take up an equity interest in Zhang Chen such that it could qualify as a foreign-invested enterprise. Ding told him he would think about it, although Ding did not want to create any more joint ventures (Ding, 2006b, p. 446). On July 26, 1998, James Schiro, Global CEO of PwC, visited Beijing. Included on his agenda was to attempt to resolve the tax and foreign exchange problems of Zhang & Chen. Ding expressed both his sympathy and his frustration to Schiro, but it was apparent that the problem was out of Ding's hands. Schiro met directly with senior officials of the State Administration of Taxation, who told him that many domestic companies were complaining about the same restrictions but that it was difficult to make an exception for Zhang & Chen CPAs.[6]

Ding (2006b, p. 140) expresses disappointment in his memoirs about the failure to resolve the regulatory problems of Zhang & Chen CPAs:

> I felt the foreigners were reasonable and open-minded. We just hit on our own icebergs – the foreign exchange accounts, payroll tax, pricing controls – which could have been solved by ourselves. The identity of the member firm of Zhang & Chen was "aborted" by these obstacles. This side of history is so unforgettable.

The difficulties of Zhang & Chen CPAs appear to have chilled the efforts of other firms to establish member firms. By 1998, when PW and Zhang & Chen CPAs were struggling with regulatory problems, China was in the final stages of negotiating membership in the WTO, and negotiations on how the Big Six would structure in China moved to this stage.

6.2.2. The Big One

Ding Pingzhun was initially optimistic that Chinese accounting firms would be able to compete effectively with the international accounting firms in China. At a 1994 meeting, Ding said that China would be like other countries, and it will be the Chinese CPA who eventually plays the major role:

> Of course we should not reject the Big Six, for they are the most excellent ones and we need to learn from them. Our attitude is: you are welcomed here, but do not monopolize. As for Hong Kong's "bigs" I am sure they will be surpassed by the mainland ones in just a few years. We are to learn from others but maintain our principles. (Ding, 2006b, p. 110)

Ding became more and more frustrated as the market developed. Local firms did not develop in a way that would allow them to compete with the Big Six. They were too small, partly a result of their connection with local government bureaus which resulted in a proliferation of firms that covered most cities, but with markets segmented based on the local government's jurisdiction. Quality was poor and skills were limited. Ding came to believe that China needed to develop a large firm capable of competing with the Big Six. He called it "the Big One." His idea was to consolidate the talent in China's local firms to create a single firm that would be of sufficient scale and quality to challenge the Big Six at home and abroad – essentially becoming a Chinese entrant to the Big Six. The institutional barriers to this quixotic adventure were huge – first he would have to overcome Chinese practices of local government ownership of most accounting firms. Then he would have to convince others, first large Chinese companies, and then the world that this firm was the equivalent of the Big Six.

Ding Pingzhun found no support for his idea when he met with Wang Jianxi, CSRC chief accountant on August 4, 1995. Wang told him it was out of question for China to develop an accounting firm that could complete for international listings because others would not accept such firm. He pointed to the United States, where he said all of the Fortune 500 firms are audited by the Big Six. "The Big Six are really too big, other firms than the Big Six would never be able to squeeze into the auditing business. Considering this, the establishment of China's Big One is of no significance" (Ding, 2006b, p. 334).

Sun Guicai, president of the Confederation of Asian and Pacific Accountants, encouraged Ding to pursue the Big One at the confederation's meeting in China on April 27, 1997. Sun, a China born Malaysian, pointed to the Philippines as an example of a market where a local firm, SGV, became the leading firm through the power of the state. In the Philippines the Marcos government essentially required local businesses to use SGV. This kept the Big Six effectively out of the market until the fall of the Marcos regime. SGV ultimately joined with AA (Dyball & Valcarcel, 1999). Sun advised Ding to first organize the profession and secure the market in China, then follow Chinese companies into Hong Kong and take over small- and medium-sized accounting firms. He claimed that the Big Six partners in Hong Kong were only in it for the money, and if the Big One began to take away their clients they would join the firm as well. After the Hong Kong market was secured the Big One could begin to acquire small and medium-sized firms in Southeast Asia (Ding, 2006a, pp. 295–297). The "Marcos solution" advocated by Sun was to use the coercive power of the state to create the Big One and to give it a monopoly over certain types of work.

Early in 1998, Ding saw an opening to push his Big One ideas. Zhu Rongji had recently made a speech where he suggested that the supervisory systems of 500 large-scale SOEs would be entrusted to the Big Six to design. Ding approached his supervisor, Vice-Minister of Finance Zhang Youcai, and observed that while this showed that the leaders put high hopes in the CPA industry, it also indicated that they also were not satisfied with the existing level of local CPAs in the country (Ding, 2006b, p. 432). Zhang asked Ding to set forth his recommendations. Ding, anticipating that response, submitted them 11 days later on January 26, 1998.

Ding concluded in his report that the problem with the CPA profession in China was that the firms were too small and talented accountants were scattered in too many firms. He reported that a briefing he had received from the Ministry of State Security had said that the Big Six are fully aware of this immature situation and make best use of it to fight over the limited market and limited human resources.[7] The solution to the problem, according to Ding, was to create the Big One, a Chinese firm that could play a major role both in the domestic market and in the international market.

Ding presented detailed plans for the Big One. He proposed assembling talent from across China to build the Big One that could compete with the Big Six within two or three years. Ding envisioned a major firm headquartered in Beijing that would admit member firms in major cities across China. The firms would be established as limited liability companies owned by the partners and CPA license holders. Ding proposed that the partners of the firms contribute 75% of total capital of 10 million Yuan (US$1.2 million) with the state providing 25% of the capital in the form of a loan. For the size of accounting firm that Ding proposed building, the firm would have been grossly undercapitalized.

Ding provided a forecast for the operations of Big One (Table 6.4).

Table 6.4. Forecast Big One Operations.

Year	Revenue	Staff
1	100	500
3	500	1,000
5	1,000	3,000

Source: Ding (1996). Revenue in RMB millions.

By 2003, the fifth year of Ding's plan, the revenue of the five largest local accounting firms in China totaled RMB432 million, less than half of Ding's forecast for the Big One. Ding's Big One proposal never went further at that time, although he had one more chance to implement it during his tenure, and it came from an unexpected corner – the Big Six firms of PW and C&L.

6.2.3. The Merger of Price Waterhouse and Coopers & Lybrand in China

On September 18, 1997, PW and C&L announced their plans to merge their global practices. The merger would be completed in 1998. While certain member firms around the world elected not to join the merged firm, the respective global firms controlled the China operations and the merger was not a local decision for the firms in China. Nevertheless, Chinese regulatory approval would be required to restructure the duplicative operating entities in China and the joint venture partners of the two firms would need to be dealt with.

Both firms had similar structures in China. Both PW and C&L were managed directly by their global firms. Each had a joint venture with a Chinese state entity – PW with Da Hua CPAs, which was owned by the SUFE and C&L with CIEC, a Beijing-based CPA firm owned by the China International Trust Investment Corporation. Each firm had representative offices in other cities, and a WFOE for consulting services. As previously discussed, PW also had a failing experiment with member firm Zhang & Chen CPAs.

When the merger was announced, Sir John Stuttard, the English chairman of C&L in China, was driving his pink 1934 Rolls Royce across Tibet in the Beijing to Paris Rally (Waller, 2006). Stuttard was legendary in Beijing for being chauffeured around in a stretched, locally manufactured *Hongqi* limousine of the type favored by politburo members. The car flew C&L flags from the front fenders in the style of diplomatic cars, a practice that usually allowed him easy access to closed areas. After his retirement from PwC, Stuttard would serve as the Lord Mayor of London and having achieved honorificabilitudinitatibus,[8] he would be knighted in 2008. Stuttard frantically called back to Beijing requesting that no contacts be made until his return. Don Menovich, American CEO of PW in China, disregarded Stuttard's request and met with Ding Pingzhun on September 26, 1997. Stuttard's grandiloquent style would grate on the Americans who managed PW's China operations, and he returned to England when Kent

Watson was selected to manage the merged firm.[9] Ding had little time for Stuttard, berating him publicly in a WTO meeting with Big Six representatives:

> You are quite the gentleman. And I heard the letter to the American government was drafted by you. But your command of the Chinese language is not good enough. Many issues which are quite clear in our eyes are made confused by you, and you almost could not correctly understand any matter in the past. It doesn't matter anyhow. Whether you understand or not, we are to carry out our policies, and you will swallow the "fruit" if you couldn't or don't want to understand. Please don't trust the so-called foreign experts of China who are actually not expert at all. It is the natural law that only Chinese could really understand China's situation.

Ding's remarks to Stuttard reflect both the cultural chasm between the Western Big Four leaders and Chinese regulators, and Ding's intense nationalism that bordered on racism. A diverse group of actors participated in the development of the profession in China. Partners from America, Hong Kong, and Europe interacted with Chinese accountants and regulators. A consistent theme present in this narrative has the Big Four leaders and Chinese regulators both puzzling over the intentions of the other. There is a Cantonese idiom for this phenomenon: a chicken talking to a duck (雞同鴨講).

Ding writes in his memoirs that he saw the opportunity in this merger to create the Big One, an international caliber firm controlled by Chinese. The firm would be established by merging four firms: Zhang & Chen CPAs, the Coopers and Lybrand-CIEC joint venture with CITIC that was managed by Zhang Ke, Yangcheng CPAs, a local firm in Guangzhou that had a loose affiliation with C&L, and PW Da Hua, PW's joint venture with SUFE in Shanghai. Ding thought that the merger would result in a firm controlled by the Chinese personnel. "We hope that this big could not be handled by the foreigners at will" (Ding, 2006b, p. 120).

Ding met with Zhang Ke on June 26, 1998. Ding said that they needed to take two steps. First, the joint ventures and Yangcheng CPAs needed to disaffiliate from their state sponsors. Zhang & Chen CPAs was never attached, and Ding saw no obstacles in completing the disaffiliation of the others. Then, Ding (2006a, p. 429) told Zhang:

> The four accounting firms should unite to form a fist. In this way when negotiating with the foreign side, the Chinese side will have strength…the foreign side consistently holds the principle of "divide and rule." We should unite like a family.

Zhang Ke was keen to follow Ding's guidance. However, the PwC partners viewed Zhang Ke as the strongest of the local partners. Zhang Ke had a strong personality and outstanding leadership traits, and the PwC partners concluded that he could not be controlled. C&L had struggled with Zhang Ke in the joint venture, and PwC was not looking to repeat that experience.

As Ding predicted, PwC followed the principle of "divide and rule." Zhou Zhongwei left Da Hua and SUFE and joined PwC as a partner. Approaching 60 years old, he had little interest in leading a large firm and was offered a comfortable position for the remaining years of his career. Following his retirement from PwC, Zhou would become CSRC's chief accountant. C&L's loose affiliation with Yangcheng CPAs was cast off. Kevin Zhang and May Chen were sent to America for two years to "further develop their skills" and conveniently remove them from the scene while PwC consolidated control. Ultimately Zhang Ke would be frozen out of the new PwC and he would take the former C&L joint venture firm, renamed Shinewing, and develop it into one of China's leading domestic accounting firms (Chan, 2008; Jones & Rabinovitch, 2013; Luk, 2010a).

Ding's hopes of creating the Big One were dashed. In his memoirs he laments: "In this way, the famous accounting firms in China at that time were swallowed by PwC. Our dream was broken by their civilized invasion" (Ding, 2006b, p. 121).

6.3. CHINA AND THE WORLD TRADE ORGANIZATION

The WTO has played a major role in the globalization of the world economy. It serves as a negotiation forum for its 133 members, provides a set of rules to govern international trade, and helps to settle trade disputes (WTO, 2010). Arnold (2005) documents how the Big Four accounting firms have used the WTO to create a global market for accounting services, and in the process undermine the effectiveness of domestic regulation. The process of China's accession to WTO is an illustration of this phenomenon.

China's accession to the WTO in December 2001 marked the conclusion of 15 years of negotiations and reforms that facilitated China's ongoing integration with the global economy (Bhattasali, Li, & Martin, 2004). While the final agreement was massive and far-reaching, the process of negotiating accession had already led to significant reforms in many areas. Most of the reforms that directly affected the accounting profession were already in place by 2001. Accountancy received early attention in the negotiating process, and key reforms such as the opening of the market to foreign competition, the licensing of foreign accountants, and the disaffiliation of local accounting firms from government sponsors had already been implemented by the time the agreement was inked.

China was one of the founding members of the General Agreement on Tariffs and Trade (GATT)[10] in 1948, but withdrew in 1959. In June 1986, China requested resumption of its contracting party status, and a working party on China was formed in May 1987. China considered that joining GATT was an important step toward the reformation of its economy, since the process of opening up to increased foreign competition would force state-owned enterprises to reform and become more competitive. In addition, low tariff access to foreign markets was increasingly important to China's growing export economy. The Uruguay Round of negotiations began a seven-and–a-half-year life in 1982. Although China was not yet a member of GATT, it took part in the negotiations. Trade in services was an important component of this round. In 1993, The Ministry of Finance designated Zhang Haixian to represent the CICPA in the negotiations. In the bilateral negotiations with the European Union, Finland, Japan, Sri Lanka, Sweden, and South Korea, Zhang found that there was great interest in the opening of China's accounting market. The negotiating parties challenged some of China's rules, including those that required CPAs to be Chinese citizens and restricted foreign involvement to the Big Six. Zhang also reported back that there was a great drawback to China's system of linking accounting firms with state-supported institutions and recommended that the industry be reformed to meet international conventions (Ding, 1993).

6.3.1. Bilateral Negotiations

In early 1997, the pace of negotiations for China to join the WTO quickened. The process had two steps: first, bilateral market-access negotiations would take place, followed by multilateral negotiations. Some 44 WTO members, including the 15 member states of the European Union as a single entity, expressed interest in participating in bilateral negotiations. The most important bilateral negotiation was with the United States, and once it was concluded in November 1999, the European Communities quickly reached agreement in May 2000. The other bilateral negotiations were rapidly concluded thereafter (Gertler, 2004).

Negotiations with the United States on accounting market access issues heated up early in 1998. On March 11, 1998, US Trade Representative (USTR) Ambassador Charlene Barshevsky held a three-hour meeting with Ding Pingzhun and Zhang Haixian of the CICPA to begin discussing the arrangements to finalize the agreements. Barshevsky told Ding that the United States wanted to conclude the negotiations before the meeting scheduled for June 21, 1998 between President Clinton and Premier Jiang. The United States had not participated significantly in earlier bilateral negotiations, where it was mainly the EU, Japan, Canada, Australia, Singapore, and South Korea that were interested in opening China's accounting markets.

Sir John Stuttard of C&L organized the Big Five[11] response to the pending negotiations. Allen Weltman, a PW partner in New York, took the lead working with the lobbyist and law firm Mayer, Brown and Platt (Sir John Stuttard, personal communication, September 1, 2009). The Big Five had submitted a report to the USTR with suggested market opening commitments and these had become the basis for the American negotiation. Barshevsky told Ding in their March 11 meeting that the United States was not bound by the Big Five requests but asked that China consider them (Ding, 2006b, p. 346).

The significant points that were raised by Barshevsky and the USTR and Ding's responses are summarized below:

1. The size restriction of firms that could enter into a joint venture should be removed.[12]

   Ding: Does not affect the Big Five. Joint ventures are going away.
2. International firms should be permitted to identify their own joint venture partners, should be allowed to have more than one joint venture, and should have no restriction on the proportion of ownership.

   Ding: China is phasing out the joint venture and is replacing it with the internationally normative member firm.
3. International firms should be permitted to set up member firms in China and there should be no restrictions on ownership or management rights.

   Ding: That is the current law. However, to own or manage a CPA firm in China one must be a Chinese CPA, the same requirement that is in place in America.
4. Member firms and joint ventures should be allowed to set up branches anywhere in the country.

   Ding: That is current law.[13]

5. International firms should be allowed to bring in foreign personnel without restriction.

   Ding: Every sovereign state has some restrictions on the entry and employment of foreigners.
6. The proposed limit on ownership in member firms to one-third by foreigners for a three-year period should be removed.

   Ding: This rule is for the benefit of foreigners. It allows them to be partners in a local firm even if they have not passed the CPA examination.
7. Foreigners who pass the CPA examination should be able to obtain a practicing qualification.

   Ding: We agree, and we are fixing the regulations.

This dialogue between Barshevsky and Ding, as recorded by Ding (2006b, p. 346), illustrates Ding's strategy with respect to the WTO negotiations. Ding saw the licensing of individual partners as the means of transferring control of the Big Five to local partners. In the United States, like most countries, ownership of a CPA firm was restricted to licensed CPAs. If China adopted this rule then all partners in a Chinese CPA firm would need to be Chinese CPAs. The proposed three-year transition period would allow foreign individual partners some time to pass the examination and become Chinese CPAs. Of course the many partners who could not read and write Chinese at a sufficient level would not be able to pass the examination. The track record for Chinese speaking partners from other countries who had attempted the examination was not good. The Big Five were not looking for their individual foreign partners to become partners in the local member firms. They were looking for institutional ownership in the member firm by the global Big Five firm, or by its Hong Kong member firm. This would allow the firms continued ownership and control of the member firms regardless of whether their foreign partners could pass the CPA examination and become licensed in China.

Two weeks later, on March 24, 1998, Ding met with representatives of the Big Five to discuss their views on the WTO negotiations. The Big Five representatives essentially reiterated the same points discussed by Barshevsky.

Barshevsky returned to Ding on May 21, 1998. The Big Five had pushed back on several issues. First, they argued that the CPA examination was too difficult and the passing rate was too low. Ding agreed that the passing rate was low, but said that was because they had so many people taking the examination. The Big Five had requested that the examination be made available in English. A Ministry of Foreign Trade and Cooperation

(MOFTEC) representative asked whether Chinese accountants could take the US CPA examination in Chinese. That exchange appears to be the last time that issue was raised.

The Big Five said they needed more time to localize the partnership. China had conceded to allow non-CPA foreign ownership until 2006 and Ding said it could be extended to 2010 or even longer. Most important to the Big Five was the issue of control of the member firm. Ding dismissed these concerns, indicating that the firms had agreed to accelerate the development of local staff, and if there were quality locals capable of managing the firm, why would the firm not use them?

On July 20, 1998, China provided its revised offer on accountancy. The revised offer extended the period under which joint ventures must be restructured into member firms from March 2001 to 2010. At the same time the provision that allowed unlicensed foreign partners to own up to one-third of a member firm was removed. No assurances were given on the other issues that had been raised by the Big Five, including the rights to set up branches and employ foreigners. In a letter to Tania Friedrichs of DG1 from the Big Five firms on August 15, 1998, the firms expressed surprise and dismay at the removal of the one-third ownership provision. Ding (2006b, p. 94) in his memoirs indicates he thought he was giving them what they wanted:

> But in the WTO negotiation, the Big Six, represented by the U.S., asked to cancel this 1/3 regulation. It seemed that they did not get this hint and theoretically speaking only fools will turn down this benefit.

The Big Five had asked that the one-third ownership provision be removed. What they meant was that the one-third limitation should be removed, and it should be replaced by a provision that allowed any level of ownership. Ding and the Big Five did not understand each other. Once again, the chicken was talking to the duck.

Unhappy with the direction of the negotiations, The Big Five took to their case to the public. On July 29, 1998, *The Asian Wall Street Journal* published an article that was highly critical of China's barriers to foreign accounting firms – "China Keeps Foreign Accountants at Bay" (MacDonald & Chang, 1998). The article quoted several Big Five partners on the difficulties they faced in the China market. On August 4, Premier Zhu Rongji demanded an explanation from MOF officials, and Ding Pingzhun presented a lengthy report on August 28, 1998, *Putting right the false report of the Asian Wall Street Journal* (Ding, 2006b, p. 458). Zhu Rongji was driving China's WTO accession and it is likely that the Big

Five planted the article as a means of signaling him as to their difficulties in the negotiations.

Somewhere about this time the decision was made to replace Ding Pingzhun as CICPA director general. He would officially retire on January 8, 1999, having worked beyond the normal retirement age. Ding would be replaced by Li Yong, who had spent most of his career in the World Bank or the MOF department responsible for the World Bank relationship, and had more finely honed diplomatic skills than Ding. The Big Five was aware of this potential development, as evidenced by a Big Five communication to Tania Friedrichs of DG1 on August 15, 1998, suggesting that it might be better to wait for Li Yong's arrival before continuing negotiations, because his "attitude towards the role of the international accounting firms may differ significantly compared to the present incumbent" (personal communication, dated August 15, 1998, obtained from Sir John Stuttard).

The Big Five altered their strategy and rather than focusing on gaining the right to own and control member firms, instead set out to preserve the right to continue with joint ventures. The disaffiliation process (see Chapter 8) had created joint ventures where the local partner was a local CPA firm owned by employees of the Big Five firm. The Big Five firm easily controlled this entity, since the local employees were dependent on the Big Five firm for compensation. The structure was better than the Zhang & Chen CPAs structure, because the joint venture would be characterized as a foreign-invested enterprise, thereby avoiding the foreign exchange, tax, and pricing problems that had doomed Zhang & Chen CPAs. Rather than being an equity joint venture where profit and management rights are dependent on equity shares, the Big Five joint ventures were structured as cooperative joint ventures under Chinese law, allowing the dominant foreign partner to exercise control and take substantially all of the profits (Folta, 2005).

6.3.2. Final WTO Agreement

Negotiations on the accession package were completed on September 17, 2001 and China officially became a member of the WTO on December 11, 2001. The final agreement contained only a few commitments with respect to accountancy. During the 15 years of negotiations for WTO accession China had substantially opened the accountancy market to foreign competition. The final agreement provided that the accountancy market was limited to partnerships or incorporated accounting firms licensed by Chinese authorities. In order to become a partner in a partnership or shareholder in an incorporated accounting firms an individual, Chinese or foreign, needed to be a CPA licensed by Chinese authorities. The agreement said foreigners who had passed the Chinese CPA examination are accorded national treatment, meaning they would be granted CPA licenses on the same basis as locals.

An important exception was included in the final package that applied specifically to the Big Five firms. Participation in existing contractual joint venture accounting firms was not limited only to CPAs licensed by Chinese authorities. The foreign partner in each of the Big Five joint ventures was not an individual foreign partner or partners of the firms. Instead it was a legal entity (foreign partnership or corporation) organized outside of China and controlled by the Big Five firm. This provision allowed this foreign entity to continue to own a controlling interest in the joint venture, despite the fact that the entity was not a Chinese CPA nor were any of its ultimate owners Chinese CPAs. This situation would change upon expiration of the joint venture terms, as is discussed in Chapter 8.

The consequence of the final WTO agreement was that the Big Four[14] abandoned efforts to create multiple member firms in China and focused instead on developing the joint venture firms. Each of the firms conducted its audit practice through the joint venture firm, and the joint ventures have established branches in the cities in which the firm establishes offices. For example, in 2010 PwC's website indicated that they had 12 branch offices of Shanghai-based joint venture PwC Zhong Tian CPAs Limited Company.[15]

The WTO agreement solved the control issue for the Big Four, allowing foreign partners to remain in control of Chinese operations. As discussed in Chapter 8, the WTO agreement was effective only through the life of the joint ventures, which terminated under Chinese law in 2012 for three firms and in 2018 for PwC. The firms were then required to restructure into limited liability partnerships.

6.4. COMPETITION BETWEEN THE BIG FOUR

When the Big Eight came to China in the 1980s, their focus was on serving their international clients. Consequently there was little, if any competition between the firms. One partner explained there was an informal understanding that the firms would not attempt to poach other firm's clients because if they were losing money serving their existing clients – why would they want to lose more money serving other firm's clients? When the market for serving domestic clients opened in the early 1990s, the firms competed aggressively for Chinese companies seeking listings because listed domestic companies were viewed as the future of the firm in China. The competition was muted by the reality that the firms continued to lose money in China. Chinese operations for each of the Big Four turned profitable around 2000 according to anecdotal evidence from Big Four partners. Increased profitability, as well as the expanded market for Chinese companies listing both domestically and abroad, introduced more aggressive competition between the Big Four firms. The failure of AA and the acquisition of its China operations by PwC was a catalyst for further increased competition.

Big Four revenue in China grew from 1.7 billion Yuan (US$205 million) in 2002 to 10.6 billion Yuan (US$1.7 billion) in 2012 (Table 6.5).

Several key competitive factors that shaped the market during the 2000s are discussed below.

6.4.1. Demise of Arthur Andersen

On March 14, 2002, the US member firm of AA was indicted by the US Department of Justice on charges of obstructing justice related to its

Table 6.5. Big Four Revenue in China, 2002–2012.

						Growth Rates	
Year	PwC	E&Y	DTT	KPMG	Total	Big Four	Local firms
2002	766	302	292	334	1,694	–	–
2003	902	388	376	432	2,099	23.9%	14.3%
2004	1,247	690	658	716	3,311	57.8%	21.4%
2005	1,803	1,083	909	915	4,710	42.3%	20.8%
2006	2,038	1,693	1,386	1,237	6,354	34.9%	18.9%
2007	2,626	2,436	2,124	1,945	9,131	43.7%	34.5%
2008	2,755	2,700	2,499	2,435	10,389	13.8%	26.5%
2009	2,578	1,961	2,370	2,221	9,130	−12.1%	23.7%
2010	2,961	2,024	2,600	1,862	9,447	3.5%	19.0%
2011	2,957	2,278	2,928	1,928	10,091	6.8%	30.3%
2012	3,226	2,236	3,044	2,136	10,642	5.5%	16.9%

Source: CICPA annual top 100 firms (Yuan in millions).

alleged shredding of audit working papers relating to failed energy giant Enron. AA would seek a speedy trial, and was convicted on June 15, 2002. AA announced it would cease auditing public companies and it began to liquidate.

The China member firm of AA had grown to become one of the market leaders in China, with revenue of $300 million and 1,400 employees in China in 2001 (de la Cruz, 2001). In late 2001, as the Enron crisis was unwrapping, AA announced its plans to open an office in every big city in China (Pan, 2001). Joe Berardino, AA's global CEO, held a regional staff meeting in Beijing in late 2001, and told the assembled staff that everything would be "ok" (Squires, Smith, McDougall, & Yeack, 2003).

AA member firms around the world began to seek a new alliance as clients began to flee in early 2002. By July 2002, E&Y had acquired 57 AA affiliates outside the United States. In Asia, the AA affiliates in Australia, Malaysia, New Zealand, the Philippines, and Singapore joined E&Y. AA affiliates in Japan and Thailand were acquired by KPMG and the Taiwan affiliate joined DTT (McBride, 2002). The most valuable prize, the fast growing China and Hong Kong practices, went to PwC.

In China and Hong Kong, AA had joined the regional talks with E&Y, but also held secret talks with Silas Yang, the new senior partner of PwC Hong Kong. One of the partners of PwC, Eddie Fong, was married to Nellie Fong of AA and they arranged for senior partners Albert Ng of AA and Silas Yang of PwC to meet at their home. They quickly reached agreement to combine their practices, with Silas Yang continuing as senior partner and Albert Ng heading up the mainland practice. At the same time, the global firm of PwC agreed to turn over ownership and management of its mainland practice to the Hong Kong member firm. E&Y was shocked and dismayed at the announcement, since Albert Ng had signaled at a regional meeting in Singapore that he would follow the other AA firms to E&Y. Anthony Wu, chairman of E&Y in China lamented: "We were also in talks with Andersen China at the time, and I thought we were close to a deal. But you know, it's like wooing a pretty young lady – one may lose for no reason at all" (Chang, 2002).

6.4.2. The New PricewaterhouseCoopers

The combination of PwC and AA resulted in the combined firm having about 6,000 staff in Hong Kong and China, more than double the size of any of the other Big Four firms (*Nikkei Weekly*, 2002; Yiu, 2002c). In several years, three of the largest accounting firms in China – AA, C&L, and PW had merged and they had also merged their China operations together with their Hong Kong operations. Integration challenges and competitor responses would make it difficult for PwC to retain its significant lead over competitors. There were huge cultural differences between AA and PwC. PwC was still working through issues related to its creation only four years earlier. AA was known for its distinctive and strong culture that was remarkably consistent globally (Squires et al., 2003). "The loyalty they had to the organization is still strong today" said Dave McCann, human resource partner for PwC in China (personal correspondence, June 11, 2009). It proved difficult for PwC to integrate the AA personnel, and a large number of them, including Albert Ng their former managing partner, left after several years to join E&Y.

Integration problems at PwC went beyond the new people from AA. A global team of partners, mostly Americans, who had an often-quarrelsome relationship with the Hong Kong firm, managed PwC in China. The global team was mostly replaced shortly after the merger, with their positions being filled by PwC Hong Kong people or former AA people. One staff member observed that the American culture that had dominated firm management had been replaced by the Cantonese culture of Hong Kong, a change so distinctive that the working language of the firm shifted from English to Cantonese. "It was a complex merger because you had three really very, very, independent cultures…I think those memories sort of went deep for some of the long-term folk here in the China firm" reflected Dave McCann (personal correspondence, June 11, 2009).

Among the most serious challenges facing the firm was retaining AA's former clients. All of AA's clients needed to select new auditors. Work related to MNCs tended to go to the new headquarters auditor. In the United States, PwC won the fewest clients and obtained the lowest total fees of any of the Big Four from former AA clients (Kohlbeck, Mayhew, Murphy, & Wilkins, 2008). While PwC in China retained most of AA's domestic clients, oil giant China National Offshore Oil Company (CNOOC) immediately switched to E&Y because of perceived conflicts with PwC service to China's largest oil company PetroChina (Chang, 2002).

If the addition of AA people created a surplus of staff in PwC, the rapid expansion of the market quickly eliminated it. Following China's accession to WTO the pace of growth in the Big Four firms rapidly accelerated due to increased foreign investment and a steady flow of IPOs of Chinese companies. PwC, accordingly, was well positioned to take on new clients in the following years.

6.4.3. Competitive Responses to the New PricewaterhouseCoopers

The dominant market position of PwC following the AA merger was untenable to the other firms in a market as potentially important as China. In 2002, the year of the merger, PwC had a 45% share of the Big Four market as measured by revenues reported to the CICPA. The other three firms had about equal market shares that were slightly below 20% each (Table 6.6). By 2008 the Big Four had roughly equal market shares, with PwC losing its significant advantage. In 2009, market shares shifted significantly as the effect of the recession was felt. In total, Big Four revenue in China fell by 12.1% in 2009 from 2008 levels.

E&Y would lose substantial market share in 2009, falling to 21.5% of Big Four revenue from 26.0% in the prior year. E&Y had been the fastest growing firm prior to recession that began in 2008, but its growth reversed sharply. In January 2009, E&Y asked its staff to take a one-month unpaid leave on a voluntary basis to reduce operating costs, and 90% agreed. In April 2009, E&Y encouraged staff to take 40 days of low-pay leave between July 2009 and July 2010 (Chen, 2009a). Another explanation for E&Y's decline related to litigation over the firm's work on Akai Holdings, which was settled for a substantial payment. The firm's litigating position, and market reputation, was significantly damaged when it was disclosed that working papers had been doctored or faked (Mitchell & Chen, 2009). The Akai scandal, which included a raid on E&Y's Hong Kong office by police, led to the replacement of E&Y senior partner David Sun Tak-Kei

Table 6.6. Market Shares of Big Four in China, 2002–2012.

Year	PwC (%)	E&Y (%)	DTT (%)	KPMG (%)	Total (%)
2002	45.2	17.8	17.3	19.7	100
2003	43.0	18.5	17.9	20.6	100
2004	37.7	20.8	19.9	21.6	100
2005	38.3	23.0	19.3	19.4	100
2006	32.0	26.7	21.8	19.5	100
2007	28.7	26.7	23.3	21.3	100
2008	26.5	26.0	24.1	23.4	100
2009	28.2	21.5	26.0	24.3	100
2010	31.1	22.0	27.3	19.6	100
2011	29.3	22.6	29.0	19.1	100
2012	30.3	21.0	28.6	20.1	100

Source: CICPA top 100 CPA firms.

by Albert Ng. Albert Ng was the former AA managing partner who had earlier left PwC and joined E&Y (Yiu, Rovnick, & Lo, 2009).

While domestic companies were increasingly important to the Big Four in China in the early 2000s, services to MNC clients remained a key component of their client portfolios. For MNC work, the China firm is largely dependent on referrals from other member firms, particularly the US firm. Table 6.7 shows that the relative market shares of the Big Four in the United States have been relatively constant, with DTT holding a larger market share and KPMG holding a smaller share than in China. DTT's larger share in the United States is in part due to the fact that the other firms disposed of their consulting practices and only recently began to rebuild them. Because of the importance of MNC clients, it would be expected that each firm's market share in China would regress toward its share in the United States and other key capital exporting markets.

In 2012, DTT had a market share in China of 28.6%, lower than its US market share of 35.7%. In 2012, KPMG had a market share in China of 20.1%, higher than its KPMG US market share of 15.7%. These differences can largely be explained by reference to the stronger performance by KPMG in China's capital markets (see Tables 5.3, 5.4, and 5.8). In addition, DTT's consulting practice in China is underdeveloped when compared to the US practice. PwC and E&Y's market shares in China are relatively comparable to their US market shares.

Table 6.7. Big Four Market Shares in the United States, 2002–2012.

Year	DTT (%)	E&Y (%)	PwC (%)	KPMG (%)	Total (%)
2002	32.2	24.7	25.8	17.3	100
2003	32.6	26.5	23.4	17.5	100
2004	32.2	25.8	24.2	17.8	100
2005	31.7	25.7	25.0	17.6	100
2006	32.5	25.5	25.6	16.4	100
2007	32.6	25.0	24.7	17.7	100
2008	33.8	25.4	23.3	17.5	100
2009	33.9	24.1	26.0	16.0	100
2010	35.3	22.9	26.0	15.8	100
2011	35.5	22.3	26.3	15.9%	100
2012	35.7	22.4	26.2	15.7	100

Source: Accounting Today annual rankings.

6.4.4. Investment

Prior to the combinations that created PwC in China, AA, PW, and C&L had all been extensively funded and managed by their global firms, whereas KPMG, DTT, and E&Y ran their mainland operations as an adjunct to their Hong Kong practices, with some level of support from the global firms. Sir John Stuttard (personal correspondence, September 1, 2009) observed:

> It is interesting to note that, some years later, prior to the merger the largest three firms were AA, PW, and C&L, in that order, benefiting from the more significant investment from their global networks and the longer term vision of building significant firms in the PRC.

The other firms quickly surmised they had some catching up to do. DTT global CEO James Copeland summoned Asia Pacific leaders to a meeting in Shanghai in July 2002 and committed to a strategy of expanding China operations (Liu, 2002). In September, 2002, DTT announced plans to double the size of its Greater China operations in the next two to five years (Yiu, 2002a). In July 2003, Bill Parrett succeeded James Copeland as global CEO of DTT and immediately made China his top investment target. Parrett said: "Our China expansion has been a personal initiative of my own" (Lee, 2007). He set a goal of having the same number of partners in China as in the United States, but admitted it might take 25 years to make that happen (Yiu, 2003). In November 2003, Parrett would announce that DTT planned to invest US$150–200 million over the next five years to expand its business in China. The money would be spent on "people and the training of people" (Sun, 2003) and to acquire competitors (Yiu, 2004b). The investment was the largest single country investment that DTT had made in its more than 100-year history (Kerrison, 2004; Pun, 2004). In April 2007, Parrett said that half of the US$150 million had been spent (Lee, 2007). The Big Four used the term "investment" loosely in China. What they called investment was typically a global subsidy to the local firm to enable it to maintain partner income while hiring and training staff in excess of current market needs. The investments enabled the firms to bring in additional expatriate talent, as well as to hire more entry level staff than currently required, all in anticipation of substantial market growth ahead. In the early years, investment funds allowed for the furnishing of offices, acquisition of technology, and provided working capital, but later investment was principally directed at funding additional staff hiring and training.

Not to be left behind the other firms, James Turley, Global CEO of E&Y declared "The commitment that we have got within E&Y is that nobody is going to out-invest us in China because it's that important to us" (Ryan, 2005). Paul Ostling, Chief Operating Officer of E&Y Global, announced in July 2006 that their investment would be at least US$200 million, most of which would be spent hiring and training additional staff as well as setting up new offices (Sun, 2006). KPMG has not disclosed any global investment in its China practice and appears to have funded its growth in China from combined China and Hong Kong operations. KPMG's nondisclosure of its investment amounts likely reflects its unwillingness to join the investment "arms race" and suggests that its investment amounts likely lagged its larger rivals. These lower investment levels likely contributed to KPMG being the smallest of the Big Four in China, despite its strong record in winning large SOE audits. KPMG experienced anemic growth in China in 2012 of only 1.2%, significantly below its global growth rate (Chiu, 2012). In 2012 KPMG was passed in size by Ruihua, the firm to be created from the merger of the China affiliates of Crowe Horwarth and RSM (Gillis, 2013b).

DTT announced, in 2010, that it had spent the US$150 million earmarked in 2004, and was planning to invest an additional US$100 million over the next three to five years (Yu, 2010). PwC, having lost its significant lead in market share, announced it would invest an estimated US $100 million on overall operations including recruiting and training of staff (Fung, 2010). In 2013, Deloitte China CEO Chris Lu reported that Deloitte had a business plan to invest US$160 million over the next three years and to expand their workforce to 15,000 people by 2015, following their total strategic investment of US$250 million made between 2004 and 2012 (Cohn, 2013). Such investment figures must be viewed skeptically, since there is accountability over whether the funds are actually expended, and there is no basis to conclude that the proposed investments were actually incremental to operating expenses the firms had already planned.

6.4.5. Mergers with Local Firms

E&Y and Deloitte both acquired local firms during the early 2000s as a means to gain size. In both cases the strategy of acquiring local firms was quickly abandoned after anticipated advantages failed to materialize.

6.4.5.1. Ernst & Young Da Hua

E&Y had pursued a more cautious approach to developing a mainland practice than the other Big Six firms in the 1990s. It had decided to serve clients from Hong Kong rather than staffing large offices on the mainland. By 1997, this had led to E&Y having a significantly smaller presence on the mainland than the other Big Six firms, with only 137 staff compared to an average of 334 for the other firms (Table 6.1).

E&Y decided that a quick way to catch up would be to acquire one of the more successful local accounting firms. Da Hua CPAs was one of the largest firms in Shanghai, formerly affiliated with the Shanghai University of Finance and Economics. Da Hua had the largest market share of companies listed on the Shanghai and Shenzhen stock exchanges in 1998 and 1999 with 46 clients (Hu, 2001). Da Hua had been PW's joint venture partner, but that joint venture had been severed during the disaffiliation process two years before when PwC formed PricewaterhouseCoopers Zhongtian CPAs Ltd., a new joint venture with a firm formed by some of its employees. Once PwC was out of the picture, E&Y stepped in and began a two-year courtship during which it provided technical assistance to Da Hua to bring it up to international standards (Hu, 2001).

The merger was announced to great fanfare on February 9, 2001 (Hu, 2001). The transaction was actually not a merger of Da Hua with E&Y's practice in China, but rather the admission of E&Y Da Hua as a full member firm of E&Y. Seven E&Y partners joined E&Y Da Hua to match the seven Da Hua partners. Anthony Wu, E&Y's China chairman became chairman of the firm, and Professor Tang Yunwei became the managing partner. Anthony Wu said in a press release:

> This merger gives both parties what they need at this juncture. Ernst & Young needs the enhanced domestic presence in Mainland China and Da Hua needs the international exposure, technical backup and resources afforded by the merger with a Big Five accounting firm. (Ernst & Young, 2001)

The CICPA supported the transaction. Ding Pingzhun had retired, but his replacement, Li Yong, saw the transaction as a means of continuing Ding's efforts to put the Big Four under local control:

> The development is in keeping with our policy of economic reform. Ernst & Young's commitment to embracing Da Hua as its member firm in China is a major step forward for development of the local accounting profession and will further help the development of the financial markets as a whole. (She, 2001)

E&Y announced shortly thereafter that it intended to replicate the Da Hua strategy. Anthony Wu said: "Negotiations are underway for possible new mergers with a number of domestic large-scale accounting firms" (Huo, 2001). In May 2002, Anthony Wu said that one or two mergers may happen that year (Yiu, 2002b). The Da Hua transaction had allowed E&Y to make a dubious claim to being the largest of the Big Four in China, although the pending merger of AA and PwC was going to create a much larger competitor. "A lot of the other local accounting firms have come to us wondering whether we'd like a merger (with them) as well because they see this as a successful exercise that has been consummated" said Wu (McCallum, 2002).

By December, E&Y announced it was in negotiations with four firms, each with about 200 staff (Wang, 2002). None of the negotiations proved fruitful, as difficulties with the Da Hua member firm forced E&Y to reconsider the strategy. In another case of "same bed, different dreams," E&Y found it impossible to integrate E&Y Da Hua into the E&Y organization. E&Y continued to separately operate its joint venture firm, now separated from the Ministry of Finance. Many partners of Da Hua found it difficult to work in the new organization and left, often taking clients with them. Within three years, 30 of Da Hua's 47 public clients had left, often citing their opinion that the new firm was less cooperative and too risk adverse (Chen, Su, & Wu, 2010). By 2004, Anthony Wu publicly admitted defeat:

> The takeover of Da Hua has been successful, but combining the businesses has been very slow. There are such huge cultural differences between us. It is much easier to integrate individual accountants into the firm. (Yiu, 2004c)

Da Hua operated separately and failed to thrive while part of E&Y (Table 6.8).

In 2007, the remnants of Da Hua would be merged into E&Y Huaming. The experiment with local member firms of the Big Four was over. They

Table 6.8. E&Y Huaming and E&Y Da Hua Revenue.

Year	E&Y Huaming	E&Y Da Hua
2002	246	55
2003	329	59
2004	628	61
2005	971	112
2006	1,598	95
2007	2,316	120

Source: CICPA. RMB in millions.

failed because it was impossible for the Big Four firms to align the strategy of local owners with their global and regional strategies. While the CICPA wanted local control of the accounting practices, the Big Four insisted on close integration of the China practice with their Hong Kong practices as well as the global firms. While the PwC merger had initially convinced E&Y to open more merger negotiations, none were consummated because of the difficulty E&Y had experienced in its failed attempt to integrate Da Hua. In 2005, James Turley, Global CEO of E&Y said that, while they were open to mergers, he expected most of their growth would be organic (Ryan, 2005).

6.4.5.2. Deloitte and Pan China

In early 2004 Peter Bowie, China CEO for DTT, said: Acquisitions of local firms will be one of our strategies to expand in the rapidly growing China market. We are exploring takeover opportunities with a few local Chinese accounting firms (Yiu, 2004b). DTT China Chairman Kenneth McKelvie hinted that DTT wanted to avoid the clash of cultures that had doomed the E&Y Da Hua transaction:

> We are not planning to merge with any of the big mainland accounting firms, as it would be hard to blend them with Deloitte's culture and management style. We are focusing on small and medium sized domestic accounting firms that either have some special skills and knowledge in particular industries, or are located in cities where Deloitte does not yet have any exposure. (Yiu, 2004a)

In March 2005, DTT announced the acquisition of Beijing Pan-China Certified Public Accountants Co. Ltd. (Beijing Pan-China). Beijing Pan-China was a member of Pan-China Certified Public Accountants group, an affiliation of local firms in six Chinese cities. The acquisition involved DTT taking over the clients and staff of Beijing Pan-China. Beijing Pan-China Managing Director James Chen said that without the merger, his company would have no chance of gaining expertise in international accounting practices or preparing public offerings in the United States or Hong Kong (Tse, 2005).

Peter Bowie indicated that DTT hoped to team up with other members of the Pan-China group but warned it could be a long process. Charles Yen, managing partner of Deloitte's northern region was more optimistic: "We do not rule out the possibility that a new name, Deloitte Pan-China, could be adopted if more Pan-China members are incorporated and the new name makes a stronger brand name" (Zhao, 2005b). DTT completed a further acquisition of a Pan-China group member in

September 2005, when it acquired Pan-China Schinda,[16] a CPA firm based in Shenzhen. There were no further acquisitions of local firms by DTT. DTT partners stated that regulators had second thoughts about concept of the Big Four acquiring local firms and discouraged the practice.

6.5. STRUCTURE OF THE ACCOUNTING MARKET IN CHINA

This section presents findings related to the structure of the CPA profession in China. This begins with a brief discussion of the branding of firms in China, proceeds to identify top firms and their geographic coverage, and then presents selected comparative market measurements.

6.5.1. Branding

Accounting firms in China face challenges in branding. Only Chinese characters are recognized for legal purposes in China. When the Big Four came to China they needed to select Chinese names for the firms. PW selected two Chinese characters (普华 – *Pu Hua*) that were viewed to be the best phonetic representation of PW, yet also had an appealing meaning in Chinese (*Pu Hua* can be translated as the essence of China). Similarly, Peat Marwick selected 毕马威 – Bi Ma Wei. This phonosemantic approach method of creating a Chinese brand name has been found to result in more positively evaluated brands (Zhang & Schmitt, 2001). Often the firms had different Chinese names in Hong Kong and Taiwan. PW in Hong Kong used a phonosemantic representation of its original English name of Lowe Bingham. The use of differing names in Hong Kong and the mainland frequently was a source of confusion with clients and regulators. Most top accounting firms in China also have brand names in English. Many have selected the names of international networks of which they are members, a practice followed by all of the Big Four. Others have romanticized their Chinese name (e.g., Shinewing, Reanda). Others have adopted new names for their English brand (e.g., Ascenda, China Audit). Table 6.9 shows the various names used by the top 20 accounting firms in China.

Table 6.9. Practice Names of Top 20 Accounting Firms in China (2012).

Ranking	Name in Chinese	Name in Pinyin	English Brand	International Affiliation
1.	普华永道中天会计师事务所	Puhua Yongdao Zhongtian	PwC	PwC
2.	德勤华永会计师事务所	Deqin Huayong	DTT	DTT
3.	瑞华会计师事务所	Ruihua	RSM/Crowe Horwath	RSM/Crowe Horwath
4.	安永华明会计师事务所	Anyong Huaming	E&Y	E&Y
5.	毕马威华振会计师事务所	Bimawei Huazhen	KPMG	KPMG
6.	立信会计师事务所	Lixin	BDO	BDO
7.	大信会计师事务所	Daxin	Daxin	PKF
8.	天健会计师事务所	Tianjian	Pan-China	Unaffiliated
9.	信永中和会计师事务所	Xinyong Zhonghe	Shinewing	Praxity
10.	大华会计师事务所	Dahua	Dahua	Unaffiliated
11.	天职国际会计师事务所	Tianzhi Guoji	Baker Tilly	Baker Tilly
12.	致同会计师事务所	Zhitong	Grant Thornton	Grant Thornton
13.	中审亚太会计师事务所	Zhongzhen Yatai	China Audit	Unaffiliated
14.	中汇会计师事务所	Zhonghui	Zhonghui	Unaffiliated
15.	众环海华会计师事务所	Zhonghuan Haihua	Union Power	Unaffiliated
16.	利安达会计师事务所	Lianda	Reanda	Reanda Int'l
17.	华寅五洲会计师事务所	Huayin Wuzhou	Huayin Wuzhou	HLB International
18.	北京兴华会计师事务所	Beijing Xinghua	Beijing Xinghua	Moore Stephens
19.	中天运会计师事务所	Zhongtianyun	Zhongtianyun	Unaffiliated
20.	中兴财光华会计师事务所	Zhongxingcai Guanghua	Zhongxingcai Guanghua	Unaffiliated

Source: CIPCA and firm websites. Measured by 2012 revenue.

6.5.2. Largest Accounting Firms in China

Table 6.10 lists the top 20 accounting firms in China in 2012 based on revenue as reported to the CICPA. The revenue reported excluded the revenue of related entities that are not registered as accounting firms, including the WFOE subsidiaries of the Big Four that engage in consulting services. The CICPA list places Ruihua at the third position, above E&Y and KPMG. Ruihua is a firm created through the merger of the China affiliates of Crowe Horwath and RSM. The merger of these firms did not take place in 2012, but is expected to be concluded by the third quarter of 2013 (RSM, 2013).

Table 6.10. Top 20 Chinese Accounting Firms in 2012.

Rank	English Brand	Revenue	Partners	CPAs	Branches
1.	PwC	3,226	2	895	15
2.	DTT	3,045	2	747	15
3.	RSM/Crowe Horwath	2,437	334	1,951	40
4.	E &Y	2,236	2	884	14
5.	KPMG	2,136	2	615	12
6.	BDO	1,774	115	1,612	28
7.	Daxin	1,366	53	1,056	13
8.	Pan-China	1,105	119	1,169	13
9.	Shinewing	1,041	106	933	18
10.	Dahua	1,003	102	960	17
11.	Baker Tilly	812	34	714	18
12.	Grant Thornton	746	120	724	16
13.	China Audit	534	33	642	20
14.	Zhonghui	529	24	269	12
15.	Union Power	441	22	353	11
16.	Reanda	426	31	525	20
17.	Huayin Wuzhou	354	16	440	11
18.	Beijing Xinghua	341	51	509	14
19.	Zhongtianyun	302	22	394	10
20.	Zhongxingcai Guanghua	261	15	563	11

Source: CICPA. Revenue in RMB millions. Big Four partners reflect only the two joint venture partners.

6.5.3. Geographic Coverage

China's economic development during the 1980s was a process that gradually opened up the country starting with special economic zones and cities near the coast. In the 1980s and early 1990s the Big Four established offices in what has come to be known as China's tier-one cities. The tier-one cities include Beijing, Shanghai, Guangzhou, and Shenzhen. As opportunities in other cities presented themselves, the Big Four began to open offices in tier-two cities. Tier-two cities, like Dalian, Qingdao, Tianjin, and Xiamen are large cities, but opened up to foreign investment later than the tier-one cities. The Big Four firms have been cautious about opening new offices. The global firms cautioned management in China not to repeat the mistake they had made in other territories of opening too many offices. One Big Four partner involved in the strategic planning for new offices remarked:

> We could see we would need more than four offices to serve such a large country, but how many would we ultimately need? Should we follow the history of the United States, where we expanded during the 1950s and 1960s to a hundred cities? One

Australian partner on our board advised us not to open offices in smaller cities as the Australian firm had done. Another partner quipped that the smallest city they were considering had a population not much less than all of Australia. This was not a situation we had ever seen before.

Table 6.11 lists the location of Big Four offices in China as of September 2013. The Big Four have maintained offices in each of the four tier-one cities in China – Beijing, Shanghai, Guangzhou, and Shenzhen. Three of the Big Four have 14 offices in Mainland China although they have not chosen the same cities. The smallest of the Big Four, KPMG, has only eight offices, and has closed several offices in recent years.

China has 33 cities with a population of over 2 million and an additional 138 with a population between 1 million and 2 million. By contrast, the United States has 51 Metropolitan Statistical Areas with a population in excess of 1 million. The Big Four have a mean of 89 offices in the United

Table 6.11. Location of Big Four Offices in China.

Location	DTT	E&Y	KPMG	PwC
Beijing	X	X	X	X
Chongqing	X			X
Chengdu		X	X	
Dalian	X	X		X
Fuzhou			X	
Guangzhou	X	X	X	X
Hangzhou	X	X	X	X
Harbin	X			
Jinan	X			
Nanjing	X	X		X
Ningbo				X
Qingdao		X	X	X
Shanghai	X	X	X	X
Shenyang		X		
Shenzhen	X	X	X	X
Suzhou	X	X		X
Tianjin	X	X		X
Wuhan	X	X		
Xiamen	X	X		X
Xi'an				X
Total	14	14	8	14

Source: Firm websites as of September 2013.

States.[17] While the stage of development of the second- and third-tier cities in China is not comparable to similar sized cities in the United States, the present level of geographic coverage in China by the Big Four and larger Chinese accounting firms is low when compared to the United States. The data in Table 6.10 evidence that no CPA firm in China has a sufficient number of offices to be considered a national firm. In 2006 the 5,671 accounting firms in China had a total number of branch offices of 618.[18] Ruihua, the Crowe Horwath and RSM affiliate, has the largest number of offices of any firm in 2013 with 40 offices.

Wang, Wong, and Xia (2008) determined that Chinese state-owned enterprises controlled by provincial, city, and county governments are more likely than non-state firms to hire small auditors within the same region. This tendency is significantly attenuated in regions with more developed institutions. This partially explains the current absence of national firms in China, yet portends opportunity for the emergence of national firms because of institutional development.

The number of offices reported in Table 6.7 for the Big Four includes only the registered branch offices of their auditing firm, and not other representative offices and offices of the firm's wholly owned consulting companies (which are not permitted to conduct audits). The Big Four firms have often opened in a new city with a representative office or branch of their WFOE because the regulatory processes for these offices is easier than establishing a branch of the CPA firm. Regulatory approval is then sought to establish a branch of the CPA firm in the same location.

6.5.4. Market Concentration

Table 6.12 presents market concentration data for the period following China's accession to WTO from 2002 to 2012. The data is based on the revenue of the 100 largest accounting firms in China based on data provided by the CICPA. The four-firm concentration ratio (CR4)[19] increases annually through 2007 where the Big Four have nearly 55% of the top 100 market. The Big Four market share drops significantly by 2012 to approximately 35%. The major reasons for the decrease appear to be the significant reduction in international IPOs following the international financial crisis in 2008 as well as the increasing competitiveness of local firms. There were many mergers of domestic accounting firms during this period, which have created some of China's largest domestic accounting firms.

Table 6.12. China Accounting Market Concentration Post WTO.

Year	CR4	CR8	HHI
2002	0.3698	0.4420	483
2003	0.3902	0.4589	506
2004	0.4571	0.5263	613
2005	0.4946	0.5630	717
2006	0.5300	0.5993	764
2007	0.5472	0.6298	798
2008	0.5281	0.6314	752
2009	0.4430	0.5670	584
2010	0.4119	0.5508	539
2011	0.3618	0.5257	470
2012	0.3480	0.5509	478

Source: CICPA Top 100.

The market for the top 100 accounting firms in China is competitive for the entire period evaluated in Table 6.12 under guidelines used by the US Department of Justice that consider any market with an HHI below 1000 to be competitive. The market is becoming increasingly competitive.

6.5.4.1. Decline in Big Four Market Shares

The Big Four increased market share steadily after China entered WTO in 2001. The trend toward increasing concentration, as measured by CR4 and HHI, reversed in 2008 and the reversal accelerated in 2009. One significant reason for the lower market shares by the Big Four in 2008 and 2009 was the decline in overseas IPOs of Chinese companies as world financial markets declined in 2008 and early 2009. By mid-2009, there was a significant rebound of IPO activities in the greater China market, but more of these listings were on Chinese stock exchanges where the Big Four has a lower market share (PricewaterhouseCoopers, 2010a).

The number of H-share IPOs began to decline after 2006 (Table 6.10). This indicates that fewer large SOEs are seeking foreign capital in part because many have already listed. As explained in this chapter, IPOs of large SOEs have been a significant portion of Big Four revenue (Table 6.13).

Chinese stock markets were also affected by the global financial crisis and there were declines in the number of IPOs in Chinese stock exchanges in 2008 and 2009. Table 6.11 shows the number of IPOs on Chinese stock exchanges from 2005 to 2009. There was a large increase in the number of IPOs on the Shenzhen Stock Exchange (including the newly formed ChiNext board) beginning in 2006. While there was a decline in the number

Table 6.13. Number of H-Share IPOs from 2000 to 2012.

Year	Number of IPOs
2000	4
2001	2
2002	6
2003	13
2004	10
2005	12
2006	23
2007	9
2008	7
2009	6
2010	7
2011	6
2012	9

Source: Hong Kong Stock Exchange.

Table 6.14. Number of IPOs on Chinese Stock Exchanges.

Year	Shanghai	Shenzhen	ChiNext
2000	88	49	–
2001	78	1	–
2002	70	1	–
2003	67	0	–
2004	61	39	–
2005	3	12	–
2006	13	52	–
2007	25	100	–
2008	6	71	–
2009	9	54	36
2010	28	205	118
2011	39	115	128
2012	26	55	74
Total	513	754	356

Source: CSMAR database.

of listings in Shenzhen in 2008, this market was less affected by the global financial crisis than other markets. A major reason for the strength of the Shenzhen Exchange was a shift in policy to encourage privately owned companies to list on Chinese exchanges. Prior to this shift, many of these companies would likely have listed overseas (Table 6.14).

Chinese regulators stopped new IPOs in October 2012. About 765 companies were awaiting approval for new offerings at March 31, 2013 (*Bloomberg News*, 2013). The market remained closed to new IPOs in December 2013 although regulators signaled they expected to allow new IPOs early in 2014.

As indicated by Tables 5.3, 5.4, and 5.8, the Big Four has a lower share of the audit market for Chinese companies listed on Chinese exchanges than those listed on foreign exchanges. In 2009, the Big Four audited only three of the nine A-share listings in Shanghai. Of the 54 IPOs on Shenzhen's SME board in 2009, and the 36 that took place on Shenzhen's ChiNext, only one was audited by the Big Four, with the remainder audited by indigenous firms (PricewaterhouseCoopers, 2010a).

The declining Big Four market shares in China as shown on Table 6.12 after 2007 reflect several important trends. Many of China's larger state-owned enterprises have already listed. All four major banks have been listed, as have the three major oil companies. While all of the major SOEs have become clients of the Big Four and provide sizable annuities to them, the number of new listings has declined. Most of the Big Four's share of A-share listings comes from larger companies that are also listed on foreign exchanges. Table 6.15 shows the market for dual listed companies. Only 61 of 156 H-share companies also have A-share listings. This reflects an opportunity for the Big Four. If the 95 H-share companies without a Shanghai A-share listing were to seek one, the Big Four market share of companies listed on the Shanghai Stock Exchange would likely increase. Table 6.15 also reports that 23 of the top 50 companies listing A-shares on the Shanghai Stock Exchange have sought dual listing in Hong Kong. The Big Four has an opportunity to obtain the large A-share companies should they choose to list in Hong Kong. As Table 6.14 indicates, there has been no recent rush for the additional H-share listings. Of greater interest to the

Table 6.15. Market for Dual Listed Companies.

Type	Number
H-share companies with A-share listings	61
H-share companies without A-share listings	95
Top 50 Shanghai A-share with H-share listing	27
Top 50 Shanghai A-share without H-share listing	23
Top 50 Shenzhen A-share with H-share listing	3
Top 50 Shenzhen A-share without H-share listing	47

Source: PricewaterhouseCoopers (2010a).

Big Four is the fact that only 3 of the top 50 companies in Shenzhen have sought H-share listings. On one hand, it presents a potentially lucrative market for the Big Four. On the other hand, it suggests that these companies have not seen the need to pursue dual listing, and may signal a decline in the importance of Hong Kong as a means of raising capital for Chinese companies.

The strong performance of indigenous auditors in 2009 listings on Chinese stock exchanges (winning 95 of 99 listings) indicates that indigenous auditors have become competitive in this market. If this trend continues, the market shares of the Big Four of audits of companies listed on Chinese exchanges will further erode. The recent trends indicate that the counterhegemonic strategies of indigenous firms that will be discussed in Chapter 8 may be beginning to pay dividends.

6.5.4.2. Comparative Market Measures

Table 6.16 compares the top 100 accounting firm markets of Australia, the United States, the United Kingdom, and China. The market for top 100 firms is significantly more concentrated in Australia, the United States, and the United Kingdom when compared to China. The Big Four firms are very small in China when compared to their US firm, with the largest Big Four firm in China less than 2% of the size of the largest US firm. The

Table 6.16. Comparison of Australia, the United States, the United Kingdom, and China Accounting Firms in 2012.

	Australia	United States	United Kingdom	China
	Top 100	Top 100	Top 100	Top 100
Concentration measures				
CR4	.5974	.7393	.7298	.3480
CR8	.7178	.8160	.8318	.5509
HHI	970	1505	1420	478
Revenue measures (US$ millions)				
Mean	83.6	494.7	167.9	49.9
Largest	1,478.9	13,067.0	3,900.2	512.1
1st quartile (25th)	43.2	125.0	37.0	41.5
Median (50th)	11.6	61.0	17.9	12.9
3rd quartile (75th)	5.7	40.0	9.0	7.4
Smallest (100th)	4.3	31.0	3.8	3.8

Sources: BRW top 100. Accounting Today top 100. Accountancy Age top 100, and CICPA top 100. RMB converted at 6.30. UK£ at 1.58. A$ at 1.04.

median local firm (the 50th) in China is about 21% of the size of the 50th largest firm in the United States. The 75th Chinese firm is about 19% of the size of the comparable firm in the United States. When compared to Australia, however, firms in China are larger than their Australian counterparts at the median and third quartiles.

The Big Four dominates the Australian, US, and UK markets to a greater extent than it does the market in China. The HHI measured by the top 100 firms in the United States and the United Kingdom in 2012 is 1505 and 1420, respectively, which indicates moderately concentrated markets. The Australian market is less concentrated, with an HHI of 970. The four-firm concentration ratios of .7393 for the United States, and .7298 for the United Kingdom, are substantially higher than the four-firm concentration ratio for China of .3480%. Significantly, unlike the other markets presented, the four firms included in the China CR4 exclude one of the Big Four.

The author determined that the HHI for the top 100 US accounting firms for 2006 is 1479.[20] This calculation was done to allow it to be compared to the HHI of 2300 calculated by the US Government Accountability Office (GAO) for the same year (Government Accountability Office, 2008). The different samples used in the respective tests explain the difference. The GAO measure looks at audit fees of public companies. A measurements based on the revenue of the top 100 accounting firms includes revenue from both public and nonpublic clients (including private companies, government, and not-for-profit entities). These findings suggest that the nonpublic market in the United States is less concentrated than the public company market. China has the same phenomenon. The HHI calculated for the fees earned from companies listed on the combined Shanghai and Shenzhen stock exchanges is 908,[21] substantially higher than the top 100 firms market HHI of 478, indicating that the nonpublic market is less concentrated than the public company market. The Big Four are not as successful at capturing the audit work of private and state-owned enterprises as they are in the public company market.

6.5.5. Participation of Chinese Firms in Global Networks

Nine of the 10 largest accounting firms in China (Table 6.10) have affiliated with an international network (Table 6.17). The member firms of the Big Four, and RSM practice in some derivation of their global network brand. Daxin joined PKF in November 2010 although as of July 2013 it was still

Table 6.17. Global Networks in China – 2012.

Global Rank	Firm	Global Revenue	China Member Firms	China Rank	China % Global Rev.
1.	PwC	31,510	PwC Zhongtian	1	1.6
2.	Deloitte	31,300	Deloitte Touche Tohmatsu	2	1.5
3.	EY	24,420	E&Y Huaming	4	1.6
4.	KPMG International	23,030	KPMG Huazhen	6	1.5
5.	BDO	6,016	BDO Shu Lun Pan	5	4.7
6.	Geneva Group International	4,386	Horizon Group	Unranked	
7.	Grant Thornton International	4,182	Grant Thornton	12	2.8
8.	RSM International	3,987	Ruihua	3	9.7
9.	Praxity Global Alliance	3,721	Shinewing	9	4.4
10.	Baker Tilly International	3,300	Baker Tilly China	11	3.9
11.	Crowe Horwath International	3,078	Ruihua	3	12.6
12.	The TAG Alliances	3,025	Lehman Brown	Unranked	
13.	Nexia International	2,827	Nexia HDDY Shanghai	79	0.3
			Beijing Yongtuo	Unranked	
14.	Leading Edge Alliance	2,769	Shinewing	9	6.0
15.	PKF International	2,683	Daxin	7	8.0
16.	Moore Stephens International	2,283	Beijing Xinghua	16	2.4
17.	PrimeGlobal	2,029	Five member firms	Unranked	
18.	Kreston International	1,965	Twelve member firms	Unranked	
19.	AGN International	1,603	Union Power	15	4.4
20.	HLB International	1,571	Huayin Wuzhou	18	3.6

Source: Accountancy Age top 35 networks 2013, CICPA.

using the brand Daxin. Ruihua, formed with the 2013 merger of Crowe Horwath and RSM in China, has indicated that it hopes to continue affiliation with both networks.

China's eighth largest firm, Shinewing, the former C&L member firm, has taken a different strategy. Shinewing has pursued a strategy of opening foreign offices directly and has offices in Australia, Japan, Hong Kong, and Singapore (Chan, 2008; Luk, 2010a). In March 2011, Shinewing joined global alliance Praxity. The International Accounting Bulletin reported that Shinewing joined Praxity because it is fiercely independent and better suited to a looser alliance model. Sixteenth ranked Reanda has created its own network, the Reanda International Network, with member firms in 12 countries and plans to expand to 14 countries in 2013 (Li, 2010; Reanda, 2013). These firms are attempting to create a competitive international firm without joining an existing international alliance.

It is notable that the China operations of the Big Four average only about 1.4% of their global revenue. This percentage may be understated due to the exclusion of consulting revenue in WFOEs from the China revenue. Second-tier firms BDO and PKF respectively earn 4.7% and 8% of their revenues from China. Newly created Ruihua constitutes 12.6% of Crowe Horwarth's and 9.7% of RSM's global revenue, illustrating the importance of retaining this firm to both global alliances.

NOTES

1. China's one-child policy was not implemented nationally until 1979, meaning that the Big Four did not begin hiring new graduates who had been born under this policy until about 2000. It is unclear what Chan is talking about.
2. The *Notice Concerning Permission for International Accounting Firms to Identify Member Firms in China* was issued by the MOF on January 22, 1996.
3. Zhou Zhongwei was an accounting professor at SUFE and a partner with its accounting firm Da Hua CPAs, which was the joint venture partner of PW. Zhou was assigned as the representative to the joint venture and later became a partner of PwC. After his retirement from PwC he became the chief accountant of the CSRC.
4. The three American partners were Donald Menovich, Kent Watson, and Johnny Chen. Menovich was the chairman of PW China until his retirement in 1998. Watson, who led PwC in China until his retirement in 2004, replaced him. Ding's memoirs noted his admiration for Watson.
5. See Chapter 5 for a discussion of how PwC developed and popularized this technique to facilitate foreign ownership in restricted industries. The controlled entities are commonly referred to as "variable interest entities" or VIEs, a term used in the relevant accounting standards.
6. The author participated in this meeting.
7. Several interviewees from Big Six firms who practiced in China during the 1990s expressed their opinion that China had conducted espionage activities related to their practice. Ding's report confirms their suspicions.
8. Honorificabilitudinitatibus, the longest word in the English language with alternating consonants and vowels, means the state of being able to be honored.

9. Cooper et al. (1998) describe how national identity is a significant source of belonging, pride, income, and conflict within expatriate populations of Big Six partners in emerging markets. The phenomenon was present in the expatriate partner groups of the Big Six firms in China.

10. GATT was transformed into the WTO in 1995.

11. Although the PW and C&L merger had not been completed at this time, it is clear from the record that PW and C&L were operating as a single firm on the WTO response. The source documents are inconsistent during this period with some referring to the Big Six and some the Big Five. I have used the Big Five except in quotations where the original usage has been preserved.

12. It is unlikely that the Big Five made this request since the size restrictions did not affect them.

13. Ding did not mention that he had refused numerous applications by the Big Six to open branch offices.

14. Arthur Andersen failed a few months after China's WTO accession reducing the Big Five to the Big Four.

15. http://www.pwc.com/gx/en/office-locations/hong-kong.html, accessed on September 15, 2010.

16. Pan-China Schinda is alternatively romanticized as Tianjian Xinde.

17. *Source*: Big Four websites.

18. *Source*: www.cicpa.org.cn.

19. The firms included in the four-firm concentration ratio are the Big Four for each year of the data, except for 2012 where Ruihua replaces KPMG.

20. The HHI of 1479 for 2006 was calculated using the 2006 list of the top 100 CPA firms in the United States as published in Accounting Today.

21. See Table 5.3.

CHAPTER 7

COUNTER-HEGEMONY

> In a word, although the "wolves" are coming, it is nothing to be afraid of. Since ten years ago they have come. And only because they came, did we start to know that there is a wider sky outside and we could quicken the system reformation of the firms. We are happy to dance with the wolves.
>
> – Ding Pingzhun, Director General of CICPA, 1998

This chapter will discuss several key aspects of the development of local certified public accountants (CPA) firms in China. The principal focus of this study is on the Big Four in China, yet understanding their role requires considering how local firms developed and how they responded to Big Four competition. Under the theoretical foundation underpinning this study, the development and reform of local accounting firms is a counter-hegemonic project directed at undermining the hegemony of the Big Four. This is done through a series of institutional reforms of the nature described by Rudi Dutschke (1969, p. 249) as "the long march through the institutions." This chapter will outline several key engagements in the long march through the institutions by Chinese accountants.

The chapter begins with a discussion of the development of accounting and auditing standards. The adoption of international accounting and auditing standards was a consequence of ideological shifts associated with the increasing globalization of China's economy. The increasing acceptance of international standards signals one of the triumphs of the Big Four ideology of globalization. In a classic Gramscian counter-hegemonic response, Chinese accountants joined standard setting bodies, gained influence in international standard setting, and finally changed international standards to fit their ideology.

Next, the discussion turns to the closure of the profession through CPA licensing. Chinese accountants attempted, largely unsuccessfully, to close the profession to foreigners through local examination and licensing. Local examination created a language and cultural barrier to the profession that few foreigners could cross, so they simply found a way around it.

Local firm reforms will be explained next. The Chinese Institute of Certified Public Accountants (CICPA), functioning both as a corporatist entity representing the domestic profession[1] and as an agent of the state (Yee, 2012), pushed through significant reforms intended to improve the competitiveness of domestic firms against the Big Four. These reforms, ongoing at the time of writing, have the potential of shaping the accounting profession in China, and the world, much differently from its current shape.

In 2012, the joint ventures of the Big Four began to reach the end of their 20-year lives. Chinese regulators took advantage of this event to force the firms to reorganize into limited liability partnerships (LLPs). Although Chinese law required that partners in LLPs be CPAs licensed to practice in China, the Big Four negotiated a compromise allowing 40% ownership by unlicensed partners that would be reduced over a transition period.

The State-owned Asset Supervision and Administration Commission of the State Council (SASAC) is responsible for managing large centrally controlled state-owned enterprises (SOEs). SASAC implemented an auditor rotation program that many believed was designed to shift the audits of SOEs away from the Big Four to local accounting firms.

Finally, I explain an important counter-hegemonic project, the opening of the market for auditing companies listed in Hong Kong to mainland accountants. This project has the potential to undermine Big Four domination of the market for Chinese companies listed in Hong Kong, and was a direct attack on the hegemonic project that helped lead to Big Four domination of the Chinese markets.

7.1. ACCOUNTING AND AUDITING STANDARDS

The environment in which a country operates shapes its national accounting practices (Radebaugh & Gray, 1997). Accounting in China during the period from 1949 to opening up in the 1980s drew principally on the Soviet model (Blake & Gao, 1995; Chen, Jubb, & Tran, 1997; Chen & Tran, 1995; Lou & Enthoven, 1987; Taussig, Yang, & Mao, 1994; Zhou, 1988). The Soviet model had been uncritically accepted in China as socialist accounting (Ezzamel, Xiao, & Pan, 2007). The approach under the Soviet model was decidedly managerial rather than financial with the primary purpose being "to assist in the implementation of state economic policy and to maintain state control over the means of production" (Adhikari & Wang, 1995, p. 27).

7.1.1. Accounting Standards

Ge Jiashu, an accounting professor at Xiamen University, first championed accounting reform in China. Ge Jiashu was born in Jiangsu Province in 1921, graduated from the Xiamen University Department of Accounting in 1945, and stayed on to teach. In 1978, as China began to open up to the outside world, Professor Ge argued that accounting should be part of China's reforms. He published an article arguing for the reinstatement of double entry accounting in China. He said that accounting methods are only a means of recording economic facts and have nothing to do with class (Ge, 1978). Ge, 57-years-old at the time, was a respected scholar and deputy president of the Accounting Society of China. His article stirred considerable discussion, with some calling it "the first round of shot in setting things right in the field of accounting" (Xiamen University, 2010). Others resisted Ge's attempts to rehabilitate the role of accounting. Li (1980) disagreed with Ge, arguing that accounting is not only a management tool, but also a class struggle tool, and accordingly should serve the needs of the proletariat. He argued that United States' generally accepted accounting principles (GAAP) was just another name for protecting capitalists. Li would have found considerable support for his position in the work of later Marxist accounting scholars (Bryer, 1999, 2005, 2006; Hopper & Armstrong, 1991). Ge's views, however, prevailed, and he continued throughout the 1980s to publish articles arguing that "accounting is in fact a methodology, a common international language of business, and that no one can change the scientific basis of accounting, the essence of which is technical" (Xiamen University, 2010). Ge played a key role in the winning of the ideological battles that enabled China to embrace international accounting and auditing standards.

The process of rebuilding accounting as an institution took shape in 1985, when the National People's Congress adopted the *Accounting Law of the People's Republic of China*, the first accounting law under the People's Republic. The law contained six chapters, which are as follows: sphere of accounting calculation, measurement and procedure, accounting supervision, accounting organization and personnel, legal responsibility, and supplementary provisions (Chow, Chau, & Gary, 1995). A key motivation for creating the accounting law was a 1984 reform to the system of taxation that replaced a profit remittance model with a corporate income tax based on net income. The same accounting rules were used to calculate profits and taxable income (Tang et al., 1994).

China's opening up exposed the need to reform accounting standards. The Soviet model was unworkable for the new foreign-invested joint ventures. The control measurements of the Soviet model were designed for a centrally planned economy and failed to provide for the rights of the respective partners in the enterprise (Blake, Gao, & Wraith, 2000). Accordingly, in 1985, the Ministry of Finance (MOF) issued *Regulations on Accounting System for Sino-Foreign Joint Ventures*, which introduced Western accounting practices to Chinese firms involved in joint ventures, yet these new regulations did not apply to most SOEs (Xiang, 1998).

While the 1985 regulations dealt with the needs of foreign investors, it became apparent that existing accounting practices were not suitable for a market economy. Tang (2000) says that China considered adapting the traditional accounting systems to meet the needs of a market economy but instead decided to adopt systems used in market economies. Mennicken (2008, p. 388) explains that international standards are fundamental instruments in the reform of a developing economy:

> Instead, it is suggested that it is at the peripheries of capitalism that new spaces for globalisation are delineated, and new elements and actors are defined and integrated. Here, international standards and models are taken particularly seriously. They are fundamental to the re-defining of organisational identities and regulatory politics. They are linked to dreams of modern development, and their adoption is seen as a way of linking up with, and becoming accepted by, Western worlds of economic and political activities.

7.1.1.1. International Participation

In 1993, the MOF signed a three-year contract with Deloitte Touche Tohmatsu (DTT) for $2.6 million to assist China to develop accounting standards in harmony with international standards (Jack, 1993a). The World Bank funded the project. DTT developed general and industry-specific standards, and established a system of continuing education for practicing accountants. Price Waterhouse (PW) was engaged for a $7.15 million World Bank-funded project to help improve the accounting, supervision, and regulatory systems of China's banks (Fung, 1993). Tom Macy, chairman of PW's worldwide financial services practice, led the PW project. These two contracts were significant for two reasons. First, they enabled the Big Four to advance their ideology in the development of standards.

This is reflected in China's relatively rapid adoption of international standards, and helped the Big Four to win consent to the view that their globalizing ideology was rightfully superior – the key element for establishing hegemony. Another significant reason was the involvement of the World Bank. This illustrated how transnational institutions help to reinforce the globalizing ideology of the Big Four.

7.1.1.2. Five Reforms

As Chinese companies corporatized and sought outside investment, investors had difficulty parsing the financial statements and the restatement of Chinese financial statements into "Western terms" was a costly process (Winkle, Huss, & Chen, 1994, p. 50). China launched a series of five significant reforms to accounting standards which brought Chinese accounting standards (CAS) in line with international standards (Peng & van der Laan Smith, 2010).

1. The first reform was launched in 1992 with the issuance of the *Accounting Standard for Business Enterprises* (1992 Standards), and *The Experimental Accounting System from Joint Stock Limited Enterprises*. These were considered revolutionary changes since they introduced a market-oriented accounting model and were the first rules to apply to domestic companies without foreign investment (Chen, Sun, & Wang, 2002; Tang, Cooper, & Leung, 1995). Some authors argued that the 1992 Standards introduced a conceptual framework that was consistent with international standards (Davidson, Gelardi, & Li, 1996) while others disagreed (Xiao & Pan, 1997; Xiao, Young, Dyson, & Pan, 1995).
2. The second reform was marked by the issuance in 1998 of the *Accounting System for Joint Stock Limited Enterprise* (which replaced the 1992 system), and 10 specific CAS (1998 Standards).
3. The third reform resulted in the 2001 issuance of the *Accounting System for Business Enterprises* (which replaced the 1998 system), as well as by 16 CAS, which consisted of six newly issued standards, five revised standards, and five original standards (2001 Standards).
4. The fourth reform stage of development is defined by the issuance in February 2006 of the Accounting Standards for Business Enterprises (ASBE). This was a major revision of accounting standards, effective on January 1, 2007. It consisted of a revised basic standard, which replaced the 1992 Standard, and 38 CAS, which replaced the 2001 system and the 16 previously issued CAS. On November 8, 2005, the MOF and Sir David Tweedie of the International Accounting Standards Board (IASB)

signed a memorandum that declared Chinese standards as being substantially in convergence with International Financial Reporting Standards (IFRS) except on three points: related party transactions and disclosure, reversal of impairment on depreciable assets, and government subsidies (the latter was subsequently aligned with IFRS) (Ding & Su, 2008).

5. The fifth state of reform, announced in 2009 by the MOF, committed China to full convergence with IFRS by 2011 (MOF, 2009).

A significant step in the reform process was an agreement between the Hong Kong Institute of Certified Public Accountants (HKICPAs) and the China Accounting Standards Board that concluded that:

> Financial statements prepared in accordance with ASBEs effective on 6 December 2007, after adjusting for the reconciliation differences ... should achieve substantially the same effect as those prepared in accordance with HKFRSs (Hong Kong Financial Reporting Standards) effective on the same date. (Ryan, 2008)

Volunteer members from the Big Four and a number of medium-sized Hong Kong firms aided in the technical analysis that was the basis of the agreement. The European Commission on December 12, 2008 decided that the GAAPs of Japan, China, Canada, South Korea, and India were equivalent to IFRS and permitted their use by companies listed in the European Union (EU). The Commission will review the situation of some of these countries (China, Canada, South Korea, and India) by 2011 at the latest (European Commission, 2008).

A number of scholars have evaluated the reform process. Hilmy (1999) examined the political influences that drove the 1992 Standards. Hilmy observed that it seemed that communism could coexist with a market economy and that accounting standards would be integrated with microeconomic and macroeconomic policies as part of a response to political pressures to improve economic conditions.

Several authors argued that reform was motivated by the increasing privatization of the economy (Tang, 2000; Winkle et al., 1994). The five reforms that led toward full convergence with IFRS have been underway for almost 20 years. Ding (2000) examined some of the reasons why full convergence was not realized earlier. He concluded that the standards reflected the will of the Chinese authorities to respect international standards yet to preserve some national characteristics. He pointed out a number of peculiarities or divergence from international practice and concluded that these peculiarities exist because of state macroeconomic considerations. He also determined that some aspects of accounting regulation lacked internal and external coherence caused by a habit of translating international standards "word for word from their English texts" (p. 38). Chen et al. (1997) picked up on this point, noting that the attempts to install Western-based accounting principles without adjustment for China's unique culture were causing problems. Chen et al. (1997) expanded on this theme, stating that the decision to adopt Anglo-American accounting principles and standards was incongruous with the socio-economic conditions and institutional arrangements that prevailed in the People's Republic of China (PRC). Specifically, they pointed to modes of enterprise management and agency problems, undelineated property rights, lack of appropriate sanctions in the legal system, lack of a central social security system, and the lack of competent accounting personnel.

Graham and Li (1997) examined situations where CAS were different than standards found in the West. They concluded that the anomalies are explainable by the principle of *guo qing*, which implies that change will be implemented only in conjunction with Chinese needs. An important implication of this conclusion is that further harmonization marks a change in Chinese needs, a change that might be spurred by the further globalization of the Chinese economy. Xiao, Weetman, and Sun (2004) explained how China's retention of a uniform accounting system (standard chart of accounts) while adopting international accounting standards was a political response to accommodate the special circumstances of the society in transition. These special circumstances included a transforming government, strong state-ownership, a weak accounting profession, a weak and imperfect equity market, and the inertial effects of cultural factors and accounting traditions.

A study of the progress of the reform in CAS was conducted by The Institute of Chartered Accountants in Scotland (2010). Some of the interviewees in this study believed that a word-by-word adoption of IFRS was unlikely to happen because of the Chinese desire to maintain sovereignty over accounting standards.

The consistent theme in this thread of research is that institutional changes in China's economy created isomorphic pressures for changes in accounting practices to meet the requirements of the changing economy. Accounting standard changes often occurred in advance of supporting institutional changes, suggesting that the introduction of new standards was used to encourage institutional change. Change did not happen immediately, but the progress was relentless. Tang (2000, p. 95) observed that: "It is not easy to introduce new and somewhat alien accounting concepts and principles in a short period of time."

7.1.1.3. Convergence with International Standards

The story of accounting standards in China is a story of increasing convergence with international standards. A series of articles have documented the convergence of Chinese standards with IFRS from the original 1992 standards to the 2006 reforms that introduced CAS (Chen, Gul, & Su, 1999; Chen et al., 2002; Chui & Wong, 1999; Haverty, 2006; Peng et al., 2008). The most current and significant research on convergence was conducted by Peng and van der Laan Smith (2010). They examined convergence through a longitudinal study from 1992 to 2006. They found that CAS converged with IFRS through direct importation of international standards or progressive changes to Chinese standards. Following metrics that they developed, they determined that convergence improved from 20% in 1992 to 77% in 2006.

Chen and Cheng (2007) examined forces for convergence and found that regulatory forces by the China Securities Regulatory Commission (CSRC) were responsible for most of the harmonization. Corporate governance was not found to be an effective enforcement mechanism for accounting standards. In contrast, Chen and Zhang (2010) (including one of the same authors) found that audit committee practices significantly influenced compliance with standards. They also found that regulatory enforcement was a more significant factor in compliance than the actual convergence of the standards. They found no evidence that international CPA firms outperformed local CPA firms with respect to IFRS compliance, leading them to caution the government against promoting international firms as a means of achieving IFRS compliance. This comment illustrates a persistent bias against the international firms by scholars in this field. The fact that at the time of their study local CPA firms were performing as well as international firms at ensuring IFRS compliance does not provide any evidence as to whether this achievement resulted from mimetic isomorphism or the independent development of IFRS skills by the local CPA firms. As this study indicates, government policy toward the international firms consistently viewed these firms as a source of technologies that would be deployed to the local firms. An alternative interpretation of Chen and Zhang's findings would indicate that local CPA firms had developed IFRS skills because of the presence of the Big Four firms. The firms could have mimicked the international firms in order to better compete with them.

The convergence literature documents a persistent effort by Chinese authorities to force the adoption of international standards. While many scholars looked for and found incidents of institutional resistance to the wholesale adoption of international standards without adjustment for the unique aspects of the Chinese institutional setting, that resistance proved temporary and ultimately futile. Accounting standards were being used as a tool to facilitate broader institutional change, and the direction of that change was to conform to globally accepted standards.

7.1.1.4. Chinese Involvement in International Accounting Standards Setting
The IASB determines international accounting standards. The IASB, formed in 2001, succeeded the International Accounting Standards Committee (IASC) that was founded in 1973. In 1982, China opened discussions about participating in IASC, but China first needed to join the International Federation of Accountants (IFAC). A major obstacle for China's membership in IFAC was Taiwan. The National Federations of Certified Public Accountants of the Republic of China was a founding member of IFAC (IFAC, 2011). China did not recognize the Republic of China as a country, and other organizations, including the United Nations and most countries, had accepted China's position. Ding Pingzhun visited CSRC chief accountant Wang Jianxi on August 4, 1995 to seek his advice on how to get the CICPA into IFAC. Wang Jianxi told him that CSRC had insisted that their Taiwanese counterpart change their name to Chinese Taipei and suggested that Ding ally with some powerful international members of IFAC to put pressure on the Taiwanese (Ding, 2006b, p. 334). Michael Sharpe, chairman of IASC, took the lead in lobbying for China's admission to IFAC (South China Morning Post, 1996). The Taiwan organization subsequently changed its name to the Federation of CPA Associations of Chinese Taiwan and the CICPA was accepted as a member of IFAC on May 8, 1997 (Xu, 1997). On July 1, 2007, Zhang Wei-Guo became the first Chinese member of the IASB, and only the second member to come from Asia or from an emerging economy (The Accountant, 2006). Zhang Wei-Guo had previously been the chief accountant of the CSRC following a career as an accounting professor at the Shanghai University of Finance and Economics (SUFE). He was required under IASB rules to sever his ties with the CSRC. Liu Zhongli, former Minister of Finance and member of the Central Committee of the Chinese Communist Party, serves as a trustee of the IFRS Foundation under which the IASB operates. Li Feilong, controller of CNOOC, serves on the IFRS Interpretations committee (IFRS Foundation, 2011a).

In February 2006, the MOF and the IASB announced plans to converge CAS with IFRS. While the new ASBE issued in 2006 had achieved a substantial degree of convergence, there were three notable areas where the standards were incompatible. Chinese standard setters easily fixed two, but the International Accounting Standards (IAS) rules on related party transactions were problematic. Before 2003, state-controlled entities were exempt from IAS 24's related party disclosure requirements. This exemption was removed in a 2003 revision, which specified that profit-oriented state-controlled entities that use IFRS must disclose transactions with other state-controlled enterprises (Ramanna, Donovan, & Dai, 2009). Chinese bureaucrats, who believed that the application of these rules would be adverse to the interests of China's large state-owned sector, resisted the IAS 24 disclosure requirements. Related party disclosures of transactions between SOEs are critical to evaluating claims of dumping, where companies face allegations of selling products in foreign markets below cost. China was the target for the largest number of antidumping measures of any country in the 2000s (Li & Whalley, 2010). In May 2006, China persuaded the IASB to open consultations about amending the requirements related to disclosures of transactions between state-controlled enterprises. The discussions, sometimes contentious, continued until IAS 24 was revised, on November 4, 2009, to address the Chinese concerns (DTT, 2011). China mobilized its accounting community to lobby for the change. Eleven major Chinese companies wrote comment letters to a 2008 exposure draft in support of the changes, as did three of China's larger local CPA firms (IFRS Foundation, 2011b). The revision of IAS 24 to address Chinese objections was the first case of Chinese influence shaping international standards, and reflected China's growing power in international institutions.

7.1.2. Auditing Standards

Xiang (1998) observed that early accounting standards reforms were undermined by the lack of professional and independent auditing, for without effective auditing practices, the standards would not lead to fairly presented financial statements. In 1995, China promulgated the first independent auditing standards, although certain voluntary standards had developed from time to time prior to that date (Xiao, Zhang, & Xie, 2000). The new standards, substantially in accord with international standards, were issued in two batches, the first effective January 1, 1996 and the second effective January 1, 1997 (Chong, 2000; Lin & Chan, 2000; Zhou, 2007). Xiao et al. (2000) observed that the development of standards was a response to the crisis of increasing fraud, similar to the manner in which the development of US standards had been a response to the McKesson Robbins fraud of the 1930s. However, unlike the US response where the profession itself created standards, in China this task fell to the government.

Cooper, Chow, and Tang (2002) examined the early development of auditing standards and concluded that a general framework had been put in place that would support further development. They found the standards were up to international practice, while the profession had yet to rise to that standard. The major remaining that would need to be addressed to bring the Chinese profession to international standards related to professional competence and experience, independence, and ethics.

The Chinese Auditing Standards Board (CASB), founded in 1988, operates under the CICPA. It is responsible for developing practice standards for Chinese accounting firms. The CASB and the International Auditing and Assurance Standards Board (IAASB) agreed in December 2005 to converge Chinese auditing standards with international standards. On November 10, 2010, the IAASB and the CASB jointly announced that full convergence had been achieved (IFAC, 2010).

7.2. LICENSING OF CERTIFIED PUBLIC ACCOUNTANTS

When the profession of CPAs was reintroduced to China in 1980, the *Provisional Regulations Concerning the Establishment of Accounting Consultancies* provided rules for the qualification of CPAs. These rules stated that CPAs were to be tested and approved by finance bureaus at the provincial level, with the MOF retaining the right to check the qualification and appropriateness of approved CPAs. Provincial finance bureaus tended to reward long-serving employees with CPA credentials rather than using a merit-based system based on relevant qualifications. Bureaucrats soon recognized that for the profession to have status in society, it would need to develop standards to raise the quality of CPAs. While the commencement of CPA licensing had begun the process of professional closure, the new profession did not achieve profession status until it broke from a system where political and bureaucratic considerations determined admission.

7.2.1. Qualifications of CPAs

The 1985 accounting law, together with the implementing regulations issued by the State Council in 1986, established provisions stipulating the qualifications of CPAs. Included in those qualifications was the requirement for a CPA examination. The first CPA examination was in 1991. Only 24,000 candidates passed out of 580,000 applicants in the first six years. By 1997, there were 250,000 annual applicants (Xu, 1997). After passing the examination, a candidate needed to join the CICPA for one year and have two years of auditing experience on the mainland prior to being offered a practicing certificate (Ding, 2006b, p. 364). Initially, only Chinese citizens could take the examination.

7.2.2. Chinese Institute of CPAs

The CICPA was formed in November 1988. The CICPA is the national organization responsible for all affairs related to CPAs. According to Yee (2012), the CICPA has all of the hallmarks of a state corporatist organization. The MOF and local government financial departments supervised the CICPA and retained regulatory power over CPAs. Zhu Rongji took an active interest in the development of the accounting profession, "emphasizing, in particular, the requirement for a high standard of professionalism" (Yee, 2012, p. 441).

A second professional body, the Chinese Association of Certified Public Auditors (CACPA) was established on September 8, 1992 under the auspices of the China National Audit Office. While the members of the CACPA were principally involved in audits of SOEs, turf battles arose between the CACPA and the CICPA (Yee, 2012). The conflicts were resolved in 1995 when the CACPA was merged into the CICPA.

7.2.3. Licensing of Foreigners

As China began its 15-year negotiation to become a member of the World Trade Organization (WTO), Zhang Haixian, who was the MOF representative to the negotiations, reported that China needed to open the CPA examination to foreigners. China had pointed out that two US states, Alabama and North Carolina, had citizenship requirements that were similar to China because they forbid foreigners from taking the US Uniform CPA Examination. US negotiators agreed to try to get those states to change the requirement, but Zhang recognized that, regardless of the outcome, China had to open its exam to foreigners. Ding was unconcerned, believing that the lack of understanding of Chinese law and the lower level of Chinese language skills of foreigners would make it difficult for them to pass the examination (Ding, 2006b, p. 319).

Foreigners first took the CPA examination in 1994. The examination was in Chinese. Within five years, there were 8,618 foreign examinees from 16 countries (including Hong Kong and Taiwan), yet only 307 passed the examination, a slightly lower pass rate than that of domestic candidates. Among those who passed, 225 candidates from Hong Kong, Taiwan, and Canada joined the CICPA and five were granted practicing certificates (Ding, 1998a, p. 366). While some Big Six foreign accountants passed the examinations, none were granted practicing certificates.

7.3. LOCAL FIRM REFORMS

Ding's conception of creating the Big One to compete with the Big Four retired with him in 1999, but the idea that Chinese accounting firms should be more competitive with the Big Four did not. The battle between the Big Four and the CICPA also subsided after Ding's retirement largely because the WTO agreement had provided the Big Four with a sustainable business form. Li Yong, Ding's successor at CICPA, was more pragmatic than Ding had been. Li Yong was in this position for only three years before being elevated to Vice Minister of Finance. Li's replacement was Chen Yugui, who remains in this position.

There have been three major campaigns to improve the quality and competitiveness of local CPA firms since the reestablishment of the profession in 1980:

1. The Structural Reform Campaign (1992–2000)

Leader: Ding Pingzhun

Key document: *Practical Guidance for Reform of Accounting Firms* (1999)

2. The Rectification Campaign (July 1997–March 1999)

Leader: Ding Pingzhun

3. The Large and Strong Campaign (2006–present)

Leaders: Wang Jun, Chen Yugui

Key documents: *Opinions on Promotion of Chinese Accounting Firms to Develop Larger and More Competitive* (2007)

The General Office of the State Council Forwarding the Announcement of Opinions on Accelerating the Development of Certified Public Accountants by the MOF (2009)

I have named the campaigns based on my interpretation of events. Those who participated in the campaigns have not used these names. I have aggregated what I see as related activities to form a campaign. The beginning and ending dates for the campaigns are ambiguous.

7.3.1. Structural Reform Campaign

The Structural Reform Campaign arose from a broader program designed to address concerns that too many SOEs had become instruments of social policy, used to provide a wide range of social services. To become efficient and competitive, the SOEs needed to adopt modern business management practices. The sweeping economic reforms that proceeded from the Third Plenum of the Fourteenth Party Congress, which was held in October 1992, established a new goal of separating enterprises from the government (Lau, 1999).

China's state-owned accounting firms were not specifically addressed when directives for the Third Plenum reforms came down in November 1993, so Lu Bing, Secretary General of the CICPA, and Ding Pingzhun went to the State Economic and Trade Commission on November 16, 1993 to ask how the reforms applied to accounting firms. They were told that accounting firms were to detach from the government, but that the process was complicated and that the MOF would have to establish guidelines (Ding, 2006a, p. 12).

The Third Plenum reforms created the opportunity for significant reforms to the accounting profession. Ding saw that they offered a solution to the most serious problem facing the profession: its lack of independence. By separating accounting firms from government, it would become possible to create independent accounting firms similar to those existing in most other jurisdictions. The process of separation also created an opportunity to propose the use of the internationally normative partnership form for the accounting profession in China.

There were three significant phases to the structural reform campaign. The first was a disaffiliation program (commonly called delinking) designed to separate accounting firms from their state sponsors in response to national policy changes and at the same time to create an independent profession. The disaffiliation program was largely completed by 2000 (Dai et al., 2000). The disaffiliation program also applied to the Big Four joint ventures.

The second phase was to introduce the partnership as the normative form of ownership of accounting firms. The concept of partnerships was new to modern China, and efforts to encourage accounting firms to adopt this form met considerable resistance.

The third thrust of the Structural Reform Campaign was to coerce accounting firms to merge in order to create larger firms. The intent of regulators in encouraging mergers was to increase market concentration in the accounting profession with the goal of improving quality and thereby enabling the indigenous firms to compete with the then Big Five. By December 31, 2000, 300 accounting firms in China had combined into 110 firms, and the original 106 firms qualified to audit public companies were reduced to 78 firms (Yuan & Li, 2003).

7.3.1.1. Delinking

China's accounting firms were initially placed under other state institutions in the same manner as all other organizations under China's centrally planned economy. The need for auditor independence was not initially recognized. Sucher and Bychkova (2001, p. 835) observed the same phenomena in Russia following the breakup of the Soviet Union:

> In this economy in transition, where there is no immediate history of a market economy, no tradition of independent external auditing and there is no great demand for the provision of financial statements for outside investors, there would seem to be little local demand for local auditors to be fully independent from the enterprises they are auditing.

The independence of CPA firms was the area where Western practices clashed most openly with deeply held institutional views as to the role of the state in China. The changes that have been made, and continue to be made, to bolster auditor independence are reflective of significant shifts in institutional logics in the broader society as the role of government in the economy is redefined.

Auditor independence has been recognized for many years as a crucial aspect to the credibility of the external audit (Antle, 1984). As some early theorists of auditing observed:

> The significance in the work of the independent auditor is so well established that little justification is needed to establish this concept as one of the cornerstones in any structure of auditing theory. (Mautz & Sharaf, 1961)

IFAC standards codified established Western definitions of auditor independence, and have often formed the basis for national codes. Western conceptions of auditor independence are often in fundamental conflict with the conception of the audit role in transitional economies. In these economies, the audit function had traditionally been an instrument of state control. Both China and the former Soviet Union began with state-owned CPA firms but in both situations, the need for an independent auditing function was ultimately recognized. Sucher and Bychova (2001) suggest that the consequence of low demand for independent auditors might lead to the perception that audit independence is only associated with Big Five firms rather than local firms. They suggested that rigorous independence rules might improve the competitiveness of local firms:

> A robust legal and professional framework covering the key aspects of auditor independence would help local audit firms compete with Big Five audit firms for audits. On the other hand, it is unclear if societal conditions would make this problematic (p. 835).

Improving the competitiveness of local accounting firms was clearly one of the motivations for the independence reforms in China. Regulators had come to understand that investors were not going to take a Chinese auditor seriously if the government controlled it.

Delinking of CPA Firms from the Government. As China began to discuss renewed participation in General Agreement on Tariffs and Trade (GATT) in the late 1980s, Chinese regulators became aware that China's state ownership of accounting firms would be an issue that would need to be resolved before China could become a member of GATT or its successor WTO. The Law on CPAs, approved on October 31, 1993, opened the door for private ownership of CPA firms in the form of partnerships or privately owned limited liability companies, yet there was great reluctance to separate existing accounting firms from the government by both the sponsors and the employees of the accounting firms. Ding complained that government units that had successful accounting firms did not want to let them go, while badly operated firms were not willing to leave the support of the state (Ding, 2006a, p. 18). The MOF issue an implementing regulation titled *Tentative measures for establishment, examination and approval of limited liability accounting firms* on December 15, 1993. The regulation restricted the ability of government entities to set up new accounting firms and indicated that approved accounting firms should detach from state organs in accordance with national regulations. Firms and local governments largely ignored the new rules. China organizes its government with a strong geographic component. Provincial and local finance bureaus typically sponsored accounting firms that operated within their geographical jurisdiction of the bureau. Accounting firms proliferated as each of these bureaus established firms, and the geocentric nature of the system, bolstered by regulatory practices that prohibited cross-provincial operations, made it impossible for any regional or national firms to arise. Large numbers of new accounting firms emerged in the early 1990s, most of which were affiliated with government entities (Table 7.1).

On July 1, 1994, Ding, recognizing that independence problems were holding back development of the CPA profession, wrote to Liu Zhongli, the Minister of Finance, recommending acceleration of the pace of reform. Specifically, Ding said there were two obstacles to the development of CPA profession: structure and talent. Structure was the most urgent problem. He recommended three actions:

1. Accelerate the approval of a group of eligible partnership accounting firms.
2. Restructure international firm joint ventures into member firms.
3. Detach existing accounting firms from their state organization within three years (Ding, 2006a, p. 17).

Table 7.1. Number of Chinese Accounting and Auditing Firms, 1992–2012.

Year	Accounting Firms	Audit Firms
1992	1,422	2,812
1993	1,836	3,374
1994	1,874	3,722
1995	2,519	3,828
1996	6,347	–
1997–2004	unavailable	–
2005	4,950	–
2006	5,800	–
2007	6,801	–
2008	7,232	–
2009	7,605	–
2010	7,790	–
2011	7,904	–
2012	8,128	–

The CICPA and Chinese Institute of Certified Auditors (CICA) merged in 1995.
Notes: Implementation of reforms was more difficult because there were two types of accounting firms that did audits, and separate regulators governed the two types. The first group was members of the CICPA. The other group was members of the CICA. The CICA was merged into the CICPA in 1995. Yee (2012) describes the circumstances that gave rise to this merger.
Source: Ding (2006a, p. 12) and CICPA. Includes branches.

China's communist legacy has created a strong public opinion that state-owned property belongs to the people, and the widely held view that if state assets are to be disposed of, the state should receive appropriate compensation. This was problematic for the process of privatizing accounting firms, since few CPAs could afford to purchase the firms. Ding suggested recycling the funds derived from the sale of state assets to the newly independent accounting firms back to the firms to cover development costs. Liu Zhongli responded to Ding on July 5, 1994, saying that "the direction is correct, but the steps are not easy" (Ding, 2006a, p.18). Ding's immediate supervisor, Zhang Youcai, wrote the next day saying: "I agree with Mr. Liu Zhongli. Please follow Mr. Liu's instruction and put forward an outline of your ideas and submit it to the Ministry of Finance for us to research" (Ding, 2006a, p. 18). The process of restructuring accounting firms was challenging. Ding (Ding, 2006a, p.19) reflected on his experience:

> At that time, I was too excited to fall asleep for several nights. I outlined many "blueprints" of system reform in my mind. To tell the truth, when I came to my office, I felt like I was trapped in a bottomless "mud puddle" and I was occupied by many contradictions that were hard to deal with. The "blueprints" on system reform seemed a "dream" far from reality. At that time, there were too many things for the CICPA to do and there was not an urgent need for system reform and the system reform of accounting firms was not in the first place of the agenda. I had some hesitations in my mind and to really do it was like Mr. Liu's instruction: "it is not easy."

In 1995, the MOF issued an exposure draft that proposed that all accounting firms disaffiliate from their government sponsors. Domestic accounting firms authorized to audit public companies were told in 1997 to break their links with government departments by the end of 1998. The remaining accounting firms were required to disaffiliate by the end of 1999. The disaffiliation program was unpopular with the firms. The uncertainty of practice without the support of a strong organization was threatening to the firms. In particular, the partners lacked the capital necessary and had come to rely on the government agency directing clients to them (Dai et al., 2000).

By 2000, the delinking process was complete. Research that has focused on the aftermath of delinking has found heterogeneous effects. Yang, Tang, Kilgore, and Jiang (2001) found evidence of increasing frequency of qualified opinions following disaffiliation. They considered possible explanations for this phenomenon, including the increasing presence of the Big Five accounting firms, new auditing standards, the cumulative experience of professionals, and the increased numbers of public companies. They concluded that the disaffiliation program was the primary reason for the increase. Gul, Sami, and Zhou (2009) reexamined these issues using a more comprehensive methodology. This paper found the same results as Yang et al. (2001) and additionally found evidence that the disaffiliation program had helped to reduce earnings management. Liu and Liu (2008) looked at the effects of auditor switching in China on the independence of successor auditors. The article was motivated by the high levels of auditor switching taking place in China's competitive audit markets between 1999 and 2004 (the years following delinking). They found evidence that companies switch auditors to manipulate earnings and that successive auditors fail to exercise the necessary prudence. This is a mixed record, with evidence that some firms were using higher standards following delinking while others appear to have used lower standards in order to win new work.

Delinking of the Big Five joint ventures. The joint ventures of the Big Five firms were subject to the same disaffiliation rules. They needed to disaffiliate the joint venture partner firm from its associated government department by the end of 1998. The Big Five enthusiastically supported the disaffiliation program. Disaffiliation would free them of a source of potential interference by the government agency to which they were affiliated. That interference had been substantially removed when the firms succeeded in getting their joint venture partners to accept a passive role soon after the ventures were established, but removing the ownership would also sever any payment arrangements that had been made to secure the passive role of the state partner. Ding was initially puzzled as to why the Big Five supported the disaffiliation program, but in his memoirs, he indicates that he came to understand that they were pragmatists. Disaffiliating from the powerful government bureaus allowed them to seize complete power over the joint ventures due to the weakness of the individual partners who took the place of the government. Ding (2006b, p. 120) recounts: "I emphasized over and over again that the China side should have some sense of danger."

Although no regulator had yet asserted the issue, some Big Five accountants were concerned that a broad interpretation of independence rules might cause the Big Five firms to lack independence on any SOE because of their joint ventures with the state. Disaffiliation would fix that potential issue. The solution was simple. The joint ventures would continue in existence, but the state would transfer its ownership of the joint venture partner to individual CPAs. The law required accounting firms to have at least five licensed CPAs. Because the Big Six had few licensed partners at that time, some of the firms needed to enlist managers to form part of the group that acquired the joint venture partner from the state.

Each of the Big Five firms disaffiliated from their state sponsors in the above fashion. The resulting organizations operated much like Zhang & Chen CPAs, with operational and financial control in the hands of the international firm. However, the problems faced by Zhang & Chen CPAs were avoided because the joint venture remained a foreign-invested enterprise that was not subject to the tax and foreign exchange restrictions that applied to local firms like Zhang & Chen CPAs.

7.3.1.2. Partnerships

The 1993 *Law of the People's Republic of China on Certified Public Accountants,* approved on October 31, 1993, but not effective until January 1, 1994, provided the legal framework for the profession that survives until today. The law restricts certain accounting work to only CPAs:

1. Examining financial statements and issuing audit opinions.
2. Verifying capital and issuing capital verification reports.
3. Performing audits or reporting related to mergers, splits, or liquidations.
4. Any other auditing activities established in laws or regulations.

The law provides that all CPAs must work for an accounting firm, and all work must be done under the firm. Firms are specifically liable for the work performed by its CPAs.

Types of entities. The law permits two types of legal entities to become accounting firms: partnerships and limited liability companies. Partnerships are required to have two or more partners, all of whom need to be CPAs. The requirement to be a CPA precludes corporate or institutional ownership.[2] Partners are responsible for the liabilities of the partnership in proportion to their capital or as otherwise provided in the partnership agreement. Partners are jointly liable for the firm's liabilities.

Alternatively, an accounting firm may be organized as a legal entity with limited liability. Such entities require registered capital of not less than 300,000 yuan (approximately US$45,000 at 2011 exchange rates), a substantial amount for many aspiring CPAs. Firms are required to have at least five CPAs. Limited liability firms are responsible for liabilities to the extent of assets.

The establishment of a CPA firm requires approval from the Finance Department of the State Council or the Finance Department of a province, autonomous region, or municipality that reports directly to the central government. Branches of CPA firms need approval from the finance department where the branch is to be located.

Ideology and limited liability. Ding Pingzhun drafted the rules to implement the CPA law. He consulted with several Big Six-trained Chinese experts and several Hong Kong partners of the Big Six. He found a professor who had studied the management of accounting firms in Britain, and obtained sample partnership agreements from friends in Taiwan. The concept of unlimited liability captivated Ding. He found it consistent with the concept in Marxist philosophy that there is a dialectical unity between being limited and being unlimited. Ding cited revolutionary hero Lei Feng, who it was claimed to have said that while people's lives are limited, serving people is unlimited (Ding, 2006a). For Ding, the structure of an accounting firm should reflect this revolutionary philosophy of life. As owners of accounting firms, partners would assume limited liability for the actions of the firm, yet as individual partners signing reports they would assume unlimited liability. Ding considered the limited liability partnership, a form that had recently emerged in the United States and which would spread globally, to be the ideal structure for accounting firms (Keatinge, Donn, Coleman, & Hester, 1995). Under a limited liability partnership, the partners would be subject to limited liability for the actions of their fellow partners, but unlimited liability for their own actions. Such a structure, however, was unavailable in China and the laws would need amendment for this to occur.

The issue of liability was key to Ding's thinking about the profession. He saw unlimited liability as something that refers to natural persons rather than legal persons. To Ding, unlimited liability was a foundation of professionalism, and consistent with Marxism. It reflected the responsibility of the young profession to serve the people. However, the structure of the profession was a contradiction – the law focused on the requirement for accounting practice to be conducted in firms that would be the focal point of liability, meaning that the liability was effectively not on the CPAs, but on the state organizations to which they were affiliated.

Ding drafted *Tentative Measures for Establishment and Examination and Approval of Partnership Accounting Firms* that the MOF issued on December 25, 1993. Implementation problems immediately arose. There was no process for obtaining business registrations for either limited liability accounting firms or partnership accounting firms. In addition, the status of the thousands of firms already established was unclear. Should these firms restructure into the new forms?

Use of partnerships. The new partnership form was slow to be taken up. In 1994, the CICPA approved three partnership accounting firms. Three CPAs in Shenzhen, Zou Zhaobao, Xue Jie, and Gao Chengjian, were the first to submit an application to establish a partnership accounting firm. The CICPA eagerly approved the application hoping that the new partnership could lead to the further development of this form of operation. Ding reports the firm operated well for two years, but then faced "irreconcilable contradictions," including the fact that the new firm continued to operate as a collection of sole proprietorships rather than a firm. Each partner did his own audits and issued his own reports. Partners formerly with state-sponsored accounting firms had formed two other firms, Chengxin in Fuzhou and Pan Chen in Shanghai. Conflicts between those firms and the related finance bureaus frustrated the development of those firms. Authorities approved five additional partnership accounting firms 1995. These eight firms, however, made little impact on a profession of several thousand accounting firms.

Ding reports that interest in partnership accounting firms came mainly from three sources. First, there were Chinese accountants who had returned from abroad. The booming Chinese economy and less attractive conditions in the West compelled many overseas Chinese to seek opportunity in China. Second, some of those who were formerly trained by the large international firms in China were considering setting out on their own. A third group came from those employed by state-controlled accounting firms, who felt oppressed by the old system and sought new opportunity.

The new independent accounting firms faced considerable market difficulty. The concept of privately owned firms was new to China, and the concept of partnership accounting firms was even newer. Ding set out on a public relations effort, teaming with the Changchun Film Studio to produce a television film on the new accounting laws called *Watchdog of Market Economy – CPAs*. Ding, a former member of the Chinese Writer's Association, wrote the commentary. He borrowed a theme from another popular TV series in China – *Beijinger's in New York:* "Do you want to become a millionaire? Please come to a partnership accounting firm, because it is heaven. Do you want to become bankrupt and sent to jail and ask your wife to bring you meals? Please come to a partnership accounting firm, because it is hell." More than 10 TV stations broadcast the show and the heaven and hell metaphor became part of the profession's vernacular.

The slow take up of the partnership structure was a result of societal and institutional forces. Private business was a new concept in China and had low social status. People considered state-owned business as more respectable, a natural consequence of the years under pure state and communal ownership. The public considered partners in CPA firms as inferior in status to government officials. Partners themselves felt that they had given up 官本位, their official rank, and had nothing to fall back upon. Ding tried to argue that people should not look at partners in accounting firms as being like the "old woman who sells cold drinks by the roadside" – the Chinese stereotype of an independent businessperson. Rather, they should be viewed like the "old foreign man who sells fried chicken," a reference to Colonel Sanders of the KFC chain of fast food restaurants that was spreading rapidly throughout China (Ding, 2006a, p. 19). The legacy of China's iron rice bowl would make change difficult.

Government institutions perpetuated the stereotypes. Government departments regularly ignored the CPA law and issued regulations restricting the kind of work that partnership accounting firms could perform, often precluding the audits of SOEs, asset valuations, or the annual inspections of foreign exchange transactions. There appears to have been a view that the only state-owned accounting firms could protect the interest of the state. Partnership accounting firms were also viewed as being of lower quality than state-owned firms. Ding reports that it was a popular view that since state-owned accounting firms were often engaged in false accounting, privately owned accounting firms were certain to do it.

7.3.2. The Rectification Campaign

Increasing numbers of accounting scandals led Vice Premier Zhu Rongji to instruct, on April 20, 1997, that "The accounting industry is to be screened and rectified." The rectification campaign was a major effort to standardize and raise the quality of accounting and auditing practices. The Big Six had been the target of two earlier examination processes. Ding describes the first examination of the Big Six in 1994 as "just a rough one which didn't focus on finance and tax, but many problems were detected" (Ding, 2006b, p. 100). A second inspection of the Big Six was conducted in August 1996, which is discussed in Chapter 6. The rectification exercise that Zhu Rongji ordered in 1997 applied to all accounting firms in China, and was the first examination of local firms. The 1997 rectification was to be completed by the end of 1998, but was actually completed in 1999 (Narayan & Reid, 2000).

The 1997 Rectification Campaign was brutal. Almost 12,700 local CPAs (25% of the total) faced discipline or eviction from the profession. Regulators closed about 580 accounting firms. Another 2,000 accounting firms received warnings or punishments (43% of the number of firms)

(Narayan & Reid, 2000). The Rectification Campaign marked the establishment of regulatory oversight on accounting firms in China.

The practice of examining CPA firms continued as an annual exercise targeting a sample of firms (Lee, 2003). While there is no disclosure of the selection process, local CPAs have said that examinations tend to occur about every third year. The examinations often disclosed significant problems. On September 28, 2005, the National Audit Office announced that a review of 16 accounting firms had found 19 deficient reports issued by 14 firms (Wall Street Journal, 2005).

7.3.3. Large and Strong Campaign

The Rectification Campaign and the Structural Reform Campaign were successful in creating a recognized, independent CPA profession in China of considerable scale. By May 2006, there were over 5,600 accounting firms with 69,700 practicing CPAs (CICPA, 2010b). Chen Yugui, CICPA Secretary General said in 2004:

> At present, China has over 170,000 SOEs, among which a considerable number are large or super large enterprises. It requires large amount of human and financial resources to audit these enterprises. As such, China needs an appropriate number of large firms. It is 20 years since China resumed the development of the CPA profession. However, there are not many firms that are capable of satisfying the needs of these enterprises. We hope that a group of large-scale quality firms will grow up in China to shoulder this significant responsibility. (Yugui Chen, 2004)

Under the direction of Chen Yugui, the CIPCA developed a comprehensive strategy to further develop the CPA profession. Wang Jun, Vice Minister of Finance, articulated that the strategy that would be deployed to develop the accounting profession would in turn upgrade the competence of Chinese enterprises and further the economic development of the country. Wang Jun said at a speech to the World Congress of Accountants in 2006 that the strategy would have three principal thrusts: (1) cultivating accounting talent; (2) converging Chinese professional standards with international standards; and (3) developing larger and more competitive firms (Wang, 2006). Regulators released a draft of the strategy to accounting firms, including the Big Four, for comment in early October 2006.

In May 2007, the CICPA strategy was released in a document entitled *Opinions on Promotion of Chinese Accounting Firms to Develop Larger and More Competitive* (CICPA, 2007). The document states that the CICPA developed the strategy under the guidance and direction of MOF and local finance bureaus with the "kind attention of the Central Committee of the Communist Party of China and the State Council." The strategy identified three key reasons for change:

> The increasing growth and scale of the Chinese economy requires a corresponding growth in Chinese accounting firms.
>
> The scope of services offered by Chinese accounting firms must expand to meet the increasing needs of a larger and more complex market.
>
> CPA firms need to be able to serve increasingly globalized Chinese companies and must expand internationally to do so.

The strategy established a 5–10 year goal for China to develop 10 internationalized accounting firms capable of serving Chinese companies globally, and 100 firms of significant scale, capable of serving large companies within China. The strategy can be categorized into three broad areas: (1) internationalization, (2) organizational and institutional reforms, and (3) talent development.

7.3.3.1. Internationalization

The strategy contemplated the internationalization of the Chinese accounting profession. The first step was the convergence of Chinese accounting and auditing standards with international standards in order to permit Chinese accountants to compete internationally. Based on the convergence of standards, the CICPA would seek the recognition of Chinese CPAs by overseas securities regulators so that Chinese CPAs would be accepted as auditors of international listings. The strategy also planned to obtain mutual recognition of Chinese CPA certificates with different countries.

Chinese accounting firms were encouraged to follow Chinese enterprises abroad and to set up foreign branches and representative offices. They were to start by providing services to Chinese companies going global. Then, they were to "work vigorously to explore ways and channels for going international" leading to their becoming "involved in overseas accounting competition on all fronts" (CICPA, 2007). Chinese accounting firms were encouraged to join international firm networks as a member firm or affiliated firm and to look for alliances with other professional service providers.

The strategy does not directly refer to the Big Four firms. There is a single comment that directly applies to them. It states that the national treatment principle should be respected for further opening up of the accounting market. The national treatment principle is the cornerstone of

WTO agreements, providing that foreigners and locals should have identical treatment. The national treatment principle normally protects foreigners from discrimination, but in China's WTO accession, the principle of national treatment was not followed to the benefit of the Big Four. The Big Four were allowed to own an interest in a Chinese accounting firm despite not being Chinese CPAs, a more favorable treatment than accorded locals. China's planned return to the national treatment rules signaled that when the Big Four joint ventures reach the end of the joint venture term all owners must be Chinese CPAs.

7.3.3.2. Organizational and Institutional Reforms

The strategy identified a number of organizational and institutional reforms that were necessary to achieve the aspirations for a larger and more competitive accounting profession. The CICPA proposed that the partnership form of organization replace the archetypal limited liability company form for accounting firms in China. This change serves two purposes: to improve governance of accounting firms and to create a partnership culture. The CICPA committed to encouraging the necessary regulatory reforms to allow the effective use of partnerships for accounting firms. The strategy sees partnerships as being a combination of people and knowledge. A partnership culture is envisioned as focusing on teamwork, a macro-perspective, a sense of mutual responsibility, tolerance, inclusiveness, and equality.

Accounting firms were encouraged to create unified brands and practice networks. Firms were encouraged to enter into partnerships among themselves and with other professional service providers. The CICPA pledged to work to remove constraints on the geographic expansion of CPA firms, and to help with issues that come up in mergers related to professional mobility, license recognition, and business registration. The CICPA recognized that local protectionism has thwarted the development of regional and national accounting firms in China.

Accounting firms were encouraged to adopt international standard practice management methods, financial systems, and information technology (IT) systems. Large firms were expected to have technical support, risk management, and IT departments. The intent of these reforms was to improve quality, service, and competitiveness.

The strategy indicates that a reasonable pricing system was needed for auditing services. In particular, it was viewed that a well-regulated public bid system would prevent excessive price-cutting, bribery, and kickbacks. The process for selecting accounting firms for SOEs and banks should set a "fair playing field for CPAs to compete in the high-end market." Presumably, a "fair playing field" is one without the coercive influence of foreign referees – investment bankers, lawyers, and foreign securities regulators, who have historically insisted on Big Four auditors.

7.3.3.3. Talent Development

The strategy set a goal to develop 1,000 CPAs capable of performing international engagements within 5–10 years. This is a curious goal, given that the Big Four firms already had 1,446 partners and senior managers who were doing international engagements at the time the strategy was released in 2007 (Table 6.2). This reveals the ambiguity with which the CICPA views the Big Four. The CICPA appears to exclude the Big Four from its conception of 10 large globalized Chinese firms. Yet, when it annually publishes a summary of the leading talents in its top 100 rankings, the leading talents of the Big Four have been included. In 2009, 20 of 165 leading talents in the top 100 CPA firms were employed by the Big Four (CICPA, 2010a).

The strategy called for improvements in undergraduate education, reforms to the CPA examination, licensing, and continuing professional education. Chinese CPAs were encouraged to obtain overseas practicing qualifications. Overseas graduates and professionals holding overseas accounting credentials were encouraged to join Chinese accounting firms.

Excellent CPAs were encouraged to join the Communist Party, and to be included in major Communist Party institutions such as the Chinese People's Political Consultative Congress and the National People's Congress. While the stated objective is to allow them to make a greater contribution to national economic development, inclusion of local CPAs in the political process will more closely align the interests of the profession with the party and the state.

7.3.3.4. Big Four Reactions

Some in the Big Four firms saw the CICPA strategy as a direct assault on their market leadership. Jim Quigley, global CEO of DTT, speculated that Chinese efforts to build competitors for the Big Four would falter once its companies grew too large:

> I think each country has its own sense of national pride, its own sense of wanting to do things its own way. (But) as Chinese companies diversify sources of their income they will need professional services firms with strong international networks. That will be the challenge of developing additional large Big Four firms in China. (Hawkes, 2008)

An internal strategy review, completed in late 2006 by another Big Four firm, saw the strategy as a positive development that would help to address the current undersupply of accountants in China. In the medium term, they did not see that the policy would result in the development of firms that could effectively compete with the global networks of the Big Four. They did not see the strategy as a significant threat to their relationship with their largest and most important clients, but recognized it would affect the market for services to smaller domestic clients.

7.3.3.5. Document 56 of the State Council

While the CICPA strategy had the support of MOF, it would remain largely aspirational without the broader support of the state. Earlier Ding had faced opposition from the CSRC in his plan to create the Big One, with the CSRC seeing the plan to develop large firms that could compete with the Big Four on international listings to be an unrealistic goal. The CSRC reported directly to the State Council and not to MOF. The CICPA would need to enlist other government bureaus to support the development of the profession. Local governments are often parochial in their administration, protecting firms under their jurisdiction while frustrating efforts to create national or regional firms. In order to make significant institutional changes the support of the State Council would be necessary. In a process that would take over two years, MOF and the CICPA sought to win State Council endorsement for their strategy. On October 3, 2009, the State Council informed the governments of all provinces, autonomous regions and municipalities, and commissions and agencies directly under State Council control that it had agreed on the now MOF strategy entitled *A Number of Opinions on Accelerating the Development of Certified Public Accountants* (State Council, 2009). Accountants in China refer to the document by its number, Document 56. The State Council in China is the highest executive organ of state power, and its approval of the MOF strategy effectively made it national policy.

The CICPA substantially revised its strategy before obtaining final State Council approval in the form of Document 56. The final document does not resemble the original CICPA strategy, although most of the concepts survived. The document segmented Chinese accounting firms into three groups: 10 large firms, 200 medium-sized firms, and a larger group of smaller firms. Document 56 sets a five-year goal to develop each of these segments, but the policy chiefly supports the quicker development of large accounting firms.

Small firms. Small firms are to provide service to small enterprises and institutions and to serve China's vast rural areas. To aid in the development of smaller CPA firms, Document 56 directs implementation of the PRC Company law that requires annual audits, and states that all hospitals, colleges, and not-for-profit organizations should be audited. Small firms are encouraged to expand the range of services to include bookkeeping, taxes, outsourcing, IT support, personal finance, and community affairs. Local firms are to actively undertake the construction of the "village accounting maintained by the town" bookkeeping business of the new socialist countryside. There are to be no geographic restrictions on CPA firms or local protectionism practices.

Medium-sized firms. Document 56 calls for 200 medium-sized firms capable of providing high-quality services to large- and medium-sized enterprises and listed companies. Medium-sized firms are encouraged to merge in order to become large firms. Smaller firms are likewise encouraged to merge in order to become medium-sized.

Large firms. Most of Document 56 focuses on the proposal to create 10 large, internationalized accounting firms with cross-border operations and the capability to provide integrated services to large Chinese companies. The firms are to expand their existing range of services, which currently include financial statement audits, capital verification reports, and tax services, to include new services such as:

1. Internal control assessment
2. Management consulting
3. Mergers and acquisitions
4. Credit investigation
5. Special audits
6. Performance evaluation
7. Forensic accounting including expert testimony
8. Investment decision support
9. Government procurement

The primary focus of large CPA firms is to provide comprehensive, internationalized services to Chinese enterprises that are pursuing China's "going-out" policy. The policy directs bureaucrats to create favorable conditions for the going-out of large accounting firms, including foreign liaison and support in obtaining recognition of qualifications. China's diplomatic efforts are to be effectively aligned with the development of the firms. The government is to provide a range of services to the large firms including market research, overseas investment promotion, foreign exchange, and security. While the latter point likely does not contemplate the deployment of the People's Liberation Army in support of the international expansion of CPA firms, it does suggest the engagement of the state security apparatus (i.e., intelligence services).

The 10 large firms are encouraged to become members in international groups, to set up foreign branches, and to acquire or merge with foreign firms. The document states that membership in international groups should be based on equality and mutual benefits. This latter point appears directed at making certain that domestic accounting firms do not become operational subsidiaries of foreign networks dominated by overseas member firms.

Document 56 proposes certain institutional reforms for large accounting firms. The document calls for improvement in the professional ethics and professional competence of CPAs, which is to be encouraged through structural and organizational reforms. Large firms are directed to establish technical, quality, and IT functions. Firms are to develop an IT function to support auditing, internal control, and related services. The decision to promote the use of LLPs for accounting firms was retained in Document 56, with an expectation that this form will promote better governance and limit personal liability.

The importance of talent development carries over to Document 56, with the Financial Departments (functional components of the MOF) and the CICPA charged to attach great importance to training, particularly of leading talents. Management teams of accounting firms are to include young and middle-aged people and firms should "smoothly realize the replacement of the old by the new." Where the CICPA encouraged excellent CPAs to join the Communist Party, Document 56 expands the involvement of the party in the profession. CPA's are extolled to:

> ... fully bring into play the role of the fighting force of the grassroots party organizations and the exemplary role of the party members, so as to provide strong political guarantee to the quicker development of the CPA industry.

MOF is to regulate large accounting firms and their CPAs. Provincial financial departments are to supervise small accounting firms. Document 56 is silent as to the regulation of medium-sized firms.

A major difference between the CICPA strategy and Document 56 is the absence of a discussion of the convergence of accounting and auditing standards. The likely reason for this is that by the time Document 56 was issued, China had already received international recognition of the substantial convergence of its accounting standards (MOF, 2009). Also omitted were the recommendations that Chinese accountants seek overseas qualifications, plans to obtain the recognition of Chinese CPAs by overseas securities regulators, and plans to seek mutual recognition of Chinese CPAs with those of other countries (although the state is directed in Document 56 to assist with these processes).

Implications of Document 56 to the Big Four. Clearly directed at the Big Four firms is a provision stating that the process of localization of the existing Big Four joint venture firms should be sped up, and that they should be required to compete fairly under the legal framework and rules of the unified market.

7.3.4. Foreign Partners in China

Similar to the policies in most countries, China restricts the practice of accounting to CPA firms owned by licensed CPAs. An exception was carved out in China for the Big Four firms, which allowed partial foreign ownership of accounting joint ventures. This allowed the Big Four firms to sidestep the issue of licensing of foreign partners working in China. Partners in China either remained partners in their home firms or became partners in the Hong Kong member firm. The CICPA records for the joint venture firms reflect only two partners for each of the Big Four firms in China – the local CPA firm, made up of selected local employees, and a foreign organization owned by some entity of the Big Four firm, typically the Hong Kong member firm. Partners working in China had the title and status of a partner, but had no direct equity interest in the China firm, and are legally employees.

In 2008, the Big Four had a total of 732 partners in mainland China, of which 199 (27.2%) were local and 532 (72.8%) were expatriates (including as expatriates the partners from Hong Kong and Taiwan). Because few of these expatriate partners had Chinese CPA licenses, they were not allowed to sign statutory audit reports in China, although they routinely signed reports used outside of China. Local partners were designated to sign statutory audits performed under the direction of foreign partners. Interviews with partners disclosed that the signing local partner typically reads the financial statements but does not usually review the underlying working papers. The local signing partner is at risk for disciplinary actions related to the financial statements and interviewees stated that there have been instances where a local partner has been disciplined by the MOF for violations related to audits that were performed under the direction of a foreign partner.

The foreign partners generally are licensed in other jurisdictions. Discussions with various Big Four partners indicate that the firms do not appear to have processes to ensure that partners are currently licensed in any jurisdiction and there appear to be no rules that would require them to be so licensed. Absent a complaint to the applicable licensing authority, it seems unlikely that a foreign licensing authority would exercise any regulatory oversight over accountants practicing in China. All partners who sign accounts for US public companies are subject to the regulatory oversight of the Public Company Accounting Oversight Board (PCAOB), but, because China forbids the PCAOB from examining the working papers of China accounting firms, this oversight is ineffective. Foreign partners who sign accounts for companies listed in Hong Kong must generally be members of the HKICPA, which retains regulatory oversight, yet the HKICPA and other Hong Kong regulators are also barred from regulatory actions within China.

The CICPA has never asserted regulatory authority over foreign CPAs practicing in China other than to prohibit them from signing statutory accounts used in China. In his memoirs, Ding (2006b, p. 94) remained puzzled as to how the Big Four operates under this restriction: "And we are still not clear how the foreign personnel could act as a partner in the joint venture firms before they get China's CPA qualification." The foreign personnel were able to act as partners because the Big Four firms allowed them to do so. The Chinese regulation requiring a Chinese CPA to sign accounts used in China was complied with by having Chinese partners sign these accounts, even when other partners had done the work. Much of the work, however, did not require Chinese opinions. Work for overseas companies was typically reported to the head office overseas, and reports on foreign listings were not considered as local reports. Chinese regulators have chosen to focus on the act of signing a report used for local statutory purposes as the act requiring local licensing. If regulators had chosen to focus instead on the act of auditing, they would have been able to claim jurisdiction over the foreign partners practicing in China. At present, the CICPA only has indirect regulatory oversight over the statutory work performed by foreign partners in China through its jurisdiction over the local signing partners. As a result, the foreign partners are essentially self-regulated in China. While they are potentially subject to regulatory oversight by the PCAOB or other foreign securities regulators, and by their home licensing authority, China has asserted its sovereign right to preclude these regulators from operating within China.

The joint venture firms that the Big Six established in 1992 had a limited life under Chinese corporate law KPMG's 20-year Sino-foreign cooperative contract signed with the approval of the MOF was the first to expire Aug. 17, 2012. Ernst & Young's (E&Y) contract expired on September 1, 2012, while Deloitte Touche's ended on February 9, 2013. PricewaterhouseCoopers (PwC) signed a 25-year cooperation agreement with the MOF, hence their contract will not expire until March 27, 2018 (Qu, 2012). The firms were permitted operate in the joint venture form because of a special provision in the WTO accession agreements that provides that existing accounting joint ventures are not subject to the rules that require all owners of an accounting firm to be Chinese CPAs. Taking advantage of this provision, the Big Four joint ventures had a foreign organization (corporation or partnership), which was a partner in the joint venture with a local accounting firm owned by some of its local employees. The termination of the joint ventures required the firms to create a new entity for their practice. This new entity was not able to use the WTO exception and all owners would be required to be Chinese CPAs.

When the Big Four firms approached Chinese regulators about the pending deadline for restructuring, they were encouraged to restructure into an LLP, which only Chinese CPAs can own. At the same time, MOF, CICPA, and SAIC have encouraged local accounting firms to reorganize from limited liability companies to LLPs to improve their governance (Armstrong, 2012a; MOF, 2010). The problem for the Big Four with the LLP approach is that they did not wish to turn over ownership of the firms to Chinese CPAs, who make up only a fraction of their partners in China. While the foreign partners in China have not had direct ownership in the joint venture firms, they have held indirect ownership typically through their partnership in the Hong Kong firm. Only 27% of Big Four partners residing in China were PRC citizens as of 2008 (Table 6.3). Anecdotal evidence suggests that few foreign partners (including those from Hong Kong and Taiwan) have passed the CPA exam and obtained a CPA certificate in China. Some of the PRC partners also are not Chinese CPAs but rather have licenses in other jurisdictions. Accordingly, if the firms were to be required to restructure into partnerships only a fraction of the firm's partners in China would be able to own the firm. Any locally unlicensed partners would need to become employees. This outcome would be unsatisfactory to the Big Four firms so they began negotiations with Chinese regulators to find a compromise.

On May 10, 2012, the MOF, SAIC, CSRC, MOC, and SAFE issued jointly *Guidance for Sino-foreign cooperation accounting firms' transition and localization* (Caikuai File No. 8. 2012). The guidance clearly indicated that the Big Four would need to restructure into LLPs. The LLPs would be required to have at least 25 partners, 100 CPAs, and registered capital of at least 10 million RMB. Partners would be required to have at least five years' experience as a CPA, with at least three in China, and have not been subject to disciplinary proceedings.

An exception was made for foreigners. Foreigners (including residents of Hong Kong, Macao, and Taiwan) who did not have a Chinese CPA qualification (or qualification as a Certified Public Valuer, Certified Tax Agent, or Certified Cost Engineer) could nevertheless become partners in the LLP if they met the following conditions:

1. Full-time practice in a Chinese accounting firm.
2. No administrative penalty in the prior three years.
3. Have a recognized foreign accounting qualification.
4. Ten years' experience after becoming licensed as a CPA in a foreign location.
5. Five years' experience with a Chinese accounting firm.
6. Between 40 and 65 years of age.

The firms had many foreign partners who met these requirements. Limits, however, were imposed on the number of unlicensed foreign partners. They could only have 40% of cumulative voting power when the LLP was formed, reducing to 20% over five years.

MOF accounting department director Yang Ming defended the new rules against widespread criticism that China was discriminating against the Big Four. "China has properly arranged a transition program for the Big Four accounting companies and taken into account the views of Chinese and overseas partners when we came up with the plan" (International Accounting Bulletin, 2012). Yang added: "The new localized offices will not only come under the supervision of the Chinese government and industrial association, but under the guidance of parent companies of the Big Four." Other commentators observed that China's new rules would be more liberal than other countries in allowing the practice of unlicensed individuals (The Economist, 2012).

Since KPMG's joint venture expired first, it was the first of the Big Four to receive permission to reorganize into an LLP on July 13, 2012. MOF announced that KPMG's LLP would have 25 partners, the minimum required under the new provisions (China Daily, 2012). KPMG China has far more partners than 25. KPMG's decision to limit the partners to 25 is curious. Chinese regulators required considerable data before approving foreign partners and limiting the foreign partners to 10 would have minimized that effort. Or perhaps KPMG had difficulty finding sufficient locally qualified partners to allow all of the foreign partners to become partners in the LLP. KPMG signaled that the low number of partners in the LLP would not change the way they conducted their practice. Stephen Yiu, senior partner of KPMG, said "the conversion will not affect our clients or staff, nor will it affect our business" (KPMG, 2012).

E&Y completed its restructuring on September 11, 2012 with Mark Weinberger, Global CEO, noting "Strong backing from the government authorities ensured that the conversion was a positive and healthy continuation of our existing business" (E&Y, 2012). Perhaps cognizant of the criticism of KPMG's low number of partners, E&Y admitted 88 partners to its LLP, said to represent the vast majority of the present partners of its audit department (China Business, 2012). Deloitte followed on January 1, 2013 (Deloitte, 2013). PwC restructured its audit practice into PwC Zhong Tian LLP on January 18, 2013 (PwC, 2013). PwC reported that its new LLP had 148 partners, with 91 having CICPA qualifications, the most of any of the Big Four. PwC was not required to move its joint venture to an LLP until 2018, but chose to do so earlier out of fears that they might be discriminated against by state owned enterprises should they fail to do so.

Each of the Big Four firms currently integrates its China practice into a larger organization that includes at least the Hong Kong and Macau firms and often includes other Asian firms. Local regulations typically prevent the cross-border combination of accounting firms, so they typically retain the legal structure of separate firms, and they operate under contracts that agree to common management processes and profit-sharing arrangements. Partners typically remain owners of their home country practice, yet their share of profits is determined based on the combined firms. Accordingly, the linkage between ownership and partner earnings has been broken, and the firms allocate profits between member firms and among partners by agreement, rather than equity ownership. The Big Four wished to continue these arrangements with the newly created LLPs in China. The present arrangements could continue under the LLP arrangements, if the LLPs entered into enforceable agreements to continue the existing management and profit-sharing practices. In a sense, this would be a return to the form used in the failed Zhang & Chen CPAs experiment conducted by PW in the late 1990s. Regulatory developments have mitigated some of the problems that Zhang & Chen CPAs faced. New tax laws have harmonized the basis for taxation between local companies and foreign companies. Liberalized foreign exchange rules for local companies make it easier to hold foreign currency. However, the scale of operations of the firms is considerably larger, and the international firms will need to be certain that agreements for management control and profit sharing are enforceable, which will likely require a level of transparency not present in the Zhang & Chen CPAs experiment. Will regulators allow the Big Four to operate in this manner? Alternatively, will they use these changes as a means to finally move the Big Four under local control? It is uncertain whether Chinese authorities would consider such an arrangement to compliant with Document 56's admonition that the arrangements confer "equality and mutual benefits," particularly if, as is the case today, foreigners hold most management positions.

The new rules requiring use of an LLP included further provisions related to the management of the firms. Members of the management committee of the firms could include only 40% foreigners at formation, reducing to 20% in five years. At the time the firms moved into the LLPs, few local partners had management positions. Local partners took control of the management committee of the LLP, but anecdotal evidence suggests that they have not asserted control over the LLP and the distribution of its profits, ceding these matters to management committee of the greater firm, which remains controlled by foreigners. Chinese regulators have yet to complain about this situation, perhaps content to wait until local partners are more senior and capable of asserting their ownership rights.

Furthermore, the new rules placed more stringent requirements for the senior partner of the LLP. This person would be required to be a Chinese national, and a Chinese CPA with at least 10 years of experience, 8 of which is in China. A special rule was provided for the initial senior partner of the LLP. This person could be a foreign national (the rules treat Hong Kong, Macau, and Taiwan partners as foreign nationals) with a foreign CPA credential. A foreign partner could serve as senior partner for the remainder of their term, or three years, whichever was shorter. Each of the firms appointed their existing Hong Kong senior partner as the LLP senior partner for a three-year term. PwC had to vote to extend the retirement age of Silas Yang, its senior partner, in order to allow the full three-year term. The requirement that the senior partner be a Chinese national arguably violates China's nondiscrimination commitments under WTO. It is uncertain whether the firms will argue this point in order to extend the terms of foreign senior partners when their present terms expire.

7.3.5. Pressure on Big Four Clients

In order to break Big Four domination of the market, companies needed to be persuaded to select local firms. Although local firms often had a price advantage that was not enough to entice firms away from the Big Four particularly for large companies with international listings.

Document 56 had a curious statement that appeared to suggest that the Big Four might not be suitable accountants for certain large SOEs:

> Overseas listed corporations, financial, energy, telecommunications and other key, large state-owned enterprises that influence the people's livelihood should have the priority to choose the services of large CPA firms that are beneficial to protecting the safety of the national economic information.

China has frequently asserted that economic information related to SOEs is a state secret (Gelatt, 1989; Narayana, 2010). The statement above seems to suggest that some large accounting firms are better suited to protecting state secrets than others. Those less suited to protecting the secrets of the state would presumably be those owned and managed by foreigners – the Big Four firms. There is a national security exception to trade agreements that could arguably allow China to exclude the Big Four from audits of state-owned and critical enterprises (Alexandroff & Sharma, 2005). At the present time it is unlikely that China's domestic CPA firms have the capability to serve most of these companies, since many of China's key enterprises are among the largest corporations in the world. However, the enunciation of this threat may gave state a considerable advantage in the negotiations over the structure and operations of the Big Four in China.

7.4. AUDIT ROTATION

There have long been arguments for mandatory rotation of auditors (Hoyle, 1978). Following the corporate crises such as Enron of the early 2000s, these calls increased in frequency and volume. Globally, companies have often retained the same auditor for lengthy periods of time. Advocates of mandatory rotation argue that it will increase auditor independence and audit quality (Catanach Jr. & Walker, 1999). Others have argued that audit rotation would lead to higher audit fees and a decline in audit quality (Petty & Cuganesan, 1996).

Until 2003, China had no rules requiring the rotation of audit firms or personnel. The Big Six tended to follow their global policies and rotated engagement partners after a set number of years, although the tenure with most clients in China was not long enough to require them to face the issue. However, more than a decade after the opening of public markets, the CSRC observed that many companies had not changed auditors. A proposal to require the periodic rotation of audit firms was met with considerable opposition from accounting firms and listed companies (Hu, 2003). In June 2003, the CSRC and MOF issued jointly *The Regulation on the Auditor Rotation of CPAs Having the Signature Qualification of Auditing Securities and Futures*, which required listed corporations to rotate their independent auditors periodically from January 1, 2004. Rather than require the rotation of firms, the new rules mandated the rotation of personnel. After five years, an individual CPA who signs an audit report and the person in charge of the audit must rotate off the audit of a listed company after five years, with a two year cooling off period. For an initial public offerings (IPO) company, those persons must rotate off in the third year after the IPO (Pacter & Yuen, 2004). The rule as finally promulgated had no meaningful effect on the Big Four, since they had similar internal policies in place.

SASAC, in a regulation issued on February 10, 2004, first required rotation of audit firms. SASAC has responsibility only for companies controlled by the Central Government, and the regulation does not apply to those companies owned by other governmental entities, which constitute the vast majority of government-controlled companies. As of July 31, 2013, there were 113 companies under Central Government management by SASAC.[3] *Rules on Financial Audit for State-Owned Enterprises* (Guozifa Pingjia File No. 173. 2004) require that the tenure of an audit firm serving as SOEs' auditor should not exceed five years. On October 7, 2005, the SASAC issued *Guidelines on improving the financial audit for State-Owned Enterprises* (Guozifa Pingjia File No. 43. 2005), which requires mandatory audit firm rotation in SOEs. Audit firms that provide audit services for SOEs should be changed every five years, and the maximum tenure for the same audit firms serving as an SOEs' auditor should no longer than ten years. SASAC directed that the rules should be strictly enforced.

On April 29, 2006, the SASAC further highlighted the regulation of mandatory audit firm rotation by issuing *Answers to Questions about Financial Audit for State-Owned Enterprises* (Guozifa Pingjia File No. 23, 2006). In 2006, the SASAC mandated that each company on a list of major Chinese SOEs rotate audit firms. SOEs whose audit firm is in the top 15 according to the top 100 audit firms issued by CICPA can keep the same audit firm for three more additional provided the total years of service is less than ten years, and no extension should be approved by SASAC. Audit firms are required to change the signing partner if rotation is delayed.

On December 29, 2011, SASAC and MOF issued jointly *Guidelines on Accounting Firms Serving Financial Auditing for State-Owned Enterprises* (Caikuai File No. 24. 2011), which requires that accounting firms serving as auditors of SOEs should be ranked among the top 50 Chinese accounting firms in the CICPA's top 100 accounting firms rankings. SOEs using accounting firms ranked in the top 15 can extend the tenure of the firms with SASAC approval, but the maximum term of service period should not longer than eight years.

The SASAC rules should have led to increased market concentration since they require the use of top 50 auditors and provide further incentives for SOEs to appoint top 15 auditors to delay rotation. Table 6.12 indicates that audit rotation has not led to greater concentration as measured by the CICPA top 100 firms. HHI for the CICPA top 100 has dropped from since 798 in 2007 to 478 in 2012. While Big Four market shares have dropped significantly during this period (Table 6.12), Tables 7.2 and 7.3 illustrate that auditor rotation policies among state-controlled companies did not result in a major shift of clients from Big Four firms to local firms. Interviews with local firm leaders indicated that they were invited to propose on large SOEs in the rotation process. SOEs rejected local firms because it was perceived that local firms did not have the necessary expertise. Some local firms declined to propose on large SOEs because they recognized they needed more time to gain the expertise to take on these large engagements.

While the data in Tables 7.2 and 7.3 suggest that SASAC did not use auditor rotation as a tool to shift audit market concentration away from Big Four firms by encouraging companies to switch to local firms, the process of auditor rotation may have the indirect effect of reducing Big Four dominance when measured by fee revenue. In late 2012, a number of large SOEs retendered their audits because their existing Big Four firms had reached the eight-year term limit allowed for top15 firms. Several companies have disclosed the results of the retender process (Table 7.4). The list contains only a portion of recent audit rotations. More complete data will become available when the companies report audit fees following the completion of the 2013 audits. What is most notable about this list is that none of these large companies selected a non-Big Four firm (although some may

Table 7.2. Auditor Rotation of State-Controlled Listed Companies.

	Rotations	Big Four Wins	Big Four Losses
2005	23	3	1
2006	38	0	1
2007	14	4	2
2008	15	0	4
2009	10	1	1
2010	6	2	2
2011	16	4	2
2012	17	2	3
Total	139	16	16

Source: CSMAR.

Table 7.3. Audit Rotation of State-Controlled Unlisted Companies.

	Rotations	Big Four Wins	Big Four Losses
2009	12	0	4
2010	7	0	1
2011	2	0	0
2012	10	4	6
Total	31	4	11

Source: SASAC.

Table 7.4. Selected 2013 Auditor Rotations.

Name	2013 Auditor	2012 Auditor	2013 Fee (RMB M)	2012 Fee (RMB M)	Fee Change
Industrial and Commercial Bank	KPMG	E&Y	133.6	160.0	−17%
Bank of China	E&Y	PwC	148.0	215.0	−31%
Ping An Insurance	PwC	E&Y	38.9	51.0	−24%
China Life Insurance	E&Y	PwC	50.7	63.9	−21%
Agricultural Bank of China	PwC	DTT	115.0	131.0	−12%

Source: Hong Kong Stock Exchange.

have appointed a local firm for certain work). Audit fees have reduced significantly, indicating the clients used audit rotation as a means to reduce fees. Although the rotation process mostly resulted in the Big Four swapping clients, the firms ended up with considerably less revenue. Initial

Table 7.5. Audit Market Concentration for Chinese Stock Exchanges.

Year	Number of Companies	Big Four	CR4	CR8	HHI
2006	1,200	59.77%	59.77%	68.13%	1,451
2007	1,232	67.88%	67.88%	76.79%	1,309
2008	1,406	62.98%	62.98%	73.19%	1,178
2009	1,581	56.70%	56.70%	72.04%	1,140
2010	1,814	57.55%	57.55%	72.59%	1,041
2011	2,080	53.36%	53.36%	71.66%	985
2012	2,465	47.95%	50.09%	71.65%	908

Source: CSMAR database (by audit fees).

audits usually involve considerable start up time to document existing practices (DeAngelo, 1981), and the lower fees are likely to put pressure on audit quality, partner earnings, or both.

Table 7.5 shows market concentration based on audit fees for companies listed on China's stock exchanges. The Big Four share of the market has declined since 2007. This is mainly a consequence of the Big Four winning a smaller share of Chinese IPOs and not from audit rotation. Only accounting firms approved by the CSRC may audit companies listed on Chinese stock exchanges.

7.5. MAINLAND CHINESE FIRMS AND THE H-SHARE MARKET

Local Chinese firms appear to have never argued that they should be auditors for the initial H-share audits. The firms had neither the scale nor the expertise in international accounting and auditing standards for these engagements and the regulatory environment in Hong Kong was hostile to outsiders. Mainland regulators realized that international firm's domination of the market for audits of large overseas listed companies was a major obstacle to the development of large Chinese accounting firms and set out to level the playing field.

The Hong Kong Stock Exchange accepted financial statements prepared under either Hong Kong Financial Reporting Standards (HKFRS) or IFRS. Since HKFRS and IFRS had substantially converged in 2005, there are normally no differences between accounts prepared on either standard.[4] Chinese companies listed on both the Hong Kong and Chinese stock exchanges were required to prepare two sets of accounts, one under CAS and the other under HKFRS or IFRS. In December 2007, the China Accounting Standards Committee and the HKICPA signed a joint declaration on the convergence of CAS and HKFRS as well as the convergence of mainland and Hong Kong auditing standards (HKICPA, 2007). The declaration concluded that CAS had sufficiently converged with HKFRS such that Chinese companies listing in Hong Kong could use it for filings in Hong Kong.

The next issue was allowing mainland auditors to issue reports accepted in Hong Kong. HKSE rules required that an accountant both qualified in and a resident of Hong Kong sign accounts. Perhaps recognizing the inevitability of change, HKICPA issued a consultation paper/exposure draft, in January 2009, that proposed changes to qualification requirements (HKICPAs, 2009a). It proposed that Hong Kong CPAs residing on the mainland could obtain practicing certificates and that mainland experience would satisfy the one-year local experience requirement. These changes would have allowed mainland-based auditors to sign reports used in Hong Kong, provided they first secured the necessary qualifications as Hong Kong CPAs. This proposal did little to pacify mainland authorities because it simply made it easier for Hong Kong CPAs to practice on the mainland. Many Hong Kong CPAs had moved to the mainland, including large numbers with Big Four firms, and the proposal would make it easier for them to use their Hong Kong qualifications.

Chinese regulators opened discussion about the Hong Kong Stock Exchange accepting reports signed by Chinese CPAs without being Hong Kong CPAs. These discussions were initiated under the Closer Economic Partnership Arrangement (CEPA), a trade agreement between Hong Kong and the mainland that was signed in 2004. CEPA was hailed in Hong Kong as opening China's markets for Hong Kong firms but was now revealing its double edge. Hong Kong CPAs complained that the proposal would jeopardize shareholders, who they claimed relied on Hong Kong's more robust system of corporate governance and auditor supervision. HKICPA came out in favor of the proposal, while expressing reservations about the effectiveness of regulation of mainland CPAs and hoping that the mainland would in turn further open its market to Hong Kong CPAs (HKICPAs, 2009b).

Hong Kong Exchange and Clearing Limited (HKEx), regulator and operator of the HKSE, issued a consultation paper in August 2009 to address the issue of whether Hong Kong should accept mainland accounting and auditing standards and permit mainland audit firms to audit companies listed in Hong Kong (HKEx, 2009). The paper recommended the acceptance of financial statements prepared using CAS, a conclusion based on the earlier agreement between the HKICPAs and the China Accounting Standards Committee that the standards had converged. It was also proposed to allow mainland CPA firms to register and seek approval from both MOF and CSRC to audit H-share companies. Once approved by Chinese regulators, the HKEx would accept them, for auditing H-share companies, without further vetting by Hong Kong regulators. Mainland regulators would be responsible for continuing oversight and would have complete responsibility for disciplinary actions and sanctions. The regulators agreed to work closely together to facilitate effective regulation. Neither Hong Kong's Financial Reporting Council nor HKICPA would have any enforcement powers against approved Chinese accounting firms. The proposal also granted rights for Hong Kong CPAs to audit the reports of Hong Kong companies listed on mainland exchanges, although no such listings presently exist. HKEx proposed the effective date of the agreements as January 1, 2010, to apply to annual accounting periods beginning on or after that date.

The CSRC and the MOF jointly announced that they were commencing a pilot program to allow a small number of Chinese CPA firms to audit H-share companies. In order to apply to participate in the program firms needed to meet certain requirements, including having total revenue of at least RMB 300 million, audit revenue of at least RMB200 million and no less than RMB50 million of which came from the auditing of public companies. Firms must have at least 400 staff and no partner can own more than 25% of the firm. In addition, mainland firms under the program must either have a member firm in Hong Kong or belong to the same international accounting firm network as a Hong Kong-based firm. Few Chinese CPA firms qualify under these standards. According to Liu Yuting, director-general of the accounting regulatory department of the Ministry of Finance, 16 accounting firms, including the Big Four's firms in China, applied for the pilot program, and the ministry completed a field study on all of them. Liu said:

> We will pick and recommend the best of the best among the participating firms. It's still unclear how many firms will be allowed to take part in the scheme, but it won't be all. (Luk, 2010c)

Regulators ultimately approved 12 firms for the pilot program, including the China member firms of each of the Big Four (Li, 2011).

The program was supposed to launch on January 1, 2010, but quickly ran into opposition in Hong Kong. Judy Wong, president of the Association of Chartered Certified Accountants (ACCA), said that while ACCA accepts the program's direction, issues needed to be resolved. "There is a confidence issue," she said. "The MOF should let the public know how they vet the applications from mainland accounting and audit firms and what the criteria are" (China Daily, 2009). Hong Kong politicians quickly jumped into the fray. Starry Lee, a legislator who was also a principal at CCIF, a Hong Kong accounting firm that holds the largest market share of H-shares and Red Chips among local firms, expressed concern in a Legco meeting in April that the changes would make it difficult for local regulators to police audit failures. Paul Chan, the legislator who represented the accountancy constituency, stated that "We should have a clear and workable mechanism on when and how the overseas regulators will help Hong Kong regulators do their investigations and carry out discipline" (Yiu, 2010). The Securities and Futures Commission, regulator of the Hong Kong Stock Exchange, delayed the implementation of the program pending further study of the effectiveness of Chinese regulation to protect investors.

On December 10, 2010, HKEx published its consultation conclusions and announced that it had decided to adopt the proposals effective on December 15, 2010 (HKEx, 2010). The first Chinese company with H-shares in Hong Kong to announce it intended to take advantage of the new rules was Tsingtao Brewery Co. Ltd. (Tsingtao) (Yiu, 2011). Perhaps not coincidentally, Tsingtao had been the first Chinese company to list in Hong Kong. Tsingtao announced that it would ask shareholders for permission to dismiss PwC in Hong Kong and engage PwC's China member firm to be its auditor. In reality, nothing changed, since PwC Hong Kong and PwC China operate as a single firm and the Qingdao office had been running the engagement for years. Tsingtao had been reporting under both CAS and HKFRS and following the new rules would report only under CAS. A review of Tsingtao's financial statements indicates that by 2009 there was no difference in the amounts of assets or profits between the accounts they prepared under CAS and HKFRS.

The limited nature of the pilot program reflects the tendency of mainland regulators to seek gradual change. However, it is likely that the beginning of this experiment portends profound changes in both the Hong Kong and mainland accounting professions. While the experiment is initially of small scale, its successful execution will likely lead to a rapid and significant expansion. While initially only H-share companies are in play, the program could easily be expanded to include Red Chips and all other companies listed in Hong Kong. It is conceivable that CPA's from anywhere in China might be competing for statutory audit work in Hong Kong well in advance of the end of Hong Kong's status as a Special Administrative Region (SAR) in 2047.

It is doubtful that in the short term many H-share companies will have to switch to local firm auditors, mainly because these firms will have limited short-term capacity to handle a huge increase in work. HKICPA president Philip Tsai Wing-chung observed:

> I do not think all 164 mainland firms will change to mainland auditors immediately, as some would like to take a wait-and-see approach to see how international investors respond to the new rule. (Yiu, 2011)

Since the Big Four audit most of the H-share companies (Table 4.1), all that will likely change in the short term is that the China member firm will replace the Hong Kong member firm as the firm of record. However, the changes level the playing field, and local firms can now effectively compete for existing and new H-share listings. Initially, the types of companies likely to switch to local firms will be the smaller H-shares, since the local firms will not have the expertise to handle large, complex companies and the regulators are unlikely to be willing to accept the risk associated with small firms auditing big companies. Over time, however, it is likely the market becomes significantly more competitive as the number of firms qualified to perform H-share audits increases as they gain experience, expertise, and size. The increased competition is likely to put significant pressure on auditing fees, even for those clients retained by the Big Four.

While the H-share market is large by itself, there would appear to be no significant barriers to expanding the rights of Chinese CPAs to audit Red Chips. While these companies are incorporated in Hong Kong, they have all of their operations on the mainland and are controlled by SOEs. Furthermore, it is conceivable that the practice rights could be extended to all accounting work in Hong Kong, particularly since audit firms based just across Hong Kong's border in Shenzhen could perform fieldwork on a commuting basis. It is this further expansion that would most threaten Hong Kong's accounting firms. At some point between now and the end of Hong Kong's status as a Special Administrative Region in 2047 this issue will likely need to be resolved, and the current developments suggest that resolution will come earlier rather than later.

NOTES

1. Richardson (1989) explained that professional associations are a form of corporatism found in advanced capitalistic societies that organize and regulate professions.

2. It would take considerable time to implement these provisions. As further discussed in Chapter 6, China's WTO accession commitments allowed the Big Four joint ventures to continue to have legal entity partners.

3. See http://www.sasac.gov.cn/n1180/n1226/n2425/index.html

4. The remaining differences between HKFRS and IFRS relate principally to the effective dates of certain provisions.

CHAPTER 8

ANALYSIS AND CONCLUSIONS

> Given the potential of China's economic growth and the volume of its capital, the nation should be able to support its own international accounting network – maybe not in five to 10 years, but in 20 years, 30 years? China has the right conditions to make this happen, although the process of building an internationally recognized brand and an international network is going to be very tough, both in terms of initial investments and efforts in moving from a familiar market to an unfamiliar one.
>
> – Chen Yugui, CICPA Secretary General (Luk, 2010b)

This study has presented a scene in the long story of globalization. Most accounts of globalization view it as a 20th century phenomenon that accelerated in the last quarter of the century. Bentley (1996) more correctly traces globalization back to Columbus's discovery of America in 1492 and to de Gama's voyage around the cape of Africa to India in 1498. Following this line of thinking, China arguably entered the process of globalization with the commencement of the silk trade and the establishment of the Silk Road during the Han Dynasty (206 BC–220 CE). For China, however, a series of foreign interventions from the opium wars of the late 19th century to the Japanese occupation from 1937 to 1945 shaped the psyche of a nation that chose to largely seclude itself from the world for the 30 years that followed the founding of the People's Republic of China in 1949. When China opened up to the forces of globalization in the late 1970s, the process of globalization in China was compressed into a period of approximately 25 years, making it the perfect laboratory to study how globalization shapes markets and institutions.

This study presents a field-level examination of the process of globalization. It has illustrated how powerful members of the transnational capital class enter and ultimately dominate local markets and in the process shape local institutions. For Gallhofer and Haslam (2006, p. 905), "globalisation as a political, economic, technological and cultural process is especially characterised by the growth and spread of suprastatism, supranationalism or supraterritoriality." This study has shown how the Big Four served as agents of globalization. They are supranational organizations, substantially unrestrained by national borders, transcending nationalistic claims, and state-based attempts to regulate them.

In recent times, there has been a significant backlash against globalization with opponents pointing out the social repercussions of globalization including the loss of jobs to low wage markets, unstable international financial markets, environmental destruction, and cultural hegemony. Proponents maintain that globalization is:

> ... natural and inevitable – an impersonal and immutable force, akin to the weather, that is beyond human intervention and control; a force that workers and companies, alike, must adapt to and accommodate, and that nations are powerless to control or subordinate to goals such as sustainable economic development or greater social equity. (Arnold, 2005, p. 299)

For much of the early development of the CPA profession in China, regulators appear to have accepted Arnold's perspective on globalization as akin to the weather. China's accession to the WTO marked its substantial submission to the forces of globalization. For the accounting profession, the first quarter century of the profession was marked by the continual acceptance of international standards. More recently nationalistic forces have arisen to challenge the fundamental assumptions of globalization and its neoliberal agenda. Recent efforts to promote the development of indigenous firms may write a new chapter in the story of the globalization of accounting.

This chapter will address three fundamental questions about the development of the CPA profession in China

1. How did the Big Four come to dominate accounting markets in China?
2. Why were the Big Four able to dominate accounting markets in China?
3. How have indigenous firms attempted to break the hegemony of the Big Four over Chinese accounting markets?

8.1. HOW THE BIG FOUR CAME TO DOMINATE ACCOUNTING MARKETS IN CHINA

The means by which China chose to reform her economy predestined the domination of the Big Four of the accounting markets. China elected to deploy three traditionally capitalistic institutions to play key roles in the reformation of the economy: (1) international capital markets, (2) foreign corporate investment, and (3) private ownership of property. In the first two institutions listed, the Big Four was already deeply entrenched and easily transferred their domination of foreign markets to China. The field of private ownership of property was not an obvious area that the Big Four would win. The slow pace of implementation of ideological change related to private property created an opening that the Big Four seized through innovation.

8.1.1. Foreign Direct Investment

Significant to the domination of the market by the Big Four was the important role that foreign direct investment (FDI) played in the reform of the economy. China received massive amounts of FDI that provided several benefits to the reforming Chinese economy. Foreign capital helped to modernize the industrial base, provided a non-state basis for employment, and the new foreign-owned businesses served both as competitors and as role models that encouraged moribund state-owned enterprises (SOEs) to reform and become competitive.

Big Four partners disclosed in interviews that work for foreign companies is now far less than half of their work in China. However, this understates the importance of foreign companies to their success. The Big Four came to China because they needed to serve their multinational clients who were investing in China. While the record indicates firms considered the long-term potential of the Chinese market to be important to their future, the primary reason they arrived in the early 1980s was that their clients were also arriving. The fact that the global coordinating entities of the firms funded the initial offices, rather than the proximate Hong Kong firm, indicates it was the importance of serving MNC clients, not developing local business, which motivated the firms. While MNC clients provided the motivation for the Big Four to enter China, they indirectly provided the funding to establish the firms. The capability to meet the needs of the client anywhere in the world forms the foundation of the Big Four's relationship with their clients. Protecting this relationship was the motivation for the member firms of the Big Four to fund the development of a practice in China that they would not ultimately own and in which they would not directly share in the profits.

The Big Four entered China with significant advantages over domestic firms. The firms easily transferred their established client relationship with investing MNCs to the new China firm. Auditing standards regarding the use of the work of other auditors create barriers to the ability of MNCs to use a firm other than their principal auditor for subsidiary operations. MNCs tend to use their international auditor even when the cost and abilities of that auditor may not be competitive with local firms. This created a significant advantage for the Big Four, giving them the ability to charge higher prices even where their capabilities fell short of domestic competitors. Over time, the ability to charge higher prices would allow the Big Four to afford to hire better personnel, ultimately resulting in the firms developing better capabilities.

The role of MNCs and FDI in the development of the Chinese accounting profession and its ultimate domination by the Big Four illustrates the mutually reinforcing behaviors of the transnational capital class in dominating new markets opened through globalization. As MNCs globalize, they bring with them other members of the transnational capital class – professionals in this case. This study has illustrated how the globalization of MNCs leads to the globalization of professional service firms because of the tendency of the MNCs to select other members of the transnational capital class as service providers in new locations rather than to use indigenous suppliers. I hypothesize that further research would determine that this mutually reinforcing behavior would extend to other supplier relationships of MNCs.

8.1.2. Foreign Capital Markets

Another key contributor to Big Four domination was the decision by Chinese regulators to allow Chinese SOEs to list on foreign stock exchanges. This decision appears to have had dual motivations: first to raise the capital necessary to modernize the SOEs in order to prepare them for global competition and second, to import foreign corporate governance practices as a means of encouraging the rapid cognitive changes that were perceived as necessary for the companies to function effectively.

The decision by Chinese policy makers to encourage large SOEs to list in Hong Kong and New York directly benefited the Big Four. SOEs began to list in Hong Kong in 1992 as H-shares and later as Red Chips. By the end of the 1990s, a number of large SOEs began to list in on the NYSE, often as part of a global offering that also included the listing of shares in Hong Kong.

Large SOEs that sought international listings soon discovered that members of the transnational professional class controlled access to the foreign markets. Big Four auditors, white shoe law firms, bulge bracket investment banks, financial printers, and valuation consultants are used as service providers on substantially all major IPOs.[1] These members of the transnational capital class engage in the mutually reinforcing practice of insisting on the participation of other members of the transnational professional class as a means of avoiding the risk of the participation of unknown professionals. Because these firms have worked together on a global basis for many years, they have established generally understood and accepted rules of interaction that provide mutual benefits. The symbiotic relationship between members of the transnational professional class had earlier led to their domination of the US and Hong Kong professional markets and it proved easy for them to extend this domination to the new Chinese market. These market-closing actions established a near insurmountable barrier to new market entrants, and that barrier was too high for indigenous Chinese CPA firms to overcome.

Language also created a barrier for indigenous Chinese CPAs that prevented them from serving Chinese companies seeking international listings. Both Hong Kong and the United States required English language prospectuses and financial statements. The Big Four in China had sought accountants with English language capabilities in order to serve MNCs, and these language skills were easily deployed to serve Chinese companies seeking international listings.

Foreign regulatory barriers also contributed to the domination of foreign listings by the Big Four. Hong Kong required until 2010 that a Hong Kong CPA must audit accounts of companies listed on the HKSE, although the HKSE granted exceptions to certain overseas companies like HSBC that used Big Four auditors. Meeting this requirement was easy for the Big Four firms, which had sizeable Hong Kong practices that they operated jointly with the mainland firms. For indigenous firms, this requirement excluded them from the market until recent years, when some of the larger mainland firms established or acquired CPA firms in Hong Kong. The 2010 removal of this requirement was a key success of the counter-hegemonic strategy of indigenous firms.

The United States also had regulatory barriers to Chinese auditors serving US-listed Chinese companies. The PCAOB requires the registration of all auditors of US-listed Chinese companies. The fact that 59 Chinese CPA firms had registered by August 13, 2010 indicates that this barrier was not significant. However, few Chinese CPA firms have become the signing accountants on US-listed Chinese companies, indicating that while the regulatory barrier might be surmountable, other obstacles including language, expertise in PCAOB auditing standards, and expertise in US GAAP and SEC rules have prevented these companies from gaining a significant share in this market.

8.1.3. Private Entrepreneurship

China's experiment with communism failed to deliver its promised prosperity to the Chinese people. A critical component of the Marxist construction of communism is the ownership of the means of production by the people. China implemented communism after 1949 by effectively eliminating the private ownership of property, especially the private ownership of productive assets. The ownership and operation of productive assets was transferred to the state or to collectives. Those who resisted were marked as "rightists" or "capitalist roaders," and faced persecution and often death.

Early in the reform process, reform minded leaders like Zhao Ziyang and Deng Xiaoping began to believe that the communal ownership of property was retarding the development of the country. These leaders began an effort to shift popular ideology toward the acceptance of a role for private ownership of property and, by extension, the acceptance of a role in Chinese society for privately owned businesses. The role of the private economy expanded with the significant economic reforms adopted at the meetings of the Fourteenth (1993) and Fifteenth (1997) Party Congresses. Jiang Zemin's 2001 Principle of the Three Representations fully rehabilitated entrepreneurs, who became eligible for Communist Party membership and the attendant access to political power.

While these political reforms established a legitimate political and legal base for entrepreneurs and resulted in increasing acceptance of the role of private enterprise among China's elite, the institutions that were needed to support the development of private enterprise changed more slowly. A persistent bias in favor of SOEs hobbled the efforts of private enterprises to develop. State-owned banks were reluctant to loan to private enterprises, a prejudice that was rooted in both ideology and prudent management. Banks perceived private enterprise as too risky, since the state effectively guaranteed loans to SOEs.

China's capital markets that developed during this ideological shift reflect the changing conditions. As shown in Tables 5.6 and 5.7, private enterprise was unable to raise substantial amounts of capital on Chinese stock exchanges until 2007, and by 2012, privately controlled enterprises only made up 26% of the market capitalization of Chinese stock exchanges.

China's late recognition of the capital needs of private enterprise unexpectedly created an opportunity for the Big Four. China's home grown entrepreneurial companies should have been the natural clients of China's domestic CPA firms. That has been the case with respect to recent listings of private companies on ChiNext, where the Big Four have an insignificant share of the audit work for recent listings. However, the absence of suitable domestic sources of capital forced entrepreneurs to look outside of China for money.

Chinese regulators had established barriers to Chinese companies that chose to list aboard. Companies were required to obtain permission from the CSRC before seeking an overseas listing, and such permission appears to have been granted only to large SOEs. Further restrictions were imposed on Chinese citizens who wished to form corporations outside of China or who wished to transfer assets to foreign companies. Rules prohibited foreign investment in many industries, and selling shares of a Chinese company abroad would result in foreign ownership, which was illegal. Working with international law firms, the Big Four helped private Chinese companies develop a structure, the variable interest entity, that allowed these companies to circumvent Chinese regulation. This has resulted in US stock markets becoming an important source of capital for Chinese private companies. In addition to developing enabling structures, the Big Four deployed expertise in US listing requirements to China. The Big Four created the market for audit services to US-listed private Chinese companies that they would dominate.

8.2. WHY THE BIG FOUR CAME TO DOMINATE ACCOUNTING MARKETS IN CHINA

It is easy to observe how the Big Four came to dominate the accounting profession in China. An examination of the current market structure for the CPA profession clearly indicates that the Big Four dominated the market overall by dominating certain key sectors – principally the market for FDI, for large SOEs listing abroad, and for private companies blocked from access to capital in China. Understanding why the firms were able to do so despite efforts by some bureaucrats to restrict their activities is more difficult.

I analyze this issue by looking at the shifting of boundaries, following Suddaby et al.'s (2007) analysis of shifting boundaries in transnational governance in accounting. First, I examine how redefined spatial boundaries influenced the debate over the pace of localization of the Big Four in China. Next, I examine shifts in ideational boundaries, and explain how changing ideologies in China created the opportunity for the Big Four to dominate the market. Third, I explain how a global shift in identification boundaries separated the Big Four and traditional accounting professionals facilitated the division of China's accounting profession into separate classes. Finally, I address shifts in power from hard actors to soft actors and explain how this shift was used to the Big Four's advantage. The shift from national to transnational governance of the profession has resulted in the creation of regulatory holes, which result in significant gaps in regulatory oversight.

8.2.1. Redefining Spatial Boundaries

Most major accounting markets developed along national lines, where strong local professions were created that later linked with other markets in the process of globalization. Even the Big Four trace their roots to strong local practices in the United Kingdom and the United States. As the Big Eight expanded to new markets, they generally found strong local firms with which to merge. The expansion of the Big Eight networks followed the rapid globalization of the world economy after World War II, and was driven by the need to serve American and British MNCs that were expanding internationally. I have traced how that happened in Hong Kong, but the same phenomenon was repeated across the world (Baskerville & Hay, 2010; Moizer et al., 2004; Wallerstedt, 2001). Ding Pingzhun (2006b, p. 96) advocated that China should develop its accounting profession the same way, telling the international firms that "localization is still the first guiding principle, and internationalization should be based on localization." The record indicates that the Big Four and Ding did not understand each other on this point. Ding was advocating for development of the profession in the way that it had historically developed in the rest of the world, with a focus on strong local firms first and integration with global networks later. Big Four partners who dealt with Ding thought he was simply advocating for fewer expatriates. This disconnect was most clear in the debate over localization during the WTO negotiations that are described in Chapter 6. The concept that the Big Four should help to develop strong local firms and wait to integrate them into their global networks was so inconceivable to them that it appears that they never understood what Ding was saying.

It is likely that emerging markets like China and Eastern Europe could not develop by following the traditional method of localization first, internationalization later. The late development of these markets happened in a heavily globalized world. In the middle of the 20th century, the accounting profession had developed in most countries to meet local market demands, and the international firms entered once the market required greater international capabilities. In China and the former Soviet Union, the need for international capabilities was immediate. In China, the need for rapid internationalization of accounting practices was mostly a result of China's decision to allow MNCs to invest in China. The Big Eight saw a need to be present in China to serve their MNC clients that would be investing in China even before regulators would have conceived of the need for indigenous CPA firms.

Ding failed to recognize that the structural boundaries of the profession were shifting or had already shifted. In their study of the transnational regulation of the accounting profession, Suddaby et al. (2007) argue that the key structural boundaries of the organizational field of professional services have shifted from the state-profession level of analysis to the transnational level.

> This view of structuration adopts a strong spatial metaphor in which the emergence of a field is likened to a definable network of activity that emerges in time and space (DiMaggio & Powell, 1983). Drawing the boundaries of the field, in this sense, involves the process of identifying the actors that interact "frequently and fatefully" (Scott, 1994, p. 208) with each other in a mutually reinforcing pattern of interactions by which mutual expectations become institutionalized in common routines, shared expectations and a growing awareness of engaging in a common project or activity (DiMaggio, 1983, 1991). Field emergence thus occurs as a result of the introduction of new actors (DiMaggio, 1991; Reay & Hinings, 2005), new practices (Leblebici, Salancik, Copay, & King, 1991) or related changes in the institutional structures, that define the spatial terrain of interaction.

This study has found considerable evidence for the shift in the boundaries of the profession. The most significant factors relate to FDI, international listings, and the adoption of international accounting and auditing standards. The shift in boundaries introduced new actors into the field – foreign regulators like the HKSE and the PCAOB, international organizations like the World Bank and the WTO, and international standard setters like the IASB. Chinese bureaucrats could not control these actors the way they could control local actors, and as a result they lost the ability to unilaterally shape the accounting profession in China.

Local boundaries precluded the rise of strong national firms. Until fairly recently, indigenous firms were locally organized and not permitted to establish branches in other cities and provinces. This artifact of China's centrally planned economy effectively blocked the development of indigenous CPA firms that could participate in the broader shift of transnational boundaries.

Ding and his fellow Chinese regulators failed to recognize these shifting boundaries until the Big Four had already dominated the profession. It is unlikely, however, that they could have done anything about it. The globalization of China's economy had increasingly shifted the boundaries of the accounting profession outside China. The Big Four was well positioned to benefit from this shift in boundaries, while domestic firms were unprepared. By the time that China's larger domestic firms were able to align with second-tier international firms and arguably build the credentials to compete internationally, the Big Four had already seized the market.

In his memoirs, Ding mourns that the Big Four came to dominate the accounting profession in China. He fails to consider whether China is better off because of this result. Certainly, China's remarkable advancement is in part attributable to the massive foreign investment into China and to the transformation of SOEs that was enabled by the reforms in corporate governance and massive capital infusions that were facilitated by foreign stock exchanges. The Big Four enabled these advances. Would the advances have been as significant if the Big Four were not present?

8.2.2. Redefining Ideational Boundaries

China has experienced a remarkable change in its ideology over the first three decades of reform. It went from a closed society with a centrally planned economy to a market-driven economy that is now the second largest on the planet. Young Chinese commonly parody once popular Communist Party slogans like "*wei renmin fu wu*" (serve the people) into "*wei renminbi fu wu*" (serve the money).

The accounting profession developed during this period of transformational ideological change in China. The rise of a market ideology created the profession, just like the rise of the communist ideology following 1949 had destroyed it. Institutional theorists have focused on how a shared ideology is the foundation of institutions (Scott, 2008). It would take considerable time for the accounting profession in China to develop a shared ideology. During the transition, competing ideologies would often come into conflict with each other before the participants would develop a shared meaning of the symbolic structures that underpin the profession (Berger & Luckmann, 1967).

The starting points of the two major participants (the Big Four and indigenous accountants) could not have been further apart. The Big Four arrived in China with a well-developed ideology of international accounting practice built on the neoliberal philosophy of globalization. They had a clear view of the importance of international standards and brought with them a methodology of practice that was near uniformly accepted in the West. For the Big Four, the role of professional accountants was well defined, particularly with respect to the independence of the profession and the way in which it worked with clients and regulators. China, on the other hand, shared none of those views, and upon inspection discovered that many of them conflicted with deeply held Chinese views of the role of institutions.

In the initial phase, regulators dealt with the irreconcilable ideologies by simply separating the profession into two groups. The foreign group was allowed to work with foreign clients, but all audit work was left to domestic CPA firms that operated under the state. This removed any real competition between the foreign and domestic firms and allowed domestic firms to develop by following Chinese ideologies. The initial ideology of the emerging accounting institution viewed CPA firms as an extension of the state regulatory apparatus and the firms effectively served as government examiners of foreign-invested enterprises. The concept of independence, which underpins Western public accounting institutions, was antithetical to Chinese society.

Deng Xiaoping's Southern Tour marked the beginning of a significant ideological shift in China that accelerated the pace of reforms. The new ideology was significantly friendlier to capitalistic institutions, leading to a rapid increase in FDI and the development of capital markets. Development of a new ideology for the accounting profession lagged developments in the broader economy, and this created an opportunity for the Big Four to introduce the Western ideology that the profession would ultimately accept.

The most significant event for the Big Four firms in China was the decision in 1992 to grant them permission to enter into joint ventures with state-owned CPA firms. This proved to be the equivalent of the Arab fable of the camel that once permitted to stick its nose into the tent, soon ends up entirely inside the tent. Joint ventures provided the Big Four with legitimacy, including the all-important license to conduct audits. Because the

Big Four were required to collaborate with state-owned CPA firms, the state should have had significant influence in the development of these firms and could have retained control of the ideological debate over the proper role of CPA firms. Instead, the Big Four succeeded in turning the state into a passive, near silent partner and the joint venture firms rapidly adopted the Big Four ideology with respect to how accounting firms should practice. At the same time, the remaining indigenous firms remained under state control and continued to practice under an ideology that saw them as an extension of state control. This assured that the domestic firms would be uncompetitive with the Big Four at one of the most critical times in the development of the profession. During the 1990s, China emerged as a powerful force in the world economy, and the domestic CPA profession, hobbled by an ideology that tied it to the past and a role as an extension of the state, fell behind. Consequently, it is during this period that the Big Four began to dominate the Chinese CPA profession.

There is ample evidence that Ding Pingzhun understood that the Chinese CPA profession needed to reform if it were to compete with the Big Four and be relevant to the changing Chinese economy. Most of Ding's reforms involved the adoption of Western concepts of professionalism, and in particular what Suddaby and Greenwood (2005) call the trustee model of professionalism, which places the public interest ahead of mercantile elements. He pushed, mostly unsuccessfully, for accounting firms to use the partnership form of organization. Against considerable resistance, he pushed through reforms to separate CPA firms from the state. This was his most significant achievement, since it changed the nature of the CPA profession from an extension of state control to a professional trusteeship that was consistent with the role of the CPA profession in the West. At the same time, China began the process of adopting international accounting and auditing standards, once again accepting the Western ideology. These reforms, however, were too slow, and by the time they were substantially implemented the Big Four "camel" was completely in the "tent" and the Big Four had come to dominate the profession.

Suddaby et al. (2007, p. 347) argued that "Ideational processes, or the means by which logics are created and reproduced, serve two seemingly contradictory purposes; they *differentiate* and *integrate* organizational actors and actions within the field." The present study is an illustration of this phenomenon. It took nearly two decades for China to implement ideological changes that would enable an independent accounting profession based on Western concepts of professional trusteeship. The process of working through those ideological changes validated the ideological foundations of the Big Four and further legitimized their claim to dominance. Many Chinese bureaucrats, particularly those involved with the CSRC, believed that the Big Four firms were superior to local alternatives, and the wholesale adoption of Western ideologies with little local adaptation convinced them that they were correct. So, rather than enabling the local firms to compete against the Big Four, the adoption of Western ideologies served to reinforce the hegemony of the Big Four.

The global accounting profession did not remain static during the period in which China's accounting profession emerged and developed. While China ultimately looked to the West for ideological guidance for the role of the profession, the ideology of the West was also changing, creating a moving target. Reviewing recent developments with respect to transnational accounting firms, Suddaby et al. (2007, p. 334) found that the dominant logic of the accounting profession had changed from a model of professional trusteeship to a model based on the commercial exchange of expertise:

> We further observe shifts in the regulatory logic of this new compact, from one based on normative principles of professional elitism to one based on neo-liberal principles of market economics (Puxty, Willmott, Cooper, & Lowe, 1987), dramatically affecting the production, consumption and control of professional expertise.

Ding focused on adopting the public trustee model of professional accountants based on the normative principles of professional elitism. He determined that this model was normative when he studied the structure of the accounting profession outside of China. In his memoirs, Ding (2006b, p. 124) writes of his growing awareness that the regulatory logic of the Big Four had shifted to a neoliberal ideology of global market competition:

> In the past, I only knew that the people in accounting firms are all accountants who are honest and steadfast. Later I knew that the accounting firm is also a merchant who has to make money. In the end I woke up and found that Andersen is not only a merchant, but also a politician, which has nothing to do with titles in the accounting world but is really something in China and even in the world.

While Ding might have been aware that the logics underpinning the accounting profession were rapidly changing, he was unable to effectively respond to the changes. Instead, the CICPA continued to strive to replicate the professional trusteeship model in China, even when Big Four had moved on to a newer globalizing ideology. As a result, the CICPA was unable to react to the significant changes that took place when the Big Four firms integrated their Hong Kong and China practices in the early 2000s and became more regionally integrated and powerful.

8.2.3. Identification Boundaries and Class

The theoretical foundation for this study posited that the Big Four and indigenous firms organized into different classes and that these classes have struggled for domination of the accounting market in China. Suddaby et al. (2007, p. 355) found that the emergence of separate class identities between elite and traditional professionals was global phenomenon: "... there has been a distinct shift in *identification* in which efforts have been made to draw a boundary between the occupational identity of elite and traditional professionals." Suddaby et al. (2007, p. 348) suggest that the separation of professionals into classes is a consequence of the shift in spatial and ideational boundaries:

> As logics and spatial boundaries of fields change, individual and organizational actors feel compelled to adopt new role structures as a means of signifying both understanding of, and compliance with, the revised "rules of the game."

In China, the shift in spatial boundaries separated the indigenous firms and the Big Four. The Big Four moved into the transnational space while indigenous firms remained within a well-defined local space that was often limited to a single community. The consequence of this separation of space was to allocate the market between the Big Four and local firms. Clients with transnational characteristics – foreign ownership, foreign listings, international activities, and large scale became Big Four clients, while smaller, locally listed, and geographically limited businesses hired indigenous firms. While there were more clients in the latter category, there were more fees in the former.

Differences in ideology, in particular the adherence to independence and international standards, initially set the Big Four apart from indigenous firms. Chinese regulators and practitioners rapidly accepted the Western ideology followed by the Big Four, yet implementation of policies based on the new ideology was too slow to allow the local firms to effectively compete with the Big Four.

For Gramsci, hegemony results because of the consent of the lower class to the perceived superior ideology of the dominant class. There is scant record of any ideological opposition to reforms that embraced Western ideologies such as international accounting and auditing standards and the independence of the profession. Opposition to the separation of CPA firms from the state was based primarily on pecuniary rather than ideological concerns. The lack of widespread ideological opposition to international standards of practice validated the perceived normative superiority of the Big Four in Chinese society, particularly with respect to serving China's largest and most important SOEs. Local firms did not present a viable alternative ideology, and consequently effectively consented to the domination of the Western ideology advanced by the Big Four. Consent came in part because local firms viewed adopting Western ideologies as a way to compete against the Big Four. Instead, the ideologies simply reinforced the hegemony of the Big Four because they validated the beliefs of many users in the superiority of the Big Four.

Even though indigenous firms consented to Western ideologies as to the manner in which the CPA profession should function, the slow pace of adoption of these ideologies would allow the Big Four to establish hegemony over them. The most significant factor was the delay until 2000 in separating CPA firms from the state. Had they separated earlier in the development of the profession, this story might be different.

8.2.4. Power Shifts

One of the consequences of the spatial and ideological shifts in the accounting profession has been a change in the way that power influences change and regulates the profession. Traditionally, accountancy is a highly regulated profession. The regulatory bargain that the profession reached provided closure and access to the coercive power of the state in exchange for adherence to professional standards and a commitment to acting the public interest. The profession is typically self-regulated through an association which develops and enforces standards (Richardson, 1997). China replicated this model with its CPA law and the establishment of the CICPA.

Globalization and the resulting shift in spatial and ideological boundaries undermine the effectiveness of the regulatory bargain between local governments and local professionals. Suddaby et al. (2007) maintain that accountancy has seen a shift from the coercive application of power by nation states and profession associations to a "soft" power exercised by the Big Four and transnational agents. A further dimension in this shift in power from nation states to transnational agents relates to increasing regulatory squabbles between "hard" actors of differing jurisdictions.

This study has presented ample evidence of this shift. The evidence falls into two broad categories: (1) shifts in power to soft actors like the IASB, the WTO, the World Bank, and the Big Four; and (2) conflicts in the exercise of power between hard actors like the CICPA, the CSRC, the SEC, and the PCAOB.

8.2.4.1. Role of Soft Actors

Soft power actors rely on normative power and the ability to shape interests and identities. Soft power is obtained, in part, through ideology and influence on international organizations (Nye, 2004). Perhaps the most powerful of soft actors in China are international standard setting bodies like the IASB. The standards setting bodies are aided in the acquisition of soft power by the World Bank, which provided the funding and leadership to encourage China on the path to adopting international standards. The Big Four also gained soft power through their participation in the activities of these organizations. In China, the selection of DTT and PW for major international projects related to international standards helped the Big Four to transfer that power to China. These projects established the Big Four as possessors of the normative ideology that China was pressured to adopt by soft power agencies like the World Bank.

The Big Four was an early beneficiary of the transfer of power from hard actors to soft actors. The increasing global acceptance of IFRS reduces the power of local standard setting bodies that once helped to ensure the closure of local markets. Hong Kong's begrudging acceptance of mainland auditors and mainland accounting standards is evidence of how international standards are reducing the hard power of national standard setting bodies.

The Big Four successfully positioned themselves as experts in the application of international standards and obtained significant influence in the setting of these standards. Global standards allow the Big Four to efficiently deploy resources globally. This allowed the Big Four to transfer experienced partners and managers from around the world to China yet have them capable of performing work to local standards without further training.

8.2.4.2. Soft Power and the WTO

An important application of soft power by the Big Four related to its successful retention of practice rights in the negotiations for China to enter the WTO. China had welcomed the Big Four to China in the apparent hope that they would transfer their knowledge and technologies to China and then depart, leaving the market to locals. Ding came to understand that they had struck a Faustian bargain and had sold the profession to the foreigners. Ding spent most of his tenure as the head of the CICPA trying to return the profession to locals, but was stymied at each step by the WTO. The Big Four demonstrated a remarkable ability to solicit the support of national governments, including the United States and the EU, to do their bidding, even when the matter was not of direct concern to these countries.

8.2.4.3. Conflicts between Hard Actors

The globalization of capital markets has created many situations where multiple state regulators are involved. For example, the listing of a Chinese company in the United States results in the SEC gaining regulatory nexus over the company and the PCAOB gaining regulatory nexus over the auditors. At the same time, Chinese regulators retain regulatory authority over companies and accountants located in China. The situation also occurs when Chinese auditors participate in the audit of overseas companies with China operations. In this situation, Chinese auditors are subject to regulatory oversight in China because they are licensed in China and they are subject to regulatory oversight by the PCAOB because they are registered with the PCAOB and participate significantly in the international audits.

China's difficult history with foreign domination from the Opium Wars to the Japanese Occupation has scarred the national memory and made China particularly sensitive anything it perceives as foreign interference in its domestic affairs. This approach has led to China converging its accounting standards rather than simply adopting IFRS as has increasingly been the practice elsewhere. When Chinese bureaucrats talk locally about the convergence process, they always make the point that they are considering China's special circumstances when converging accounting standards. In practice, however, they have tended to adopt international standards without modification, sometimes on a word for word translated basis.

China has been consistent in its position that foreign regulators cannot act in China. China considers the presence of foreign regulators acting on Chinese soil to be a breach of China's sovereignty. China has prohibited the PCAOB from coming to China to inspect China-based auditors who are registered with the PCAOB. This prohibition includes Hong Kong-based auditors to the extent that the work examined relates to clients based on the mainland. While China has largely stayed out of Hong Kong's affairs since its return to China in 1997, it has used its sovereignty over Hong Kong to keep the PCAOB at bay.

China's position is that it alone should be responsible for the regulation of accountants within its borders. It took the same position in negotiations with Hong Kong regarding the acceptance of the reports of Chinese auditors of H-share companies. Hong Kong regulators agreed that Chinese regulators would have sole authority over Chinese auditors. In the case of H-shares that report in Hong Kong under Chinese accounting standards and using Chinese auditors, the situation may prove workable. Chinese regulators have the expertise to regulate these situations. Because Chinese regulators pushed to allow Chinese companies to report under Chinese accounting standards and to use Chinese auditors, they have an interest in making the regulative processes work.

Chinese regulators likely have less interest with respect to US listings of Chinese companies. Chinese regulators do not have the expertise in US accounting and auditing standards to effectively inspect the work of Chinese firms in this area. Although Chinese companies seeking US listings are supposed to seek prior approval from the CSRC, private companies commonly circumvent this requirement by using offshore holding companies incorporated in the Cayman Islands or the British Virgin Islands. Consequentially, the CSRC has no regulatory power over these firms. The MOF has regulatory power over Chinese accounting firms that audit US-listed Chinese companies, which it administers together with the CICPA. The Big Four dominate the market for auditing US-listed Chinese companies. The Chinese member firms that do these audits register with both the CICPA and the PCAOB. Chinese regulators, however, have shown no interest in audit reports used abroad. Inspections of Chinese accounting firms by Chinese regulators focus on statutory filings in China that are prepared under Chinese accounting principles. Consequently, there are several situations where Chinese regulators are not exercising regulatory oversight on audit work conducted in China:

1. Foreign partners practicing in China without a local license
2. Foreign firms that operate in China through consulting firms
3. Audit work performed by Chinese CPA firms on financial statements prepared using IFRS or foreign GAAP for use outside of China.

Unlicensed foreign partners. The majority of the partners of the Big Four in China are foreign nationals (including Hong Kong and Taiwan partners who are treated as foreigners by the CICPA). Few have passed the Chinese CPA examination that is a necessary first step to obtaining a practicing certificate in China. Based on discussions with partners, most audits of overseas-listed Chinese companies are done under the direction of a foreign partner resident in China. These partners are not directly subject to regulatory oversight in China because they are not licensed as certified public accountants in China. This situation may change because of the move to limited LLPs in 2012. China will have the ability to regulate foreign partners who are admitted to the LLPs, although it remains uncertain whether they will do so.

Chinese regulators choose to focus on the act of signing a report that would be used in China as the act that would require licensing as a certified public accountant. Foreign partners do not sign such reports, and if clients require them, the firm arranges for a partner with a practicing CPA license to sign on behalf of the unlicensed foreign partner. These accommodation signatures are not required for reports used outside of China, such as inter-office reports on MNCs or audit opinions of foreign-listed companies. In these cases, the foreign engagement partner signs and takes full responsibility for the opinion. Because Chinese regulators do not apparently consider audits used for foreign purposes to fall under their regulatory responsibility, they have not exercised any regulatory authority over foreign partners in China. The foreign partners may have a license in another jurisdiction, and that jurisdiction might have regulatory authority over the partner. However, there are no rules to require this unless the firms choose to regulate this internally.

Regulatory holes. I argue that the shift in power away from national regulators to hard and soft transnational regulators has resulted in the formation of regulatory holes. In defining a regulatory hole, I draw on structural hole theory, a mid-range theory within the genre of network theory. A structural hole is a gap between two individuals with complementary resources or information. Entrepreneurs can exploit structural holes by stepping into this gap and connecting the two separated individuals. Structural holes in markets give rise to competitive advantage to entrepreneurs who can identify and exploit them (Burt, 1992; Walker, Kogut, & Shan, 1997).

Regulatory holes function similarly to structural holes. They are the gap between two regulators with complementary mandates. Complementary mandates mean that two regulators have a reason to regulate the same activity. This overlapping jurisdiction could exist within a state, and a good example of that in China would be the oversight of auditors of public companies, where both the MOF/CICPA and the CSRC have regulatory authority. Complementary mandates may also be a multijurisdictional mandate that arises when an activity involves more than one state. An example of multijurisdictional mandate arises from the audits of US-listed companies by Chinese auditors. If both regulators with a complementary mandate fulfill their regulatory role without restriction, there is no regulatory hole. There may, instead be duplicative regulatory activities because both regulators might regulate the same activity.

Regulators, of course, do not always completely fulfill their regulatory mandate. Regulatory holes emerge when two or more regulators have the responsibility to regulate an activity, but fail to do so. This could occur when both regulators choose to not regulate a particular activity because of a lack of resources, disinterest in the activity, or political pressures to minimize regulation. Regulatory holes of this nature can arise in the transnational space because of the high cost of regulating far-flung activities, the lack of visibility of these activities (the out-of-sight, out-of-mind syndrome) or domestic political pressures. The regulation of individual foreign partners in China by their home jurisdiction is often inadequate for these reasons. Home country regulators have little information about the activities of their accountants who are practicing in foreign countries and are likely to deal with them only on an exception basis. Foreign partners in China have not been subject to regulation in China, although those that become partners in the Big Four's LLPs may. Because foreign partners are usually not Chinese CPAs, they are not members of the CICPA or directly subject to regulation by the MOF. While the MOF and CICPA could have reasonably have argued that China's CPA law prohibits foreign partners from performing audit services in China, they have not chosen to do so. Consequently, a regulatory hole is created where foreign CPAs practice in China without regulation by either China or their home jurisdiction.

Another type of regulatory hole is created where a regulator blocks a complementary regulator from regulating an activity yet fails to regulate the activity themselves. This situation typically arises out of regulatory "turf battles" where regulators spat over which should regulate a particular activity (Buxbaum, 2003; Partnoy, 2000). Regulatory turf battles can erupt between domestic regulators with overlapping jurisdictions, and they can arise between national regulators with respect to transnational activities that fall within the jurisdiction of two or more national regulators. The regulatory hole is created when a regulator successfully asserts that regulation of a particular activity is the sole responsibility of that regulator to the exclusion of the second regulator, followed by the first regulator then failing to exercise its regulatory responsibility. China's restrictions on the ability of the PCAOB to inspect Chinese accounting firms are an example of this type of regulatory hole. China has made a national sovereignty claim to block the PCAOB from coming to China, yet has failed to assert regulatory authority over audits that are done in China for use abroad. The same conditions exist with respect to the audit of H-share companies, where China has excluded Hong Kong regulators from oversight on Chinese accounting firms. In this case, however, Chinese regulators have promised to regulate these accounting firms, and it is too early to assess their performance in doing so. To the extent that China blocks foreign regulators from performing their regulatory activities and Chinese regulators do not step in, the activities fall into a regulatory hole and are essentially unregulated.

Structural hole theory posits that the existence of structural holes creates opportunity for entrepreneurs who can identify and exploit them. Extending this theory to regulatory holes suggests that the existence of regulatory holes creates opportunities for accountants to identify and exploit them. This has happened in China, where accounting firms have created a significant market serving overseas-listed companies that is essentially unregulated. The absence of regulation creates an opportunity for the firms to increase profitability by decreasing audit quality. While there is little regulatory risk in doing so, there remains substantial risk to malpractice claims (which may be subject to similar holes when prosecuted) and to reputation within and outside of China. Consequently, there is a significant incentive for the firms to self-regulate. In the case of the Big Four in China, I found considerable evidence that they do so. Each of the firms had large risk and quality functions, and teams assembled by the global firms regularly inspect each. Burt (1992, p. 2) argues that "holes create inequality between organizations as they create inequality between people." This is because the distribution of holes around an organization determines the organization's entrepreneurial opportunities. The Big Four is uniquely positioned to take advantage of the regulatory holes related to foreign-listed companies. Because of China's failure to regulate the activities of foreign partners in China who were signing international audit reports, the Big Four was able to transfer significant numbers of foreign partners to China in order to seize this market. The Big Four was closest to the regulatory hole, since it had access to partner resources that were capable of doing work related to foreign listings. Local firms, more distant from the regulatory hole, were less capable of seizing the market for overseas-listed companies. Had China decided to close the regulatory hole by claiming regulatory jurisdiction over the activities of foreign partners, including requiring local licensing before signing any audit opinions regardless of where the reports are used, the market might have developed differently.

8.3. HOW HAVE INDIGENOUS FIRMS TRIED TO BREAK THE DOMINANCE OF THE BIG FOUR?

Concerns arose among Chinese bureaucrats about the growing hegemony of the Big Four shortly after the Big Four entered into joint ventures.

Chinese bureaucrats saw the joint ventures as a mechanism to transfer technologies from the Big Four to China. They expected that once this was complete, the Big Four would leave and China would have its own accounting profession. The Big Four never shared that vision. They came to China expecting to ultimately build large practices that would become key members in their global firms. All of the Big Four partners I interviewed stated that it was always their intent that local accountants would ultimately own and manage their practices in China. They also said that they expected that the China firm would be more closely integrated with their global operations than many member firms had been in the past. This expectation developed in part because the global organization had provided the capital to develop the practice in China, and in part because of aspirations for a more globally cohesive entity.

Ding Pingzhun soon recognized that there were no meaningful technologies involved in public accounting and that the Big Four intended to take up the market. Ding and the CIPCA represented the interests of the indigenous firms, who do not appear to have developed class-consciousness until after they had separated from the state. The CICPA is part of political society with its power principally derived from the coercive power of the state rather than the consent of the led. There are indications, however, that the indigenous profession accepted the leadership of the CICPA. This observation is consistent with Yee's (2009) portrayal of the state-accounting profession relationship as a father–son relationship as encompassed within the Confucian notion of *wu lun*. However, Yee's conflation of the CICPA and the state ignores the fact that the state did not operate as a monolith. The CICPA consistently looked out for the interests of indigenous firms, while other branches of the state, notably the CSRC, often worked at cross purposes by implementing policies that favored the Big Four. The failed attempt by the CSRC to require the Big Four to serve as an auditor of all public companies is an example of the difference in ideological outlook between various Chinese bureaucracies. In this case, the CSRC believed that Big Four auditors would improve the quality of information available to investors and thus enhance China's capital markets, but the CICPA saw the proposal as a threat to indigenous firms.

Ding chose a path of reform based on mimetic and normative isomorphism. Ding appears to have accepted at an early date the inevitability of the neoliberal agenda of globalization, and focused his efforts on conforming China's accounting profession to globally accepted practices. Several of Ding's key initiatives evidence this, including the separation of CPA firms from the state and efforts to promote the use of the partnership form of organization. Ding also used normative arguments with mixed success in WTO negotiations in an attempt to return domination of the profession to domestic firms. Ding successfully pushed back on a Big Four proposal to offer the Chinese CPA examination in English, but he was unsuccessful with his arguments that China should require that locally licensed CPAs own all CPA firms. On this last point, however, Ding's position ultimately prevailed in 2012 when the Big Four were required to restructure into LLPs controlled by Chinese CPAs.

China's steady adoption of international accounting and auditing standards is another example of normative and mimetic isomorphism. Throughout the 1990s and into the early part of the 2000s, China put in place institutions that mimicked international institutions and those of other states. The China Accounting Standards Board, CICPA, and CSRC are good examples of this activity. This demonstrates that in China's case, the "long march through the institutions" was a process of normative and mimetic isomorphism. Many of the steps in the long march were a consequence of China's efforts to join the WTO, yet it does not appear that China was always coerced into making changes in its accounting institutions, but rather the changes appear to have been greeted as progressive changes that would modernize China's institutions. The cumulative effect of the changes in China's accounting institutions served to deepen contradictions, enabling indigenous firms to argue that they do the same work following the same standards, so why does most of the work go to the foreigners?

The Big Four has failed to successfully position their China member firms as being Chinese. Although they substantially localized the staff levels below partner, the firms are seen in China as being foreign. It appears unlikely this perception will change until local partners control the firms and hold most senior leadership positions. The transformation into LLPs in 2012 does not seem to have changed the foreign perception of the firms. For local firms, it does not appear that the mere affiliation with a foreign network results in society considering a CPA firm to be foreign. Interviewees consistently considered firms like BDO and Grant Thornton to be local firms because of their local ownership and management.

Members of the American Chamber of Commerce in China indicated their perspective that reform and opening up slowed dramatically following the completion of China's WTO accession process in 2006 (American Chamber of Commerce in the People's Republic of China, 2011). Jeffrey Immelt, CEO of General Electric accused the Chinese government of becoming increasingly protectionist: "I am not sure that in the end they want any of us to win, or any of us to be successful" (Dinmore & Dyer, 2010). US Commerce Secretary and China Ambassador appointee Gary Locke said that "There are real frustrations within this administration and among business and congressional leaders about the commercial environment in China" (Cai, 2011). Protectionism increased during and following the global downturn. Western companies have been reluctant to complain because, as one lawyer observed, "They have shown themselves to be retaliatory, and it really has the intended effect" (Bradsher, 2010). These observations may mark a change in China's view toward the role of foreign investment and indicate an increasing interest in the success of China's own businesses. This rise in economic nationalism is contemporaneous with rising nationalism in China (Bajoiria, 2008). Hall (2000, p. 64) argues that "… there is much to be said for seeing nationalism as a strategy of late development, which is to say that this protean force is often modern and modernizing … ." China must comply with the market opening commitments it made when it joined the WTO, but it is increasingly using the national security exceptions included in WTO agreements to its advantage (American Chamber of Commerce in the People's Republic of China, 2011).

China's efforts to build 10 large accounting firms, capable of serving Chinese companies globally, fits in this recent trend of economic nationalism. Earlier reforms laid the groundwork for the rise of the indigenous firms, providing a normative framework for their operation. China is now seeking to exploit this framework for the benefit of its local CPA firms. Document 56 establishes the State Council approved plan for breaking the hegemony of the Big Four. One of the first skirmishes was over the acceptance of Chinese accounting standards and auditors for H-share companies listed in Hong Kong, a fight easily won by mainland regulators over opposition in Hong Kong. Document 56 portends further attacks on Big Four hegemony in future years. In 2012 the expiration of the operational periods for the Big Four joint ventures in China forced the firms to restructure into LLPs that are controlled by locally licensed partners. While this may ultimately result in local control of the Big Four, early indications are that the firms have found a way to continue business as usual such that the leadership of the firms remains firmly in foreign hands. Mandatory audit rotation is probably the biggest threat to Big Four dominance in China. The initial round of rotations does not appear to have resulted in a shift of clients from the Big Four to local firms. The next rotation, in 2020, may have a different result. If large local firms are able to develop the expertise to audit large SOEs, the government may pressure certain large SOEs to change from the Big Four to large local CPA firms. Large local firms may be encouraged to poach key partners from the Big Four in order to serve these large SOEs. The next decade promises to be very interesting for the Big Four in China.

NOTE

1. White shoe law firms refer to a group of prestigious, generally New York based, law firms. The white shoe refers to a type of suede shoe once popular among Ivy League graduates. Bulge bracket investment banks refer to a group of large global investment banks that lead most global offerings and whose names bulge into larger print on a prospectus.

CHAPTER 9

IMPLICATIONS AND TOPICS FOR FURTHER RESEARCH

> But as Marx noted long ago, the role of philosophy is not to describe the world but to change it, and the aspirations of critical accountants should be no less.
>
> – Neimark, 1990, p. 111

This chapter offers strategic recommendations to the three major groups of actors in the Chinese accounting profession today: the Big Four, large domestic firms, and regulators. I have drawn on the findings in this study to create these recommendations. The recommendations are not findings; they are simply my opinion about actions that the various actors who do and will play a part in the development of the accounting profession in China could take to enhance their respective positions.

I also provide suggestions for further research. I provide a list of possible research topics that either extend this study or address interesting issues that I came across during the study. I believe that the Chinese accounting profession will be an important global institution. As such, it will merit considerable attention by scholars in the future.

9.1. WHAT THE BIG FOUR NEEDS TO DO

I believe that the Big Four will face significant challenges in China in the coming years, primarily because political forces have lined up against them (Gillis, 2010b). Official State policy, as explained in The State Council's Document 56, envisions a larger role for domestic firms at the expense of the Big Four. This policy reflects China's growing nationalism. After two decades of integrating China into the world economy by encouraging foreign involvement, China appears to have changed its focus to promoting its own companies. The biggest problem the Big Four face is the perception that they are foreign firms when China has chosen to favor local firms.

The number of local partners in the Big Four has grown significantly, yet local partners remain in the minority. Frank Lyn of PricewaterhouseCoopers (PwC) said "We already have a number of PRC partners – their percentage will continue to increase" (Chen & Luk, 2010, p. 24). Table 5.11 supports Lyn's assertion. However, few local partners have found leadership positions and none are in senior leadership positions. That is partly because of age, since most local partners were only recently admitted to the partnerships and do not have the level of experience that has typically been required for leadership roles in the Big Four. It is partly because the firms have purged many young local certified public accountants (CPAs) with strong leadership traits. I found evidence through my interviews that the socialization process of the Big Four has driven out many locals with leadership characteristics and has retained those who would readily submit to the leadership of Hong Kong partners. Consequently, many Big Four partners that I interviewed questioned whether local partners in China would be capable of becoming future leaders of the Big Four firms. One of PwC's key local partners departed in 2009 when he became unhappy with the pace at which he was being given leadership responsibilities (Chen, 2009b). PwC lost its most senior PRC national, Charles Feng, who left to join Morgan Stanley as its Vice Chairman in China. In my interviews, I met many impressive young PRC partners of Big Four firms, but they were early in their partner careers and would likely need a decade of seasoning before they would be prepared for major leadership roles in the firms. In my view, the Big Four will localize at the partner level, including senior management positions, but it is likely to take a decade or two for that to happen naturally. The deck has been stacked against local partners, with current governance practices heavily favoring incumbent Hong Kong partners. PwC has even reduced voting rights for younger partners that will delay the transfer of power to locals for some time. Big Four localization efforts are unlikely to meet the expectations of Chinese bureaucrats and politicians. They may not meet the expectations of staff and clients, particularly state-owned enterprises (SOEs) subject to political pressures.

The Big Four point out that the process of localization at the partner level takes considerable time, and the rapid growth of the firms has created the need for more partners than local ranks can provide. To deflect criticism over the pace of localization, the Big Four have taken to conflating Hong Kong and PRC partners. A good example of that was present in an interview with *A Plus* by Frank Lyn of PwC in which he said that 80–90 percent of partners are mainland Chinese or Hong Kong people, but declined to provide a breakdown that would allow scrutiny of this (Chen & Luk, 2010). The basis for this reasoning is that Hong Kong is now part of China, albeit a self-governing special administrative region. On the mainland, however, Hong Kong is treated much like any other foreign country, and Hong Kong accountants are not permitted to practice on the mainland without passing the mainland CPA examination and obtaining a practicing certificate. Hong Kong accountants face a dilemma – they wish to be treated as Chinese when there is an advantage to being Chinese, but they wish to remain foreign for other purposes, including regulation and the tax advantages given to expatriates. This contradiction will increase for Hong Kong until its period of separate governance ends in 2047 and it is fully absorbed as part of Mainland China. It is likely that this is an early example of the pressures that the profession in Hong Kong will face. Hong Kong accountants will wish to become more integrated with the mainland in order to gain greater market access, yet it will resist the integration of the Hong Kong and mainland professions in order to protect their local market. At present, however, it appears that Chinese regulators are not accepting the argument that the Hong Kong leaders of the Big Four in China should be considered Chinese. Regulators will be wise to continue this approach in order to create pressure on Hong Kong for early integration with the mainland.

I believe that the Big Four will fail to win widespread support for their arguments that Hong Kong partners should be considered Chinese in the localization debate. I believe their success in maintaining their dominance of the markets in China will depend heavily on how well they handle the perception of localization. It is likely to be a key factor in China's plans under Document 56 to create 10 large internationalized accounting firms. The Big Four firms need to be considered as among those 10 large, internationalized firms, and not as the obstacle to the development of these firms.

The Big Four firms know that they need to develop local partners for future leadership positions, but it is perhaps understandable that most incumbent leaders would like that to happen after their retirement. There is likely to be increasing conflict between the expatriate and local partners as the transition of power begins. This was the case in the Big Four firms in Singapore and Hong Kong when they faced the handover of power from expatriates to locals, and the example set in those locations indicates that the transfer of power can take a very long time, and will not turn out well for the expatriates. However, because a delayed transfer of leadership threatens the firm's dominance of the China market, I suggest that the global firms need to intervene and develop plans for a more rapid transfer of power to local partners.

The transition of the Big Four's audit practices to limited liability partnerships (LLPs) in 2012 was a big step toward localization. In practice, however, it appears that the Big Four are undermining the localization of the LLPs by allowing the expatriate-dominated management committee of the greater firm to make most operating decisions for the LLP. In form, the audit practices are now under the control of local partners, but in practice, the Hong Kong senior partner sets the agenda. Until local partners replace the Hong Kong senior partners no meaningful progress toward localization is likely. The Big Four would be wise to accelerate this process, and to make certain that the LLP makes all of the important decisions for the audit practice, including setting partner compensation.

The most significant challenge for the Big Four firms is that it is likely there will not be any qualified local senior partner candidates in this decade. A senior partner candidate is likely to need at least 25 years of experience to do the job. Given that the Big Four only began to hire significant numbers of local staff in 1992, it indicates that the first candidates would become available about 2017. However, the numbers of staff hired in the early years were small, and the odds that a senior partner caliber individual was among them are slim.

An alternative that firms might consider is to bring in a senior partner from the outside. The needed attributes – Chinese nationality, deep professional experience, strong government connections, and sterling reputation are also rare outside the Big Four. A bold move would be to merge one of the Big Four firms with Zhang Ke's Shinewing. Zhang Ke is widely respected as the dean of China's accounting profession, and there is deep respect for him in both government and business. But he was badly burned by his prior affiliation with C&L, and the only conceivable way he would join a Big Four would be as its senior partner. It is unlikely that the Hong Kong partners of the Big Four would accept this. That is a shame, since a Big Four firm run by Zhang Ke would likely dominate the market.

The Big Four escaped an expected nationalist push in the recent round of mandatory audit rotation of large SOEs. These large enterprises just shifted between Big Four firms, although audit fees appear to have dropped substantially. The next round, likely in 2020,[1] may not be so kind. Local firms will have had another eight years to build capability, and there is likely to be increased political pressure to switch SOEs to local firms. As discussed below, local firms and their global networks should see this as the most important event in the history of their networks.

The Big Four firms need greater political power in China. The domination of these firms by foreigners has left them with poor political connections. They need to get local partners more actively involved in the Communist Party and in boards and commissions that support the development of the accounting profession and the capital markets. This has happened to a certain extent, but it appears that the efforts have been more opportunistic than strategic and the partners involved have often been too junior to have a meaningful impact.

The Big Four have done a poor job positioning themselves as Chinese firms. Interviews with local staff at the Big Four indicate that their own people consider the firms to be foreign, yet second-tier firms like BDO and RSM are uniformly considered local. I believe that the firms have underinvested in public relations. They need to change the public perception of them as foreign. That will be difficult, but they should be able to soften the popular opinion of them as foreign companies that have invaded and taken up the market in China. The public relations and philanthropic activities of the Big Four in China appear to have focused heavily on business development rather than on building a corporate image of good citizenship. I suggest that the Big Four should develop a sustained grassroots public relations campaign that positions them as an important, local, and patriotic institution in China. The Big Four established hegemony by bringing an ideology to China that was accepted by key institutions. If they are to maintain their hegemony they need to broaden the acceptance of their "Chineseness" (Wang, 1991), which will ensure their legitimacy in Chinese society.

9.2. WHAT LOCAL FIRMS NEED TO DO

The objective for local CPA firms in China is to break the dominance of the Big Four. Counter-hegemonic theory suggests that a direct assault on the Big Four by local firms, even with the support of local regulators, would likely fail. The Big Four are too heavily entrenched, with strong support both within and outside of China. Instead, the theory calls for what Dutschke (1969) described as the "long march through the institutions." Much of that long march is finished. It involved conforming the domestic CPA profession with international norms, particularly those with respect to the adherence to international standards and model of practice. The goal of the long march is to deepen contradictions – "since we do the same work to the same standards, why do we, the Chinese firms, not do the Chinese work?" Local firms have done a remarkable job in the past few years reducing the Big Four dominance of the market. Despite the distance already covered on the long march, the Big Four still dominate the high end of the market because many do not accept that local firms can do the same work to the same standards.

I offer two strategies for indigenous firms to break the hegemony of the Big Four in China. The first is to complete the long march through the institutions by infiltrating the final and most important institution, the Big Four. This strategy caps the long march with a revolution. Chairman Mao (1927/1961) said:

> A revolution is not a dinner party, or writing an essay, or painting a picture, or doing embroidery; it cannot be so refined, so leisurely and gentle, so temperate, kind, courteous, restrained, and magnanimous. A revolution is an insurrection, an act of violence by which one class overthrows another.

I am not advocating physical violence, which would be inappropriate, ineffective, and unnecessary. Physical violence is unnecessary because local accountants can use the coercive power of the state as a substitute for physical violence. The insurrection proposed is the overthrow of the present foreign leadership of the Big Four in China by local partners with the aid of the state. The objective is to localize the ownership and leadership of the Big Four, and to align the Big Four practices with the agenda of the state. This is a bold strategy, and I am not certain that either local accountants or regulators have the stomach for it. It has elements of Ding Pingzhun's failed attempt to create a Chinese Big One at the time of the Price Waterhouse (PW) and Coopers & Lybrand (C&L) merger. Conditions for success may be better today.

The alternative strategy is to use the second-tier of global accounting firms to build Chinese accounting firms that can challenge the hegemony of the Big Four in China, and perhaps globally. This strategy is also a continuation of the long march, but rather than the revolutionary step of infiltrating and overthrowing Big Four power structures, it involves infiltrating and coopting second-tier global firm institutions. This is essentially the strategy that China is currently following, and I have suggestions on how to improve its effectiveness. Before explaining these two strategies, it is necessary to first examine why China wants a locally owned profession.

9.2.1. Why does China want a Locally Owned Profession?

Chinese bureaucrats have consistently pined for a CPA profession under the control of local nationals, although they have never articulated the reason why this would be ideal. This aspiration appears grounded in nationalism. Document 56 refers to the need to consider protecting national secrets when selecting accounting firms, a clear reflection of the view that only a patriot can be trusted to look out for the interests of the state. China is playing the national security card mostly because it is a legitimate defense against open markets, but I believe the underlying motivation is not national security, but nationalism.

Major accounting firms are powerful institutions with wide ranging influence on society. It is reasonable that Chinese leaders would want people leading these organizations are aligned with the agenda of the state. It is understandable why they are concerned about foreigners controlling powerful institutions like the Big Four within China. Chinese leaders appear to believe that if local nationals own and manage these businesses, they will be more likely to support state initiatives. Chinese leaders are likely naïve in this matter, for the assumption that private businessmen will always align their interests with the state is dubious.

9.2.2. How to Stage a Revolution

Conditions are auspicious for an assault on the Big Four firms by Chinese nationalists. The expiration of the joint ventures under which the firms operated expired and were replaced by LLPs has created an opportunity to seize control of the firms. In a major concession to the foreign partners of the Big Four, Chinese regulators permitted partners with foreign accounting qualifications to own up to 40% of the LLP, reducing to 20% over five years. The firms were also permitted to retain a foreign senior partner for three years.

The Big Four firms are likely to wish to continue to operate their practices as they have in recent years. Each of the firms combines for operational purposes with the Hong Kong member firm and in some cases with other firms in Asia. The managing partner in each case is a Hong Kong partner, and Hong Kong partners dominate management of the firms. The Hong Kong managing partner became the senior partner of each of the LLPs. If Chinese bureaucrats wish to change the Big Four into locally controlled firms, they will need to change the management of the firms.

While the rules will require a local senior partner in three years, it is likely that the firms will attempt to keep operational control at a firm-wide level where decisions will be made by a board of partners and management committee that is presently dominated by Hong Kong partners. It is likely that the firms will attempt to make the LLP a puppet entity that reports to the firmwide management committee.

Document 56 gives bureaucrats direction for achieving management control of the Big Four. It encourages large Chinese CPA firms to join international accounting alliances, but directs that equality and mutual benefits underpin the relationship. Based on this principle, bureaucrats can organize and incentivize local partners to further the objectives of Document 56 by asserting control over the LLPs and rejecting attempts by Hong Kong partners to control the LLP. Such an appeal to local partners could be based on patriotism and include prestigious appointments in Chinese institutions, including the Communist Party. The strategy would be to indoctrinate the local partners into the ideology expressed by Document 56 and to enlist them to fulfill an important role in China's future. The key means of gaining control over the firms is to gain control over the allocation of profits to partners. The audit practice is the most profitable of business segments for the Big Four in China. If the LLP controls partner compensation, it will control the Big Four firms in China.

I do not believe that there are many, or perhaps any, local partners in the Big Four who are currently capable of serving as the senior partner of the firms. The Big Four is likely to dwell on this point, supporting the concept of transfer of control to local partners, while indicating that the time is not yet right. Chinese regulators will be familiar with this refrain, having heard it for the past 20 years, and will question whether the firms believe that local partners will ever be ready for leadership. However, the Big Four are likely correct. While today's partners might well be ready to run a firm of the size that the Big Four were a decade ago, the firms have grown significantly in size and complexity and more experienced partners are required to lead them. Of course, current leadership is concerned about self-preservation, and that is likely to persist to delay the transfer of leadership to locals. However, the question of whether local partners are ready to run the firms is a valid question.

A possible solution to the leadership issue is to merge some of the more successful local firms into the Big Four. As discussed above, a merger with Zhang Ke's Shinewing would likely create the dominant Big Four firm in China. Several of the other large domestic firms would also be candidates for this strategy. Most of these firms are members of second-tier firms, and this strategy would seriously undermine the strategy of the second-tier firms. Rather than creating an alternative to the Big Four, it would further extend Big Four hegemony over the market, but put it under Chinese control. Pursuit of this strategy would likely prevent the second-tier from effectively challenging the Big Four anywhere in the world. The global Big Four organizations would likely resist this strategy, viewing the changes as potentially reversing attempts to create a more globally cohesive organization (Greenwood et al., 2010). Several of the firms have had trouble with certain member firms that resisted tight integration with global initiatives. Asian firms, particularly those in Japan and Korea, were noted for this behavior, although the Singapore and Hong Kong firms often came under criticism. The Big Four would benefit, however, by the significant weakening of the second-tier in China and in the diminished prospects for the second-tier globally.

The transfer of ownership to local partners threatens the significant numbers of expatriate partners presently working in China. Because they would be unable to share in the ownership of the firm, they would need to become employees of the firm and the local partners would determine their compensation. They would face reduced career opportunities if leadership roles go to locals. They may face reduced income or even loss of position depending on the decisions of the local partners. Ultimately, the proportion of foreign partners would likely decrease as local partners develop the skills to take those responsibilities. The Big Four, however, are multinational enterprises and diverse talents will be required to serve both foreign and domestic clients in China. The firms and regulators must be careful to not weaken the firm's capabilities by localizing too quickly or too completely.

The strategy proposed here is a takeover of the Big Four practices in China by Chinese nationals. Such a takeover arguably would result in firms that are better aligned with the strategic objectives of China. Because the China member firms of the Big Four will remain critical components of the Big Four's global strategy, China would gain significant influence in Big Four strategies, giving it a larger voice in global accounting institutions, and by extension a larger role in global financial markets. This strategy would not disturb existing Big Four client relationships, which would be to the advantage of the large SOEs that currently use the Big Four. It would also ensure that large Chinese companies would have high-quality global accounting resources available as they expand internationally. This strategy would seriously undermine the second-tier firms, relegating them to a permanently minor role.

9.2.3. Upgrading the Second-Tier

The second strategy I see for China is to make large domestic firms more competitive by strengthening the second-tier firms. China had initially made it difficult for the second-tier firms to establish themselves in China, but in recent years has encouraged their development (Godfrey, 2011). Second-tier firms BDO, RSM/Crowe Horwarth, and PKF are already among the 10 largest CPA firms in China (Table 6.17). Baker Tilly and Grant Thornton, ranked 11th and 12th in China, are also members of the second-tier. Frank Lyn of PwC observed: "At first, people think that the Big Four are competing with the mainland CPA firms, but we really are competing with the same second-tier international networks" (Chen & Luk, 2010, p. 24). The second-tier firms offer two key advantages to local Chinese CPA firms. First, they have expansive international networks. While China had hoped that Chinese firms would expand abroad to build their own networks, the firms that have attempted that route, mostly Shinewing and Reanda, have had only modest success. It does not appear realistic that China's local CPA firms could develop an international network quickly enough to serve China's rapidly internationalizing companies. The second advantage from the perspective of Chinese firms is that the second-tier firms are less globally cohesive than the Big Four, and allow the Chinese member firms greater latitude in how the practice is conducted. While this may be attractive to Chinese firms concerned about foreign dominance, it is also a weakness of the second-tier firms. The strict adherence to globally defined standards is a competitive advantage for the Big Four, and inconsistent service delivery standards in the second-tier undermine their brands.

European regulators have been determining whether to institute measures to reduce Big Four dominance (Cafolla, 2011; Castle, 2010; European Commission, 2010; House of Lords, 2011; Huber, 2011; Jones, 2013). Measures under consideration include mandatory audit rotation or mandatory tenders, joint audits, restrictions on non-audit services, and addressing bias toward use of Big Four firms (Oxera, 2011). China is likely to jump on this bandwagon, using it as further justification for implementing Document 56 reforms.

China's mandatory audit rotation program for SOEs did not result in a major shift of clients from the Big Four to local firms in the first round of rotations that concluded at the end of 2012. Mandatory auditor rotation programs have often been suggested as a means of improving audit quality (Myers, Myers, & Omer, 2003; Petty & Cuganesan, 1996). Audit rotation, or a related requirement that companies periodically seek competitive bids, serves to increase turbulence in the market. Turbulence is a measure of market volatility, which is a necessary condition for shifts in market shares (Davies & Geroski, 1997). Chinese regulators could use auditor rotation as a means of creating opportunity for local firms to compete for work currently held by the Big Four.

In the first round of audit rotations, Chinese regulators encouraged SOEs to consider appointing large local firms. This was resisted by SOEs and often by the local firms. Many of the SOEs in the program are among the world's largest corporations, and local firms correctly surmised that they were not yet up to the task. The next round of rotations of large SOEs will take place in 2020, and this round will be critical for both local firms and the Big Four. If local firms are unable to win large SOEs in the 2020 rotation, the practice of engaging only Big Four firms for large SOEs will likely become an institutional logic precluding local firms from further consideration in future rotations.

For local firms, winning large SOEs will not be easy, even with ideological winds at their backs. If they can maintain current growth rates, the firms should be of sufficient size to do the work. The local firms face the logical paradox of not being able to win large Chinese companies as clients because they have no experience with large Chinese clients; experience that they cannot obtain because they have no large Chinese clients. The solution to the paradox is to acquire the required expertise from outside the organization.

The expertise to audit large Chinese companies currently resides in the Big Four. Second-tier firms, supported by the state, could target the recruitment of seasoned audit partners with experience in auditing large SOEs from the Big Four firms. This recruitment will not be easy, since the relevant partners are likely to be highly compensated and to hold prestigious positions. The second-tier firms need to be prepared to offer competitive compensation and may need support from their global networks to do so. The state could play an important role in recruiting, appealing to patriotic sentiments, and offering prestigious appointments to party and government positions. Currently, however, few of the major Chinese corporations have a lead Big Four audit partner who is a local. Most are expatriates, or Hong Kong nationals, because few local partners have enough experience to lead a major engagement. The Big Four would be wise to "raise the ante" by significantly increasing the compensation of qualified local partners to make this strategy more difficult for local firms to adopt.

China may be the best hope for second-tier firms to break the global hegemony of the Big Four. If they are successful at first breaking the hegemony in China, they will be well positioned to benefit from the expected continued rise in outbound Chinese FDI. Through serving Chinese MNCs globally, the second-tier firms may develop the credentials to compete in other countries for MNC work. This will not be a rapid change, but as China grows in global influence, it is likely to be a persistent change.

The second-tier firms have less cohesive international networks than the Big Four. The second-tier firms will need to focus on the effectiveness of their network in delivering transnational services if they are to make progress at breaking Big Four hegemony. One of the strengths of the Big Four is their established process for the monitoring of quality standards of member firms, a practice that the second-tier likely will need to enhance in order to be competitive with the Big Four.

Joint audits are another way that local firms could gain the expertise to compete with the Big Four. Joint audits exist when a company appoints two or more auditors. The auditors divide the work between them. Joint audits could provide the opportunity for domestic firms to gain experience on large SOEs that are currently audited by a single Big Four firm. Joint audits have largely fallen out of favor in the world because they are viewed as inefficient. Joint audits have persisted in France, and have led to France having a much lower level of market concentration than other European countries (Piot, 2007). Joint audits could be a powerful tool to improve the market share of domestic firms while giving them the expertise to audit large companies.

European regulators are contemplating restrictions on non-audit services rendered by auditing firms. Sarbanes–Oxley introduced these restrictions in the United States and three of the Big Four disposed of their consulting practices. Since then, however, most have rebuilt the consulting division, including the firms in China (Chen & Luk, 2010). Restricting non-audit services attempts to improve audit quality through enhancing independence, but it is not likely to have a significant impact on market concentration for audit services.

The second-tier firms have long complained of "Big Four clauses" present in loan agreements that force companies to select a Big Four auditor. I found evidence of this practice in China in two loan agreements from the State Council's China Development Bank. However, the institutional bias of the transnational capital class toward the Big Four operates much the same way. I see little that regulators can do to address this bias.

9.3. WHAT REGULATORS NEED TO DO

Chapter 8 discussed the problem of regulatory holes. Certain types of regulatory holes are a result of the globalization of capital markets. I have identified two key regulatory holes related to the accounting profession in China, and I recommend that Chinese and US regulators take steps to close them.

The first regulatory hole relates to foreign accountants who are practicing in China. Many of these foreign accountants are partners with the Big Four member firms in China. They are licensed in foreign jurisdictions, most frequently Hong Kong, which is considered foreign for licensing purposes, and are not licensed as CPAs in China. They practice as partners in China, but only sign reports that are used outside of China, such as interoffice opinions on subsidiaries of foreign companies or opinions related to Chinese companies listed on foreign exchanges. If an opinion is required for use in China, a local partner signs it as an accommodation to the foreign partner. The Big Four audit many of the largest SOEs in China and the lead engagement partner is typically a foreigner who does not hold a Chinese CPA license. Chinese accounting regulators (the CSRC, CICPA, and MOF) regulate the Big Four firms, but the foreign partners typically are not licensed or registered in China and their work is unregulated by Chinese authorities. Foreign partners who have become partners in the Big Four's LLP in China are technically subject to Chinese regulation, yet it is too soon to determine whether this oversight will be effective. At the same time, China prohibits foreign regulators, specifically the HKICPA and the PCAOB, from exercising their regulatory responsibilities in China.

Certain foreign CPA firms, mostly from the United States, audit the accounts of small Chinese companies listed on US exchanges or on the over-the-counter bulletin boards. Some of these firms have opened offices in China that are registered as consulting firms rather than accounting firms, while others travel to China to do their work. These firms do not register as accounting firms with Chinese regulators and accordingly escape regulation by Chinese accounting regulators.

Chinese accounting regulators should bring all foreign accountants practicing in China within their jurisdiction. Foreign individuals who are performing audit services in China at the partner and manager level should be required to register with the CICPA. The registration should include the presentation of current credentials from a foreign regulator and the agreement to be subject to Chinese regulation with respect to work done in China. Chinese regulators should establish rules that limit the work that foreign accountants can perform in China, and that establish appropriate rules for the oversight of foreign accountants by local CPAs.

The second regulatory hole relates to Chinese companies listed abroad where China refuses to allow foreign regulators to come to China to inspect the work of China-based accountants, many of whom are unregulated foreigners as discussed above. Bringing these accountants within the regulatory span of Chinese regulators helps to fill this hole, but Chinese regulators also have to take responsibility for foreign filings if they are to successfully argue that foreign regulators should rely upon their oversight.

The CSRC has asserted that the PCAOB should fully rely on the work of the CSRC (2009). The PCAOB is unlikely to accept the CSRC position that they should accept the inspections of Chinese regulators unless they can be convinced that Chinese regulators have both the interest and the expertise to perform these reviews. They are unlikely to be able to do so. First, the regulatory power of the CSRC extends only to Chinese CPA firms with securities licenses in China. Some of the Chinese firms registered with the PCAOB do not have securities licenses in China and are not subject to CSRC inspections, although they do remain under CICPA and MOF jurisdiction. Hong Kong CPA firms are not subject to the regulatory jurisdiction of either MOF or the CSRC, although they are subject to regulation by the HKICPA. As a result, the CSRC is unable to fulfill the PCAOB role with respect to all registered firms in China and Hong Kong. While registered firms are subject to either MOF or HKICPA regulation, there are no processes in place at these institutions that would require inspections of the nature required by the PCAOB. Second, CSRC inspections relate only to audits of issuers of securities on Chinese exchanges and would not include the many Chinese companies that, while listed on US exchanges, are not listed in China. MOF examiners focus on reports prepared under CAS and do not examine the audits of financial statements prepared for use outside of China. Third, CSRC, MOF, and HKICPA examiners are not expert in PCAOB auditing standards or US GAAP and would be unable to assess compliance with these standards. It is highly doubtful that examiners from these agencies would be willing to enforce foreign rules that are stricter than local rules. It is also unlikely that employees of these agencies, already struggling with the implementation of IFRS, would devote the training resources to develop the necessary skills to evaluate the auditing of US public companies.

The PCAOB reached a deal to share information in connection with investigations, but investigations are a small part of the PCAOB agenda. The investigation deal has likely made it more difficult for the PCAOB to reach a deal to do inspections. Chinese regulators are seen as having met the PCAOB half way. They are probably not willing to go any further, and the PCAOB likely does not have the political capital in the United States to take the extreme action of deregistering accounting firms that it cannot inspect. This has left the accounting firms in a regulatory hole and it has left investors vulnerable. The PCAOB and Chinese regulators need find another way to compromise.

I suggest that the PCAOB and Chinese regulators seek a compromise on the inspection of Chinese accounting firms registered with the PCAOB by instituting peer reviews of Chinese firms registered with the PCAOB with respect to the work on US-listed companies. The compromise could also be extended to H-share engagements audited by mainland firms where the HKICPA is similarly blocked from inspections in China. The Sarbanes–Oxley Act replaced peer reviews with independent inspections conducted by the PCAOB because of arguments that peer reviews lacked credibility. However, there is evidence that peer reviews were effective (Hilary & Lennox, 2005). Peer reviews in China could be conducted with teams of partners and managers from the Big Four firms, including experts in US accounting from the US member firms. The peer review teams could work under the oversight of the CSRC, which would also supply the regulatory power needed to sanction adverse findings.

9.4. FURTHER RESEARCH TOPICS

This study ambitiously examined the development of the CPA profession in China over the past 30 years. The delimitations of the study necessarily excluded many interesting topics that have influenced the development of the profession, or which would reflect on how the new profession affected the development of China. I often found myself chasing an interesting issue down a path that I found could lead to a different book than the one I have completed. In this section I will set forth some of those potential research projects. In the remainder of my research career, I may choose to pursue some of these projects, but I offer them here for adoption by other scholars.

9.4.1. Updating and Extending This Study

I have broadly evaluated the development of the CPA profession in China through 2012, with a focus on the role of the Big Four. The topic is so fast moving that this study should be updated, most likely after the next round of SOE rotations in 2020. The update would evaluate the success of the Chinese government policy articulated in Document 56 for the development of large domestic CPA firms. The Big Four will likely face significant changes during the next five years, such as adaption to the LLP form and transition to local leadership. Recent trends indicating a rise of second-tier firms may result in a dramatically different market structure than we see today. This topic nests within the field of work that will examine the globalization of Chinese enterprises. The rapid increase in outbound FDI from China suggests that China will become a major force in globalization in this century.

A native English speaker conducted this study, and it focused on the role of the Big Four in the development of the CPA profession in China. A complementary study, conducted by a native Chinese speaker and focused on the development of local firms, would provide a harmonizing, and perhaps critical, response to this work. Little is known about the development of local firms, particularly after their separation from the state. How these firms have joined with the second-tier and the impact that the China member firm is having on the global networks of the second-tier is an important topic.

9.4.2. Comparative Studies

Comparative institutional analysis is a powerful methodology for understanding institutional practices (Aoki, 2001). China is not comparable to most markets. No other developing market situations have had the scale of China. Brazil and India, two of the members of the BRICS[2] group, were not communist countries and developed differently than China. Nevertheless, comparative studies of the modern development of the CPA profession comparing other countries with China could tease out interesting observations. In particular, India appears to have been more protective of its market than China. The Big Four are not permitted to practice in their own names in India.[3] The recent Satyam scandal raises the question of whether limitations on Big Four practice have affected audit quality.

Russia and other countries of the former Soviet Union would form an excellent basis for a comparative study with China, since these countries all have roots in communism. The CPA profession in Russia has developed a different market structure, with market leader PwC being to only Big Four among the top ten firms. China has had considerably greater success in tapping international capital markets. Is there a relationship between the presence of the Big Four and the ability of companies to raise capital? Why were domestic firms better able to capture the market in Russia?

The legal profession in China is an excellent field for study. It faces many similar issues to accounting (Morgan & Quack, 2006), and has taken different approaches to internationalization (Beaverstock, 2004). In China, international law firms have been more restricted in the form of practice in China than accounting firms. A study that compares the development of these professions in China would help to explain differences in the professions, their relationship to other institutions, and their respective roles in the development of China's economy. A significant common issue between the professions is transnational regulation. In China, regulators of the legal profession appear to focus more on the license of the individual practitioner while accounting regulators appear to focus more on the license of the firm. This has led to the Big Four easily accessing local markets, while international law firms are prohibited from hiring local lawyers or performing Chinese legal work.

9.4.3. China Focused Studies

China has already become a rich accounting research site. This is likely to expand as China's influence in the world economy grows. Databases that include financial data for Chinese-listed companies such as the CCER and CMOS databases that I used in this study are useful for replicating studies done in other markets. The relative ease in accessing data from multiple markets should lead to scholars testing hypotheses using multiple sources of data.

Chinese bureaucrats have relentlessly pushed for the adoption of the partnership form of operation for CPA firms, hoping that this would lead to a partnership culture. These efforts seem to be based on the assumption that the partnership form is a normative way to professionalize the profession, consistent with Greenwood et al.'s (1990) P2 model of partnership and professionalization. I challenge the assertion that the P2 model is appropriate for Chinese culture. The firms I observed in my study, both Big Four and local, did not appear to be embracing that form, but rather tended to have leadership focused on a strong, domineering, senior partner. Can partnerships prosper in Chinese culture, or will firms require a strong, even dictatorial leader? What are the implications for independence and quality of the partnership culture that develops in China?

The accounting practices of privately owned firms (as contrasted with SOEs) are significantly understudied in China. I have found no studies (until this one) that have even considered that private companies have until recently been forced to seek capital overseas. There is now considerable data available on Chinese companies that have listed abroad, and for the increasing numbers of private companies listing in ChiNext. Comparative studies of the accounting practices of private and owned companies could provide significant insight into the private/public debate around the world.

9.4.4. Studies of Globalization and Accounting

This study extends a significant body of research that addresses globalization and accounting. One of the findings in this study, the existence of regulatory holes because of gaps in the transnational regulation of accounting, should be further examined. Focused on China, research could determine whether existing regulatory holes related to US-listed Chinese companies result in lower audit quality. Expanding this research to other settings where the PCAOB has faced restrictions in its ability to inspect local CPA firms will help to understand the problems of transnational regulation.

The Big Four have been strong supporters of the global adoption of IFRS. A study could determine whether the convergence of international accounting and auditing standards improves the competitiveness of international accounting firms. Do they achieve cost advantages from the ability to share training and technical resources and does this give them a competitive advantage over local firms? Are second-tier firms as capable as the Big Four at leveraging convergence for local market advantages?

A phenomenon discovered in this study was the migration of a large number of Chinese-speaking accountants from Hong Kong, Malaysia, and Singapore to serve the rapidly expanding market in China. These accountants often received substantial increases in compensation, and many have become partners with the Big Four in China or serve as financial managers with listed companies. What impact did this large migration have on the accounting professions in the sending countries? Does this migration lead to declines in the accounting quality of companies in Hong Kong, Malaysia, and Singapore? Did the experience of accountants who worked in China help companies from these countries take advantage of opportunities in China?

The role of international accounting institutes in China is a developing issue. Asian jurisdictions with a British colonial heritage have long relied upon British institutions like ACCA and ICAEW to grant qualifications that are locally recognized. More recently, CPA Australia has joined those venerable institutions as major international credentialing agencies. In Japan and Korea, the AICPA and the American CPA credentials are more prevalent. China has chosen to not recognize foreign qualifications, requiring aspiring accountants to qualify locally. However, there remains significant interest in foreign credentials, with ACCA, ICAEW, and CPA Australia all actively operating in China. The competition between credentialing agencies in China and the impact of these institutions on Chinese accounting would be an interesting research topic.

9.4.5. Studies of Auditor Rotation

China's program of mandatory auditor rotation for SOEs has completed its first cycle. While mandatory auditor rotation has taken place in other markets, the rotation in China involves some of the world's largest corporations. Preliminary evidence points to the Big Four retaining these companies as clients, but with substantial fee reductions. Scholars should examine the effect the audit rotation policy has on audit quality and market competitiveness.

NOTES

1. As is more completely discussed in Chapter 8, SOEs must rotate auditors every five years, although those that appoint auditors in the Top 15 may apply for an additional three years before rotation.
2. Brazil, Russia, India, China, and South Africa are the BRICS countries, commonly considered the key emerging markets.
3. In India, PwC practices in its former name PW. DTT practices as Deloitte, Haskins, and Sells and also as Touche Ross, both premerger names. The firms have not been permitted to update the names. KPMG and E&Y practice under local names.

REFERENCES

2010 annual directory of CPA firm associations and networks. (2010). *Public accounting report*, February 15, Extra, pp. 1–15.

Abbott, A. (1988). *The system of professions: An essay on the division of expert labor*. Chicago, IL: University of Chicago Press.

Abbott, A. (1999). *Department and discipline: Chicago sociology at 100*. Chicago, IL: University of Chicago Press.

Accountancy Age. (1989). Big accountancy firms "cautious" over China conflict. *Accountancy Age*, June 8.

Accountancy Age. (1995). Chinese walls come down. *Accountancy Age*, April 26.

Ackerman, A. (2011). SEC probes backdoor mergers by Chinese firms. *The Wall Street Journal*, April 4.

Adhikari, A., & Wang, S. Z. (1995). Accounting for China. *Management Accounting*, *76*(10), 27–32.

Ahmed, Z., Hopper, T., & Wickramsinghe, D. (2010). *Hegemony, counter hegemony and NGO accountability change: BRAC in Bangladesh*. Paper presented at the Sixth Asia Pacitic Interdisciplinary Research in Accounting Conference, Sydney, Australia.

Al-Qahtani, A. K. (2005). The development of accounting regulation in the GCC: Western hegemony or recognition of peculiarity? *Managerial Auditing Journal*, *20*(3), 217–226.

Alawattage, C., & Wickramasinghe, D. (2008). Appearance of accounting in a political hegemony. *Critical Perspectives on Accounting*, *19*(3), 293–339.

Alexandroff, A. S., & Sharma, R. (2005). The national security provision – GATT article XXI. In P. F. J. Macrory, A. E. Appleton, & M. G. Plummer (Eds.), *The world trade organization: Legal, economic and political analysis*. New York, NY: Springer.

Allen, W. T., & Shen, H. (2010). *Assessing China's top-down securities markets*. Working Paper No. 10–70. Public Law and Legal Theory Research Paper Series. New York University School of Law, New York, NY.

Alpert, B., & Norton, L. P. (2010). Beware this Chinese export. *Barron's*, August 28.

American Chamber of Commerce in the People's Republic of China. (2011). *American Business in China: 2011*. White Paper. Beijing.

Annisette, M. (2000). Imperialism and the professions: The education and certification of accountants in Trinidad and Tobago. *Accounting, Organizations and Society*, *25*(7), 631–659.

Antle, R. (1984). Auditor independence. *Journal of Accounting Research*, *22*(1), 1–20.

Aoki, M. (2001). *Comparative institutional analysis*. Boston, MA: The MIT Press.

Arevalo, A. (2013, May 1). *Declaration of Alberto Arevalo*. Retrieved from http://lawprofessors.typepad.com/china_law_prof_blog/2013/06/more-documents-in-the-case-of-sec-vs-deloitte-touche-tohmatsu-cpa-ltd.html

Armstrong, P. (1991). *The influence of michel foucault on historical research.* Paper presented at the 3rd Interdisciplinary Perspectives on Accounting Conference, University of Manchester.

Armstrong, R. (2012a). "Big Four" auditors brace for big changes. *Reuters Canada*, February 28. Retrieved from http://ca.reuters.com/article/businessNews/idCATRE81R07V20120228?pageNumber = 2&virtualBrandChannel = 0&sp = true

Armstrong, R. (2012b). Deloitte's Boshiwa exit a precursor to more China auditor resignations. *Reuters*, March 16.

Arnold, P. J. (2005). Disciplining domestic regulation: The World Trade Organization and the market for professional services. *Accounting, Organizations and Society*, *30*(4), 299–330.

Ash, R. F., & Kueh, A. Y. (1996). *The Chinese economy under Deng Xiaoping*. Oxford: Oxford University Press.

Asian Development Bank. (2002). *The development of private enterprise in the people's republic of China*. Asian Development Bank, Manila.

Asthana, S., Balsam, S., & Kim, S. (2009). The effect of Enron, Andersen, and Sarbanes-Oxley on the US market for audit services. *Accounting Research Journal*, *22*(1), 4–26.

Aubin, D. (2011). Chinese accounting scandals spur auditor upgrades. *Reuters*, March 11.

Aubin, D. (2012a). U.S. audit watchdog in tentative deal to observe in China: Official. *Chicago Tribune*, September 21.

Aubin, D. (2012b). U.S. sees talks with China on corporate audits. *Reuters*, November 8. Retrieved from http://www.reuters.com/article/2012/11/08/us-usa-audit-china-idUSBRE8A71DR20121108

Aubin, D. (2013). U.S. audit regulator reaches deal with China on document access. *Reuters*, May 24.

Auyeung, P. (2002). A comparative study of accounting adaptation: China and Japan during the nineteenth century. *Accounting Historians Journal*, *29*(2), 1–30.

Bai, Z. L. (1988). Accounting in the people's republic of China: Contemporary situations and issues. In V. K. Zimmerman (Ed.), *Recent accounting and economic developments in the far east* (pp. 27–50). University of Illinois, Center for International Education and Research in Accounting.

Bailey, D. (1995). Accounting in transition in the transitional economy. *European Accounting Review*, *4*(4), 595–623.

Bailey, W., Karolyi, A., & Salva, C. (2006). The economic consequences of increased disclosure: Evidence from international cross-listings. *Journal of Financial Economics*, *81*(1), 175–213.

Bain. (2013). *China briefing: The great IPO freeze*. Retrieved from http://www.bain.com/about/press/bain-news/2013/china-briefing-the-great-ipo-freeze.aspx

Bajoiria, J. (2008). *Nationalism in China*. Retrieved from http://www.cfr.org/china/nationalism-china/p16079. Accessed on April 29, 2011.

Balfour, F. (2007). NASDAQ–NYSE rivalry comes to China. *Bloomberg Businessweek*, December 3.

Ballas, A. A. (1998). The creation of the auditing profession in Greece. *Accounting, Organizations and Society*, *23*(8), 715–736.

Ballas, A. A. (1999). Privatizing the statutory auditing services in Greece. *Accounting, Business & Financial History*, *9*(3), 349–373.

Barboza, D. (2010). China passes Japan as second-largest economy. *The New York Times*, August 15.

Barrett, M., Cooper, D. J., & Jamal, K. (2005). Globalization and the coordinating of work in multinational audits. *Accounting, Organizations and Society*, *30*(1), 1–24.
Bartlett, C. A., Ghoshal, S., & Birkinshaw, J. M. (1995). *Transnational management*. Homewood, IL: Irwin.
Baskerville, R., & Hay, D. (2006). The effect of accounting firm mergers on the market for audit services: New Zealand evidence. *Abacus*, *42*(1), 87–104.
Baskerville, R., & Hay, D. (2010). The impact of globalization on professional accounting firms: Evidence from New Zealand. *Accounting History*, *15*(3), 285–308.
Bassnet, S. (1994). *Translation studies*. London: Routledge.
Bates, T. R. (1975). Gramsci and the theory of hegemony. *Journal of the History of Ideas*, *36*(2), 351–361.
Bayron, H., & Ng, I. (2010). Closer scrutiny: China's new internal control standard puts Chinese companies under the microscope. *A Plus*, (August), 14–18.
Beaver, W., McNichols, M., & Price, R. (2007). Delisting returns and their effect on accounting-based market anomalies. *Journal of Accounting and Economics*, *43*(2/3), 341–368.
Beaverstock, J. V. (2004). "Managing across borders": Knowledge management and expatriation in professional service legal firms. *Journal of Economic Geography*, *4*(2), 157–179.
Bentley, J. (1996). Cross-cultural interaction and periodization in world history. *American Historical Review*, *101*, 749–770.
Berger, P. L., & Luckmann, T. (1967). *The social construction of reality*. New York, NY: Doubleday Anchor.
Bhattasali, D., Li, S., & Martin, W. (Eds.). (2004). *China and the WTO: Accession, policy reform, and poverty reduction strategies*. Washington, DC: The International Bank for Reconstruction and Development.
Birmingham Post. (2007). Ernst & Young looking for four-fold expansion. *Birmingham Post*, September 5.
Blake, J., & Gao, S. (Eds.). (1995). *Perspectives on accounting and Finance in China*. London: Routledge.
Blake, J., Gao, S., & Wraith, P. (2000). Joint ventures in China: Accounting implications. *Managerial Finance*, *26*(5), 1–11.
Bloomberg Businessweek. (2013). IPO-eager Chinese companies await new regulations. *Bloomberg Businessweek*, August 1.
Bloomberg News. (2013). IPO bankers become frogs in hot water amid China market halt. *Bloomberg News*, April 8.
Bockus, K., & Gigler, F. (1998). A theory of auditor resignation. *Journal of Accounting Research*, *36*(2), 191–208.
Boland, R. (2006). Numbers stretched to limit – China needs 300,000 accountants and the demand keeps rising. *South China Morning Post*, July 22.
Borkenau, F., & Aron, R. (1962). *World communism: A history of the communist international*. Ann Arbor, MI: University of Michigan Press.
Boussebaa, M. (2009). Struggling to organize across national borders: The case of global resource management in professional service firms. *Human Relations*, *62*, 829–850.
Bradsher, K. (2010). Sitting out the China trade battles. *The New York Times*, December 23.
Brahm, L. J. (2003). *Zhu Rongji and the transformation of modern China*. Singapore: Wiley.
Brandenberg, M. (1987). Top international firms in China. *Accountancy Age*, March 31.

Brilliance China. (2007). *Form 6-K, report of foreign issuer, July 5, 2007*. Washington, DC: U.S. Securities and Exchange Commission.

Brock, D. M., & Powell, M. J. (2005). Radical strategic change in the global professional network: The "Big Five" 1999–2001. *Journal of Organizational Change Management*, *18*(5), 451.

Brown, J., Cooper, D. J., Greenwood, R., & Hinings, C. R. (1996). Strategic alliances within a Big Six accounting firm. *International Studies of Management and Organization*, *26*(2), 59–79.

Bryer, R. (1999). Marx and accounting. *Critical Perspectives on Accounting*, *10*(5), 683–709.

Bryer, R. (2005). A Marxist accounting history of the British industrial revolution: A review of evidence and suggestions for research. *Accounting, Organizations and Society*, *30*(1), 25–65.

Bryer, R. (2006). Accounting and control of the labour process. *Critical Perspectives on Accounting*, *17*(5), 551–598.

Burchell, S., Clubb, C., Hopwood, A. G., Hughes, J., & Nahapiet, J. (1980). The roles of accounting in organizations and society. *Accounting, Organizations and Society*, *5*(1), 5–27.

Burke, R. J. (1996). Sources of job satisfaction among employees of a professional services firm. *Psychological Reports*, *78*(3), 1231.

Burrage, M. (1990). Introduction: The professions in sociology and history. In M. Burrage & R. Torstendahl (Eds.), *Professions in theory and history: Rethinking the study of professions*. London: Sage.

Burt, R. S. (1992). *Structural holes: The social structure of competition*. Cambridge, MA: Harvard University Press.

Buttery, E. A., & Wong, Y. H. (1999). The development of a guanxi framework. *Marketing Intelligence and Planning*, *17*(3), 147–155.

Buttigieg, J. A (Ed.). (1991). *Antonio Gramsci: Prison notebooks*. New York, NY: Columbia University Press.

Buxbaum, H. L. (2003). Jurisdictional conflict in global antitrust enforcement. *Loyola Consumer Law Review*, *16*(4), 365–377.

Bychkova, S. (1996). The development and status of auditing in Russia. *European Accounting Review*, *5*(1), 77–90.

Byrnes, N., & Lynch, S. (2012). U.S. watchdog downplays deadline on China audit inspections. *Chicago Tribune*, December 21.

Cafolla, L. (2011). Breaking up the big players. *A Plus*, (April), 32–36.

Cai, J. (2011). China shutting out American firms, says Locke. *South China Morning Post*, May 5.

Calantone, R. J., & Zhao, Y. S. (2001). Joint ventures in China: A comparative study of Japanese Korean, and U.S. partners. *Journal of International Marketing*, *9*(1), 1–23.

Caramanis, C. V. (1997). The enigma of the Greek auditing profession: Some preliminary results concerning the impact of liberalization on auditor behaviour. *European Accounting Review*, *6*(1), 85–108.

Caramanis, C. V. (1998). Assessing the impact of "liberalisation" on auditor behaviour: Accounting research in politically charged contexts. *Accounting, Auditing & Accountability Journal*, *11*(5), 562–592.

Caramanis, C. V. (1999). International accounting firms versus indigenous auditors: Intra-professional conflict in the Greek auditing profession, 1990–1993. *Critical Perspectives on Accounting*, *10*(2), 153–196.

Caramanis, C. V. (2002). The interplay between professional groups, the state and supranational agents: Pax Americana in the age of 'globalisation'. *Accounting, Organizations and Society*, *27*(4/5), 379–408.

Caramanis, C. V. (2005). Rationalisation, charisma and accounting professionalisation: Perspectives on the intra-professional conflict in Greece, 1993–2001. *Accounting, Organizations and Society*, *30*(3), 195–221.

Carcello, J., Hollingsworth, C., & Mastrolia, S. (2011). The effect of PCAOB inspections on Big 4 audit quality. *Research in Accounting Regulation*, *23*(2), 85–96.

Carnegie, G. D., & Napier, C. J. (2010). Traditional accountants and business professionals: Portraying the accounting profession after Enron. *Accounting, Organisations and Society*, *35*(3), 360–376.

Carroll, W. K., & Carson, C. (2003). The network of global corporations and elite policy groups: A structure for transnational capitalist class formation? *Global Networks*, *3*(1), 29–57.

Carter, C., & Spence, C. (2013). Being a successful professional: An exploration of who makes partner in the Big Four. *Contemporary Accounting Research*.

Caso, R. G. (2002). Andersen: The evolution of a global professional services firm. *Review of Business*, *23*(1), 6–9.

Castle, S. (2010). E.U. concerned by Big Four's dominance in auditing. *The New York Times*, October 13.

Catanach Jr., A. H., & Walker, P. L. (1999). The international debate over mandatory audit rotation: A conceptual research framework. *Journal of International Accounting, Auditing and Taxation*, *8*(1), 43–66.

Center for Audit Quality. (2012). *Guide to PCAOB inspections*. Retrieved from http://www.thecaq.org/resources/pdfs/GuidetoPCAOBInspections.pdf

Chan, A. (2005). Two-thirds of SAR accountants work for mainland companies, *China Daily*, September 9.

Chan, C. (2008). *Against the Big 4: Growth strategies for indigenous Chinese CPA firms Poon Kam Kai Series*. Hong Kong: Asia Case Research Centre, University of Hong Kong.

Chan, M. K. (1996). Hong Kong: Colonial legacy, transformation, and challenge. *Annals of the American Academy of Political and Social Science*, *547*, 11–23.

Chan, M. W. L., & Rotenberg, W. (1999). Accounting, accounting education, and economic reform in the People's Republic of China. *International Studies of Management & Organization*, *29*(3).

Chan, N. (2004a). Overworked: Accountants may get more holidays. *South China Morning Post*, July 16.

Chan, N. (2004b). We've been short-changed, say accountants. *South China Morning Post*, July 14.

Chan, N. (2005). Accounting firms raise audit fees as business improves: Some clients grumble about the higher charges, but overworked staff are happy with salary increases. *South China Morning Post*, January 12.

Chang, T. (2002). Ernst & Young gets most out of Andersen. *Business Weekly*, July 9.

Che-Ahmad, A., Houghton, K., & Derashid, C. (1996). The pricing of audit services: Evidence from the KLSE listed companies. *Jurnal Analisis*, *4*(1), 33–45.

Che-Ahmad, A., Houghton, K., & Yusof, N. (2006). The Malaysia market for audit services: Ethnicity, multinational companies and auditor choice. *Managerial Auditing Journal*, *21*(7), 702–723.

Chen, C., Gul, F. A., & Su, X. (1999). A comparison of reported earnings under Chinese GAAP vs. IAS: Evidence from the Shanghai stock exchange. *Accounting Horizons*, *13*, 91–112.

Chen, C. J. P., Su, X., & Wu, X. (2010). Auditor changes following a Big 4 merger with a local Chinese firm: A case study. *Auditing: A Journal of Practice & Theory*, *29*, 41.

Chen, G. (2009a). Ernst & Young China staff to take low-pay leave. *Reuters*, April 16.

Chen, G. (2009b). Top PwC China M&A partner Xie quits. *Reuters*, August 24.

Chen, H., & Tran, A. V. (1995). Recent accounting reform in China. *Asian Review of Accounting*, *3*(1).

Chen, J., & Cheng, P. (2007). Corporate governance and the harmonisation of Chinese accounting practices with IFRS practices. *Corporate Governance: An International Review*, *15*(2), 284–293.

Chen, J., & Zhang, H. (2010). The impact of regulatory enforcement and audit upon IFRS compliance – Evidence from China. *European Accounting Review*, *19*(4), 665–692.

Chen, K. (1994a). Entry made easier for accountants. *South China Morning Post*, January 11.

Chen, K. (1994b). H-share listings offer new area for accountants. *South China Morning Post*, January 20.

Chen, M., & Luk, H. (2010). Balance of power with the Big 4. *A Plus*, *6*(6), 20–24.

Chen, S. (1998). The rise and fall of debit-credit bookkeeping in China: History and analysis. *Accounting Historians Journal*, *25*(1), 73–92.

Chen, S., Sun, Z., & Wang, Y. (2002). Evidence from China on whether harmonized accounting standards harmonize accounting practices. *Accounting Horizons*, *16*(3), 183–198.

Chen, Y. (2004). *Opportunities and opening-up of China's accounting market, speech at Jaipur, India*. Retrieved from http://www.cicpa.org.cn/english/news_alert/200804/t20080428_4183.htm. Accessed on March 1, 2009.

Chen, Y., Jubb, P., & Tran, A. (1997). Problems of accounting reform in the people's republic of China. *The International Journal of Accounting*, *32*(2), 139–153.

Chien, K. (2009). E&Y says crisis speeds move to emerging markets. *Reuters*, May 14.

China Business News. (2012). *Ernst and Young approved to localize China Operations. China Business News*, August 1.

China Daily. (2008). Most of world's top companies invest in China. *China Daily*, May 5.

China Daily. (2009). Mainland accounting coming to the city. *China Daily*, December 31.

China Daily. (2012). KPMG localization program approved. *China Daily*, July 17.

China Daily. (2013). Big Four accounting firms no longer biggest. *China Daily*, August 26.

China Mobile Limited. (2013). *Company profile*. Retrieved from http://www.chinamobileltd.com/about.php

Chinese Institute of Certified Public Accountants (CICPA). (2007). *Opinions on promotion of Chinese accounting firms to develop larger and more competitive*. Retrieved from http://www.cicpa.org.cn/english/news_alert/200808/W020080812590118592750.pdf. Accessed on November 25, 2009.

Chinese Institute of Certified Public Accountants (CICPA). (2010a). *Comprehensive evaluation of top 100 accounting firms in 2010*. Chinese Institute of Certified Public Accountants, Beijing.

Chinese Institute of Certified Public Accountants (CICPA). (2010b). *Overview*. Retrieved from http://www.cicpa.org.cn/english/. Accessed on September 29.

Chiu, K. (2012). KPMG plays down China audit spat. *The Wall Street Journal*, December 14.

Chong, G. (2000). Auditing framework in the People's Republic of China and international auditing guidelines: Some comparisons. *Managerial Finance, 26*(5), 12–20.

Chow, L., Chau, G., & Gary, S. (1995). Accounting reforms in China: Cultural constraints on implementation and development. *Accounting and Business Research, 26*(1), 29–49.

Christensen, M., Newberry, S., & Potter, B. N. (2010). *The role of global epistemic communities in enabling accounting change: Creating a 'more business-like' public sector*. Paper presented at the 6th Accounting History International Conference, Wellington, New Zealand.

Chu, D. (1992). Judgement day for accountants. *South China Morning Post*, December 6.

Chua, W. F., & Poullaos, C. (1993). Rethinking the profession-state dynamic: the case of the Victorian charter attempt 1885–1906. *Accounting, Organizations and Society, 18*, 691–728.

Chua, W. F., & Poullaos, C. (1998). The dynamics of 'closure' amidst the construction of market, profession, empire and nationhood: An historical analysis of an Australian accounting association, 1886–1903. *Accounting, Organizations & Society, 23*(2), 155–187.

Chua, W. F., & Sinclair, A. (1994). Interests and the profession-state dynamic. *Journal of Business Finance and Accounting, 21*(5), 669–705.

Chui, A. P. L., & Wong, D. S. N. (1999). A comparison of earnings based on Chinese and international accounting standards: The case of PRC enterprises. *Advances in International Accounting, 67*.

Citron, D. B., & Manalis, G. (2001). The international firms as new entrants to the statutory audit market: An empirical analysis of auditor selection in Greece, 1993 to 1997. *European Accounting Review, 10*(3), 439–459.

Clarke, D. C. (2003). Corporate governance in China: An overview. *SSRN eLibrary*. doi:10.2139/ssrn.424885

Cogman, D. (2013). Due diligence in China: Art, science and self-defense. *McKinsey Quarterly* (July).

Cohn, M. (2012a). PCAOB chair Doty warns against auditing shortcuts. *Accounting Today*, November 30.

Cohn, M. (2012b). PCAOB makes tentative progress on Chinese audit firm inspections. *Accounting Today*, September 24.

Cohn, M. (2013). Deloitte revamps structure of China firm. *Accounting Today*, January 14.

Communist Party of China. (2007). *Constitution of the Communist Party of China.* Retrieved from http://english.cpc.people.com.cn/65732/6758063.html. Accessed on November 19, 2010.

Cooper, B., Chow, L., & Tang, Y. (2002). The development of auditing standards and the certified public accounting profession in China. *Managerial Auditing Journal, 17*(7), 383–389.

Cooper, C. (1995). Ideology, hegemony and accounting discourse. *Critical Perspectives on Accounting, 6*, 175–208.

Cooper, D. J., Greenwood, R., Hinings, C. R., & Brown, J. L. (1998). Globalization and nationalism in a multinational accounting firm: The case of opening new markets in Eastern Europe. *Accounting, Organizations & Society, 23*(5/6), 531–548.

Cooper, D. J., & Robson, K. (2006). Accounting, professions and regulation: Locating the sites of professionalization. *Accounting, Organizations and Society, 31*(4/5), 415–444.

Cooper, D. J., & Robson, K. (2009). Practitioners, work and firms. In J. R. Edwards & S. Walker (Eds.), *The Routledge companion to accounting history research* (pp. 274–296). Oxford: Routledge.

Covaleski, M. A., Dirsmith, M. W., Heian, J. B., & Samuel, S. (1998). The calculated and the avowed: Techniques of discipline and struggles over identity in Big Six public accounting firms. *Administrative Science Quarterly*, *43*(2).

CSRC. (2009). *Comments RE: Public Company Accounting Oversight Board: Notice of filing of proposed amendment to board rules relating to inspection*. Retrieved from http://www.sec.gov/comments/pcaob-2008-06/pcaob200806-1.pdf

Dai, X., Lau, A., & Yang, J. (2000). Hooking-up: A unique feature of China public accounting firms. *Managerial Finance*, *26*(5), 21–30.

Daniel, P., Suranova, Z., & De Beelde, I. (2001). The development of accounting in Slovakia. *European Accounting Review*, *10*(2), 343–359.

Daniels, J. D., Pitts, R. A., & Tretter, M. J. (1984). Strategy and structure of US multinationals: An exploratory study. *Academy of Management Journal*, *27*(2), 292–307.

Daniels, P. W., Thrift, N. J., & Leyshon, A. (1989). Internationalization of professional provider services: Accountancy conglomerates. In P. Enderwock (Ed.), *Multinational service firms* (pp. 79–105). London: Routledge.

Darrough, M. N., Huang, R., & Zhao, S. (2012). The spillover effect of Chinese reverse merger frauds: Chinese or reverse merger? *SSRN*, September 9.

Davidson, R., Gelardi, A., & Li, F. (1996). Analysis of the conceptual framework of China's new accounting system. *Accounting Horizons*, *10*(1), 58–74.

Davies, S. W., & Geroski, P. A. (1997). Changes in concentration, turbulence, and the dynamics of market shares. *The Review of Economics and Statistics*, *79*(3), 383–391.

DeAngelo, L. E. (1981). Auditor size and audit quality. *Journal of Accounting and Economics*, *3*(3), 183–199.

de la Cruz, R. (2001). Andersen seeks more in China. *The Wall Street Journal Europe*, November 23.

Deloitte. (2013). *Deloitte successfully completes localization conversion in China*. Retrieved from http://www.deloitte.com/view/en_cn/cn/2d833ea7a473c310VgnVCM1000003256f70aRCRD.htm

Deloitte Touche Tohmatsu. (2011). *IASB agenda project: Amendments to IAS 24 related party disclosures*. Retrieved from http://www.iasplus.com/agenda/relatedparty.htm. Accessed on March 8.

DeMond, C. W. (1951). *Price Waterhouse and Company in America: A history of a public accounting firm*. New York, NY: Comet Press.

Démurger, S. (2000). *Economic opening and growth in China*. Paris: Organisation for Economic Co-operation and Development.

Deng, P. (2001). WFOEs: The most popular entry mode into China. *Business Horizons*, *44*(4), 63.

Deng, S., & Macve, R. (2012). *The origination and development of China's accounting firms: 'translation' meets self-determination*. Paper presented at the Interdisciplinary Perspectives on Accounting Conference 2012, Cardiff University, UK.

Denzin, N. K., & Lincoln, Y. S. (2000). Introduction: The discipline and practice of qualitative research. In N. K. Denzin & Y. S. Lincoln (Eds.), *Handbook of qualitative research* (pp. 1–28). Thousand Oaks, CA: Sage.

Dezalay, Y., & Garth, B. G. (2002). *The internationalization of palace wars: Lawyers, economists, and the contest to transform Latin American states*. Chicago, IL: The University of Chicago Press.

Diamond, S. F. (2003). *The PetroChina syndrome: Regulating capital markets in the anti-globalization era*. Cornell Law Faculty Working Papers. Cornell Law Library, Cornell Law Faculty Working Papers, Ithaca, NY.

DiMaggio, P. J. (1983). State expansion and organizational fields. In R. H. Hall & R. E. Quinn (Eds.), *Organizational theory and public policy*. Beverly Hills, CA: Sage.

DiMaggio, P. J. (1991). Constructing an organizational field as a professional project: U.S. art museums, 1920–1940. In W. W. Powell & P. J. Dimaggio (Eds.), *The new institutionalism in organizational analysis*. Chicago, IL: The University of Chicago Press.

DiMaggio, P. J., & Powell, W. W. (1983). The iron cage revisited: Institutional isomorphism and collective rationality in organizational fields. *American Sociological Review*, *48*(2), 147–160.

Ding, P. (1993). Report on attending the GATT service trade negotiations in Uruguay Round, October 28, 1993. In P. Ding (Ed.), *The wind and rain travels at double speed: The road of Chinese CPAs* (Vol. Opening up, p. 316). Dalian: The Publishing House of Dongbei University of Finance and Economics.

Ding, P. (1996). Interview with CCTV journalist, February 13, 1996. *The wind and rain travels at double speed: The road of Chinese CPAs* (Vol. Opening Up, p. 339). Dalian: The Publishing House of Dongbei University of Finance and Economics.

Ding, P. (1998a). Report on the opening-up situation of the accounting market to Ministry of Finance. In P. Ding (Ed.), *The wind and rain travels at double speed: The road of Chinese CPAs* (Vol. Opening up, p. 590). Dalian: The Publishing House of Dongbei University of Finance and Economics.

Ding, P. (1998b). Response to the report given by Beijing institute of CPAs. In P. Ding (Ed.), *The wind and rain travels at double speed: The road of Chinese CPAs* (Vol. Opening up, p. 441). Dalian: The Publishing House of Dongbei University of Finance and Economics.

Ding, P. (2006a). *The wind and rain travels at double speed: The road of Chinese CPAs – Reform volume*. Dalian: The Publishing House of Dongbei University of Finance and Economics.

Ding, P. (2006b). *The wind and rain travels at double speed: The road of Chinese CPAs – Opening-up volume*. Dalian: The Publishing House of Dongbei University of Finance and Economics.

Ding, P. (2008). *The wind and rain travels at double speed: The road of Chinese CPAs – Legal volume*. Dalian: The Publishing House of Dongbei University of Finance and Economics.

Ding, Y. (2000). Harmonisation trends in Chinese accounting and remaining problems. *Managerial Finance*, *26*(5), 31–40.

Ding, Y., & Su, X. (2008). Implementation of IFRS in a regulated market. *Journal of Accounting and Public Policy*, *27*(6), 474–479.

Dinmore, G., & Dyer, G. (2010). Immelt hits out at China and Obama. *Financial Times*, July 1.

Doty, J. (2013). *Remarks on the global audit*. Retrieved from http://pcaobus.org/News/Speech/Pages/02082013_Texas.aspx

Dugdale, L. (2011). The expanding empire of Zhang Ke. *INTHEBLACK*, December 1.

Dutschke, R. (1969). On anti-authoritarianism. In C. Oglesby (Ed.), *The new left reader*. New York, NY: Grove Press.

Dyball, M. C., & Valcarcel, L. J. (1999). The "rational" and "traditional": The regulation of accounting in the Philippines. *Accounting, Auditing & Accountability Journal*, *12*(3), 303–327.

E&Y. (2012). *EY Hua Ming embarks on a new era in China.* Retrieved from http://www.ey.com/CN/en/Newsroom/News-releases/2012_Ernst-Young-Hua-Ming-embarks-on-a-new-era-in-China

Ebrey, P. B. (1996). *The Cambridge illustrated history of China.* Cambridge: Cambridge University Press.

Edwards, J. D. (1960). *History of public accounting in the United States.* East Lansing, Michigan: Bureau of Business and Economic Research, Michigan State University.

Ernst & Young. (2001). Ernst & Young announces merger with mainland China accounting firm Da Hua. *Business Wire*, February 9.

European Commission. (2008). *Accounting: European Commission grants equivalence in relation to third country GAAPs.* Retrieved from http://europa.eu/rapid/pressReleasesAction.do?reference=IP/08/1962&format=HTML&aged=0&language=EN&guiLanguage=en. Accessed on May 1, 2011.

European Commission. (2009). *Consultation on control structures in audit firms and their consequences on the audit market.* Directorate General for Internal Market and Services, Brussels.

European Commission. (2010). *Audit policy: Lessons from the crisis.* Brussels.

Ezzamel, M., Xiao, J. Z., & Pan, A. (2007). Political ideology and accounting regulation in China. *Accounting, Organizations and Society*, *32*(7/8), 669–700.

Fang, Z., & Tang, Y. (1991). Recent accounting developments in China: An increasing internationalization. *The International Journal of Accounting*, *26*(2), 85–103.

Fédération des Experts Comptables Européens. (2008). *Trans-national organizations and practices within the accountancy profession.* Brussels: Fédération des Experts Comptables Européens.

Femia, J. (1986). Hegemony and consciousness in the thought of Antonio Gramsci. *Political Studies*, *23*(1), 29–48.

Ferguson, L. (2012). *Investor protection through audit oversight.* Retrieved from http://pcaobus.org/News/Speech/Pages/09212012_FergusonCalState.aspx

Ferner, A., Edwards, P., & Sisson, K. (1995). Coming unstuck? In search of the 'corporate glue' in an international professional service firm. *Human Resource Management*, *34*(3), 343–361.

Feuerwerker, A. (1976). *The foreign establishment in China in the early twentieth century.* Ann Arbor, MI: Center for Chinese Studies, The University of Michigan.

Fisher, L. (1994). Go east, brave firms: Accountancy in China. *Accountancy*, *June*, 45.

Fleischman, R. K., & Radcliffe, V. S. (2003). Divergent streams of accounting history: A review and call for confluence. In R. K. Fleischman, V. S. Radcliffe, & P. A. Shoemaker (Eds.), *Doing accounting history: Contributions to the development of accounting thought* (Vol. 6, pp. 1–29). Oxford: Elsevier Science, Ltd.

Folta, P. H. (2005). Cooperative joint ventures. *The China Business Review*, (January/February), 18–23.

Fryxell, G. E., Butler, J., & Choi, A. (2004). Successful localization programs in China: An important element in strategy implementation. *Journal of World Business*, *39*(3), 268–282.

Fu, P. (1974). Governmental accounting in China during the Chou Dynasty. *Journal of Accounting Research*, *9*, 40–51.

Fung, E. (2010). PwC to spend around US$100 million on China hiring, training in 3–5 years. *The Wall Street Journal*, September 15.

Fung, H., Liu, Q., & Yau, J. (2007). Financing alternatives for Chinese small and medium enterprises: The case for a small and medium enterprise stock market. *China & World Economy*, *15*(1), 26–42.

Fung, K. C., Iizaka, H., & Tong, S. Y. (2004). Foreign direct investment in China: Policy, recent trend and impact. *Global Economic Review*, *33*(2), 99–130.

Fung, N. (1993). Accounting firm appointed advisor. *South China Morning Post*, September 17.

Gaidar, Y., & Gaidar, E. T. (2003). *State and evolution: Russia's search for a free market*. University of Washington Press, Seattle.

Gallhofer, S., & Haslam, J. (2006). The accounting-globalisation interrelation: An overview with some reflections on the neglected dimension of emancipatory potentiality. *Critical Perspectives on Accounting*, *17*(7), 903–934.

Gant, T. (Ed.). (2005). *International directory of company histories* (Vol. 68), Farmington Hills, MI: St. James Press.

Gao, D. Y. (1982a). *Chinese accounting history* (Vol. 2), Beijing: China Finance and Economics Press.

Gao, D. Y. (1982b). *The general history of Chinese accounting* (Vol. 1), Beijing: China Finance and Economics Publishing House.

Gao, D. Y. (1988). *The general history of Chinese accounting* (Vol. 2), Beijing: China Finance and Economics Publishing House.

Gardella, R. (1992). Squaring accounts: Commercial bookkeeping methods and capitalistic rationalism in late Qing and Republican China. *The Journal of Asian Studies*, *51*(2), 317–339.

Garnaut, R., Song, L., Tenev, S., & Yao, Y. (2005). *China's ownership transformation: Process, outcomes, prospects*. Washington, DC: International Finance Corporation.

Ge, J. S. (1978). The reputation of debit/credit bookkeeping method must be restored: On the so called 'capitalist bookkeeping method'. In J. S. Ge (Ed.), *Issues on basic accounting theory and methods* (pp. 110–124). Beijing: Economic Science Press.

Ge, Z. (1993). Economic reforms and accounting internationalization in the People's Republic of China. *Journal of International Accounting, Auditing and Taxation*, *2*(2), 129–143.

Gelatt, T. A. (1989). The new Chinese state secrets law. *Cornell International Law Journal*, *22*, 255.

General Accounting Office. (2003). *Public accounting firms: Mandated study on consolidation and competition*. Washington, DC: United States General Accounting Office.

Gertler, J. L. (2004). What China's WTO accession is all about. In D. Bhattasali, S. Li, & W. Martin (Eds.), *China and the WTO: Accession, policy reform, and poverty reduction strategies* (pp. 21–28). Washington, DC: The International Bank for Reconstruction and Development.

Ghoshal, S., & Bartlett, C. A. (1990). The multinational corporation as an interorganizational network. *Academy of Management Review*, *15*(4), 603–625.

Gilbert, J. (1999). *The hard centre: New labour's technocratic hegemony*. Retrieved from http://www.signsofthetimes.org.uk/pamphlet1/The Hard Centre.html. Accessed on February 14, 2011.

Giles, J. P., Venuti, E. K., & Jones, R. C. (2004). The PCAOB and convergence of the global auditing and accounting profession. *CPA Journal*, *75*(3), 36–39.

Gillis, P. (2010a, November 14). *The emperor's new suit: VIEs in China*. Retrieved from http://www.chinaaccountingblog.com/weblog/the-emperors-new-suit-vies-.html

Gillis, P. (2010b, November 21). *The perfect storm: Big challenges face the Big Four in China*. Retrieved from http://www.chinaaccountingblog.com/weblog/the-perfect-storm-big-chall.html

Gillis, P. (2011a). *The big four in China: Hegemony and Counter-hegemony in the development of the accounting profession in China.* Ph.D. thesis, Macquarie Graduate School of Management, Australia.

Gillis, P. (2011b, March 20). *Explaining VIE structures.* Retrieved from http://www.chinaaccountingblog.com/weblog/explaining-vie-structures.html

Gillis, P. (2011c, April 1). *The reverse merger problem.* Retrieved from http://www.chinaaccountingblog.com/weblog/the-reverse-merger-problem.html

Gillis, P. (2011d, April 11). *Statistics on VIE usage.* Retrieved from http://www.chinaaccountingblog.com/weblog/statistics-on-vie-usage.html

Gillis, P. (2013a). *The end game.* Retrieved from http://www.chinaaccountingblog.com/weblog/the-end-game.html

Gillis, P. (2013b, July 10). *KPMG kicked out of Big Four in China.* Retrieved from http://www.chinaaccountingblog.com/weblog/kpmg-kicked-out-of-big-four.html

Goddard, A. (2002). Development of the accounting profession and practices in the public sector: A hegemonic analysis. *Accounting, Auditing & Accountability Journal, 15*(5), 655–688.

Godfrey, M. (2011). China's second-tier firms target the Big Four's Achilles heel. *Accountancy Age*, May 10.

Godwin, A. (2009). The professional "tug of war": The regulation of foreign lawyers in China, business scope issues and some suggestions for reform. *Melbourne University Law Review, 33*(1), 133–162.

Gold, T., Guthrie, D., & Wank, D. (2002). An introduction to the study of guanxi. In T. Gold, D. Guthrie, & D. Wank (Eds.), *Social connections in China: Institutions, culture and the changing nature of guanxi.* Cambridge: Cambridge University Press.

Gomes, D. (2008). The interplay of conceptions of accounting and schools of thought in accounting history. *Accounting History, 13*, 479–509.

Government Accountability Office. (2008). *Audits of public companies: Continued concentration in audit market for large public companies does not call for immediate action.* (GA0-08-163). Washington, DC: United States Government Accountability Office.

Graham, L., & Li, C. (1997). Cultural and economic influences on current accounting standards in the People's Republic of China. *The International Journal of Accounting, 32*(3), 247–278.

Gramsci, A. (1935/1971). *Selections from the prison network* (Q. Hoare & G. N. Smith, Trans.). London: Lawrence and Wishart.

Green, S. P. (2004). *The development of China's stock market, 1984–2002: Equity politics and market institutions.* London: RoutledgeCurzon.

Greenlees, D. (2007). PetroChina tops $1 trillion in value, an all-time record. *The New York Times*, November 5.

Greenwood, R., & Empson, L. (2003). The professional partnership: Relic or exemplary form of governance? *Organization Studies, 24*(6), 909.

Greenwood, R., Hinings, C. R., & Brown, J. (1990). "P2-Form" strategic management: corporate practices in professional partnerships. *Academy of Management Journal, 33*(4), 725–755.

Greenwood, R., Morris, T., Fairclough, S., & Boussebaa, M. (2010). The organizational design of transnational professional service firms. *Organizational Dynamics, 39*(2), 173–183.

Gregory, N., Tenev, S., & Wagle, D. (2000). *China's emerging private enterprises: Prospects for the new century.* Washington, DC: International Finance Corporation.

Gul, F., Sami, H., & Zhou, H. (2009). Auditor disaffiliation program in China and auditor independence. *Auditing: A Journal of Practice and Theory, 28*(1), 29–51.

Gunny, K. A., & Zhang, T. C. (2013). PCAOB inspection reports and audit quality. *Journal of Accounting and Public Policy, 32*(2), 136–160.

Haas, P. M. (1992). Introduction: Epistemic communities and international policy coordination. *International Organization, 46*, 1–35.

Hall, J. A. (2000). Globalization and nationalism. *Thesis Eleven, 63*(1), 63–79.

Hall, S. (1983). The problem of ideology – Marxism without guarantees. In B. Matthews (Ed.), *Marx: A hundred years on* (pp. 57–84). London: Lawrence & Wishart.

Hall, S. (1984). *State and society in contemporary Britain: A critical introduction*. Cambridge: Polity.

Hao, Z. P. (1999). Regulation and organisation of accountants in China. *Accounting, Auditing & Accountability Journal, 12*(3), 286–302.

Haverty, J. L. (2006). Are IFRS and US GAAP converging? Some evidence from people's republic of China companies listed on the New York stock exchange. *Journal of International Accounting, Auditing and Taxation, 15*(1), 48–71.

Hawkes, A. (2008). Deloitte dismisses China growth plans. *Accountancy Age*, July 31.

He, C. (2003). Entry mode and location of foreign manufacturing enterprises in China. *Eurasian Geography and Economics, 44*(6), 443–461.

Heim, K. (1997). Using local staff is key to profitability for firms in China. *The Wall Street Journal*, December 12.

Hempton, J. (2012, June 10). *The macroeconomics of Chinese kleptocracy*. Retrieved from http://brontecapital.blogspot.com/2012/06/macroeconomics-of-chinese-kleptocracy.html

Hiebert, P. G. (2008). *Transforming worldviews: An anthropological understanding of how people change*. Grand Rapids, MI: Baker Academic.

Hilary, G., & Lennox, C. (2005). The credibility of self-regulation: Evidence from the accounting profession's peer review program. *Journal of Accounting and Economics, 40*, 211–229.

Hilmy, J. (1999). Communists among us in a market economy: Accountancy in the People's Republic of China. *The International Journal of Accounting, 34*(4), 491–515.

Hinings, C. R., Brown, J. L., & Greenwood, R. (1991). Change in an autonomous professional organization. *Journal of Management Studies, 28*(4), 375–393.

Hinings, C. R., Brown, J. L., & Greenwood, R. (2007). Change in an autonomous professional organization. *Journal of Management Studies, 28*(4), 375–393.

Hinings, C. R., Greenwood, R., & Cooper, D. (1999). The dynamics of change in large accounting firms. In D. M. Brock, M. Powell, & C. Hinings (Eds.), *Restructuring the professional organization: Accounting, healthcare and law* (pp. 131–153). New York, NY: Routledge.

Hitt, M. A., Bierman, L., Uhlenbruck, K., & Shimizu, K. (2006). The importance of resources in the internationalization of professional service firms: The good, the bad, and the ugly. *Academy of Management Journal, 49*(6), 1137.

Hobbs, A. (2011). Muddy waters target urges action. *Bloomberg News*, June 20.

Hong Kong Exchanges and Clearing Limited. (2009). *Consultation paper on acceptance of mainland accounting and auditing standards and mainland audit firms for mainland incorporated companies listed in Hong Kong*. Hong Kong: Hong Kong Exchanges and Clearing Limited.

Hong Kong Exchanges and Clearing Limited. (2010). HKEx Publishes Consultation Conclusions on Acceptance of Mainland Accounting and Auditing Standards and

Mainland Audit Firms for Mainland Incorporated Companies Listed in Hong Kong. Retrieved from http://www.hkex.com.hk/eng/newsconsul/hkexnews/2010/101210news.htm. Accessed on March 19, 2011.

Hong Kong Exchanges and Clearing Limited. (2013). *China dimension*. Retrieved from http://www.hkex.com.hk/eng/stat/smstat/chidimen/chidimen.htm

Hong Kong Institute of Certified Public Accountants. (2007). *Joint declaration of the China Accounting Standards Committee and the Hong Kong Institute of Certified Public Accountants on the converged China accounting standards for business enterprises and Hong Kong financial reporting standards* (Vol. 2010). Hong Kong: Hong Kong Institute of Certified Public Accountants.

Hong Kong Institute of Certified Public Accountants (2009a). *Consultation paper on proposed changes to the practising certificate regime*. Hong Kong: Hong Kong Institute of Certified Public Accountants.

Hong Kong Institute of Certified Public Accountants (2009b). *Response to consultation paper on acceptance of Mainland accounting and auditing standards for Mainland incorporated companies listed in Hong Kong*. Hong Kong: Hong Kong Institute of Certified Public Accountants.

Hopper, T., & Armstrong, P. (1991). Cost accounting, controlling labour and the rise of conglomerates. *Accounting, Organizations and Society*, *16*(5/6), 405–438.

Hopwood, A. G. (1978). Editorial: Accounting research and the world of action. *Accounting, Organizations and Society*, *3*(2), 93–95.

Hopwood, A. G. (1987). The archaeology of accounting systems. *Accounting, Organisations and Society*, *12*(3), 207–234.

Hopwood, A. G. (1988). *Accounting from the outside*. New York, NY: Garland Publishing Inc.

House of Lords. (2011). *Auditors: Market concentration and their role* (2nd Report of Session 2010–11). Select Committee on Economic Affairs.

Hoyle, J. (1978). Mandatory auditor rotation: The arguments and an alternative. *Journal of Accountancy*, *145*(5), 69–78.

Hu, B. (2001). Ernst & Young in merger. *South China Morning Post*, February 9.

Hu, B. (2002). Tough audit rules eased after outcry from interest groups. *South China Morning Post*, March 2.

Hu, B. (2003). Mainland to begin auditor rotations. *South China Morning Post*, November 1.

Huang, A., & Ma, R. (2001). *Accounting in China in transition: 1949–2000*. London: World Scientific.

Huber, N. (2011). Big Four break-up threat. *Accountancy Age*, January 27.

Hunt, A. (1990). Rights and social movements: Counter-hegemonic strategies. *Journal of Law and Society*, *17*(3), 309–328.

Huo, H. (2001). Accounting mergers thriving. *Business Weekly*, February 27.

Hutcheon, R. (1998). *High-rise society: The first 50 years of the Hong Kong housing society*. Hong Kong: Chinese University Press.

Hwang, K. (1987). Face and favor: The Chinese power game. *American Journal of Sociology*, *92*(4), 944–974.

International Accounting Bulletin. (2005). IAB research – Hong Kong: The market where strategy is king. *International Accounting Bulletin*, September 8.

International Accounting Bulletin. (2012). Chinese official defends localisation rules. *International Accounting Bulletin*, May 24.

IBM. (2010). *Career development: Career paths*. Retrieved from http://www-935.ibm.com/services/us/gbs/bus/html/bcs_careers_development.html. Accessed on May 25.

IFAC. (2010). *Chinese accounting standards board and international auditing and assurance standards board issue joint statement regarding convergence of international standards.* Retrieved from http://press.ifac.org/news/2010/11/chinese-auditing-standards-board-and-international-auditing-and-assurance-standards-board-issue-joint-statement-regarding-convergence-of-international-standards. Accessed on May 4, 2011.

IFAC. (2011). *IFAC history in brief: Founding members of IFAC.* Retrieved from http://www.ifac.org/History/founding_member_bodies.php

IFRS Foundation. (2011a). *About the IFRS Foundation and the IASB.* Retrieved from http://www.ifrs.org/Home.htm. Accessed on March 4.

IFRS Foundation. (2011b). *Related party disclosures: Comment letters.* Retrieved from http://www.ifrs.org/Current + Projects/IASB + Projects/Related + Party + Disclosures + %28IAS + 24%29/Exposure + Draft + and + Comment + Letters/Comment + Letters/Comment + Letters.htm. Accessed on March 8.

Jack, A. (1993a). China signs accounting standards contract. *Financial Times*, February 9, p. 3.

Jack, A. (1993b). Chinese practitioners ready for their great leap forward. *Financial Times*, August 12.

Jacobs, J. B. (1979). A preliminary model of particularistic ties in Chinese political alliances: Kan-ching and Kuan-hsi in a rural Taiwanese township. *The China Quarterly*, *78*, 237–273.

James, K. (2010). "Who am I? Where are we? Where do we go from here?" Marxism, voice, representation, and synthesis. *Critical Perspectives on Accounting*, *21*(8), 696–710.

James, M. (2008). Surge in demand for professionals: An acute shortage of qualified personnel in the mainland leads to excellent career prospects and higher wages, *South China Morning Post*, January 18.

Jiang, Z. (2001). *Speech at the meeting celebrating the 80th anniversary of the founding of the Communist Party of China.* Retrieved from http://www.china.org.cn/e-speech/a.htm. Accessed on August 1, 2010.

Jiao, X. (2002). New accounting policy unwise. *China Daily*, January 18.

Jindra, J., Voetmann, T., & Walkling, R. (2012). *Reverse mergers: The Chinese experience.* Fisher College of Business Working Paper Series. Charles A. Dice Center for Research in Financial Economics, Columbus, OH.

Jones, A. (2013). Regulator drops threat to force audit rotation. *Financial Times*, July 22.

Jones, A., & Rabinovitch, S. (2013). Accounting: Stalking the big four. *Financial Times*, April 16.

Jopson, B. (2006a). Big Four firms plan to boost China staff. *Financial Times*, June 5.

Jopson, B. (2006b). Cultural revolution leaves void among China's number crunchers. *Financial Times*, June 5.

Joseph, J. (2002). *Hegemony: A realist analysis*. London: Routledge.

Kanamori, T., & Zhao, Z. (2004). *Private sector development in the people's republic of China.* Tokyo: Asian Development Bank Institute.

Karmel, S. M. (1994). Emerging securities markets in China: Capitalism with Chinese characteristics. *The China Quarterly*, *140*, 1105–1116.

Kaup, B. Z. (2013). Transnational class formation and the spatialities of power: The case of elite competition in Bolivia. *Global Networks*, *13*(1), 101–119.

Kauppi, N., & Madsen, M. R. (Eds.). (2013). *Transnational power elites: The new professionals of governance, law and security*. New York, NY: Routledge.

Keatinge, R., Donn, A., Coleman, G., & Hester, E. (1995). Limited liability partnerships: The next step in the evolution of the unincorporated business organization. *Business Lawyer*, *51*, 147–187.

Kerrison, O. (2004). Deloitte targets 500% increase in Chinese fees by 2009. *International Accounting Bulletin*, June 17.

Kilzer, L. (2012). Paper dragons. *Pittsburg Tribune*, February 26.

King, N., Beattie, A., Cristescu, A. M., & Weetman, P. (2001). Developing accounting and audit in a transition economy: The Romanian experience. *European Accounting Review*, *10*(1), 149–171.

Kiong, T. C., & Kee, Y. P. (1998). Guanxi bases, *xinyong* and Chinese business networks. *The British Journal of Sociology*, *49*(1), 75–96.

Kipnis, A. (2002). Guanxi production and ganqing avoidance. In T. Gold, D. Guthrie, & D. Wank (Eds.), *Social connections in China: Institutions, culture and the changing nature of guanxi* (pp. 21–34). Cambridge: Cambridge University Press.

Kirsch, R. J., Laird, K. R., & Evans, T. G. (2000). The entry of international CPA firms into emerging markets: Motivational factors and growth strategies. *The International Journal of Accounting*, *35*(1), 99–119.

Kleinman, G., Lin, B., & Palmon, D. (2013). *Audit quality: A cross-national comparison of audit regulatory regimes.* Paper presented at the American Accounting Association, Anaheim, CA.

Kohlbeck, M., Mayhew, B. W., Murphy, P., & Wilkins, M. S. (2008). Competition for Andersen's clients. *Contemporary Accounting Research*, *25*(4), 1099–1136.

Koven, P., & Shecter, B. (2012). OSC accuses Ernst & Young as firm settles Sino-Forest class action suit. *Financial Post*, December 3.

Koza, M. P., & Lewin, A. Y. (1999). The coevolution of network alliances: A longitudinal analysis of an international professional service network. *Organization Science: A Journal of the Institute of Management Sciences*, *10*(5), 638–652.

KPMG. (2012). *KPMG: Localisation "best thing for KPMG in China"*. Retrieved from http://www.kpmg.com/CN/en/PressRoom/PressReleases/Pages/press-20120731-KPMG-Huazhen-SGP.aspx

Kraar, L., & McGowan, J. (1995). The death of Hong Kong. *Fortune*, June 26.

Lai, R. (1994a). Accountant firms shed the shackles of joint ventures. *South China Morning Post*, November 30.

Lai, R. (1994b). Cracking the code. *South China Morning Post*, June 8.

Lai, R. (1996). Fate sealed for accounting firms. *South China Morning Post*, July 5.

Larrain, J. (1983). *Marxism and ideology*. New York, NY: MacMillan Publishing Company.

Larson, M. S. (1977). *The rise of professionalism: A sociological analysis*. Berkeley, CA: University of California Press.

Lau, A., & Yang, J. (1990). Auditing in China: Historical perspective and current developments. *The International Journal of Accounting*, *25*(1), 53–62.

Lau, W. K. (1999). The 15th Congress of the Chinese communist party: Milestone in China's privatization. *Capital & Class*, *23*(2), 51–87.

Leblebici, H., Salancik, G., Copay, A., & King, T. (1991). Institutional change and the transformation of the U.S. radio broadcasting industry. *Administrative Science Quarterly*, *36*, 333–363.

Lee, D. S. (2005). The impact of Big 8 mergers on market power: Evidence from the Hong Kong market. *Journal of International Financial Management & Accounting*, *16*(1), 69–96.

Lee, J. L. (2007). Deloitte sets China path - Firm aims to have 10,000 employees by 2010. *The Wall Street Journal Asia*, April 3.

Lee, L. (2003). China launches investigation into accounting companies. *The Asian Wall Street Journal*, November 25.

Lee, S. S. (2006). S'pore accountants can earn up to 40% more in China. *Straits Times*, June 7.

Lee, T. A. (1990). *The closure of the accounting profession*. New York, NY: Garland Press.

Left, A. (2011, April 26). *Citron reports on Longtop Financial (NYSE:LFT)*. Retrieved from http://www.citronresearch.com/citron-reports-on-longtop-financial-nyselft/

Legislative Council of Hong Kong. (2010). *Mansard, April 28, 2010*. Hong Kong: Retrieved from http://www.legco.gov.hk/english/index.htm

Lehman, C., & Tinker, T. (1987). The "real" cultural significance of accounts. *Accounting, Organisations and Society*, *12*(5), 503–522.

Lenz, H., & James, M. (2007). International audit firms as strategic networks: The evolution of global professional service firms. In G. Cliquet, G. Hendrikse, M. Tunnanen, & J. Windsperger (Eds.), *Economics and management of networks: Franchising, strategic alliances and cooperatives* (pp. 367–392). Heidelberg, Germany: Physica-Verlag.

Levitt, A. (2002). *Take it on the street*. New York, NY: Pantheon Books.

Lewis, T. (2005). *In partnership: KPMG's 60 years in Hong Kong and 20 years in China*. Hong Kong: KPMG.

Li, B. (1980). Are bookkeeping methods of a class nature. *Accounting Research*, *1*, 23–24.

Li, B. Z., & Wang, J. Z. (1989). *Chinese accounting history*. Beijing: Science of Economics Publishing House.

Li, C., & Whalley, J. (2010). Chinese firm and industry reactions to antidumping. *Vox*. Retrieved from http://www.voxeu.org/index.php?q=node/5770

Li, J. (2011). Mainland accounting standards get green light from local bourse. *China Daily*, December 11.

Li, J., Xin, K. R., Tsui, A., & Hambrick, D. C. (1999). Building effective international joint venture leadership teams in China. *Journal of World Business*, *34*(1), 52–68.

Li, K. (1997). *A glossary of political terms of the people's republic of China* (M. Lok, Trans.). Hong Kong: The Chinese University Press.

Li, T. (2010). Reanda International Network takes aim at the Big 4. *China Daily*, September 16.

Li, Y. (2011). *State-led financialization: Political economy of the ChiNext, China's NASDAQ*. Paper presented at the Global Governance: Political Authority in Transition, Montreal, Canada.

Lin, K. Z., & Chan, K. H. (2000). Auditing standards in China: A comparative analysis with relevant international standards and guidelines. *The International Journal of Accounting*, *35*(4), 559–577.

Lin, Z. J. (1992). Chinese double-entry bookkeeping before the nineteenth century. *The Accounting Historians Journal*, *19*, 103–122.

Lin, Z. J. (1998). Internationalization of public accounting: Chinese experience. *Managerial Auditing Journal*, *13*(2), 84–94.

Liu, Q. (2002). Deloitte gears up for bigger role in expanding mainland market. *The Standard*, July 2.

Liu, W., & Liu, X. (2008). Auditor switching, earnings manipulation and auditor independence: Evidence from A-share listed companies in China. *Frontiers of Business Research in China*, *2*(2), 283–302.

Liu, Y. Z., & Wang, J. (1994). A review of the development of double-entry bookkeeping in China. *Accounting Research (in Chinese)*, *15*(3), 43–44.
Loong, P. (2001). Power, politics and philanthropy. *Asiamoney*, September 1.
Lorsch, J., & Tierney, T. (2002). *Aligning the stars: How to succeed when professionals drive results*. Boston, MA: Harvard Business School Press.
Lou, E., & Enthoven, A. J. H. (1987). *Accounting and auditing in the people's republic of China*. New York, NY: Coopers & Lybrand Foundation.
Lowendahl, B. (2000). *Strategic management of professional firms*. Copenhagen, Denmark: Handelshojskolens Forlag.
Lu, H. (1995). Bowler hat and pinstripe men head for Shenyang. *China Daily*, March 6.
Lu, J., & Saunders, G. (2005). Chinese public accounting: From the 1900's to present. *Journal of Accounting and Finance Research*, *13*(4), 27–37.
Lu, W., & Aiken, M. (2003). Accounting history: Chinese contributions and challenges. *Accounting, Business & Financial History*, *13*(1), 1–3.
Lu, W., Ji, X., & Aiken, M. (2009). Governmental influences in the development of Chinese accounting during the modern era. *Accounting, Business & Financial History*, *19*(3), 305–326.
Luk, H. (2010a). Blazing the trail: Shinewing's Zhang Ke on the thorny path of building a Chinese accounting brand. *A Plus*, *6*(8), 20–24.
Luk, H. (2010b). China's big accounting plan. *A Plus*, *6*(7), 14–18.
Luk, H. (2010c). China's new accounting epoch. *A Plus*, *6*(6), 14–18.
Luo, X., & Liu, X. (1996). Report on the finance-tax inspection on the joint venture firms. In P. Ding (Ed.), *The wind and rain travels at double speed: The road of Chinese CPAs* (Vol. Opening up, pp. 415–416). Dalian: The Publishing House of Dongbei University of Finance and Economics.
Lynch, S., & Yukhananov, A. (2013). U.S. Treasury Secretary says China to hand audit work to SEC. *Reuters*, July 12.
MacDonald, E., & Chang, L. (1998). China keeps foreign accountants at bay. *The Asian Wall Street Journal*, July 29.
Mackerras, C., Taneja, P., & Young, G. (1994). *China since 1978: Reform, modernization and socialism with Chinese characteristics*. New York, NY: St Martin's Press.
Maddison, A. (2003). *The world economy: Historical statistics*. Paris: OECD.
Maister, D. H. (1982). Balancing the professional service firm. *Sloan Management Review*, *24*(1), 15–29.
Malhotra, N., & Morris, T. (2009). Heterogeneity in professional service firms. *Journal of Management Studies*, *46*(6), 895–922.
Malsch, B., & Gendron, Y. (2013). Re-theorizing change: Institutional experimentation and the struggle for domination in the field of public accounting. *Journal of Management Studies*, *50*(5), 870–899.
Mao, Z. (1927/1961). *Report on an investigation of the peasant movement in human selected works of Mao Tse-Tung* (Vol. I). Beijing: People's Publishing House.
Mao, Z. (1961). *Selected works of Mao Tse-Tung* (Vol. IV), Beijing: People's Publishing House.
Marosi, A., & Massoud, N. (2008). "You can enter but you cannot leave...": US securities markets and foreign firms. *The Journal of Finance*, *63*(5), 2477–2506.
Marx, K. (1867). *Capital: The process of production of capital* (Vol. 1). F. Engels (Ed.). Retrieved from http://www.marxist.org

Marx, K. (1867/1981). *Capital* (D. Fernbach, Trans. Vol. III). London: Penguin Books.
Marx, K., & Engels, F. (1846/1974). *The German ideology*. New York, NY: International Publishers.
Mautz, R., & Sharaf, H. (1961). *The philosophy of auditing*. New York, NY: American Accounting Association.
McBride, S. (2002). Questioning the books: US verdict has little effect on Andersen's Asia operations – Most affiliates have linked with new firms. *The Asian Wall Street Journal*, June 18, p. A-5.
McCallum, K. (2002). Ernst & Young wants to merge with China firms. *Dow Jones International News*, July 4.
McFarland, J. (2013). OSC accuses Ernst & Young of shoddy audit of TSX Venture-listed Zungui Haixi. *The Globe and Mail*, June 24.
McKee, D. L., & Garner, D. E. (1997). *Accounting services, growth, and change in the pacific basin*. Westport, CT: Quorum Books.
McNally, M., & Schwarzmantal, J. (2009). *Gramsci and global politics: Hegemony and resistance*. New York, NY: Routledge.
Mennicken, A. (2008). Connecting worlds: The translation of international auditing standards into post-Soviet audit practice. *Accounting, Organizations and Society*, *33*(4/5), 384–414.
Mennicken, A. (2010). From inspection to auditing: Audit and markets as linked ecologies. *Accounting, Organizations and Society*, *35*(3), 334–359.
Ministry of Finance. (2009). *Roadmap for continuing and full convergence of the Chinese accounting standards for business enterprises with the international financial reporting standards*. Beijing: Ministry of Finance, People's Republic of China.
Ministry of Finance. (2010). *Interim regulations on the promotion of the use of special general partnership form for medium and large accounting firms*. Beijing: Ministry of Finance.
Minyard, D. H., & Tabor, R. H. (1991). The effect of Big Eight mergers on auditor concentration. *Accounting Horizons*, *5*(4), 79–90.
Mitchell, T., & Chen, X. (2009). Ernst & Young settles Akai case. *Financial Times*, September 23.
Moizer, P., Benau, M. A. G., Humphrey, C., & Martinez, A. V. (2004). The corporate image of auditors in a developing audit market within the EU: The case of Spain. *European Accounting Review*, *13*(3), 561–582.
Morgan, G. (2001). Transnational communities and business systems. *Global Networks*, (1), 113–130.
Morgan, G., & Quack, S. (2006). The internationalisation of professional service firms: Global convergence, national-path dependency or cross-border hybridization. *Research in the Sociology of Organizations*, *24*, 403–431.
Morris, T., & Pinnington, A. (1998). Promotion to partner in professional service firms. *Human Relations*, *51*(1), 3.
Morrison, A. D., & Wilhelm, W. J. Jr. (2004). Partnership firms, reputation, and human capital. *American Economic Review*, *94*(5), 1682–1692.
Morse, K. A. (2005). Much ado about nothing: Looking past the drama of the Sarbanes–Oxley Act and reevaluating the US delisting trend among non-US firms. *International Law and Management Review*, *2*, 87–99.
Mouffe, C. (1979). *Gramsci and Marxist theory*. London: Routledge & Kegan Paul.
Muddy Waters Research. (2010). *Muddy Waters initiating coverage on ONP – Strong sell*. Retrieved from http://www.muddywatersresearch.com/research/orient-paper-inc/initiating-coverage-onp/

Mueller, F., Carter, C., & Ross-Smith, A. (2011). Making sense of career in a Big Four accounting firm. *Current Sociology*, *59*(4), 551–567.

Murphy, C. (1991). Hong Kong: A culture of emigration. *The Atlantic Monthly*, *267*(4), 20–26.

Murphy, R. (1984). The structure of closure: A critique and development of the theories of Weber, Collins and Parkin. *The British Journal of Sociology*, *35*(4), 547–567.

Muzio, D., & Faulconbridge, J. R. (2013). The global professional service firm: "One firm" models versus (Italian) distant institutionalized practices. *Organizational Studies*, *34*(7), 897–925.

Myers, J. N., Myers, L. A., & Omer, T. C. (2003). Exploring the term of the auditor–client relationship and the quality of earnings: a case for mandatory auditor rotation? *The Accounting Review*, *78*(3), 779–799.

Nakamoto, M. (2009). Deloitte puts China staff on unpaid leave. *Financial Times*, June 11.

Napier, C. J. (1998). Giving an account of accounting history: A reply to Keenan. *Critical Perspectives on Accounting*, *9*(6), 685–700.

Narasimhan, R., & Chung, S. (1998). Auditor concentration of listed public companies on international stock exchanges. *Journal of International Financial Management & Accounting*, *9*(3), 201–215.

Narayan, F. B., & Reid, B. (2000). *Financial management and governance issues in the people's republic of China*. Manila: Asian Development Bank.

Narayana, N. (2010). China 'state secrets law' set to widen ambit soon. *International Business Times*, July 5.

Naylor, E. (1993). Auditors may "qualify" some China listings. *South China Morning Post*, June 6.

Neimark, M. (1990). The king is dead. Long live the king! *Critical Perspectives on Accounting*, *1*(1), 103–114.

Newquist, C. (2013, May 29). *Deloitte is the audit firm that has had the most trouble in China... by far*. Retrieved from http://goingconcern.com/post/deloitte-audit-firm-has-had-most-trouble-china-far

Nikkei Report. (2007). Big 4 auditors eye major staff increases on IPO, M&A boom. *Nikkei Report*, August 3.

Nikkei Weekly. (2002). Accounting demand soaring in China. *Nikkei Weekly*, November 25.

Noble, J. (2013). End of the road for China's "B" market. *Financial Times*, January 9.

Nokia Corporation. (2009). *Notes to consolidated financial statements*. Retrieved from http://www.nokia.com/about-nokia/financials/financial-statements. Accessed on February 14, 2011.

Norris, F. (2011). The audacity of Chinese frauds. *The New York Times*, May 26.

Nye, J. S. (2004). *Soft power: The means to success in world politics*. New York, NY: Public Affairs.

O'Neill, M. (1996). China tells foreign accountants to find partners. *Reuters*, July 4.

Ollman, B. (1993). *Dialectical investigations*. New York, NY: Routledge.

Oqvist, F. (2013, May 29). *China Finance: Updated data on auditors linked with issues*. Retrieved from http://www.tradingfloor.com/posts/china-finance-updated-data-auditors-linked-issues-606252080

Oxera. (2011). *Auditors and the financial crisis: Beyond the status quo*. Retrieved from http://www.oxera.com/cmsDocuments/Agenda_April 2011/Auditors and the financial crisis.pdf. Accessed on May 1.

Pacter, P., & Yuen, J. (2004). *China financial reporting update: 2003 year-end review*. Retrieved from http://www.iasplus.com/china/04-01e.pdf. Accessed on August 17, 2010.

Pan, H. (2001). Andersen due a nation-wide expansion. *Shanghai Star*, November 29.

Park, S. H., & Luo, Y. (2001). Guanxi and organizational dynamics: Organizational networking in Chinese firms. *Strategic Management Journal*, *22*, 455–477.

Park, S. H., & Russo, M. V. (1996). When competition eclipses cooperation: An event history analysis of joint venture failure. *Management Science*, *42*(6), 875–890.

Parker, J. (1992). Arthur Andersen claims first in China service. *Reuters*, August 18.

Partnoy, F. (2000). Multinational regulatory competition and single-stock futures. *Journal of International Law and Business*, *21*, 641–661.

Patten, C. (1998). *East and West: The last governor of Hong Kong on power, freedom and the future*. London: Macmillan.

PCAOB. (2007). *PCAOB meets with Asian counterparts to discuss cooperation on auditor oversight*. Retrieved from http://pcaobus.org/News/Releases/Pages/03232007_AsianCounterparts.aspx

PCAOB. (2009). *Docket 027: Rule amendments concerning the timing of certain inspections of non-U.S. firms, and other issues relating to inspections of non-U.S. firms*. Retrieved from http://pcaobus.org/Rules/Rulemaking/Pages/Docket027.aspx

PCAOB. (2010). *Staff audit practice alert No. 6: Auditor considerations regarding the work of other auditors and engaging assistants from outside the firm*. Retrieved from http://pcaobus.org/Standards/QandA/2010-07-12_APA_6.pdf. Accessed on August 15.

PCAOB. (2011). *Activity summary and audit implications for reverse mergers involving companies from the China region: January 1, 2007 through March 31, 2010*. Washington, DC: Public Company Accounting Oversight Board.

PCAOB. (2013a). *About the PCAOB*. Retrieved from http://pcaobus.org/About/Pages/default.aspx

PCAOB. (2013b). *Global networks*. Retrieved from http://pcaobus.org/Registration/Firms/Pages/RegisteredFirms.aspx

PCAOB. (2013c). *Issuers that are audit clients of PCAOB-registered firms from non-U.S. jurisdictions where the PCAOB is denied access to conduct inspections*. Retrieved from http://pcaobus.org/International/Inspections/Pages/IssuerClientsWithoutAccess.aspx

PCAOB. (2013d). *Memorandum of understanding on enforcement cooperation between the Public Company Accounting Oversight Board of the United States and the China Securities Regulatory Commission and the Ministry of Finance of China*. Retrieved from http://pcaobus.org/International/Documents/MOU_China.pdf

PCAOB. (2013e). *Non-U.S. firm inspections*. Retrieved from http://pcaobus.org/International/Inspections/Pages/default.aspx

PCAOB. (2013f). *Non-U.S. registered firms*. Retrieved from http://pcaobus.org/International/Registration/Pages/InternationalRegisteredFirms.aspx

PCAOB. (2013g). *Registered firms*. Retrieved from http://pcaobus.org/Registration/Firms/Pages/RegisteredFirms.aspx

PCAOB. (2013h). *Settled disciplinary orders*. Retrieved from http://pcaobus.org/Enforcement/Decisions/Pages/default.aspx

Pearson, R. (2012). Deloitte's China problem comes to a head. *Forbes*, April 2.

Peng, S., Tondkar, R. H., van der Laan Smith, J., & Harless, D. W. (2008). Does convergence of accounting standards lead to the convergence of accounting practices? A study from China. *The International Journal of Accounting*, *43*(4), 448–468.

Peng, S., & van der Laan Smith, J. (2010). Chinese GAAP and IFRS: An analysis of the convergence process. *Journal of International Accounting, Auditing and Taxation.*

Perera, H. B., Rahman, A. R., & Cahan, S. F. (2008). Globalisation and the major accounting firms. *Australian Accounting Review, 13*(29), 27–37.

Petty, R., & Cuganesan, S. (1996). Auditor rotation: Framing the debate. Companies could face higher fees and a decline in audit quality if law changes force them to rotate their auditors. *Australian Accountant, 66*, 40–42.

Piehwe, D., Walpen, B., & Neunhoffer, G. (2007). *Neoliberal hegemony*. London: Routledge.

Piot, C. (2007). Auditor concentration in a joint-auditing environment: The French market: 1997–2003. *Managerial Auditing Journal, 22*(2), 161–176.

Poon, H. F., & Rowley, C. (2007). Contemporary research on management and human resources in China: A comparative content analysis of two leading journals. *Asia Pacific Business Review, 13*(1), 133–153.

Post, H. A. (1996). Internationalization and professionalization in accounting services: The cases of BDO Binder and BDO CampsObers. *International Studies of Management & Organization, 26*(2), 80–103.

Poullaos, C. (2004). Globalisation, accounting critique and the university. *Critical Perspectives on Accounting, 15*(4–5), 715–730.

Previts, G. J. (1985). *The scope of CPA services*. New York, NY: Wiley.

PricewaterhouseCoopers (PwCs) (2010a). *Greater China IPO watch*. Hong Kong: PricewaterhouseCoopers.

PricewaterhouseCoopers (PwCs). (2010b). *Our history*. Retrieved from http://www.pwc.com/gx/en/about-pwc/facts-and-figures.jhtml. Accessed on May 21.

PricewaterhouseCoopers (PwCs). (2011). *About us*. Retrieved from http://www.pwccn.com/home/eng/aboutusindex.html. Accessed on March 15.

PricewaterhouseCoopers (PwCs). (2013). *PricewaterhouseCoopers Zhong Tian charts another milestone in China*. Retrieved from http://www.pwccn.com/home/eng/pr_250313.html

Proctor, K., & Qui, T. (2006). With boom, China faces work force shortages: Firms poach for skills and English fluency. *International Herald Tribune*, August 16.

Pun, P. (2004). Deloitte in US$150 million mainland investment plan. *The Standard*, June 2.

Puxty, A. G., Willmott, H. C., Cooper, D. J., & Lowe, T. (1987). Modes of regulation in advanced capitalism: Locating accountancy in four countries. *Accounting, Organizations and Society, 12*(3), 273–291.

Qu, Y. (2012). Challenges of localizing the "Big Four". *Caijing*, July 3.

Radebaugh, L., & Gray, S. (1997). *International accounting and multinational enterprises* (4th ed.), New York, NY: Wiley.

Radebaugh, L. H., Krylova, T. B., & Rahman, Z. (1994). The evolution of accounting in the former Soviet Union: Historical perspectives and global influences. In V. K. Zimmerman (Ed.), *The New Europe: Recent political and economic implications for accountants and accounting*. Urbana, IL: University of Illinois Center for International Education and Research in Accounting.

Ralston, D. A., Gustafson, D. J., Cheung, F. M., & Terpstra, R. H. (1993). Differences in managerial values: A study of US, Hong Kong and PRC managers. *Journal of International Business Studies, 24*(2), 249–275.

Ramanna, K., Donovan, G. A., & Dai, N. (2009). *IFRS in China*. Cambridge MA: Harvard Business School Publishing.

Ramirez, C. (2012). Promoting transnational professionalism: forays of the "Big Firm" accounting community into France. In M.-L. Djelic & S. Quack (Eds.), *Transnational communities: Shaping global economic governance*. Cambridge: Cambridge University Press.

Rask, K. J., Chu, D. K. W., & Gottschang, T. R. (1998). Institutional change in transitional economies: The case of accounting in China. *Comparative Economic Studies*, *40*(4), 76–77.

Reanda. (2013). *Annual review 2012: Reanda International*. Retrieved from http://www.reanda-international.com/News_Photo/pdf/Annual_Review_2012.pdf

Reay, T., & Hinings, C. R. (2005). The recompostition of an organizational field: Health care in Alberta. *Organization Studies*, *26*, 351–383.

Redding, G., & Witt, M. A. (2007). *The future of Chinese capitalism*. Oxford: Oxford University Press.

Reed, K. (2012). PKF Chinese firm to join BDO. *Accountancy Age*, November 13.

Reeves, J. (2012). Largest IPO in history? Facebook won't even crack the Top 10. *InvestorPlace.com*, January 30. Retrieved from http://investorplace.com/ipo-playbook/facebook-public-offering-10-biggest-ipos-in-history/

Ribstein, L. E. (2003). Limited liability of professional firms after Enron. *Journal of Corporate Law*, *29*, 427–437.

Richardson, A. J. (1989). Corporatism and intraprofessional hegemony: A study of regulation and internal social order. *Accounting, Organizations and Society*, *14*(5/6), 415–431.

Richardson, A. J. (1997). Social closure in dynamic markets: The incomplete professional project In accountancy. *Critical Perspectives on Accounting*, *8*(6), 635–653.

Robinson, W. I., & Harris, J. (2000). Towards a global ruling class? Globalization and the transnational capital class. *Science and Society*, *64*(1), 11–54.

Rose, N. (1999). *The powers of freedom: Reforming political thought*. Cambridge: Cambridge University Press.

Rose, T., & Hinings, C. (1999). Global client's demands driving change in global business advisory firms. In D. M. Brock, M. Powell, & C. Hinings (Eds.), *Restructuring the professional organization*. London: Routledge.

RSM. (2013). *RSM International and Crowe Horwath International accounce member firm merger*. Retrieved from http://www.rsmi.com/en/press/rsm-international-and-crowe-horwath-international-announce-member-firm-merger.aspx

Ryan, J. (2008). The clouds part – China converges. *A Plus*, (January), 16–19.

Ryan, S. (2005). Ernst & Young CEO sees China as 2nd biggest practice in 10 years, *AFX Asia*, October 26.

Said, E. (1983). *The world, the text, and the critic*. Cambridge, MA: Harvard University Press.

Sallach, D. L. (1974). Class domination and ideological hegemony. *Sociological Quarterly*, *15*(1), 38–50.

Salleh, A., Rose, R. C., Kumar, N., & Peng, L. C. (2007). Readiness in meeting globalization challenges: A case of accounting firms in Malaysia *Journal of Social Sciences*, *3*(4), 176–184.

Samsonova, A. (2009). Local sites of globalisation: A look at the development of a legislative framework for auditing in Russia. *Critical Perspectives on Accounting*, *20*(4), 528–552.

Sanchanta, M., & Mavin, D. (2013). Deloitte tightens its client screening. *The Wall Street Journal*, January 17.

Sasson, A. S. (1991). Hegemony. In T. Bottomore, L. Harris, V. G. Kiernan, & R. Miliband (Eds.), *A dictionary of Marxist thought*. Maiden, MA: Blackwell Publishing Ltd.

Scapens, R. W., & Hao, Z. P. (1995). Chinese accounting reform: Reasons and effects. In J. Blake & S. S. Gao (Eds.), *Perspectives on accounting and finance in China*. London: Routledge.

Schulzke, K. (2013, April 3). *What lurks in Deloitte's Longtop Financial audit work papers?* Retrieved from http://whistleblowercentral.com/2013/04/03/what-lurks-in-deloittes-longtop-financial-audit-work-papers/

Schumer, C. (2011). *Letter to James Doty, Chairman, public company accounting oversight board.* Retrieved from http://www.chinaaccountingblog.com/111122schumer-ltr-pcaob-re.pdf

Scott, W. R. (1994). Conceptualizing organizational fields: Linking organizational and societal systems. In H. U. Derlien, U. Gerhardt, & F. W. Scharpf (Eds.), *Systemrationalitat und partialinteresse [System Rationality and Partial Interests]*. Baden-Baden: Nomos-Verlagsgesellschaft.

Scott, W. R. (2008). *Institutions and organizations: Ideas and interests* (3rd ed.), Thousand Oaks, CA: Sage.

Seal, W., Sucher, P., & Zelenka, I. (1996). Post-socialist transition and the development of an accountancy profession in the Czech Republic. *Critical Perspectives on Accounting*, *7*(4), 485–508.

SEC. (2011a). *Adopting additional listing requirements for companies applying to list after consummation of a "reverse merger" with a shell company*. Release No. 34-65708.

SEC (2011b). *Investor bulletin: Reverse mergers.* Washington, DC: Securities and Exchange Commission.

SEC. (2011c). *SEC files subpoena enforcement action against Deloitte & Touche in Shanghai.* Retrieved from http://www.sec.gov/news/press/2011/2011-180.htm

SEC. (2011d). *U.S. and Chinese regulators meet in Beijing on audit oversight cooperation.* Retrieved from http://www.sec.gov/news/press/2011/2011-164.htm

SEC. (2012a, December 3). *SEC charges China affiliates of Big Four accounting firms with violating U.S. securities laws in refusing to produce documents.* Retrieved from http://www.sec.gov/News/PressRelease/Detail/PressRelease/1365171486452-.UhACNhZ4jGk

SEC. (2012b). *Securities and Exchange Commission's reply memorandum in support of its application for order requiring compliance with subpoena.* Retrieved from http://media.complianceweek.com/documents/42/courtlink_document_us-dis-dcd_10371.pdf

SEC. (2013). *Order instituting administrative proceedings and notice of hearing pursuant to Section 12(j) of the Securities Exchange Act of 1934*. Release No. 70042.

Securities and Futures Commission. (2012). *SFC commences legal proceedings against Ernst & Young over access to accounting records.* Retrieved from http://www.sfc.hk/edistributionWeb/gateway/EN/news-and-announcements/news/doc?refNo=12PR92

Selmer, J. (2003). Staff localization and organizational characteristics: Western business operations in China. *Asia Pacific Business Review*, *10*(1), 43–57.

Shalia-Esa, A., & Lynch, S. (2011). Justice Department probing Chinese accounting. *Reuters*, September 29.

Shanghai Daily. (2004). PwC strike may widen. *Shanghai Daily*, July 13.

She, B. B. (2001). Ernst & Young, China accounting firm form venture. *Reuters*, February 8.

Shen, Y., Shen, M., Xu, Z., & Bai, Y. (2009). Bank size and SME lending: Evidence from China. *World Development*, *37*.

Shu, Z. (2000). Auditor resignations: Clientele effects and legal liability. *Journal of Accounting and Economics*, *29*(2), 173–205.

Sikka, P., & Willmott, H. C. (2009). All offshore: The sprat, the mackerel, accounting firms and the state in globalization. In C. S. Chapman, D. J. Cooper, & P. B. Miller (Eds.), *Accounting, organizations, and institutions*. Oxford: Oxford University Press.

Silver, C. (2007). Local matters: Internationalizing strategies for US law firms. *Indiana Journal of Global Legal Studies*, *14*(1), 67–93.

Simon, R. (1982). *Gramsci's political thought*. London: Lawrence & Wishart.

Simunic, D. A., & Wu, X. (2009). China-related research in auditing: A review and directions for future research. *China Journal of Accounting Research*, *2*(2), 1–25.

Sklair, L. (1995). *Sociology of the global system*. Baltimore, MD: John Hopkins University Press.

Sklair, L. (1997). Social movements for global capitalism: the transnational capitalist class in action. *Review of International Political Economy*, *4*(3), 514–538.

Sklair, L. (1998). The transnational capitalist class and global capitalism: The case of the tobacco industry. *Political Power and Social Theory*, *12*, 3–43.

Sklair, L. (2002). Democracy and the transnational capitalist class. *Annals of the American Academy of Political and Social Science*, *581*(May), 144–157.

Smith, P. (2008). Global risk: Is it a good time to operate in a network of firms? *Accountancy Age*, November 6, p. 18.

South China Morning Post. (1992). Arthur Andersen helping China firms with listing. *South China Morning Post*, October 18.

South China Morning Post. (1993). Andersen post to Li. *South China Morning Post*, May 7.

South China Morning Post. (1996). Accounting chief pushes for China recognition. *South China Morning Post*, May 23.

Spence, C. (2007). Social and environmental reporting and hegemonic discourse. *Accounting, Auditing & Accountability Journal*, *20*(6), 855–882.

Spence, C. (2009). Social accounting's emancipatory potential: A Gramscian critique. *Critical Perspectives on Accounting*, *20*(2), 205–227.

Squires, S. E., Smith, C. J., McDougall, L. M., & Yeack, W. R. (2003). *Inside Arthur Andersen: Shifting values, unexpected consequences*. Upper Saddle River, NJ: Prentice Hall.

State Council. (2009). *The general office of the state council forwarding the announcement of opinions on accelerating the development of certified public accountants by the ministry of finance*. Document No. 56. Beijing.

Steger, I. (2012). Examining muddy waters' track record. *The Wall Street Journal*, November 28.

Stender, N. A., She, S., & Jin, M. (2007). SAFE plugs holes of China/offshore round-trip investments. *China Law & Practice*, (July/August), 58–60.

Stevens, M. (1981). *The big eight: An incisive look behind the pinstripe curtain of the eight accounting firms whose practices affect the pocketbooks of every American*. New York, NY: Macmillan Publishing Company.

Sucher, P., & Bychkova, S. (2001). Auditor independence in economies in transition: A study of Russia. *European Accounting Review*, *10*(4), 817–841.

Suddaby, R., Cooper, D. J., & Greenwood, R. (2007). Transnational regulation of professional services: Governance dynamics of field level organizational change. *Accounting, Organizations & Society*, *32*(4/5), 333–362.

Suddaby, R., Gendron, Y., & Lam, H. (2009). The organizational context of professionalism in accounting. *Accounting, Organizations and Society*, *34*(3/4), 409–427.

Suddaby, R., & Greenwood, R. (2005). Rhetorical strategies of legitimacy. *Administrative Science Quarterly*, *50*(1), 35–67.

Sun, M. (2003). Deloitte invests heavily. *China Daily*, November 21.

Sun, M. (2006). Ernst & Young to invest US$200 million to expand business. *China Daily*, July 18.

Suzuki, T., Yan, Y., & Chen, B. (2007). Accounting for the growth and transformation of Chinese businesses and the Chinese economy: Implications for transitional and development economics. *Socioeconomics Review*, *5*(4), 665–694.

Tabakoff, N. (1996). Deloitte head to step down following vote. *South China Morning Post*, August 16.

Talley, E. L. (2006). Cataclysmic liability risk among Big Four auditors. *Columbia Law Review*, *106*, 1641–1651.

Tam, J. (2002). Locals miss mainland accounting jobs. *The Standard*, July 22.

Tang, Q., & Lau, A. (2000). Accounting reforms in China: A transition from a state plan and control-oriented system to capital market-oriented system. *Managerial Finance*, *26*(5), 80–98.

Tang, R. Y. W., Metwalli, A. M., & Marie Smith, O. (2010). Foreign investment: Impact on China's economy. *Journal of Corporate Accounting & Finance*, *21*(6), 25–40.

Tang, T., Cooper, B. J., & Leung, P. (1995). Accounting in China: Developments and opportunities. In J. B. Black & S. S. Gao (Eds.), *Perspectives on accounting and finance in China* (pp. 23–40). London: Routledge.

Tang, Y. (1997a). The development of the accounting profession in China. *Research in Accounting Regulation*, *11*, 295–312.

Tang, Y. (1997b). The recent accounting development and internationalization of accounting education in China. *Issues in Accounting Education*, *12*(1), 219–227.

Tang, Y. (1999). Issues in the development of the accounting profession in China. *China Accounting and Finance Review*, *1*(1), 21–36.

Tang, Y. (2000). Bumpy road leading to internationalization: A review of accounting development in China. *Accounting Horizons*, *14*(1), 93–102.

Tang, Y., Chow, L., & Cooper, B. J. (1994). *Accounting and finance in China: A review of current practice*. Hong Kong: Longman.

Taussig, R. A., Yang, D. C., & Mao, X. (1994). Financial accounting standards in contemporary China. *Advances in International Accounting*, *7*, 29–42.

Thakur, M., Burton, G. E., & Srivastava, B. N. (1997). *International management: Concepts and cases*. New Delhi: Tata McGraw Hill.

The Accountant. (2006). IASB appoints full-time members. *The Accountant*, November 30.

The Asian Wall Street Journal (AWSJ). (1996). China sets new accountant rule. *The Asian Wall Street Journal*, July 5.

The Asian Wall Street Journal (AWSJ). (1996). Asian-Pacific brief: Price Waterhouse. *The Asian Wall Street Journal*, December 24.

The Economist. (2012). Internal controls. *The Economist*, May 19.

The Economist. (2012). Rotten eggs and gadflies. *The Economist*, September 15.

The Institute of Chartered Accountants of Scotland. (2010). *Chinese accounting reform: Towards a principles-based global regime*. The Institute of Chartered Accountants of Scotland, Edinburgh.

The Wall Street Journal. (2005). WSJ Briefing: Beijing turns an eye on accounting firms. *The Wall Street Journal*, October 20.

Thomas, W. A. (2001). *Western capitalism in China: A history of the shanghai stock exchange*. Aldershot: Ashgate.

To, E. (1989). Emigration crisis for accountants. *South China Morning Post*, December 16.

Toffler, B. (2003). *Final accounting: Ambition, greed and the fall of Arthur Andersen*. New York, NY: Broadway Books.

Tong, D., & Zhou, Z. H. (2009). *Re: PCAOB rulemaking docket matter No. 27*. Retrieved from http://pcaobus.org/Rules/Rulemaking/Docket 027/024_Csrc.pdf

Tong, I. (1992a). Auditors to scrutinise Chinese firms. *South China Morning Post*, July 24.

Tong, I. (1992b, October 8). China's listings plan a bonus for accountants. *South China Morning Post*.

Tong, I. (1992c). Peat Marwick to audit Shanghai Petrochem. *South China Morning Post*, November 10.

Tong, I. (1993). Framework agreed for mainland listings. *South China Morning Post*, May 15.

Torres, D. (1991). What, if anything, is professionalism? Institutions and the problem of change. *Research in the Sociology of Organizations*, *8*, 43–68.

Triedman. (2013). China and SEC reach agreement on Deloitte audit docs. *The Litigation Daily*, July 15.

Tsai, K. S. (2002). *Back alley banking: Private entrepreneurs in China*. Ithaca, NY: Cornell University Press.

Tsang, E. (1998). Can guanxi be a source of sustained competitive advantage for doing business in China? *The Academy of Management Executive*, *12*(2), 64–73.

Tse, V. (2005). Deloitte China to merge with Beijing Pan-China. *Dow Jones International News*, March 21.

Tydd, J. (2008). Global strategy pays off for E&Y. *Accountancy Age*, October 9.

US Department of Treasury. (2009). *The First U.S.–China strategic and economic dialogue economic track joint fact sheet*. Retrieved from http://www.treasury.gov/press-center/press-releases/pages/tg240.aspx

US Department of Treasury. (2010). Second meeting of the US – Strategic & economic dialogue joint US–China economic track fact sheet.

US Department of Treasury. (2011). *Third meeting of the U.S.–China strategic and economic dialogue joint U.S.–China economic track fact sheet*. Retrieved from http://www.treasury.gov/press-center/press-releases/Pages/tg1170.aspx

US Department of Treasury. (2012). *Joint U.S.–China economic track fact sheet – Fourth meeting of the U.S.–China strategic and economic dialogue (S&ED)*. Retrieved from http://www.treasury.gov/press-center/press-releases/Pages/tg1567.aspx

US Department of Treasury. (2013a). *Joint U.S.–China economic track fact sheet of the fifth meeting of the U.S.–China strategic and economic dialogue*. Retrieved from http://www.treasury.gov/press-center/press-releases/Pages/jl2010.aspx

US Department of Treasury. (2013b). *Remarks of Treasury Secretary Jacob J. Lew at the close of the fifth U.S.–China strategic and economic dialogue*. Retrieved from http://www.treasury.gov/press-center/press-releases/Pages/jl2008.aspx

US Department of Treasury. (2013c). *U.S.–China strategic and economic dialogue*. Retrieved from http://www.treasury.gov/initiatives/Pages/china.aspx

Universum. (2011). *The Universum Chinese student survey 2011*. Retrieved from http://www.universumglobal.com/IDEAL-Employer-Rankings/The-National-Editions/China. Accessed on April 29, 2011.

van de Vijver, F. J. R., & Leung, K. (1997). *Methods and data analysis for cross-cultural research*. Thousand Oaks, CA: Sage.

van der Pijl, K. (1984). *The making of an Atlantic ruling class*. London: Verso.

van der Pijl, K. (1998). *Transnational classes and international relations*. London: Routledge.

Verghese, K. (2013). Accounting and accountability. *Asian Legal Business* (February 1).

Viswanatha, A., & Aubin, D. (2012). SEC delays court action seeking Deloitte China audit papers. *Reuters*, July 18.

von Nordenflycht, A. (2010). What is a professional service firm? Toward a theory and taxonomy of knowledge-intensive firms. *The Academy of Management Review*, *35*(1), 155–174.

Walker, G., Kogut, B., & Shan, W. (1997). Social capital, structural holes and the formation of an industry network. *Organization Science*, *8*(2), 109–125.

Walker, K. B., & Johnson, E. N. (1996). A review and synthesis of research on supplier concentration, quality and fee structure in non-U.S. markets for auditor services. *The International Journal of Accounting*, *31*(1), 1–18.

Walker, S. P., & Shackleton, K. (1998). A ring fence for the profession: Advancing the closure of British accountancy 1957–1970. *Accounting, Auditing and Accountability Journal*, *11*(1), 34–71.

Waller, M. (2006). Globetrottter set for the challenge. *The Times*, November 11.

Wallerstedt, E. (2001). The emergence of the big five in Sweden. *European Accounting Review*, *10*(4), 843–867.

Walter, C. E., & Howie, F. J. T. (2001). *To get rich is glorious: China's stock markets in the '80s and '90s*. New York, NY: Palgrave Macmillan.

Wang, G. (1991). *The Chineseness of China – Selected essays*. Oxford: Oxford University Press.

Wang, H., & Zweig, D. (2008). *China's diaspora and returnees: Impact on China's globalization process*. Paper presented at the Globalization of Chinese Enterprises: Transformational Politics, Business Strategies and Future Paths, Cambridge, MA.

Wang, J. (2006). *Innovating development philosophy: Serving economic and social development*. Paper presented at the 17th World Conference of Accountants, Istanbul, Turkey. Retrieved from http://www.cicpa.org.cn/english/news_alert/200804/t20080428_4796.htm

Wang, O. (2002). Ernst & Young in acquisition talks with 4 Chinese accounting firms. *Xinhua Financial Network*, December 9.

Wang, Q., Wong, T. J., & Xia, L. (2008). State ownership, the institutional environment, and auditor choice: Evidence from China. *Journal of Accounting and Economics*, *46*(1), 112–134.

Wang, X. (2000). PetroChina sets out stall of sweeteners for investors. *South China Morning Post*, January 24.

Ward, S. (1992). China gives CPA firm joint-venture approval. *South China Morning Post*, August 17.

Warin, F. J., Diamant, M. S., & Pfenning, J. M. (2010). FCPA compliance in China and the gifts and hospitality challenge. *Virginia Law and Business Review*, *5*(1), 34–80.

Warsame, H. A. (2006). The evolutionary advances in tax education in Canada and the hegemonic leadership of the accounting profession. *Journal of Economic & Administrative Sciences*, *22*(1), 60–84.

Watanabe, Y. (1939). Accountancy profession in Japan. *The Accounting Review*, *14*(4), 430–432.

Way, D., & Nield, R. (2002). *Counting house: The history of PricewaterhouseCoopers on the China coast*. Hong Kong: PricewaterhouseCoopers.

Weber, M. (1922/1978). *Economy and society: An interpretive sociology* (Vol. 1), Berkeley, CA: University of California Press.

Wei, M., & Young, D. (2009). NASDAQ sees over 30 China listings in 2010. *Reuters*, December 14.

Weisbrot, M. (2011). 2016: When China overtakes the US. *Guardian*, April 27.

West, B. P. (1996). The professionalization of accounting: A review of recent historical research and its implications. *Accounting History*, *1*(1), 77–102.

Wikileaks. (2009, June 1–2). *Treasury secretary Geithner's meetings with Chinese officials*. Retrieved from http://www.wikileaks.org/plusd/cables/09BEIJING1635_a.html

Wilhelm, W. J., & Downing, J. D. (2001). *Information markets*. Harvard: Harvard Business School Press.

Williams, G. (1960). Egemonia in the thought of Antonio Gramsci: Some notes on interpretation. *Journal of the History of Ideas*, *21*(4), 586–599.

Wilpert, B., & Scharpf, S. Y. (1990). Intercultural management: Joint ventures in the People's Republic of China. *International Journal of Psychology*, *25*, 643–656.

Winkle, G. M., Huss, H. F., & Chen, X. Z. (1994). Accounting standards in the People's Republic of China: Responding to economic reforms. *Accounting Horizons*, *8*, 48–57.

Wong, C. S., & Law, K. S. (1999). Managing localization of human resources in the PRC: A practical model. *Journal of World Business*, *34*(1), 26–40.

Worth, O. (2002). The Janus-like character of counter-hegemony: Progressive and nationalist responses to neoliberalism. *Global Society*, *16*(3), 297–315.

WTO. (2010). *What is the World Trade Organization?* Retrieved from http://www.wto.org/english/thewto_e/whatis_e/tif_e/fact1_e.htm. Accessed on September 16.

Wu, Z. (2003). Accounting crackdown uncovers widespread fraud. *The Standard*, January 17.

Wyatt, A. R. (2004). Accounting professionalism – They just don't get it! *Accounting Horizons*, *18*(1), 45–54.

Xiamen University. (2010). *Professor Ge Jiashu's unique life in accounting*. Retrieved from http://ice.xmu.edu.cn/english/showletter.aspx?news_id=2634. Accessed on March 1, 2011.

Xiang, B. (1998). Institutional factors influencing China's accounting reforms and standards. *Accounting Horizons*, *12*(2), 105–119.

Xiao, G. (2004). *People's republic of China's round-tripping FDI: Scale, causes and implications*. ADB Institute Discussion Papers. Working Paper No. 24. Latin America/Caribbean and Asia/Pacific Economics and Business Association.

Xiao, Z., & Pan, A. (1997). Developing accounting standards on the basis of a conceptual framework by the Chinese government. *The International Journal of Accounting*, *32*(3), 279–299.

Xiao, Z., Weetman, P., & Sun, M. (2004). Political influence and coexistence of a uniform accounting system and accounting standards: Recent developments in China. *Abacus*, *40*(2), 193–218.

Xiao, Z., Young, D. O., Dyson, J. R., & Pan, A. (1995). Development of accounting standards and conceptual framework in China. *Advances in International Accounting*, *8*, 177–199.

Xiao, Z., Zhang, Y., & Xie, Z. (2000). The making of independent auditing standards in China. *Accounting Horizons*, *14*(1), 69–89.

Xu, B. (1997). Opportunity knocks for successful CPAs. *Business Weekly*, June 1.

Xu, L., Cortese, C., & Zhang, E. (2013). Exploring hegemonic change in China: A case of accounting evolution. *Asian Review of Accounting*, *21*(2), 2–24.

Xu, X. (1997). Chinese CPAs join key global association. *China Daily*, May 14.

Xu, X. (2000). Firms OK'd for audit business. *China Daily*, December 6.

Xu, Y., & Xu, X. (2003). Becoming professional: Chinese accountants in early 20th century Shanghai. *Accounting Historians Journal*, *30*(1), 129–154.

Yan, A., & Zeng, M. (1999). International joint venture instability: A critique of previous research, A reconceptualization, and directions for future research. *Journal of International Business Studies*, *30*(2), 395–414.

Yang, L. Q., Tang, Q., Kilgore, A., & Jiang, Y. (2001). Auditor-government associations and auditor independence in China. *The British Accounting Review*, *33*(2), 175–189.

Yang, M. (1994). *Gifts, favors, and banquets: The art of social relationships in China*. Ithaca: Cornell University Press.

Yapa, P. W. S., & Hao, Z. P. (2007). An analysis of current trends in accounting professional development in People's Republic of China. *Asian Review of Accounting*, *15*(1), 25–44.

Yee, H. (2009). The re-emergence of the public accounting profession in China: A hegemonic analysis. *Critical Perspectives on Accounting*, *20*(1), 71–92.

Yee, H. (2012). Analyzing the state-accounting profession dynamic: Some insights from the professionalization experience in China. *Accounting, Organisations and Society*, *37*(6), 426–444.

Yeoh, B., & Willis, K. (2005). Singaporean and British transmigrants in China and the cultural politics of contact zones. *Journal of Ethic and Migration Studies*, *31*(2), 269–285.

Yiu, E. (1997). Deloitte tailors its services for Chinese. *South China Morning Post*, October 14.

Yiu, E. (2001). Big Five win Beijing mandate in audit of listed financial firms. *South China Morning Post*, May 25.

Yiu, E. (2002a). Deloitte Touche Tohmatsu to double size of its operations in the Greater China region within the next two to five years. *South China Morning Post*, September 2.

Yiu, E. (2002b). Ernst & Young targets mainland partners for expansion strategy. *South China Morning Post*, May 22.

Yiu, E. (2002c). Merged firm to triple workforce. *South China Morning Post*, May 13.

Yiu, E. (2003). Incoming Deloitte chief has sights set on China. *South China Morning Post*, March 31.

Yiu, E. (2004a). Deloitte sets sights on mainland push: China expansion plan includes mergers with specialized accounting practices. *South China Morning Post*, November 22.

Yiu, E. (2004b). Deloitte unveils US$150 million expansion strategy for China; The accounting firm intends to acquire competitors and boost staff numbers, *South China Morning Post*, March 3.

Yiu, E. (2004c). E&Y poaches staff on the mainland. *South China Morning Post*, July 2.

Yiu, E. (2008). Big 4 accounting companies lift mainland hiring. *South China Morning Post*, June 9.

Yiu, E. (2009). Who's got the best no-pay leave deal among China's accountants? *South China Morning Post*, April 27.

Yiu, E. (2010). SFC resists mainland audit plan: Securities regulator worried proposal means investor protections cannot be enforced. *South China Morning Post*, May 10.

Yiu, E. (2011). New rules for mainland firms to affect accountants. *South China Morning Post*, February 7.

Yiu, E. (2013). Ernst & Young in court over secrets kept from the SFC. *South China Morning Post*, March 28.

Yiu, E., Rovnick, N., & Lo, C. (2009). Ernst & Young chief steps down amid probe. *South China Morning Post*, October 1.

Yu, R. (2010). Deloitte to spend more money in China for business expansion. *Dow Jones International News*, April 11.

Yuan, H., & Li, H. (2003). Organization form, size and audit quality of accounting firms. *Auditing Research*, *1*, 32–34.

Zeff, S. A. (2003). How the US accounting profession got where it is today: Part II. *Accounting Horizons*, *17*(4), 267–287.

Zhang, L. Y. (2004). The roles of corporatization and stock market listing in reforming China's state industry. *World Development*, *32*(12), 2031–2047.

Zhang, S., & Schmitt, B. H. (2001). Creating local brands in multilingual international markets. *Journal of Marketing Research*, *38*(3), 313–325.

Zhao, Q. (2009). SME board turns 5. *The Global Times*, May 26.

Zhao, R. (2005a). Deloitte plans merger with local firms. *China Daily*, January 17.

Zhao, R. (2005b). Mainland merger for accounting giant. *China Daily*, March 21.

Zhao, S. (1993). Deng Xiaoping's southern tour: Elite politics in post-Tiananmen China. *Asian Survey*, *33*(8), 739–756.

Zhou, H. (2007). Auditing standards, increased accounting disclosure, and information asymmetry: Evidence from an emerging market. *Journal of Accounting and Public Policy*, *26*(5), 584–620.

Zhou, Z. H. (1988). Chinese accounting systems and practices. *Accounting, Organizations and Society*, *13*(2), 207–224.

Zhu, R. (2013). *Zhu Rongji on the record* (J. Y. Mei, Trans.). Washington, DC: Brookings Institution Press.

Zhu, T. (1999). China's corporatization drive: An evaluation and policy implications. *Contemporary Economic Policy*, *17*(4), 530–539.

ABOUT THE AUTHOR

Paul L. Gillis, Ph.D. CPA, is Professor of Practice at Peking University's Guanghua School of Management. He was with PricewaterhouseCoopers for 28 years, retiring in 2004 to pursue a doctorate at Macquarie Graduate School of Management in Sydney, Australia. He has resided in China since 1997, and is a member of the Standing Advisory Group of the US Public Company Accounting Oversight Board.

INDEX